DRAFTING FOR SUCCESSION

AUSTRALIA
LBC Information Services
Sydney

CANADA and USA
Carswell
Toronto

NEW ZEALAND
Brooker's
Auckland

SINGAPORE and MALAYSIA
Sweet & Maxwell Asia
Singapore and Kuala Lumpur

DRAFTING FOR SUCCESSION

By

John Kerrigan, MA, LL.B. (Hons), MSI, Solicitor

THOMSON
™
W. GREEN

Published in 2004 by
W. Green & Son Limited
21 Alva Street
Edinburgh EH2 4PS

Reprinted 2005

www.wgreen.thomson.com

Typeset by LBJ Typesetting Ltd, Kingsclere

Printed in Great Britain by MPG Ltd, Bodmin, Cornwall

No natural forests were destroyed to make this product;
only farmed timber was used and replanted.

A CIP catalogue record of this book is available from the British
Library.

ISBN 0414 01546 0

DEDICATION

For the most part, those who have assisted me with their time, ideas and criticisms are too many to mention individually. To all those who have contributed (and they know who they are), many thanks. I do, however, feel that a special mention must be made of certain individuals who have greatly contributed to the production of this book. The staff at Maxwell MacLaurin (particularly, Emily, Sharon, Charlotte and Lesley) are due a huge vote of thanks. Most of all, however, I dedicate this book to my long suffering wife, Linda whose support in producing the final text has been invaluable.

PREFACE

The Practice of Law—what are the essential features? I have always held
the view that a legal practitioner should be both professional and
practical. Our clientele take our professionalism for granted. Our ability
to be practical, *i.e.* present appropriate solutions to client's problems
might, from the client's point of view, remain debatable. The essential
thrust of this book is two-fold. First, I hope to demonstrate to the reader
methodologies by which he/she can demonstrate the value of his/her
services to the client, and thereby secure that the advisor is appropriately
remunerated. Of equal importance, I am concerned to bring to the
attention of all of those who practice in this field the risks which we now
undertake. Hopefully, the "hints and wrinkles" which I have outlined in
this work will assist the reader to ensure that the provision of his/her
services is not only both professional and practical but also, dare I say it,
risk averse.

John Kerrigan
2004

CONTENTS

CONTENTS

TABLE OF CASES

TABLE OF STATUTES

TABLE OF STATUTORY INSTRUMENTS

PART I—ADVISING CLIENTS

CHAPTER 1

WHY MAKE A WILL?

INTRODUCTION

The entitlement to make a will is regarded in Scotland as a fundamental **1–01** freedom. It is not a wholly unrestricted freedom, as certain requirements of a particular testator might be void owing to uncertainty or repugnancy or being contrary to public policy, and the will, itself, requires to meet certain basic formalities of execution. Strangely, however, it is not a right that we as a society generally make use of. Every year, those who die without leaving a will of any description greatly outnumber those who have made a will before their death. Whether or not an individual has strong religious beliefs, no one likes to contemplate the end of their earthly existence, and this is perhaps one reason why many individuals baulk at making a will. Historically speaking, the author considers that it would not be an unfair criticism of the legal profession to propound that it has not been sufficiently proactive in persuading clients of the benefits of making a will. This is, perhaps, a reflection of what the author considers to have been a traditional viewpoint within the legal profession (*i.e.* that will making for clients was really only a peripheral service). In recent years, the attitude of the legal profession has changed. The legal profession, charities, trade unions and financial advisers (amongst others) have increased their efforts in seeking to persuade the general public of the desirability, if not the necessity, of making a proper will.

BENEFITS OF HAVING A WILL

If you take the time to explain the benefits of a will to a client, you will **1–02** often persuade the client of the folly of not having an appropriate will in place. The benefits include the following (not necessarily set out in order of importance):

Freedom of choice

The making of a will is an exercise of freedom of choice on the part of **1–03** the client. Few lay people have any great familiarity with the Laws of Intestacy in Scotland. Our society is much more jealous in guarding individual rights, and the making of a will is, after all, the exercise of just one such right. In a philosophical sense, it is important that clients should be encouraged to exercise their rights.

Laws of Intestacy

The making of a will involves a series of different choices. An **1–04** individual who does not make a will is therefore leaving the succession to his estate to devolve in accordance with the provisions of the

Succession (Scotland) Act, 1964, as amended. Any practitioner who has regularly made wills over a period of time for clients will know that, often, their clients have little or no knowledge of the Laws of Intestacy and in fact may well be operating on the basis of a gross misconception as to what would happen on the client's death without having made a will. Common misconceptions are:

- Where one spouse dies without leaving a will, the surviving spouse automatically succeeds to the whole Estate of the predecessor. This is, of course, not the formula provided by sections 8 and 9 of the 1964 Act, as amended, and an explanation that this is so may often be sufficient to persuade a married client that, if only to protect his or her spouse, a will is vital.
- Clients operate under various misconceptions as to when children become entitled to payment. Most clients still believe that children will not be entitled to payment until the age of 18 years (which is, of course, not the position in terms of the Age of Legal Capacity (Scotland) Act, 1991). In some cases, the author has found that many clients still believe that the law in this area still applies the old "key of the door" approach (*i.e.* that vesting does not take place until someone is 21 years of age). Older clients will certainly remember when the age of majority was, indeed, 21 years. With effect from January 1, 1970, the age of majority was reduced to 18 years—The Age of Majority (Scotland) Act 1969.
- Many clients have only a clouded perception of who might benefit from their estates if they were to pass on unmarried and without issue. In many cases, a brief examination of the family tree of the client will lead the client to conclude that there are certain individuals who would otherwise succeed under the Laws of Intestacy whom the client would not wish to see obtaining any benefit. Again, therefore, the making of a will means the exercise of specific choice in this area.

Choice of executors or trustees

1–05   If a will involves an element of *delectus persona* in so far as choice of beneficiaries is concerned, it equally involves choice also in relation to the appointment of executors or trustees. A feature of many home-made wills is that no valid appointment of executors is made. It is important that clients should choose individuals in whom they repose faith and trust for the administration and winding up of their estate. For various reasons, the testator might not wish to appoint his or her surviving spouse as executor (perhaps as they conceive that this would be an undue burden on a grief-stricken widow or widower, or because of the advanced age of both spouses). A client can choose a number of executors, can appoint substitutes and can decide on the full range of powers to be entrusted to the executors. Where a discretionary power is granted, the client can rely on their chosen executors to exercise that power in a manner in which the client would have approved, and in respect of which the client can leave guidance or direction in terms of a Letter of Expression of Wish.

Range of beneficiaries

A client making a will can choose to benefit a wide range of **1–06** individuals or concerns. For example, if the client is unmarried and has no issue, then that client could choose to bestow benefits on old friends or indeed upon a range of charities whom the client favours, or with whom the client may have had some relationship during his or her lifetime. Employees and charities are not within the Rules of Succession as applied to the "Free Estate" of an intestate deceased. These Rules are contained in sections 1 to 7 of the 1964 Act.

Financial provision protection

In making a will, a client also has a choice as to when and how their **1–07** chosen beneficiaries will be entitled to succeed/vest. This facility of a properly made will is of great importance. A will can be constructed so as to provide specific formulae for the financial protection of a young or financially naïve beneficiary, or beneficiaries suffering from mental incapacity. Most clients are horrified to discover that a child, on attaining the age of 16 years, can demand as a right that the benefit left to them under a deceased relative's will should be made over to them absolutely. In the case of mentally incapax beneficiaries, not only can appropriate provision be made for their financial support, but this can also be effected on a basis which will not otherwise imperil the incapax beneficiary's rights to any valuable social security benefits.

Tax planning

A properly thought out and constructed will can form a very valuable **1–08** part of the client's tax planning. A client's estate, without such planning, might otherwise be liable to inheritance tax (IHT). Great increases in property values over the past few years have moved many individuals to a position where their estates would exceed the nil-rate band of inheritance tax. Where the will-making process is properly approached, an examination of the nature and composition of the client's estate is required. Many individuals still fail to appreciate the actual "cash" value of their dwelling-houses; when the potential liability is put to the client, he or she will often see the benefits which can be obtained from making a suitably drafted will, making use of at least part of that client's nil-rate band.

Non-beneficial provisions

A will can include "non-beneficial provisions" which may be of **1–09** particular concern to the client. These can include specific funeral directions, for which there is no provision under the 1964 Act in relation to an intestate estate. Interpersonal relationships within a family can often be strained or difficult, and on occasions, disputes and arguments can arise amongst adult children of the deceased as to the proper disposal of their late parent's remains. Such disputes can, to a large extent, be avoided if the client specifically directs what should happen to his or her remains on death. Equally, some clients may wish to donate their bodies (or parts of the same) for scientific or medical research, etc. Again, no provision for such ancillary matters appears in the 1964 Act.

Last statement

1–10   Above all else, it should be pointed out that a will can be the last statement of love, respect and affection which that client has for members of his or her family or others. It is a lasting testament of such feelings and in the author's view, it is entirely valid to make this essentially philosophical point to the client.

CLIENT RESISTANCE

1–11   Clients very often put forward reasons as to why they have not made, and do not wish to make a will. The legal profession should be in a position to address the client's viewpoint and to put forward reasoned arguments as to why the client is wrong. The most common arguments put forward by clients might be characterised by the following phrases:

"I am too young to make a will"

1–12   It is a common misconception that the making of a will lies within the province of older generations. In fact, the right to test is a freedom available to all individuals who are capax and of full age (see Chapter 2). A 30-year-old who is married and has young children may be a high earner. The client may be operating under the type of misconception detailed above (*i.e.* that the surviving spouse will inherit everything even where there is no will). In such circumstances, the potentially adverse effect of intestacy upon the surviving spouse should be carefully explained to the client, as should the rights of young children who might be left to vest in their legal rights and the free estate at 16 years of age, and thereafter possibly squander their inheritance.

"I have nothing to leave"

1–13   Clients notoriously undervalue their estates. Some clients fail to take into account, for example, the value of life assurance policies which only pay out upon their deaths. One reason for this is, perhaps, that the client does not perceive that he or she will benefit in any way from the funds in question. Similarly, clients will often fail to take into account a legitimate *spes successionis* as, understandably, clients do not wish to value elderly parents in terms of "pounds and pence". Clients who are members of an occupational pension scheme or who have their own personal pension plans often overlook, or do not appreciate, that death while still in employment or prior to attainment of the normal retirement age (under the relevant personal pension plan) is likely to result in a sizeable sum of money becoming available. If the will-making process is approached in a proper, detailed, information-gathering basis, it can often be demonstrated to the client that he or she has a net worth of which he or she was unaware, and which would justify making a will.

"I have no one to leave my estate to"

1–14   An individual who is widowed and has no issue might feel that there is no point in making a will. It should be explained to such a client that even where there is no will, the 1964 Act sets out Rules of Succession.

This could mean that fairly distant relatives, who have not been in contact for many years, benefit. The possible time and expense involved in tracing such beneficiaries should also be explained to the client. In such circumstances, the draftsman might consider it appropriate to ask such a client whether or not he or she would wish to see the benefit of his or her estate going to a charity or charities, or "deserving" old friends, etc.

"My family will do the right thing"

A small number of clients may believe that in making a will they may **1–15** be doing no more than precipitating a dispute within their family after death. Such a viewpoint should be seen as a denigration of responsibility and assumes that, notwithstanding the Rules of Succession, the client's family will ensure a fair outcome, perhaps reflecting the respective financial positions of adult children, etc. It should be pointed out that such an outcome can never be guaranteed and that the entitlement of a beneficiary on intestacy is, in fact, a legal right. Having been put to beneficiaries in that manner, it might be unlikely that they would agree to division of the intestate estate differing from that for which provision is made under the 1964 Act (even although this would be possible in terms of section 142 of the Inheritance Tax Act, 1984)—"After all, I am only taking what the law says I am entitled to".

"If I made a will I would be signing my own death warrant"

There often appears to be reluctance to make a will amongst **1–16** particularly elderly clients, as some wrongly assume a causal connection between the signature of the will and their time of death. This is, of course, nonsensical and the client should be dissuaded from maintaining such a superstitious outlook. If the client has fears in this area, then perhaps one way to seek to address them (quite apart from bringing some of the arguments outlined above to bear) is to persuade the client that, given his or her feelings, it would only be appropriate for the client to put his or her affairs in order.

"My affairs are too complex"

Many individuals will find that, over a period of time, they have been **1–17** "sold" investments and financial products which they do not fully understand. Such clients often find themselves being intimidated by complex investments, and instead of seeking advice in relation thereto, the client chooses to "stick his head in the sand". This can result in inertia across the board, with the client not really knowing what to do with such investments and how they might fall to be handled upon the client's death. In truth, this is no excuse for not making a will and, in fact, is a real incentive to consult with an appropriately skilled draftsman who can not only prepare the client's will, but also offer advice in relation to lifetime planning, perhaps utilising (dependent upon his or her tax profiles) the complex investments in question.

"I cannot afford to make a will at this time"

Such a statement is not normally a reference to the legal fees which **1–18** may be charged by the draftsman for preparation of the relevant document. It tends to reflect a misunderstanding on the part of particularly older clients who know nothing of the Rules of Ademption, etc. Clients sometimes have a gross misconception that if they make a will incorporating specific bequests then they must, at all costs, preserve and retain the items so bequeathed until their death. Obviously that is not the case (unless of course the client has contractually bound himself in some way to specifically bequeath the item in question, in which case he may be under some obligation to retain the item), and such a client should be told that they are free to deal with their property as they wish.

It is important that will draftsmen are able not only to produce documentation which meets the requirements of the willing testator, but are also in a position to reason with and persuade the unwilling as to why a will should be made.

THE LAW OF INTESTACY PRIOR TO THE SUCCESSION (SCOTLAND) ACT, 1964

1–19 The Law of Intestate Succession prior to September 10, 1964 tended to be a confusing patchwork, based largely on the common law as amended by various statutes passed at different times. This meant that prior to 1964, offering succinct advice on an intestacy was not a simple task. As Meston pointed out, whilst the Act did not purport by itself to be a new code of intestate succession, it was nonetheless "the first attempt to look at the law of intestate succession as a whole and to re-state most of it in the light of modern conditions and in a readily accessible form".[1]

THE PRIOR RIGHTS

1–20 Whilst the essential thrust of this work is to deal with appropriate drafting techniques, it is important that the draftsman should be able to explain in a reasonably succinct way the likely outcome to the client if the client were to decide not to make a will.

Under the system worked out by the 1964 Act it was essential to "carve out" certain prior rights for the surviving spouse after settlement of debts. As implied by their name, these rights took priority over all other claims on the estate. Thereafter, the first in line were those entitled to claim legal rights from the deceased's estate, and finally the 1964 Act provided rules as to who was entitled to succeed to the free estate.

Dwelling-house

1–21   Under section 8(1), when a person dies intestate leaving a spouse and the intestate estate includes a relevant interest[2] in the dwelling-house to which the section applies, the surviving spouse shall be entitled to receive out of the intestate estate:

(a) If the value of the relevant interest does not exceed £130,000[3]

---

[1] M.C. Meston, *The Succession (Scotland) Act, 1964* (1st ed., W. Green, 1964).
[2] Which can involve a tenancy—see s.8(6)(d) the 1964 Act.
[3] This is the current figure.

(i) If subsection (2) of this section does not apply to the relevant interest;

(ii) If the said subsection (2) applies, a sum equal to the value of the relevant interest;

(b) In any other case the sum of £130,000 provided that, if the intestate estate comprises a relevant interest in two or more dwelling-houses to which this section applies, this subsection shall have effect only in relation to which one of them as the surviving spouse may elect for the purposes of this subsection within six months of the date of death of the intestate.

Section 8(4) made it clear that the right applied to any dwelling-house in which the surviving spouse of the intestate was ordinarily resident at the date of death of the intestate.

Furniture and plenishings

In terms of section 8(3), the surviving spouse is entitled to receive out **1–22** of the intestate estate:

(a) Where the value of the furniture and plenishings does not exceed £22,000[4] the whole thereof;

(b) In any other case such part of the furnishings and plenishings to a value not exceeding £22,000 as may be chosen by the surviving spouse.

Provided that if the intestate estate comprises furniture and plenishings of two or more such dwelling-houses, the subsection shall have effect only in relation to the furniture and plenishings of such one of them as the surviving spouse may elect for the purposes of this subsection within six months of the date of death of the intestate.

Note that the figures of £130,000 and £22,000, respectively, are the most recent limits set for prior rights under the 1964 Act as amended (the original value of the housing right with effect from September 10, 1964—when the Act came into effect—was £15,000 and the furnishings right £5,000).

Section 8(6) defined "furniture and plenishings" as including garden effects, domestic animals, plates, plated articles, linen, china, glass, books, pictures, prints, articles of household use and consumable stores; but does not include any article or animal used at the date of death of the intestate for business purposes, or money, or securities for money, or any heirloom.[5]

Financial right

The financial right is contained in section 9 of the Act. In section 9(1) **1–23** it was *originally* provided that the surviving spouse shall be entitled to receive out of the intestate estate:

---

[4] This is the current figure.

[5] Compare the 1964 Act definition with *Millers Trustees v Miller*, 1907 S.C. 833, where "furniture" was held not to include consumable items.

(a) If the intestate is survived by issue, the sum of £2,500 or;
(b) If the intestate is not survived by issue the sum of £5,000.

The present figure where there is no issue is £58,000, and where there is issue £35,000. It should be noted that where the balance of the deceased's estate exceeds either of those figures, then the relevant sum is taken rateably from heritage and moveables.

LEGAL RIGHTS

1–24 Where there is no issue, the surviving spouse is entitled to one-half of the net moveable estate as at the date of death of the deceased spouse. Where there is issue, the entitlement of the surviving spouse is one-third of the net moveable estate as at the relevant date of death.

THE FREE ESTATE

1–25 Thereafter the free estate is divisible in terms of the Rules set out in essentially sections 1–7 (Pt I) of the 1964 Act. These Rules of Succession are set out in succinct tabular form in Meston.[6]

CRITICISMS OF THE STATUTORY FORMULA FOR INTESTACY

1–26 The 1964 Act was an attempt to rationalise the pre-existing law on intestacy. Whilst representing a rationalisation and an improvement upon the previous position, the framework set out under the 1964 Act still remains substantially in place and is not free from criticism.

House prices

1–27   The limits set out in sections 8 and 9 are reviewed from time to time. However, particularly in view of increases in house prices over recent years, it is arguable that the amount of the housing right is now far too low. A similar comment applies to the financial right under section 9 of the 1964 Act.

"Relevant interest"

1–28   In terms of section 8(6)(d) of the 1964 Act, the "relevant interest" in a dwelling-house is subject to any heritable debts secured over the interest. This, of course, means that the surviving spouse might be required to bear the added burden of, perhaps, a considerable mortgage just at a point in time where he or she is at his or her most financially vulnerable.

Definition of "dwelling-house"

1–29   The definition of "dwelling-house" is specified in section 8(6)(a) of the Act as including any garden or portion of ground attached to and usually occupied with the dwelling-house, or otherwise required for the

---

[6] M.C. Meston, The Succession (Scotland) Act, 1964 (5th ed.), Appendix 1.

amenity or convenience of the house. However, in light of changes in society, the question has to be raised as to whether or not the definition set out in the 1964 Act is sufficient.[7]

Children

Where children are entitled to claim their entitlement to *legitim* and/or **1–30** have right to the free estate, the framework set up by the 1964 Act does not prevent vesting at the age of 16 years. Even where section 9 of the Children (Scotland) Act, 1995 applies, vesting at the age of 16 years is not prevented. In particular, an executor dative is not specifically empowered by the 1964 Act to pay the benefit over to the parent or guardian for the time being of the child in question. This has been the attitude adopted by indemnity insurers issuing bonds of caution, who invariably required that the executor dative should retain the benefit in question until the beneficiary attained full age.

Impersonal and inflexible

The Rules of Intestacy are entirely impersonal. There is little or no **1–31** room for flexibility and clients should not place any reliance on their family "doing the right thing" and being prepared to enter into a Deed of Variation under section 142 of the Inheritance Tax Act, 1984. In some cases application of the Rules of Intestacy can result in what might be considered to be a wholly inequitable situation. Take the position of two spouses who have enjoyed a loving, mutually supportive relationship for several years. They have never had children and have never adopted a child. One spouse dies, leaving a substantial estate, survived by the other spouse, an elderly parent and brothers and sisters. Under the Rules of Succession referred to above, the spouse would receive her housing and financial prior rights and also one-half of the net moveable estate by way of legal rights. However, the elderly parent and brothers and sisters of the pre-deceasing spouse would succeed to the remainder of the pre-deceasing spouse's estate. This would apply whether or not there had been any estrangement at any time between the pre-deceasing spouse and the elderly parent or one or more of his collaterals. Given that the spouses may have striven during the course of their marriage to build up their asset base, is the foregoing outcome equitable?

Distortion

Application of the 1964 Act can involve a degree of distortion in **1–32** relation to the division of *legitim*. In that connection, sections 11(1) and 11(2) require to be read together. This can have the effect of passing a larger portion of a deceased's grandparents' estate to one "branch" of the family to the disadvantage of the other (which is something which most testators will normally seek to avoid).[8]

---

[7] The definition is unclear as to whether mobile or temporary residences such as caravans or houseboats are included. It would seem strange that there should be any doubt on this point given that the Matrimonial Homes (Family Protection) (Scotland) Act, 1981, expressly includes such temporary residences within the definition of a "matrimonial home". Meston is of the view that the definition can include such temporary residences: see Meston (4th ed.), p.39.

[8] See Meston, cited above, pp.56 and 57.

Trap for the unwary

1–33   There is also a trap for the unwary practitioner. At the time of writing nearly 40 years have passed since the 1964 Act came into effect. However, situations may still arise where familiarity with the pre-Act law will be required. It is not beyond the bounds of possibility that title to a heritable property of an individual who died prior to September 10, 1964 has not been fully made up. The pre-1964 law would still apply, and given the great increases in the value of heritable properties over the past 40 years or so, the possibility of a dispute within a family remains.

COMPARISON OF OUTCOMES—TO TEST OR NOT TO TEST

1–34   As can be seen from the above criticisms, for a large number of reasons, and perhaps with one exception,[9] there are hardly any situations in which intestacy will be preferable. The making of a will allows an individual much greater flexibility and can avoid the complexities (which few lay clients really understand) of the calculation of an appropriate Scheme of Division. The example below helps to illustrate the complications.

Example

Facts

1–35   A dies, survived by his spouse, B, and two children, X and Y. A's estate comprises the following:

(i) A dwelling-house worth	£100,000
(ii) A holiday cottage worth	£40,000
(iii) Furniture and personal effects in the dwelling-house worth	£10,000
(iv) Bank and building society deposits	£60,000
(v) A portfolio of shares worth	£300,000
(vi) A life policy (assigned in connection with A's mortgage over his dwelling-house)	£30,000

A has a mortgage of £50,000 on his dwelling-house, and his funeral expenses and other debts amount to £5,000.

Scheme of Division

1–36   Because A did not make a will before his death, a Scheme of Division is required to calculate:

- The entitlement of each beneficiary
- The IHT liability.

The methodology in calculating an appropriate Scheme of Division is, in truth, reasonably straightforward. However, it requires an understanding of how the Rules set out in the 1964 Act operate, thus:

---

[9] *Kerr, Petitioner*, 1968 S.L.T. (Sh. Ct.) 61.

1. In any estate, debts due by the deceased take priority over the rights of beneficiaries therein. That being so, debts form a first deduction in the calculation.
2. Under the 1964 Act, prior rights of the surviving spouse take priority over all other rights. Thus, after deduction of debts, prior rights require to be calculated.
3. Once that calculation has been properly effected (taking into account detailed provisions of the Act), the legal rights of surviving spouses then require to be calculated.
4. Only once this has taken place can the value of the free estate be ascertained.
5. Proper calculation of the rights of the surviving spouse is vital to the accurate ascertainment of any inheritance tax liability arising in respect of the estate passing to beneficiaries other than the spouse.

In relation to the facts detailed above the Scheme of Division would be as follows:

Scheme of Division example

Estate	*Heritable*	*Moveable*	**1–37**
Dwelling-house	£100,000		
Holiday cottage	£40,000		
Furniture and personal effects		£10,000	
Life policy		£30,000	
Other assets		£360,000	
	£140,000	£400,000	

Less debts

(i) Proportion of mortgage **1–38**
Heritable estate £100,000 x £50,000   £38,461.54
        £130,000

Moveable estate £30,000 x £50,000   £11,538.46
        £130,000

(ii) Other debts   £5,000.00
        £101,538.46   £383,461.54

Net estate for division   £485,000

	Heritable	*Moveable*
	£101,538.46	£383,461.54

Deduct prior rights

House (s.8)   £100,000.00   **1–39**
Less proportion of mortgage   £38,461.54
                £61,538.46
Furniture (s.8)   £10,000.00
        £40,000.00   £373,461.54

Cash right (s.9)	£35,000	
Born by heritable estate £40,000.00 x £35,000	£3,386.04	
£413,461.54		
Born by moveable estate £373,461.54 x £35,000		
£413,461.54	£31,613.96	
	£341,847.58	

Deduct legal rights

1–40 Spouses *ius relictae* (1/3 x £341,847.58)   £113,949.19
Legitim fund   £113,949.19
                                              £36,613.96   £113,949.20

Free estate is therefore £36,613.96 + £113,949.20 = **£150,563.16**

IHT calculation

1–41 *Net estate for division*   £485,000.00

Spouse entitled to:	£100,000.00	
(a) Dwelling-house (s.8)		
(b) Furniture (s.8)	£10,000.00	
(c) Cash right (s.9)	£35,000.00	
(d) Legal rights	£113,949.19	
	£258,849.19	
Less proportion of mortgage	£38,461.54	
		£220,487.65
		£264,512.35

IHT on £264,512.35	Nil	
Tax on first £255,000		
Tax on first £9,512.35	£3,804.94	£3,804.94
Divisible between X and Y		**£260,707.41**

Comments on example

Life policy

1–42   In this case, as there is a life policy assigned to the heritable creditors, the mortgage requires to be apportioned between the heritable property and moveable estate. For the heritable proportion the calculation (the value of the heritable property over which the mortgage is secured) is divided by the value of that property combined with the value of the relevant life policy, multiplied by the amount of the mortgage. The apportionment of the mortgage liability between heritable and moveable estate arises owing to the principle that, if the creditor holds securities over both heritable and moveable property for the same debt, then that debt requires to be apportioned as being partly heritable and partly moveable.[10] The actual assignation of endowment policies to building

---

[10] See the case of *Graham v Graham* (1898) 5 S.L.T. 319 O.H.

societies and banks is a practice which has been increasingly departed from over the past 15 years or so. Increasingly, vendors have adopted a perhaps less paternalistic view of their borrowers, and have allowed the latter to arrange interest-only mortgages, making it clear to the borrowers that it falls to them to ensure that they arrange a suitable investment to repay the capital balance of the sum borrowed at the relevant maturity date. Thus, even if a policy has been arranged to meet ,or at least partially defray, the capital repayment at maturity of the loan, if that policy has not been assigned, then the creditor has no security over the same, and the apportionment detailed in the foregoing Scheme of Division will not be required. An equal consideration might apply if, although an assignation of the policy had been signed by the borrower, intimation of that assignation had never been effected (intimation of the assignation being required in order to effect the right of the assignee).

Dwelling-house

Bear in mind that the heritable right of the surviving spouse relates to **1–43** a "relevant interest in a dwelling-house" to which section 8 applies. In paragraph (d) of section 8(6) "relevant interest" in relation to a dwelling-house means the interest therein of an owner, or the interest therein of a tenant, subject in either case to any heritable debts secured over the interest (*i.e.* the surviving spouse takes the relevant property subject to any outstanding mortgage).

Holiday cottage furnishings

Note that no value is given for furnishings in the holiday cottage. The **1–44** furnishings in question are situated in the dwelling-house to which the spouse has right under section 8 of the 1964 Act. However, had the holiday cottage been furnished and the furniture belonged to A, under section 8(3) the right to furniture and plenishings of a dwelling-house applies to a dwelling-house to which section 8 applies (*i.e.* the spouse would not have been entitled to claim the furniture and plenishings in both the section 8 dwelling-house and the holiday cottage, even if the combined value of the same is less than £22,000).

Financial right

The cash right again has to be apportioned between the heritable and **1–45** moveable property in view of the provisions of section 9(3):

> "the amount which the surviving spouse is entitled to receive by virtue of Subsection 1 of this Section shall be borne by and paid out of, the parts of the intestate Estate consisting of heritable and moveable property respectively in proportion to the respective amounts of those parts".

Common mistakes

These are: omitting to properly apportion the mortgage as a debt **1–46** where there is a life policy assigned to the lender and omitting to apportion the cash right as required by section 9(3).

Solution—if only A had made a will

As can be seen from the above Scheme of Division, because A did not **1–47** make a will, he has allowed his young children to succeed to a sum of £260,707.41 after payment of inheritance tax. This situation:

- could seriously prejudice the financial position of his surviving spouse who may live for many years after he has died;
- builds in no financial protection whatsoever for his children, both of whom will succeed to a very sizeable sum of money upon attaining the age of 16;
- may require the surviving spouse to consider consulting with the Accountant of Court in terms of section 9 of the Children Act, 1995.

Had he consulted with a solicitor, the latter may well have been able to offer advice which would have protected, in financial terms, both herself and her children, and allowed for mitigation over a period of time of the anticipated IHT liability on death of B.

Possible Changes to the Law of Intestacy

1–48 In its 1990 Report (No.124), the Scottish Law Commission recommended reform of the existing law on legal rights including Rules on intestate succession, the intention being to greatly simplify matters.

Briefly, the Commission proposed that the existing prior rights of the surviving spouse should be replaced by the surviving spouse's "legal share", a new legal concept.

Legal share proposals

1–49
- The legal share would extend to heritable property as well as moveable property.
- The spouse's legal share would be 30 per cent of the first £200,000 of net estate and 10 per cent of any excess.
- In relation to intestate succession, the surviving spouse should receive the whole intestate estate if the deceased left no issue. If the deceased was survived by issue, then the surviving spouse should receive the first £100,000 with any excess being divided 50/50 between the surviving spouse and the issue.
- If the surviving spouse claimed his or her legal share, then he or she would forfeit all other rights of testate or intestate succession. This proposal has a resonance with the equitable compensation provisions of section 13 of the 1964 Act which provided that:

> "Every testamentary disposition executed after the commencement of this Act by which provision is made in favour of the spouse or any issue of the Testator and which does not contain a declaration that the provision so made is in full and final satisfaction of the right to any share in the Testator's Estate to which the spouse or the issue as the case may be is entitled by virtue of *ius relicti*, *ius relictae* or *legitim* shall (unless the disposition contains an express provision to the contrary) have effect as if it contains such a declaration."

These proposals have not yet been acted upon. Unfortunately, this appears to reflect the historical provenance of the 1964 Act itself. In

1950, the Mackintosh Committee on "the Law of Succession in Scotland" published its report. This bemoaned the fact that whilst legislative change had taken place in England in 1925 (the Administration of Estates Act), relative to the Law of Intestate Succession in that jurisdiction, no progress had been made over intervening years for any similar amendment to the Law of Intestacy in Scotland, and that notwithstanding increasing pressure for change during that time. England in fact saw other legislative change in this area when the Intestate Estates Act, 1952, received the Royal Assent in October, 1952. Given the criticisms of the regime set up under the 1964 Act, it is to be hoped that it does not take the Scottish Executive more than 30 years to modernise the Law of Intestate Succession in Scotland.

PROFESSIONAL CONSIDERATIONS IN MAKING A WILL

The making of an appropriate will for a client is a task redolent with **1–50** responsibility on the part of the draftsman. This should always have been the case, but the decision in *Holmes v Bank of Scotland* (See Chapter 3) merely re-emphasises the heavy responsibility incumbent upon the draftsman. When the client instructs the preparation of a will, then the draftsman should ensure that he follows certain fundamental tenets:

- Is the draftsman satisfied as to the capacity of the client? In that connection, see the fuller discussion on this point in Chapter 2.
- Is there any sign of the client being under some form of duress or undue influence? Again, for a fuller discussion of this point see Chapter 2.

Most draftsmen will be aware of concerns in relation to the above matters. However, there are other areas where the draftsman should be on his guard. A solicitor should never take instructions for preparation of a will from a third party. While this might seem to be obvious, circumstances can arise where the draftsman might be less vigilant than he would normally be.

For example, a solicitor has acted for a client for many years. During that time, the client has demonstrated that he is an individual of personal and financial integrity. The solicitor receives a telephone call from the client indicating that he has an elderly uncle whose physical health has failed, but, in so far as his mental capacity is concerned, he is still "all there". The client's uncle wishes to make a will but is reclusive and unable to travel, owing to his health. The uncle does not trust solicitors. The client passes on his uncle's instructions and suggests that he (the client) will take the will out to his uncle for signature. A draftsman who succumbs to the temptation to trust his client in those circumstances may well face problems further down the line. The draftsman should always meet with the testator and confirm his instructions. At the same time, the draftsman can form his own view in the capacity of "the old uncle". Where the draftsman does not follow that practice, he is asking for trouble. The draftsman must always be vigilant to observe his duty of client confidentiality.

The Code of Conduct of the Law Society of Scotland (Art.5(a)) indicates that a solicitor must act on the basis of his client's proper instructions or on the instructions of another solicitor who acts for the client. Whilst an elderly or infirm client may be willing to have his instructions conveyed to the draftsman by a trusted relative, the draftsman must always be aware of his responsibilities in relation to his duty of client confidentiality. The fact that the contact has been initiated by a relative of the testator does not mean that the draftsman is thereby entitled to make that relative privy to the advice which the draftsman has offered to the testator, nor to the format of the will to be granted by the testator. Article 4 of the Code makes it clear that it is a fundamental duty of a solicitor to observe client confidentiality.

1–51   Another similar area of difficulty is where a trusted client indicates that he has an old relative who wishes to make a will, and the client wishes to bring his relative into the draftsman's office to issue instructions. To avoid embarrassment, the draftsman should explain immediately that he needs to speak to the elderly relative in private. This will allow the draftsman to ensure that there is no question of undue influence being brought to bear on the older relative. The draftsman should always bear in mind that his responsibility is not to the "introducing client", but to the potential testator.

Perhaps the most awkward situation for the draftsman relates to the making of wills for spouses. It is suggested that the draftsman should not assume that spouses wish to make "mirror image" wills. Whilst in the great majority of cases this will prove to be the case, this should never be assumed. Again, to avoid embarrassment at the meeting itself, it might be appropriate for the draftsman to suggest that appropriate practice would be for the spouses to consult separately with the draftsman, unless, of course, they have already decided that they have no objection to having a "combined" meeting with the draftsman—and this presupposes that their wills will be true "mirror images". This is a particularly difficult area—clients may feel that an insistence on the part of their solicitor that they be interviewed separately is "overkill". There are two particular areas where difficulties can arise:

1. The spouses may have no children, and may not have addressed in discussions between themselves who should benefit on death of the survivor of them. Such clients may have no difficulty whatsoever in the survivor of them succeeding to the whole estate of the pre-deceasor. However, they may have entirely different views as to who the ultimate beneficiary should be.
2. Younger clients may often not have considered the question of guardianship if they should both pass on whilst their children are still in minority. Again, this can be a particularly difficult area for the draftsman where the spouses are at odds as to who should be appointed.

There are no practice Rules governing the above situations, and it is not clear to the author that either of the situations above would necessarily be characterised as being a "conflict of interest". It should always be borne in mind that the individual testator has freedom (within recognised limits) to make the will which he or she sees fit. If spouses have irreconcilable differences as to how each other should make their wills, then the best course for the draftsman would be to suggest that they seek separate advice.

SOLICITOR AS BENEFICIARY

Where a solicitor has for many years provided valued services to a client, **1–52** it is perhaps understandable that the client may wish to recognise this service in his will. However, this is a particular danger area for the draftsman, as an examination of the records of the Scottish Solicitors' Discipline Tribunal indicates. At all times, the draftsman should be aware of the risks to him in preparing a will in which he might be a beneficiary. The best advice is that the draftsman should not prepare a will in which he, or any partner or member of his firm or of his family, will benefit in a material (or, perhaps, any) way. Whilst this may appear to be extreme, it is a practice which the draftsman would be advised to follow. Over the years, it has been accepted that, above all else, a solicitor should put the interest of his client before his own. At all times, the draftsman must steer clear of any suggestion of undue influence.

This can be a difficult area for a solicitor who has acted for a particular client for many years. The client may not be aware of the necessary, ethical standards incumbent on his solicitor, and may not understand (and may take offence) when a longstanding legal agent (whom he may come to regard a friend) declines the proposed benefit. However, unless the benefit in question is no more than a "token", the best practice would be for the solicitor to indicate that he cannot make the will (nor can any of his partners), and if the client still wants the benefit in question in his will, then the client will need to consult another and independent firm of solicitors.[11] Whilst the temptation might be to accede to the client's request, the draftsman should be aware of various decisions of the Scottish Solicitors Discipline Tribunal in this area. These decisions are a matter of record and claimed ignorance of the same will be no excuse.

The particular difficulty in this area is what amounts to a "token" bequest. It has been suggested that the figure of £100 to £150 might be regarded as being acceptable. However, the draftsman should consider whether or not it is appropriate for any question as to his integrity to be raised over such a small sum.

Increasingly, solicitors are required to have greater social and interpersonal skills than perhaps possessed by our antecedents. This is an area where an acquisition of such skills is a necessity. For a comprehensive consideration of the issues arising in this particular area, the author would refer the reader to Barr, etc.[12]

IMPORTANCE OF REVIEWING AN EXISTING WILL

Many clients, perhaps not fully concerned about the possible tax **1–53** mitigation benefits of a properly drafted will, may find the will-making process to be intrusive, if not unpleasant. This is very often due to the

---

[11] See Webster, *Professional Ethics and Practice for Scottish Solicitors.*
[12] Barr, etc., *Drafting Wills in Scotland*, (Butterworths/Law Society of Scotland, 1994) paras 6.150–156.

fact that clients, of necessity, are required to contemplate not only their own death, but also that of loved ones. In particular, no client wishes to envisage a situation where his or her children will die before him or her. Quite apart from saving legal expense, the foregoing represents a reason why many clients, once the will has been signed, regard themselves as having "done their duty" and are happy that the will should be consigned in safe custody, largely out of mind, until it is required to be put into effect. Again, however, it is important that clients should be encouraged to review their wills regularly (perhaps once a year). A client should be advised:

- That changes of address of anyone named in the will have no effect on the validity of the same, although a note of the new address should be placed with the will. Whilst the death of someone named in the will might not affect the essential thrust of the document, a brief discussion with the client's solicitor might be indicated.
- That changes (for better or for worse) in the client's financial position should be discussed with the client's solicitor—the will may have been made at a point in time where the client was reasonably wealthy and felt able to spread some of that wealth beyond his own immediate family. Business or a financial disaster might greatly affect the client's viewpoint, and where the beneficiaries in question are members of the family, the usual way of bestowing a benefit upon them will be by way of legacy. In such circumstances, the client does need, for example, to be aware of the priority of legacies over residuary bequests.
- That if a will incorporates tax mitigation measures, obvious changes to capital taxation in the UK should precipitate a professional review of the will.
- Most importantly, that it is the client's responsibility (and not that of the drafting solicitor) to ensure that the will remains an up-to-date and accurate statement of the client's testamentary wishes and intentions. The solicitor should remind the client of the necessity of the client regularly reviewing his will. In the Appendix of Styles, the author has reproduced a copy of the note issued to his clients when they have completed the making of a new will.

SAFE CUSTODY

1–54 Once a will has been made/reviewed for the client the following course of action should be considered/advised:

- A will should not be retained by a client at home. If, for example, there was a serious fire in which the client died, it is likely that the will would also be destroyed. Whilst a copy of the last will could be set up, this is unnecessary and expensive. Clients should therefore be encouraged to leave their executed will with a solicitor, or at the very least place it in safe custody with their bank (although this will result in an annual safe custody fee being charged by the bank).

- A copy of the completed will should be sent out to the client with a recommendation that it be placed with his or her other important papers. Many clients are well organised and will in any event advise their families that a will has been made and has been placed with a particular solicitor. Other individuals are private and do not particularly wish to inform their families that a new will has been made as, perhaps, they fear that this might elicit some enquiry (perhaps for the wrong motive) on the part of adult children, etc. as to why a new will has been made. Such a client should nonetheless be encouraged to keep a copy of the will (bearing the name and address of the custodian of the same), where it will be found with other important papers.

CHAPTER 2

THE DRAFTSMAN'S RESPONSIBILITY TO THIRD PARTIES

BACKGROUND

2–01 "May you live in interesting times"—apparently an old Chinese curse. We certainly do live in interesting times. The motto of the Law Society of Scotland—*Nihil Humani Alienum* (roughly translated "nothing in human affairs is strange to us")—is increasingly relevant. In every aspect of professional practice, solicitors are encouraged to take more care, be risk aware (and at the same time risk averse), whilst maintaining a reasonable profitability. The legal profession has become more aware of those areas of practice wherein, as the ancient mariners would say, "here be dragons". For many years, however, Scottish solicitors were comforted (and comfortable) in the knowledge that they could not be held to account by disappointed beneficiaries for the negligent drafting of a client's will. Essentially, for many years Scottish solicitors were responsible to their clients—and only their clients. This was based on a decision given over 150 years ago in the *Robertson v Fleming* case.[1] This case involved a claim by cautioners against the solicitor employed by the debtor to prepare and to have intimated (which the solicitor did not do) a bond of relief and assignation in favour of the pursuers. This case did not therefore involve a "disappointed beneficiary", but arose out of a commercial document. The views of the court are of interest:

- Lord Cranworth stated that "the doctrine contended for at the Bar, that where A employs B, a professional man, to do some act professionally, under which, when done, C would derive a benefit, if, then, B is guilty of negligence towards his employer so that C loses the contemplated benefit, B is, as a matter of course, responsible to C, is evidently untenable. Such a doctrine would, as pointed out by my noble friend, lead to the result that a disappointed legatee might sue the Testator's Solicitor for negligence in not causing the Will to be duly signed and attested, though he might be an entire stranger to both the Solicitor and the Testator."
- Lord Wensleydale stated that "whenever an Attorney or Agent is employed by anyone to do an act which when done will be beneficial to a third person and that act is negligently done, an action for negligence may have been attained by the third person against the Attorney or Agent. I cannot think that any such proposition is made out to be part of the Law of

---

[1] (1861) Macq. 4 at 167.

Scotland. . . . It is rightly said on behalf of appellant that if that proposition was true, numberless legatees and heirs on entail, disappointed of their expectations by erasures and informalities, would have invoked its aid to indemnify them, but no one ever did."

It should be noted that these comments were *obiter dicta*. Clearly, in 1861 the view was firmly held that solicitors ought to have no liability to a disappointed beneficiary. The protection which the *Robertson v Fleming* case offered Scottish solicitors alleged to have been negligent in making a will was for many years applied in later cases.[2]

The position in England changed some years ago. In *Ross v Caunters*[3] Sir Robert Megarry had held that solicitors did owe a duty of care to disappointed beneficiaries. This view was repeated in the House of Lord's decision in *White v Jones*.[4] Interestingly, in the English case of *White v Jones*, reference was made to the Scottish decision in *Robertson v Fleming*. Lord Goff pointed out that the comments of the learned judges referred to above had been *obiter*.

THE PRESENT LAW IN SCOTLAND

In *Weir v J.M. Hodge & Son*,[5] Lord Weir somewhat unhappily found **2–02** himself to be bound by the decision in *Robertson v Fleming*, although he expressed great concern that the decision in *Robertson v Fleming* was out of kilter with the current view in Scottish society, and with the modern law of negligence.

Lord Cameron of Lochbroom also perceived in *MacDougall v MacDougall's Executors*[6] that he was bound by the decision in *Robertson v Fleming*. Lord Cameron decided that a solicitor who was careless in execution of a will owed no duty or care to a party whom the testator intended to benefit thereunder and, even if he did, the ambit of that duty would not extend to one who was not an intended beneficiary under the will, but a mere successor in title to an intended beneficiary. However, the unreported case of *Robertson v Messrs Watt & Co*[7] appears to have proved to be a watershed in Scottish law in this area, even though its significance may not have been realised at the relevant time. In the latter case, the whole issue of whether or not a solicitor could be liable in negligence to a disappointed beneficiary was reserved, pending proof of the facts. It would seem that in *Robertson v Watt & Co* a Scottish Court had at long last recognised that not only should *Robertson v Fleming* not be regarded as binding and that the law had moved on, but also that, as in *White v Jones*, the law of Scotland could recognise a claim by a disappointed beneficiary.

---

[2] *Tully v Ingram* (1891) 19 R. 65; *Auchindoss v Duncan* (1894) 21 R. 1091.
[3] (1980) Ch. 297.
[4] [1995] 2 A.C. 207.
[5] 1990 S.L.T. 266.
[6] 1994 S.L.T. 1178.
[7] July 4, 1995.

Robertson v Watt & Co was an Appeal from Arbroath Sheriff Court. The deceased's wife had raised an action against her late husband's solicitors on the basis that, having been instructed by him prior to his death, they failed to advise him to make another will in circumstances where the will previously made by him (and in terms of which it was alleged the pursuer had been left the whole estate) could not be found. The pursuer contended that it had remained her late husband's position that she should inherit the whole of his estate. No will was made, and on his death the wife received only her prior and legal rights under the Laws of Intestacy. The solicitors in question disputed liability to Mrs Robertson, claiming that they were not instructed in connection with the deceased's testamentary intentions, but only in relation to a dispute concerning access to a drainpipe. It is clear that the court took the view that the claims of the pursuer should be put to proof, *i.e.* they did not simply dismiss the action as being irrelevant.

2–03 We turn now to the case of *Holmes v the Governor and Company of the Bank of Scotland* (also known as *Davidson v Bank of Scotland*).[8] Again, Lord Kingarth having considered all of the authorities (and giving particular importance to the case of *Robertson v Watt & Co*), refused to dismiss the action on the grounds of relevance, but allowed a proof before answer. Although, again, the facts in this case were disputed, the message from this case is clear—Scottish courts will no longer tolerate delay in the making of a will for a client, particularly as the family of the deceased client of the bank had alleged that the bank had been told on at least two occasions that their client's health was failing, and that if they did not get a move on she would not be able to sign the will (which turned out to be the case).

It would therefore appear that the "shield" protecting solicitors against claims by disappointed beneficiaries, provided by *Robertson v Fleming*, has at long last gone. The *Robertson v Watt & Co* case is also of interest, as there appears to have been an implication that even if the solicitors were instructed only to deal with a dispute regarding a drainpipe, if they knew of the testamentary position in respect of Mr Robertson they should have offered appropriate advice. In that connection, the case of *John J. Smith v Gordon & Smyth and Others*[9] is of note. In this case, the seller of heritable property was unaware that if he did not reinvest the proceeds within a certain time, he could not claim rollover relief for capital gains tax purposes. He was not advised of this by his solicitor. His solicitor was found liable. In the opinion of Lady Paton, the solicitor should have advised his client at the very least to seek the view of his accountant, or the opinion of a specialist tax adviser.

The legal profession is moving under full sail into increasingly risk-laden waters. Is a solicitor now under an obligation to make a specific enquiry as to whether or not all of his clients have made wills? If he does not do so, can he be liable? One might hesitate to adhere to that suggestion, but best practice would indicate that appropriate advice should be offered, if only on a "defensive" basis.

Those who do make wills are increasingly going to find themselves under pressure and their actings under retrospective scrutiny, sometimes

---

[8] 2002 S.L.T. 544; and 2002 S.C.L.R. 481.
[9] See *www.scotcourts.gov.uk/opinions/pat1607.html*

several years after the will has been made. Human nature being what it is, questions might be raised even where, on the face of it, a will has been properly drafted. For example, in a substantial estate, questions might arise as to whether or not, when drafting the will for the relevant client, the client was advised on IHT mitigation strategies.

RISK-MANAGEMENT RECOMMENDATIONS

The following recommendations might help to avoid difficulty at a later stage. **2–04**

1. Gather as much information as possible regarding a client and properly retain the same.
2. Avoid making wills on the basis of a telephone conversation. The legal profession is notorious for not keeping detailed notes of telephone conversations.
3. Endeavour whenever possible to meet with the client and retain detailed notes of the meeting(s) in question, confirming matters discussed at the meeting in a subsequent letter to the client.
4. Demonstrate from the file that the question of IHT mitigation has been raised. In particular, do not rely on an assurance on the part of the client that IHT will never be an issue in so far as his or her estate is concerned. Clients often misidentify the composition, nature and value of their personal estates. The manner in which house prices have increased over recent years has resulted in many more individuals coming into the realm of IHT liability. In the Appendix of Styles, the author has included a note on IHT sent to all clients who wish to make a will (whether for the first time or not). The purpose of this is to focus the mind of the client, and also to demonstrate that the point has been raised.
5. Always ensure that the client is advised (in properly recorded fashion) of the effect of legal rights upon his or her estate (again, see the author's note on legal rights, for issue to clients making wills, etc). Few clients know about the doctrine of legal rights, and a claim in respect of the same can have a distorting effect on the thrust of a client's will. Failure to advise the client of the nature and effect of legal rights may result in a complaint that the client was not put in a position where he or she could have considered strategies for mitigating the effect of such a claim upon their estate, particularly by a "black sheep".
6. Once the client has issued what appear to be final instructions, do not delay in the preparation of a draft will for approval by the client. A question of delay in preparation of the will was considered in both *White v Jones*[10] and also in *Holmes v Bank of Scotland*.[11] Although in the latter case facts were disputed, the court took the view that it was prepared to consider whether

---

[10] Cited above.
[11] Cited above.

there had been a delay which might lead to liability on the part of the bank.

7. Always have a copy of the draft approved by the client before it is executed. Send a copy of the draft with a suitable commentary to the client.

8. So far as possible and within the draftsman's power, he should ensure that there is no delay in proper execution of the will itself.

9. It is of course the responsibility of the draftsman to ensure that the will has been fully and properly executed. This includes checking that the client has made no unauthenticated alterations, deletions or additional changes which might affect the whole of the relevant section of the will.

10. Unless a firm offers a "will reviewing" service (which few firms do), always make it clear to the client that it remains his or her responsibility to ensure that the will remains an up-to-date statement of their testamentary wishes and intentions. Although clients may think differently, the legal profession as a whole is not telepathic and does not know what is happening in a client's private life. Clients should be advised to review their wills once a year (once again see the Appendix of Styles, which includes the note issued by the author to clients who have just completed the execution of a will). In addition, there are "life events" or circumstances which might occasion a client to carry out an unplanned annual review, namely:

    (i) additions to the family
    (ii) the death of someone named in a will
    (iii) a windfall by way of inheritance or otherwise
    (iv) conversely, a financial disaster
    (v) a perceived change in the laws relating to capital taxation in the UK.

11. Above all else, proper records should be retained on file. Professional indemnity insurers take a dim view of failure to "properly write up" a file.

It remains to be seen to what extent there will be a burgeoning of claims arising from the *Holmes* case. However, one point is clear. Even if the legal profession has not yet realised the same, the days of treating the making of a will as a peripheral, loss-leading service have to be consigned to the past. Those who draft wills for clients need to be able to demonstrate, from this point onwards, that they have applied appropriate standards of care to the task.

CHAPTER 3

INFORMATION GATHERING (INHERITANCE TAX AND OTHER COMMON PROBLEMS)

BACKGROUND TO INFORMATION GATHERING

The adage "know your client" is extremely important. The information-gathering process is vital, and an almost forensic approach is required. Most firms now use information sheets, which are often sent out to clients who indicate a wish to make a will, to be completed and returned to the draftsman solicitor before meeting with the client in question.[1] **3–01**

It is, however, essential that the draftsman should not regard even a seemingly fully-completed information sheet as being the end of his responsibilities. The information provided by the client has to be considered in detail and, where appropriate, additional questions need to be raised. A will cannot be made properly without having full information from the client. In order to properly frame a will for a client, it is important to ascertain his or her financial position, the general family circumstances of the client, and his/her wishes.

The early information-gathering process is an important one and, if carried out properly, can itself be not only a means of demonstrating appropriate good practice, but also a source of generation of additional business for the solicitor. An example of this might be where a client has an obvious "inheritance tax timebomb". Many wealthy clients do not realise the likely effect of inheritance tax on their deaths, and may be delighted to know that there is a range of strategies available to mitigate IHT. For example, an appropriate life policy written in trust could be obtained to at least partially address the effect of inheritance tax on the death of the client.

If the information-gathering process is properly carried out, it can throw up various "interesting" areas where not only the draftsman can add real value for the client, but also additional business can be generated for the solicitor preparing the will.

Areas to be aware of are:

- Business interests
- Partnership interests
- Marriage contracts
- Lifetime gifts (including the creation of *inter vivos* trusts)
- Survivorship destinations

---

[1] See suggested format in the Appendix of Styles.

- Bank accounts
- Powers of apportionment or appointment
- Care home fees
- Powers of attorney
- Inheritance tax issues
- Sensitivity issues
- Special destinations

We will now take a look at each of these areas in turn.

BUSINESS INTERESTS

3–02 Quite apart from bearing in mind the question of business property relief for inheritance tax purposes, further investigation of the relevant business interest might prove to be of value to the client. Many worthwhile businesses effectively die with their owners, mainly because the latter have not planned any appropriate succession to the interest in question during their lifetimes. The value of a small business may in fact be entirely dependent on the goodwill generated by the client himself/herself.

When making a will for such a person, it might be appropriate to suggest that the client now begin to take steps to ensure an orderly succession to his or her business on death. This may mean bringing in other parties who will themselves begin to attract a clientele and generate goodwill, and may not appeal to some clients. However, if the business fails then the value represented thereby may be almost entirely lost to the client's family, with the executors being left to carry out no more than an asset stripping exercise.

PARTNERSHIP INTERESTS

3–03 If the client is a partner then a check on the terms of the partnership agreement is indicated. The danger area here relates to how the interest of a deceased partner is to be handled.

Business property or agricultural relief

3–04   If the surviving partners are obliged to purchase the interest of a deceased partner (as opposed to being given the option to do so), then the Inland Revenue will deem that such a clause in the partnership contract is an agreement for sale reached before death and will thus disentitle the estate of the deceased from claiming business property or agricultural relief.[2]

A property does not qualify for business or agricultural relief if it is subject to a binding contract for sale (except a contract relating to the conversion of an unincorporated business to a company, or a company reconstruction). A "buy and sell" agreement made by partners or

---

[2] Sections 113 and 124 of the Finance Act 1987.

company directors to take effect on their death is considered by the Inland Revenue to constitute such a contract.

Transfer of shares

There are of course other considerations to be taken into account in **3–05** relation to the preparation of a will for a testator who has a shareholding in a private company or who is a partner. The memorandum and articles of a company may well have specific provisions regarding transfer of shares, including to the deceased's shareholder's beneficiaries. In the case of a partnership, it is trite law that owing to the presumed element of *delectus persona*, unless a partnership agreement provides otherwise, a deceased partner cannot bequeath his place in the partnership as such to a third party (in effect introduce a new partner without the consent of the existing partners). A bequest of an individual's interest in a partnership is really a legacy of the value of the partner's interest in the partnership as at the date of death. Where the memorandum and articles of a private company restrict transfers in certain circumstances, then once again the bequest is really a value of those shares, and not the shareholding itself. These are matters which can truly only be established by examination of the relevant documentation, in order that the client may be under no illusion as to what the nature of the bequest will in fact amount to.

Bequeath of business property

A further problem may arise where the client wishes to bequeath, for **3–06** example, a building which he owns (and from which there is a conducted business in which he had an interest). Such an asset will attract business property relief for IHT purposes at 50 per cent. However, the beneficiary to whom the building has been bequeathed may have no interest in the business whatsoever, and may have little concern as to the degree of disruption which might be occasioned by the loss of that building to the business. The scope for, to say the least, friction between the relevant beneficiary and the remaining principals in the business is obvious.

Such a difficulty should be pointed out to the client and a strategy developed, if possible, to avoid potential problems. A solution might be for the will to contain a direction to executors to offer the building to the business at current open market value, with a direction that the net proceeds of such a sale (if carried through) be paid to the relevant beneficiary.

MARRIAGE CONTRACTS

Many hold the view that what happens in America eventually impacts on **3–07** UK lifestyles. Marriage contracts are again increasingly in vogue in the USA, and there may well be a resurgence in their use in this country where, for example, individuals who have previously been married and have, perhaps, adult families of their own, are marrying again late in life. In such circumstances, they may have already agreed and have entered into a contract in terms of which they effectively waive legal rights in one or other's estates. If you are making a will for such a client, then the existence of such a marriage contract is of obvious relevance.

LIFETIME GIFTS (INCLUDING THE CREATION OF *INTER VIVOS* TRUSTS)

3–08 Where appropriate, a client could be encouraged to make sensible lifetime gifts. This is of obvious and particular relevance where inheritance tax may be an issue. It is also of obvious relevance where married clients may wish to consider making use of first death/nil-rate band legacies.

SURVIVORSHIP DESTINATIONS

3–09 It is important to bear in mind that special destinations between spouses are not revoked by divorce. In some cases, it might be appropriate to consider whether or not a particular special destination might be evacuated. This can be achieved in a will, but not where the destination is contractual (where the co-owner has contributed equally to the price), or where the property was gifted from a third party.

   If one co-owner paid the whole price but then directed that the property should be taken in joint names with a survivorship destination, the paying co-owner can revoke, but not the person who did not make a contribution towards the price. There may be circumstances in which it would be appropriate to revoke a special destination as part of a general inheritance tax planning exercise.

BANK ACCOUNTS

3–10 Beware of the common misconception that the survivor is entitled to all of the funds held in a joint bank or building society account. This is not the case.[3] Note, however, that under section 26 of the Family Law (Scotland) Act 1985, money in a housekeeping account is regarded as belonging to husband and wife in equal shares.

   Similarly, at the time of writing, the financial assessment of elderly people entering nursing homes is a real "hot potato". Interestingly, the National Assistance (Assessment of Resources) Regulations 1992 allow a local authority to regard bank accounts in joint names as being jointly owned by the spouses, even if this is not in fact the case.

A modern (but real) problem

3–11 Many clients now operate online banking accounts. In order to instruct transactions, the client has to have a specific password. The advice which a client receives from most online banks is that they should memorise their password and not write it down. This raises a specific problem once a client has passed on. If a client has followed the advice then how do the executors, in the first instance, know about the account and in the second instance, obtain details regarding the same without having the appropriate password. In the short-term, pending banks adopting a suitable approach to such problems, clients should be advised to ensure

---

[3] *Dennis v Aitchison*, 1923 S.C. 819.

that details of such accounts are recorded in written form with the details being placed with their wills, (including the relevant password). Many millions of pounds are still held as "unclaimed assets". An appropriate approach to online banking (and recording the information in some suitable confidential way) will ensure that funds at credit of an online bank account will not simply be added to those many unclaimed millions.

POWERS OF APPORTIONMENT OR APPOINTMENT

Where such a power is vested in the testator, its nature and effect should **3–12** be considered. It may be advisable that the power should be referred to specifically in the testator's will and expressly exercised.

Classification

Powers of appointment are generally classified as either *general* or **3–13** *special*.

General power of appointment

A general power of appointment could in theory provide an unlimited **3–14** choice as to the eventual donee. However, this should be avoided, as a very broad power may be alleged to be void as delegating the right to making a will to someone other than the testator.[4]

Special power of appointment

A special power of appointment is more common. In effect, it is **3–15** normally a legacy to a class of beneficiaries with instructions, for example, that the legacy should be divided in such a manner, and subject to such terms and conditions, as the person holding the power may direct. The holder of the power cannot move out with the class of the beneficiaries defined by the testator when exercising the power.

Relation to trusts

It should also be noted that a power of appointment may be granted **3–16** in relation to an asset under a trust. The truster can empower an individual to dispose of trust assets to particular individuals.

Such a power can be exercised in the will of the person so empowered. In the case of *Hyslop v Maxwell's Trustees*[5] the testator had bequeathed a life rent of his estate to his niece. He empowered the niece to dispose of the life rented property by will or other deed in such manner as she saw fit. Although the will of the niece made no specific reference to the power of appointment, it was held that the power had been exercised by her in terms of a general will made by her.

POWERS OF ATTORNEY

Many solicitors now recognise that it is good practice to raise, with older **3–17** clients who are making wills, the question of whether or not they should consider at the same time granting "protective" powers of attorney. A

---

[4] *Bannerman's Trustees v Bannerman*, 1915 S.C. 398.
[5] 1834 12 S. 413.

power of attorney need not become effective immediately (it can contain a "springing" clause). In particular, the power of attorney, once properly granted, can avoid the necessity for seeking the appointment of a financial guardian.

The intention of the Adults with Incapacity (Scotland) Act 2000 (which substantially came into force in April 2001) was to modernise the previous law in relation to intervention in the financial affairs of an incapacitated person; where there is no continuing or continuing/welfare power of attorney, the family of an incapacitated person will need to petition the court for appointment of a suitable person as financial guardian.

In that regard the following has to be borne in mind:

- As indicated above, a court petition is required;
- Three different reports need to be obtained and lodged with the petition;
- A person nominated as a financial guardian cannot take up his or her appointment until the court so finds;
- In comparing costs, the granting of a power of attorney is still much less expensive than having a financial guardian appointed;
- A financial guardian appointed by a court does not have the same width or range of powers as an attorney under a continuing or continuing/welfare power of attorney;
- There remains an element of delectus persona in relation to the appointment of an attorney. The same cannot necessarily be said of the appointment of a financial guardian.

The advice which a solicitor will offer to the client will obviously depend to a large extent on his knowledge of the client, that is, upon the information-gathering process. If a minimalist or perfunctory approach is adopted opportunities are being lost, both for the solicitor, but even more so for the client.

Composition and value of the client's estate

3–18   Some of the above pointers touch on what is arguably the most important area, the composition and value of the client's estate. Clients tend to know little about inheritance tax. Given recent house price increases throughout the UK, and unless there are great changes to inheritance tax (which is always a possibility), the solicitor's role in advising on IHT will become even more important.

In 2000, inheritance tax was payable in respect of 19,000 estates. In 2001 it was 18,000. Why should that be? One reason might simply be that more clients were beginning to take appropriate tax mitigation steps. Five years ago the value of an individual's house meant that only one in 40 relevant estates "ranked" for inheritance tax. Within a couple of years, if house prices continue to rise, it is estimated that the value of dwelling-houses alone will bring one in every eight people within the range of inheritance tax. In fact, the Inland Revenue estimate that 29,500 estates will be liable to IHT in 2003, probably due to house price rises in the UK (particularly in the south-east).

As suggested earlier, it is extremely important that, in the will-making **3–19** process, the solicitor should cover the question of inheritance tax. If he fails to do so, non-exempt beneficiaries may, at least in theory, seek to claim against the will-making solicitor on the basis that the benefit to them would have been the greater had the advice in question been offered at the outset. The legal profession may face a public relations difficulty with its clients. Older clients have, over the years, become accustomed to the will-making process being a simple, non-intrusive process. Those days have gone.

Ascertainment and valuation of the client's estate

Misconceptions

When an individual dies, the value of the whole of his or her estate **3–20** needs to be ascertained for IHT purposes. However, a number of common misconceptions exist:
  (i) *The value of furnishings, personal effects and even jewellery is not taken into account.* This is not so, and where inheritance tax is an issue, all such items need to be properly valued (normally by a skilled valuer).[6]
  (ii) *Many clients believe that where they hold property jointly with another (usually their spouse) such joint assets are excluded.* This is not so; even where an individual has only a "partial" interest in an asset (such as a heritable property or a bank account), if inheritance tax is chargeable, then the value of the interest of the deceased is taken into account in calculating the charge.
  (iii) *Clients commonly forget to take into account monies which would be payable under life assurance policies, death in service schemes or personal pension policies.* Where such benefits come directly back into the estate of the relevant client, this can in fact move the client from a position of having no liability into perhaps having a substantial liability.

Reasons for misconceptions

The simple reason that many clients forget about such benefits is that **3–21** they are not available to them during their lifetime. On other occasions, clients may not fully know or understand that these benefits may well become payable on their death. Payment of the benefits is triggered only on death.

  Example
  A client has assets totalling £200,000. If the client is employed and is a member of his employer's occupational pension scheme, then very often a sum equivalent to four times the annual salary of the employee at death is payable by way of death in service benefits. If

---

[6] See the relevant supplementary pages of the IHT 200. Beware of s.213 of the IHTA 1984.

the client in question is earning £30,000 per annum, the death in service benefits could be £120,000. If these benefits are added to the client's other assets (totalling £200,000), the IHT liability will be £320,000 minus the nil-rate band (£263,000) which equals £57,000 taxed at 40 per cent—which gives an IHT liability of £22,800.

Personal pension or occupational pension scheme

3–22   Where death benefits under personal pension or occupational pension schemes are in fact payable at the discretion of the relevant fund trustees, then such payments will normally be exempt from inheritance tax.[7]

However, this is another area where the solicitor can add value to the services which he can provide. Not all such payments are discretionary. If not, then the lump sum payment will form part of the estate of the testator.

The problems which could arise here are:

- The death benefits will be taxable to IHT, and will need to be detailed in the Form C1 and the IHT 200.
- Being moveable, the benefits will be subject to a legal rights claim.

Thus, when a client has a personal pension or is a member of an occupational pension scheme, then the client should be advised:

- To check whether or not the payments are discretionary. Bear in mind that there are some schemes which have regulations allowing for both discretionary and non- discretionary payment. If the payment is discretionary then the client should check requirements of the fund trustees in order to ensure that the benefits go to those whom the client would wish to nominate. Many schemes have specific forms which are fairly straightforward and which they will ask the contributor to complete. In other cases a simple letter of nomination may suffice.
- The client may have granted a nomination many years before, the terms of which he or she no longer considers to be appropriate. The client should be reminded that such nominations may need to be updated. This is an important point that the client should be reminded of.

Overlooked assets

"Potential" assets

3–23   There are a number of "potential" assets which are more often than not overlooked by a client. These include:

- *Life insurance policies.* Whether or not the value of a policy comes back into the estate of the individual will depend on

---

[7] s.151 of the IHTA 1984.

whether the proceeds of the policy are payable to the executors/ personal representatives of the deceased (in which case they will be taxable), or whether the benefit is expressed to be payable to some other person (in which case they may avoid taxation). Proceeds of policies written under the Married Woman's Policies of Assurance (Scotland) Act will not form part of the estate of the deceased, and therefore should not be shown in the Form C1. They should not be regarded as forming part of the residue of a deceased's estate, and a client should not seek to bequeath a policy to an individual other than the assured under the policy itself (in any event, such a bequest in a will is unnecessary in view of the terms of the above legislation).

- *Death in service benefits* (see the example above).
- *Sums payable under retirement annuity or personal pension policies.* Normally such policies will provide for payment of a sum where the person who has purchased the relevant policy dies before reaching retirement age. The sum which is payable will depend on the terms of the policy. Some older policies provide simply for return of the premiums paid. Others provide for return of the premiums paid with interest at an agreed rate thereon. Most favourably from the point of view of the individual, more modern policies provide for payment of the value of the pension fund at date of death. This can amount in any case to a substantial sum of money, which again may well be payable to the executors or personal representatives of the deceased. If it is, then again it will be taxable to IHT.

Other "potential" benefits

There are other "potential" benefits which many people overlook. **3–24** Classic examples are:

- *A potential direct inheritance from an elderly relative.* No one really wants to contemplate the death of a loved one, particularly a parent or other elderly family member. However, as wealth within our society has increased, a greater proportion of the population does have a reasonable inheritance expectation. Thus, a situation might be encountered where a client is not *per se* liable to inheritance tax, having assets of £200,000. If, however, the client has a reasonable expectation of inheriting another, say, £100,000 from a parent or other relative, then the receipt of such an inheritance will move the client from having no liability to having a substantial liability (in the example given above IHT would amount to £18,000).
- *Beneficiary under a trust.* Clients often fail to mention that they are already beneficiaries under a trust, but that the capital benefit due to them has not yet been paid.
- *Damages claim.* Although not particularly common, it is possible that the client is involved in a litigation (for example, arising out of personal injury) which, if resolved in the client's favour, could amount to a substantial sum of money being paid

to the client. Most individuals involved in such claims, particularly where a litigation has been ongoing for a period of time, tend not to "count their chickens" and therefore to overlook the potential benefits of a successful outcome.

Bear in mind also the provisions of the Damages (Scotland) Act 1976 as amended by the Damages (Scotland) Act 1993. Section 2 of the 1976 Act allows the executor of a deceased person to bring or to continue an action for personal injuries. If money is recovered it will belong to the estate of the deceased. That being so, a special enquiry may be necessary—asbestos claims require particular care. Some of these claims were settled on the basis that a further sum might be payable in the event of the claimant dying within a certain period, and it being demonstrated that the claimant had died as a result of an asbestos-related cause.

Full and frank disclosure required

3–25   From the adviser's point of view, it can therefore be seen that the client has to be encouraged to be full and frank in his or her disclosure of assets and potential assets. Some clients can see this as unduly intrusive, but the fact of the matter is that without having all the details, an adviser cannot properly advise. An adviser might first conclude that there was no IHT liability when in fact, with a little more information, the adviser would have reached an entirely different conclusion. Again, if the draftsman does not ask the correct questions, can he/she be held liable?

Insurance

3–26   As people get older, the willingness to purchase an insurance product decreases. However, there are some very valuable insurance products which can be purchased to mitigate the effect of inheritance tax on death (including some which can be "combined" to cover care home fees whilst still allowing scope for IHT mitigation).

It is important that clients should bear in mind that even a minimalist approach can have value. There is no need or requirement to arrange an insurance product which will cover the whole of the anticipated IHT liability. It should also be noted that for the most part, with a possible exception of a discounted bond trust, the arranging of an insurance product will not reduce the IHT liability. It does, however, provide a fund outwith the personal estate of the deceased which can be utilised to address the liability, thereby ensuring that principally residuary beneficiaries obtain a greater benefit from the estate than would otherwise have been the case.

Perhaps the simplest way of making use of an insurance product is for the client to take out a term assurance policy and write the proceeds of the policy in trust. On an actuarial basis, certainly for younger clients, the possibility of the insurer having to pay out on, say, a 10-year policy is small. A term policy is pure "protection". If the insured survives to the end of the term, then unless the policy is unitised or is convertible, the policy lapses with no value. That being so, when any client adopts this strategy, he or she must clearly understand that if they survive to the end of the relevant term, the "protection" which they have arranged will cease.

The most common way for spouses to address this matter is for the clients to arrange a joint life second death policy. The policy does not pay out on first death but rather on second death.

Bear in mind that all such policies must be written in trust, normally at **3–27** the outset. If this step is not taken then the value of the policies will form part of the estate of the deceased (in the latter example the estate of the second spouse to die), and far from providing some cushioning effect in respect of IHT, will simply increase the IHT liability. Thus, if the adviser encounters a situation where there is a joint life second death policy which has not been written in trust, the question of whether or not there has been some negligence on the part of a previous adviser has to be considered (on the premise that as neither spouse will benefit from the policy, what was the point in taking it out in the first place?).

Some IHT policies are arranged on a regular premium basis, others on a single premium basis. All such premiums will be potentially exempt transfers. They may be immediately exempt on the normal expenditure out of income basis. If the client adopts a strategy of assigning an existing policy into trust, then the policy needs to be valued at the time the trust is created and intimated. The value of the policy at that time will of itself be the potentially exempt transfer value. The benefit of this approach is that when the policy grows in value over a period of time, that growth will be outwith the personal estate of the testator (provided it has been properly written in trust), and the benefit of that growth can therefore be passed to beneficiaries of the relevant trust free of IHT.

There is another important point here—if the beneficiaries chosen under the policy trust differ from the residuary beneficiaries under the will, then there will be no cushioning of the effects of IHT for residuary beneficiaries under the will.

Again, as part of the overall service which a solicitor should be capable of providing, where a client wishes to arrange a new policy or to write an existing policy in trust, the legal profession should be involved in offering advice as to the appropriate format of trust. Clients are in general not experienced in dealing with trusts, and, if left to their own devices, might adopt a wholly inappropriate format of trust. Most insurers have pre-printed trust forms which could be adopted. The insurers themselves will not seek to advise on this matter, however, and, left to their own devices, clients may make the wrong choice and adopt a format of trust which is not appropriate for IHT purposes.

Potential pitfalls

The mitigation of inheritance tax is a worthwhile aim, but, as with **3–28** everything else in life, the process is a balance. There are various important considerations which need to be taken into account:

- *Gifts*. A gift made unthinkingly with a view to saving inheritance tax could simply result in an immediate capital gains tax (CGT) liability. Capital gains tax arises in respect of a "disposal"—many clients wrongly think that it is only of relevance when an asset is sold—this is not the case. This consideration is of particular importance in relation to investment such as stocks and shares. A gift of a shareholding is a

disposal for capital gains tax purposes. If the gain in that
holding exceeds the donor's annual exemption for CGT purposes, an immediate capital gains tax liability will have been
crystallised.

- *Lifetime gifts.* Apart from capital gains tax considerations, care
is required in relation to lifetime gifts. While such a gift can
substantially reduce an anticipated inheritance tax liability on
death, the nature of the asset needs to be carefully considered.
For example, if the asset in question is an investment which is
producing valuable income, then the effect of loss of that
income will need to be properly considered.
- *Surviving spouse.* Spouses engaging in IHT planning should
always bear in mind the likely financial position of the survivor
(and the possibility that the survivor may need to take up
permanent residence in a care home—see Chapter 16). This
applies with particular force nowadays given the increasing
longevity of our population. An individual retiring at 60 could
easily have another 35 years or so ahead of him or her. Given
recent advances in genetic medicine, there are some geneticists
who have indicated that within 10 years, individuals might be
born who might reasonably be expected to have a life expectancy of 120 years!
- *IHT planning cannot be carried out in isolation.* An individual
who makes a gift with a view to IHT mitigation might, several
years later, find themselves being "penalised" (under the
"deprivation" rules set out in the National Assistance (Assessment of Resources) Regulations 1992) if he or she needs to go
into a nursing home and applies for financial assistance from
the local authority in relation to payment of fees.

IHT: appropriate steps

3–29   Bearing in mind the cautionary note outlined above, there are
numerous steps which an individual can take with a view to mitigating
inheritance tax. These include:

Step 1 Understanding and making full use of the various small
exemptions/reliefs which are available.

Step 2 Making carefully considered potential exempt transfers, *i.e.*
gifts.

Step 3 Writing existing life insurance benefits, death in service
benefits and personal pension funds in trust. Such policies/
benefits are often capable of being written in trust for selected
beneficiaries. (Policies already assigned to a lending institution
in connection with a mortgage cannot be written in trust or
assigned to other third parties without consent of the lenders).

- *Life insurance policies.* The value of the policy as at the
date of assignation (by way of gift) into a trust would be a
potentially exempt transfer. If a period of seven years from
the date of the third party assignation or writing in trust
passes before death of the original policy owner, the
potentially exempt transfer will be wholly free of inheritance tax, as will growth within the value of the policy
during the seven-year period in question.

- *Death in service benefits.* Those under occupation of pension schemes are often subject to an "internal" trust which would keep the benefits out of the estate of the employee on death. This is not necessarily the case and a check should be made with the scheme administrators. Very often the step can be taken by simply writing a letter of expression of wish. In some cases a more complex trust declaration might be required.
- *Personal pension funds in trust.* As indicated above, if a pension policy holder dies before retirement age there can be substantial benefits payable under the relevant policy. Again, it is very often possible to write these benefits in trust, thereby ensuring that a large sum of funds does not come bouncing back into the estate of the deceased. If the benefits are written in trust then they will not form part of the estate of the deceased's personal estate, and will be free of IHT.

Step 4 One of the simplest ways of mitigating IHT is to ensure that both spouses make at least partial use of their respective nil-rate bands. In many cases, spouses adopt the "traditional approach" of bequeathing their respective estates to each other, or if both of them die together, equally between their children. Whilst often that might be wholly appropriate, it is important that the spouses realise that they are effectively giving one "nil-rate band" (£267,000) back to the Treasury. Transfers between spouses are exempt. However, transfers to other members of the family are not so exempt. There is a common misconception that only one tranche of £267,000 is available to spouses. This is not the case as each spouse has his/her own nil-rate band allowance.

Step 5 Clients should therefore be encouraged to look at their wills. If they have bequeathed their whole estates to each other, then they should assess whether or not the survivor of them would require the whole estate. The scenarios below help to illustrate potential outcomes.

- *Scenario 1*: A husband (H) has an estate worth £300,000. His wife (W) has an estate of her own worth £100,000. They have two adult children, A and B. If H passes on, bequeathing his estate to W, she will then have an estate worth £400,000. There is no tax on the estate (£300,000) passing from H to W as it is spouse exempt. When W passes on, her nil-rate band can be brought into play, reducing the taxable estate (£400,000) to £137,000. The IHT payable on this before A and B take their benefit will be £54,800.
- *Scenario 2*: Having carefully considered their joint financial position, H amends his will to the effect that on his death, his children, A and B, each receive a legacy of £72,500. H passes on. £145,000 passes tax free (being below H's nil-rate band) to his children. The remainder (£155,000) passes to W. She then has an estate worth £255,000. When

she passes on, her total estate will be £255,000. As this is below the amount of the nil-rate band, there will be no tax payable on her death. So, by a simple alteration to the will, a tax bill of £54,800 has been avoided.

- *Scenario 3*: Not all spouses are in a position to take advantage of the "extreme" example detailed above. However, H and W, having considered their respective financial positions, might conclude that it would not be safe to bequeath £145,000 to their children on H's death. They do, however, feel that they are comfortable with their children each receiving £25,000 on each other's death. This would mean that on the death of H, a total of £250,000 would pass to W. When she passed on leaving £350,000, her taxable estate would be £87,000, on which the tax bill would be £34,800. Thus, in this third scenario, a tax bill of over £20,000 has been saved.

Other points to note

Commorientes clause

3–30   The commorientes clause is normally 30 days. However, in certain circumstances, the 30-day period of survivorship might be considered to be insufficient. The maximum period under section 92 of the IHTA 1984 is six months.

Destinations over on renunciation

3–31   It is considered to be good practice to include destinations over on renunciation. For example, an adult child (particularly a reasonably wealthy one) may wish to pass part of his inheritance to his children to effect some inheritance tax planning of his own. A client should therefore be asked what he or she would like to happen to a bequest in the event of the legatee pre-deceasing. In addition, it is important to consider who should benefit in the event of a legatee surviving but renouncing the legacy, and whether a substitute legatee should be named and should also be given.

Whilst a deed of variation is a very valuable means of effecting post-death inheritance tax planning, the question of a destination over on renunciation has two possible advantages:

- It has been suggested that the entitlement of a family or other beneficiaries to enter into a deed of variation might be revoked by the Chancellor.
- A variation under section 142 of the Inheritance Tax Act by a parent in favour of his children who are aged under 18 and unmarried is treated as a settlement by a parent, and accordingly the income derived from the "varied estate" is regarded by the Inland Revenue as being the parent's income under section 663 of the Income and Corporation Taxes Act 1988. However, the Inland Revenue do not adopt the same view where the bequest is redirected by means of over destination following renunciation.

Claiming legal rights

The possibility of children claiming their legal rights is itself a valuable **3–32** inheritance tax planning tool.

Disabled persons

The provisions of the IHTA 1984, section 89, coupled with Schedule 1, **3–33** paragraph 2 of the Taxation of Chargeable Gains Act 1992, give valuable tax concessions for disabled persons who are unable to administer their property or manage their affairs by reason of a mental disorder in terms of the Mental Health Act 1986, or who receive an attendance allowance or a disability living allowance.

The qualifying conditions are:

- That not less than half of the trust property that has applied is applied for the disabled person; and
- That there is no interest in possession in the trust property.

In appropriate circumstances, the client should be advised of the terms of section 89, in order that an appropriate testamentary trust which qualifies as a "disabled trust" can be properly created in terms of the client's will.

SENSITIVITY ISSUES

Dark intentions?

A will can be the last written expression of love, care and support **3–34** which an individual can leave to his family. Equally, it can be used as a very blunt weapon to cause distress, or at least to make a point. The draftsman's solicitor has to consider whether he is willing to prepare a will which has the latter intention. Common areas of difficulty (very often not recognised as such by the client) are as follows:

Disinherit a "black sheep"

The client wishes to disinherit a "black sheep" child—in such circum- **3–35** stances it is imperative that the child's entitlement to claim legal rights is fully explained. Where appropriate, strategies for mitigating, if not avoiding that claim have to be put forward to the client.

Dwelling-house bequests

The client may wish to bequeath a dwelling-house to a particular **3–36** beneficiary. Here, care has to be taken over whether it is a particular house nominated by the client, or whether in fact it is any dwelling-house owned and occupied by the client as his or her home at the date of death. The client's perception is not necessarily the same as that of the solicitor drafting the will, and this point must be clarified. Similar considerations can apply where the property is subject to a mortgage—is the bequest to be free of, or subject to, the mortgage liability?

Previous marriage with children

Particular care needs to be taken where the client is unmarried, living **3–37** with a long-term partner, or where the client and his present spouse have been previously married before to others and perhaps have children both to each other, but also to their previous spouses. This is a very difficult area where client misconceptions can cause havoc and can, if proper drafting techniques are not applied, lead to one of the party's children by their first marriage being effectively disinherited (see Chapter 7).

The solution which many clients seek to adopt is to leave a life rent of their estates to the surviving partner/spouse in a second marriage. If, however, the life rent is of a house, then you must check whether or not there is an existing mortgage in respect of that house. If there is, what are the client's wishes and intentions in respect of the same? (Again, see the warning note in Chapter 7).

"Rose-tinted glasses"

3–38   Beware of the client who views the world with "rose-tinted glasses". Inheritance tax mitigation is a laudable aim. It is not, however, necessarily the most important aspect of the making of a will, although the client may not realise this. For example, clients, in an effort to save IHT on second death may be overly generous in the use of first death legacies in favour of children/other issues. Such over generosity could leave the surviving spouse in financially straightened circumstances, just at a point in his or her life where some degree of financial comfort would have been wholly appropriate.

Inequality of benefit between children or other beneficiaries in the same class requires care on the part of the draftsman. A client may have entirely valid reasons for leaving a larger share of his or her estate to one child rather than to others. However, when a client expresses such a wish, then his or her reasons for so doing should be properly explored. A client may think that his or her children will fully understand the rationale for inequality of benefit between them, but this is very often not the case. If one child is to receive more than another, then there may be a case for suggesting to the client that he or she call a "family meeting" to explain his or her reasons for doing so. Whilst this would not be normal practice (many clients are jealous of the confidentiality of their wills), an appropriate explanation to children may, although not avoiding a degree of hurt, find more acceptance, particularly where the reasons for adopting such an approach are explained in detail, with an assurance being given that any inequality of benefit does not indicate greater love for one than the other. Beware in particular when a client says "my children are not like that"—that is the very situation where professional warning bells should start to ring.

SPECIAL DESTINATIONS

3–39   When taking instructions for a will, the draftsman cannot lose sight of the possibility that certain assets of the client's estate might be subject to special destinations. In the case of heritable properties, this may mean that the titles are required to be checked. A client may have forgotten (or indeed may not have been told in the first place) that a particular heritable property is subject to a special destination. If the client is aware of the existence of a special destination, this begs the question as to whether or not the client understands that, unevacuated, the special destination will effectively prevent the client from passing his interest in that property to someone other than the joint title holder or holders.

Special destinations are most commonly found in:

- *A destination over provision in a will*: identifying a substitute beneficiary who will take either in succession to the original institute, or in place of the latter should he fail to inherit, for example by pre-deceasing the testator;
- *The title to a heritable property*: for example "in favour of X and Y and the survivor of them".

The latter type of special destination is not of itself a will, or indeed a testamentary writing, but has testamentary effect. In the foregoing example is seen the true nature of a special destination—it alters the normal rules of intestate succession—thus, even where an individual dies in intestate, if he has taken title to a heritable property in the joint names of himself and another and the survivor of them, the survivor will, through operation of the special destination, become owner of the whole property.

It should be noted that special destinations can also relate to moveable property.[8] The question of the nature and extent of a special destination in relation to moveable property was considered in the case of *Denis v Aitchison*.[9] In that case, however, it was decided that taking title to a bank account in joint names of the survivor did not raise any presumption of gift, and did not carry the beneficial ownership in the funds in the account to the survivor on death of the other.

Draftsmen beware

As a general point, in the author's view a survivorship destination **3–40** should not be utilised in relation to a heritable property without specific authorisation from clients. Whilst, historically, the use of a survivorship destination where spouses where purchasing together might have been considered to be convenient (and in many cases entirely appropriate), the author is aware of at least one complaint of inadequate professional services. The allegation being that the solicitor in question some 15 years ago incorporated a survivorship destination title in favour of a husband and wife without explaining the import of the same to them, and without seeking their specific instructions on use of that destination.

The use of a survivorship destination may not be appropriate where parties in question are not married—however, whatever their marital status, specific instructions should be obtained.

Equally, there may be a professional risk to the draftsman if he does not check the title position in respect of heritable properties which the testator wishes to specifically bequeath. In the English case of *Kecsmeki v Rubens Rabin & Co*,[10] the draftsman was instructed to include a provision in the client's will leaving to a third party a share of heritage

---

[8] *Connell's Trustees v Connell's Trustees* (1886) 13 R. 1175.
[9] 1923 S.C. 219.
[10] Reported in *The Times*, December 31, 1992.

owned by the testator. Unfortunately for the draftsman, he failed to inform his client that the title in question contained the English equivalent of a survivorship destination. The court held that the drafts-man owed the potential beneficiary a duty of care and had been in breach of that duty, thereby allowing the disappointed beneficiary to pursue a claim against the draftsman.

Given that Scottish and English law in the area of responsibility to third parties is now on the face of it on the same footing, following the decision in *Holmes v Bank of Scotland*,[11] the message to the Scottish draftsman is clear—the relevant title should be checked. Reliance on an assurance by the client that there is no survivorship destination (his recollection may be faulty or incorrect), may not exculpate the draftsman.

Debts and liabilities (including inheritance tax)

3–41   The fact that a particular property is subject to a special destination and therefore does not pass either under the testator's will or under the laws of intestacy does not mean that heritable property will escape liability to charge inheritance tax (unless of course the "survivor" is an exempt beneficiary such as a spouse). Equally, passing of title under a survivorship destination does not allow the survivor to escape liability for the deceased's debts.

Evacuation

3–42   Whether or not a particular special destination has been validly evacuated has been a fruitful source of litigation for some time.[12] Quite apart from checking whether or not there is a survivorship destination in the first place, the draftsman of the will needs to have the relevant skills to advise a client in a variety of circumstances, as follows:

- *A client who is involved in a divorce or is recently divorced.* He may wrongly believe that the effect of the divorce will be to evacuate the special destination, but this is not the case. The will draftsman cannot advise in isolation. He needs to establish what steps may have been taken, if any, *inter vivos*, to effectively and properly evacuate the special destination.

  Failing such steps being taken by the draftsman, he may find himself liable to a disappointed beneficiary at some future point in time.

  Example
  A husband and wife, A and B, purchase a property together, taking title in their joint names and the survivor of them. They become divorced, and as part of the divorce settlement, A conveys to B his one half *pro indiviso* share in, and to, the matrimonial home. He then seeks to make a will bequeathing

---

[11] 2002 S.L.T. 544; and 2002 S.C.L.R. 481, cited above.
[12] *Perrett's Trustees v Perrett*, 1909 1 S.L.T. 302. See also *Steele v Caldwell & Others*, 1979 S.L.T. 228.

the whole property to third parties (very often children). However, the disposition of a one half *pro indiviso* share by A to B will not be sufficient to completely evacuate the survivorship destination. On B's unexpected and perhaps untimely death, the survivorship destination still lurks in the background, with the effect that unexpectedly A might inherit B's "original" one half *pro indiviso* share. In that (and other) situation(s), the proper way of fully discharging the survivorship destination would have been for A and B to convey the property jointly to B.

- *Evacuate an existing survivorship destination.* The will-making client may for a number of reasons wish to evacuate an existing survivorship destination. The draftsman needs to be aware of the circumstances where unilateral action on the part of the client will evacuate the destination, and also where something further may be required.

  1. *Contractual destination.* Where both parties have contributed to the price paid for the property, the destination is contractual and may not be evacuated by one at his own hand. In *Perrett's Trustees v Perrett*,[13] Lord President Dunedin stated that where the destination was contractual:

     "Each took the chance of getting the half of the other, and accordingly . . . the property stands upon its own destination and is not carried, and could not be carried, by any testament whatsoever. . . this destination could (not) have been altered except by joint consent of the spouses".

  2. *Contributed in kind.* Where the parties have contributed in kind, the rule enunciated by Lord President Dunedin also applies.[14]

  3. *Revocation.* If one paid the whole price then he is entitled to revoke, but not the other co-owner who has contributed nothing. The terms of the conveyance are crucial. In one case, there was an admission that the terms of the deed did not accurately reflect the true position.[15] The court felt that further investigation was appropriate, and extrinsic evidence was allowed to prove who actually paid the price. However, in a later case,[16] no such admission was made and therefore the court found itself unable to admit extrinsic evidence as to the true position.

  4. *Gift.* If a special destination in favour of A and B and the survivor of them appeared in a deed granted by a third party by way of gift, then neither co-owner can evacuate.

Where unilateral evacuation by will cannot be achieved, then the draftsman has to be able to advise the client that, to test effectively in

---

[13] Cited above, p.527.
[14] *Shand's Trustees v Shand's Trustees*, 1996 S.L.T. 306.
[15] *Hay's Trustees v Hay's Trustees*, 1951 S.C. 329.
[16] *Gordon-Rodgers v Thomson's Trustees*, 1988 S.L.T. 618.

respect of his one-half share, there will need to be steps taken on an *inter vivos* basis.

Evacuation by will

3–43   Even where it is possible to evacuate by will, care still needs to be taken that this is effected in an appropriate way. Prior to commencement (September 10, 1964) of the Succession (Scotland) Act, 1964, common law in relation to what was required to revoke a special destination was inconclusive, relying on various presumptions in an attempt to discover the testator's intentions. As Meston points out, many difficulties arose from the common practice of taking a title to heritage in the names of husband and wife and the survivor, and then subsequently, possibly even on the same day, executing a will which took no account of the survivorship destination. A question of implied revocation frequently arose.

Those problems were substantially addressed by section 30 of the 1964 Act. Section 30 relates to a testamentary disposition executed after commencement of the Act, and provides that such a disposition shall have no effect so as to evacuate a special destination unless it contains a specific reference to the destination, and a declared intention on the part of the testator to revoke it.

The terms of section 30 are quite clear and easy to implement. However, they are also strictly construed. In the case of *Stirling's Trustees and* Others,[17] the court had to consider the terms of a will executed on February 2, 1966. The court took the view that, even although the case largely related to a life rent under a deed of entail granted many years before, the relevant deed was the will of 1966, and as it had not complied with the strict terms of section 30, the 1966 will had not evacuated the special destination of the deed of entail.

The draftsman should note that he will need to have some familiarity with the pre-1964 law in relation to deceased testators whose wills pre date September 10, 1964.

Survivorship destinations and the incidence of debt

3–44   Clients should not believe that use of a survivorship destination will allow relevant assets to pass to the survivor free of debt. In the case of *Fleming's Trustee v Fleming* (also known as *Jackson v Fleming*),[18] the trustee in bankruptcy sought a declarator that he was vested in a one-half share of a heritable property, where, at the date of grant of sequestration, the title to the property had stood in the joint name of a bankrupt (who had subsequently died) and his wife, Mrs Fleming, equally between them and the survivor of them. The trustee in bankruptcy argued that his act and warrant defeated the special destination and that registration of the act and warrant was not essential. As an alternative, the trustee sought declarator that Mrs Fleming was personally liable to her late husband's creditors to the extent of the value of her husband's share in the property. The Court of Session felt that the

---

[17] 1977 S.L.T. 229.
[18] 2000 S.L.T. 406.

trustee's act and warrant, being effectively an *inter vivos* deed and not recorded, it could not evacuate the special destination. However, the court also felt that Mrs Fleming only had the same right in the share as her late husband had, and that by virtue of his sequestration, his share had vested in the trustee and was liable for her late husband's debts.

Possible reform

In its Report on Succession,[19] the Scottish Law Commission proposed **3–45** restriction of the scope of special destinations. The Commission recommended:

- That simple survivorship destinations should remain valid. However, where a document of title to a property (whether moveable or heritable) contained a destination in favour of some person other than the original grantee, the destination would be invalid in respect of that person.
- The Commission proposed that a destination other than will instructing conditional substitution should be ineffective in respect of the substitute beneficiary, with the original institute taking a full and indefeasible right.

The proposals of the Commission remain unimplemented.

---

[19] Scottish Law Commission 124 January, 1990; 2000 S.L.T. 406.

CHAPTER 4

MARRIAGE, COHABITATION AND CHILDREN

Prior rights

4–01   Marriage itself brings automatic rights of succession. These are of course the rights detailed in sections 8 and 9 of the Succession (Scotland) Act 1964 as amended. These statutory rights, which have already been considered in Chapter 1, have common features:

- They apply only where a person dies intestate (but this includes partial intestacy)[1] and is survived by a spouse;
- They entitle the surviving spouse to receive the relevant rights only out of the intestate estate;[2] and
- They are subject to the long negative prescription of 20 years.[3]

What about legal rights?

4–02   In fact *ius relictae/relicti* and *legitim* are not strictly speaking rights of succession. They are:

> "In the nature of debts which attach to the free succession after the claims of onerous creditors have been satisfied. Hence, it has been frequently said judicially that, in respect of their legal claims, the widow and children are heirs in competition with onerous creditors, and are creditors in competition with heirs."[4]

As a first point, the existence of *ius relictae/relicti* should not be overlooked if the client in question is living with another party to whom he or she is not married. It is possible that the client has been married, has been separated from his or her spouse for many years and has never divorced, with no separation agreement ever having been put in place. In such circumstances, on death of that individual, the estranged and perhaps long-lost spouse will still have an entitlement to claim his or her legal rights. Legal rights are a difficult concept for many clients to

---

[1] Section 36 of the 1964 Act.

[2] Section 36(1) of the 1964 Act, which defines intestate estate as "so much of his estate as is undisposed of by Testamentary Disposition".

[3] Sections 6 and 7, and Sch.1, para.2(f) of The Prescription Limitation (Scotland) Act 1963.

[4] *Naismith v Boyes* (1899) 1 F. (H.L.) 79.

understand. In truth they are really a way of providing family protection for both a surviving spouse and children.

In *Hutton's Trustees v Hutton's Trustees*,[5] Lord Salvesen stated that:

> "I regard the right which our law gives to children in their father's estate, in common with the laws of most civilised countries except England, as a very important check on capricious and unjust treatments."

We should bear in mind that England has a statutory provision to provide protection (see below). It is important also to bear in mind that legal rights vest as at date of death in spouses and children.[6] If the party entitled to claim legal rights dies after the date of vesting (*i.e.* the date of death of the other spouse or parent), but before the right has been satisfied or extinguished, the right to claim passes to the executors of that spouse or child.[7] In the situation given above (the client living with another party, having been separated for many years but not divorced), if the long-lost spouse is alive at the client's date of death, but subsequently passes on before he or she has claimed his or her entitlement to legal rights, the claim is still exigible at the instance of the executors of that long-lost spouse. **4–03**

BALANCING PERCEIVED OBLIGATIONS

Where a client has previously been married, and has remarried or is living with a partner of long standing, there are different pressures and perceived obligations which he or she can have difficulty in balancing. The first is that, in most cases, the client will wish to be sure that the financial provision for the current spouse/partner is provided/protected. Equally, however, the client may not wish to see his or her children by the first marriage become totally disinherited. Such an unfortunate outcome (for the children) can happen with astonishing ease. **4–04**

A simple example is as follows:

- Two divorcees who have children by their previous marriages become married to each other.
- Both spouses grant what they regard as being "equitable" wills, *i.e.* they bequeath the residue of their respective estates to each other, provision being made that on second death, residue of the second to die will be split into two equal halves, and those halves then divided equally between the children of the earlier marriages (thus endeavouring to ensure fairness as between the two families).
- One of the spouses passes on. His or her children get on well with the surviving step-parent. They do not wish to adversely affect the financial position of the surviving step-parent and

---

[5] 1916 S.C. 60.
[6] *McMurray v McMurray's Trustees* (1852) 14 D. 1048.
[7] *MacGregor's Executrix v MacGregor's Trustees*, 1935 S.C. 13.

they may be aware of the fact that there is in place a will of that step-parent which is generally equitable, *i.e.* on his or her death, one-half of his or her estate will come to the children of the predecessor. They discharge their entitlements.

- Several years go by. The step-children fall out of contact with the surviving step-parent. He or she interprets this as being an indication that the step-children do not care for him/her, or alternatively, the natural children of the step-parent begin to work on their parent—"Bob and Willie aren't your children, they're not part of our family—why should they get anything?"
- The surviving spouse makes a new will revoking the earlier will. In terms of the new will, only his or her natural children are the beneficiaries. The surviving spouse then dies. The step-children have effectively been disinherited—they discharged their entitlement to legal rights on their natural parent's death, and they have no similar rights in the estate of the step-parent.

It is of vital importance that, when acting for clients faced with this difficult balancing act, the draftsman should point out potential difficulties that the above type of scenario may bring. There is no doubt that many people in the above situation simply decide to trust one another. Reposing of such trust in the other spouse/partner may often be justified. However, it is the solicitor's responsibility to point out to the clients as tactfully as possible that a right of an individual to revoke an existing will is regarded as a fundamental freedom in our society. The surviving spouse, acting as detailed above, is not regarded as contravening public policy. On occasions, such clients might suggest that their respective wills include a provision that the will in question is to be irrevocable. Unfortunately, such a clause is not binding.[8]

OPTIONS

4–05 Although the possibilities outlined above are explained to clients, many will opt to make mirror-image wills and rely on trust. Often, this stems from a wish not to offend the other spouse or partner. However, what other options are available?

Life-rent

4–06 This is often the route adopted by one spouse/partner who wishes to provide financial protection for the other, at the same time preserving the inheritance of the testator's children. From the client's point of view, there may be a seeming equity in adopting such an approach. From a testator's point of view, the surviving spouse/partner will have a roof over his or her head, and an income deriving from the estate of the testator.

Reasonable use

4–07 Such an approach might be reasonable if:

---

[8] *Dougall's Trustees v Dougall* (1789) M. 15949.

- The testator's dwelling-house is modern and requires little maintenance.
- The surviving spouse/partner already has a reasonable income of his or her own.

Potential pitfalls

There are, however, downsides which may not be appreciated at the **4–08** time the relevant will is prepared.

1. *The dwelling-house may be old and requiring considerable repair and maintenance.* Erskine[9] states that:

> "Life-renters as they are entitled to the profits, must also bear the burdens attending the subjects life-rented, as taxations, duties payable to the Superior, Minister's Stipend and all other yearly payments chargeable on the lands, which may fall due during the liferent."

In his Principles 2, 9-33, Erskine also states that:

> "Life-renters are not answerable for the ordinary wear and tear, nor for the result of accident or vis major. Neither they nor the feuars are bound to build or repair in such circumstances. . . ordinary repairs necessary to keep the subjects in existing tenantable condition are a burden on the life-renter; but a life-renter who makes improvements in the subjects is presumed to do so for his own benefit and cannot recover the expenditure from the feuar."

This can leave the life-renting spouse/partner in an awkward situation. For example, there can be disputes as to the liability for particular repairs. If it is agreed that the liability does not fall on the life-renter, then if the cost of repairs is borne by the remaining life-rented estate, this will reduce the size of the income produced by that estate for the life-renting spouse/partner.

2. *Liabilities for heritable property.* The liabilities for which the life-renter can be liable include council tax, water charges, feuduties, and also interest payments on any debts secured over the property.[10] Thus, if the property is already subject to a mortgage, the surviving spouse/partner who is to enjoy the liferent may find himself/herself subject to an unexpected liability. If clients are determined to make use of a life-rent, then there needs to be clear discussion at an early stage as to what is to happen in respect of the mortgage on death. It may be that one practical solution is for one or both parties to take out term assurance policies, which would ensure production of funds to fully repay the mortgage on death during the currency of the same.

---

[9] Institute II—9.61.
[10] *Glover's Trustees v Glover*, 1913 S.C. 115.

3. *Furniture and plenishings in the life-rented property.* The right of the life-renter is to use, but not to consume or destroy, the subjects life-rented. If the client intends to make provision for a life-rent, then consideration should be given to the furnishings and plenishings of the relevant dwelling-house being bequeathed absolutely to the life-renter. This can avoid difficulties further down the line, particularly where the adult children of the pre-deceasing spouse/partner do not get on well with the life-renting spouse/partner. It has to be conceded that particular problems can arise if the plenishings include intrinsically valuable family heirlooms. In such circumstances, it might be prudent not to subject them to the life-rent, but rather bequeath them direct to the intended ultimate beneficiary.

4. *A life-renter is entitled only to the fruits of possession.* That being so, given very low interest rates at the time of writing, it would be appropriate to point out to the client the likely level of income which might be generated by his or her estate. Some of the difficulties here might be addressed by empowering the trustees under the will to advance capital to the life-renter. Again, whilst that approach has a seeming equity, if the testator appoints his/her adult children as the trustees, then possibilities for conflict or difficulties arising are obvious.

5. *The use of the life-rent vehicle could unexpectedly create an IHT liability.* For example, if a testator leaves an estate worth £240,000 in life-rent to his partner, on her death, the life-rented estate will fall to be aggregated with the personal estate of the partner on his/her death. Whilst the personal estate of the partner may itself be below the nil-rate band, a charge to tax may arise. This will need to be borne by the life-rented estate and is likely to lead to the fiars questioning the advice given at the relevant time.

6. *The ages of the spouses/partners are also of relevance.* Where one or both are still relatively young, the life-rent may postpone the rights of the fiars for many years. Again, this itself might be a source of conflict/ill-feeling. However, if this point has been made clear and the client is content, then the solicitor framing the will has done his/her job. Remember, at all times the will belongs to the client.

7. *Both the life-renter and the fiars may be unhappy at the course adopted by the testator.* The life-renter may feel that less than full financial provision has been made for him/her. The fiars will perceive that the inheritance which they had anticipated has been denied them, for possibly an inordinate period of time.

8. *Sale proceeds.* Without proper drafting, questions may arise as to whether or not the life-renter is entitled to require sale of the originally life-rented house and purchase of another dwelling-house to be subject to the same life-rent provisions. Similarly, if, for example, the life-renter needs to go into a nursing home, is he/she entitled to the income from the sale proceeds of the dwelling-house which he/she has left?

Joint bank accounts

Owing to what is essentially a fundamental misunderstanding as to **4–09** how "joint and survivor" bank accounts operate, spouses/partners very often seek to offer one another protection by opening such an account or accounts, and perhaps placing significant sums of money there. Leaving aside the wisdom of placing significant sums of money into low earning (albeit low risk) deposits, many clients wrongly believe that on death of one of them, the survivor will become the unchallengeable owner of the whole sum in the relevant account or accounts. If the draftsman encounters clients who have joint accounts of this type, then he should explain to them that a joint and survivor account does not involve any presumption of gift. Whilst the bank will allow the survivor to uplift (to the point of closure) from the account, the bank has no liability to the executor of the deceased account holder, and does not need to adjudicate upon the question of beneficial interest/ownership of the funds.

With this in mind, the following points are important for the client to consider:

- If all the funds in the account belong to the deceased, then the funds remain part of his or her estate.
- If all the funds in the account belong to the surviving spouse/partner, then no part of the funds fall to be included in the deceased's estate.
- If the funds are jointly owned, then a decision needs to be taken as to appropriate division of those funds between the surviving account holder and the estate of the deceased account holder. The fact that one spouse or partner opens an account in joint names of survivor and places funds therein is not to be interpreted as donation to the other account holder.[11]

Discretionary trusts

Use of discretionary trusts can have value in various different situa- **4–10** tions. Again, use of a discretionary trust will to protect a spouse/partner has some attractions, but also has a downside. The will could create a trust in terms of which the surviving spouse/partner is, along with the children/issue of the pre-deceasing spouse/partner, included in the range of discretionary beneficiaries.

Attractions

A discretionary trust offers flexibility, particularly where the couple **4–11** are reasonably young and there is considerable uncertainty as to the likely financial situation over the longer term of the survivor.

Owing to this flexibility, a couple do not need to commit themselves to any particular "fixed" scheme of division and, subject to setting out appropriately worded letters of expression of wish, can give general guidance to their trustees as to their wishes.

---

[11] *Dennis v Aitchison*, 1923 S.C. 819, cited above in Ch.3. This case also considered survivorship destinations in a wider context.

From a psychological point of view, the type of discretionary trust envisaged may appeal to the couple, as each may see himself/herself as making appropriate provision not only for the survivor of them, but also of his/her natural children/issue.

Potential downsides

4–12   Again a careful, appropriate choice of trustees is required. Conflict can arise if one or more of the natural children of the predecessor is/are trustees.

A discretionary trust provision is a difficult one for clients to fully understand. The surviving spouse/partner and the children of the pre-deceasing spouse/partner may find it difficult to conceive that a trust has been created in which none of them have any specific, enforceable rights.

As indicated above, careful choice of trustee is indicated, and it is of equal importance that the letters of expression of wish granted clearly design and explain the intentions of the testator.

The fact that income within a discretionary trust will bear income tax at 40 per cent (from April 6, 2004) can be seen by many as a disincentive. The IHT treatment of a discretionary trust is difficult for the lay person to understand, and can for that reason be a "turn off".

Prenuptial marriage contracts

4–13   Such contracts are really more designed to protect the assets of one party on divorce from the other. For many years, marriage contracts fell out of favour in Scotland, and for several years the validity of such contracts in England has been the subject of some doubt.

England

4–14   The Family Law Committee of the English Law Society recommended in May 1991 that ante-nuptial marriage contracts might be used to avoid disputes about the division of property on divorce. The Committee indicated that such contracts would:

> "provide a means whereby the parties can decide for themselves how their property should be divided between them. This reduces or removes the possibility of involvement and the imposition of a solution by the Court which may be completely contrary to the parties' wishes. This would further the current trend. . . of reducing Court interference in family life, wherever possible, and encouraging the parties to take. responsibility themselves."

However, the Family Law Committee thought that in England, without legislative intervention, such marriage contracts might not be recognised and held to be enforceable, as:

(1) They might be regarded as being contrary to public policy.
(2) There might be no proper consideration stated.
(3) There might be no intention to create legal relations.
(4) The courts might not recognise an attempt by the parties to oust their jurisdiction.

Scotland

Eric Clive[12] is highly critical in some respects of the use of marriage **4–15** contracts:

". . . It must be said that this type of arrangement does seem rather old fashioned. What man or woman of spirit and independence of mind would marry someone who was so pathetic as to require this type of protection? What man or woman capable of marrying would consent to be protected in such a demeaning way? What sort of basis is this for a viable and satisfying marriage?"

Notwithstanding his criticisms, Clive[13] recognises that the concern of the Family Law Committee in England would not be tenable in Scotland when he states:

"marriage contracts which, among other things, regulated the position on divorce have never been regarded as contrary to public policy in Scotland. Consideration is irrelevant. The terms of the contract could easily make it clear that it was intended to create legal relations. It is clearly recognisable in Scotland that the parties to an ante-nuptial marriage contract can oust the jurisdiction of the Courts in relation to financial provision on divorce. The Court at the time of divorce has a statutory power to vary or set aside an agreement relating to financial provision on divorce but only if the agreement was not fair and reasonable at the time it was entered into."[14]

Clive also points out an alternative to an ante-nuptial marriage contract which ousts the jurisdiction of the court. There might be a contract which sets out certain agreed principles of property division and also deals with minor and quite specific points of a potential dispute, with the view to the contract being taken into account by the court at the time of a divorce. Section 10 (6)(a) of the Family Law (Scotland) Act 1985 expressly provides that a court may justify departure from the norm of equal sharing, where there is "any agreement between the parties on the ownership or division of the matrimonial property".

Whilst not of direct relevance to the immediate question of succession, in the author's view Clive's comments on the use of such contracts in Scotland are worthy of more detailed consideration, in conjunction with a re-examination of the freedom of an individual to revoke his or her will (see below).

COHABITATION

Background

Statistics indicate that an increasing number of couples favour **4–16** cohabitation without entering into the formality of marriage. However, as marriage opens up rights of succession, it is important that couples

---

[12] E. Clive, *The Law of Husband and Wife in Scotland*, (W. Green) p.314.
[13] *ibid.*, p.315.
[14] Family Law (Scotland) Act 1985, s.16(1)(b).

who are not married to each other (whether or not of the same sex) are encouraged to consider the financial position of the survivor of them on death of the other. Unfortunately, historically, Scottish law has not looked kindly on couples who have chosen to live together in a relationship approximately equivalent to, but short of, marriage. There is very little provision for cohabitees in Scottish law. Perhaps the prime example is section 18 of the Matrimonial Homes (Family Protection) (Scotland) Act 1981 as amended. It might be argued that the protection offered by section 18 is itself minimal, and hedged in with conditions. The "non entitled partner" may apply to the court for occupancy rights for a period not exceeding six months. Although the Court has power to extend the period in question, the rights afforded by section 18 are not automatically afforded to all cohabitees. It requires that the couple must live together with each other as if they were man and wife. The court is to regard all the circumstances of the case, including the time during which the couple have been living together, and whether or not there are any children from the relationship.

Unlike England, in the absence of a suitable will by the pre-deceasing partner, Scottish cohabitees have no rights of succession.

Marriage by cohabitation with habit and repute

4–17   Unfortunately, over the years, this has resulted in what some might perceive to be injustice, with (normally female) petitioners failing to prove marriage by cohabitation with habit and repute.

Eric Clive[15] sets out the requirements for a successful petition, namely:

1. There must be cohabitation.
2. The cohabitation must be as husband and wife.
3. The cohabitation must be in Scotland
4. The cohabitation must be for a sufficient time.
5. The parties must be reputed to be husband and wife.
6. The repute must be sufficiently general.
7. The parties must be free to marry each other.

Clive also points out two further matters which fall to be considered:

(a) Whether the presumption of tacit consent which might arise has in fact been rebutted.
(b) At what date marriage should be regarded as having taken place.

The tests set out by Clive were approved by the court in the recent case of *Dallas v Dallas*.[16] The pursuer and her partner, Mr McEwan, had cohabited between October 1989 and Mr McEwan's death in June 1993.

The court accepted that Mr McEwan and the pursuer had cohabited. However, whether they had cohabited as man and wife was an entirely different question. As the court pointed out, cohabitation with regular

---

[15] *The Law of Husband and Wife in Scotland*, cited above, pp.52 *et seq.*
[16] 2002 G.W.D. 207.

sexual relations and even the birth of a child does not necessarily, in present day circumstances, "point even presumptively to matrimonial consent having been exchanged". The judge expressed the view that there was a distinction between those persons living together as husband and wife, and "persons living together as a husband and wife would". Ms Dallas failed, perhaps partly owing to the fact that there was evidence that she had on occasions declined to be referred to as a wife.

England

Unfortunately, and yet again, Scotland appears to be lagging behind **4–18** England where there is a statutory form of protection for cohabitees. This can be found in the Inheritance (Provision for Family and Dependants) Act 1975. In terms of that Act, it is possible for an English cohabitee to make application to the court for financial assistance on the estate of the deceased's partner if he or she was being "wholly or partly maintained by the deceased when he died". This section is not absolute as most courts do require that where the claimant is an unrelated dependent, he or she must establish a moral claim over that which a blood relation has, and that "to be in necessitous circumstances" is not itself sufficient to establish a claim under the Act. Interestingly, the 1975 Act also allows a former spouse who has not remarried on death of the other former spouse to apply to the Court for an order for financial provision on death of the other.

A further example of English law being ahead of Scottish law can be seen in the case of *Grant v Edwards*.[17] A man and woman lived together for over 20 years. He was employed, whilst she stayed at home keeping house and bringing up their children. Title to the house stood in the man's name alone. When the relationship broke down, the woman was unable to seek any financial provision on divorce, as there could be no divorce. However, the court held that the man held the house on a "constructive trust" for the benefit of both himself and his co-habitee, and she was therefore entitled to claim one-half of its value. Are we beginning to move towards the English position?

In the case of *Shilliday v Smith*,[18] a man and woman began to live together, and became engaged to be married. A house was purchased for them to live in, but title was taken in the sole name of the man. The woman paid for renovations to the house. The engagement was then broken off and she claimed back the money which she had paid for the renovations. The court took the view that she was entitled to succeed. The woman had paid in the expectation of marriage, and that expectation being frustrated, the man should not be allowed to keep the benefit of the renovations without cost.

Until the recent intervention of the Scottish Executive (see below), there remained a sexual bias in respect of cohabitation in Scotland. In the case of *Edmonds v Edmonds*,[19] in offering a definition of cohabitation, the court stated that it was a heterosexual and not a homosexual

---

[17] (1986) 2 All E.R. 426.
[18] 1998 S.C.L.R. 502.
[19] 1971 S.L.T. (Notes) 8.

relationship. It is vital that you should encourage clients who are cohabiting (whether of the same sex or not) to make appropriate wills.

SEPARATION AND DIVORCE

Effects of separation

4–19   Separation does not itself affect intestate rights of succession of the estranged spouse, or (unless the will specifies) an entitlement to a bequest under the will of the other estranged spouse. However, some care is needed here. Whilst it may be entirely appropriate to indicate to a client that *de facto* separation will not affect the testate or intestate rights of succession of the other spouse, it is important to remember that a client may still hope for a reconciliation with the other party. For several years, the profession has encouraged mediation for clients undergoing marital difficulties, and it might be seen to be inconsistent with that more conciliatory approach for the legal profession (perhaps unfairly) to be perceived as encouraging clients to alter with immediate effect their wills, to the possible detriment of the estranged spouse. It has of course become normal practice to incorporate specific discharges of rights of succession in properly framed separation agreements.

Existing wills on divorce

4–20   A will made "inside" a marriage may no longer be appropriate once the client is "outside" that marriage. A client undergoing a divorce should be advised to revisit the terms of his or her will. Bearing in mind that a divorce is one of the most stressful times of an individual's life, a client may have wholly overlooked the terms of an existing will made several years beforehand. This is again an area where tact and diplomacy on the part of the draftsman is required. Not all clients who become divorced regard their former spouses in an unkindly way. It may well be that, in the absence of any other suitable candidates, a divorced client would still wish his former spouse to benefit. Even if that is so, a new will (in absolutely specific terms) may be required in order to avoid the types of difficulties outlined below.

As a first point, divorce does not itself automatically revoke prior wills[20](and of equal importance it should be noted that marriage does not itself have that effect on a prior will). If a client makes a will in favour of his or her spouse and then is divorced from that spouse, the court will have to consider, for example, whether the provisions in favour of "my wife" were intended for the woman who was wife at the time the will was signed, or whether intended for the woman who was wife at the time of death. There is no presumption as to the meaning of the word "wife" in this connection.[21] The question (again one of construction) may turn on the whole terms and language of the deed, and whether the bequest was in some way conditional on the woman in question being wife at the time of death, or whether the word "wife" was merely an

---

[20] *Westerman's Executor v Schwab* (1905) 8 F. 132.
[21] *Burn's Trustees*, 1961 S.C. 17.

identifying description. The leading case here is *Pirie's Trustees v Pirie*.[22] In this case, the testator directed his trustees to allow his wife a life-rent of his estate "and that for her own maintenance and support of my children so long as they shall continue to reside in family with her and be unable to maintain themselves". The husband divorced his wife and married again, but the second wife pre-deceased him. It was held that the bequest to the first wife was "in her capacity as his wife" and thereby subject to a condition that she should be his wife at the time of his death. It was considered important that the life-rent was declared to be alimentary and in full satisfaction of legal rights. The court considered that the settlement was in the nature of a family provision. Equally, if the use of the word "wife" is merely descriptive and there are no factors which indicate that the bequest was conditional on the woman remaining the testator's wife as at the date of his death, then its terms will be given effect notwithstanding divorce.[23]

Reform

It should be noted that the Scottish Law Commission (the Report on **4–21** Succession Number 124 in 1990) recommended that divorce or annulment of marriage should have the effect, unless the contrary intention appears, of revoking a testamentary provision in favour of the former spouse. The Commission did not recommend any change to the existing rule that a testator's marriage will not revoke his or her will. Similarly, the Commission recommended that nomination of the former spouse as executor or trustee should be revoked, again unless the contrary intention applied. The proposals of the Commission (as yet unimplemented) appear to reflect a recognition that not all divorces are bitter battles which end in eternal enmity.

"Spouse exemption"

Inheritance tax has sometimes been described as being a "voluntary **4–22** tax". This may be something of an overstatement of the true position, but probably stems from a comment made many years ago by Lord Jenkins (when he was Chancellor of the Exchequer), when he stated that inheritance tax was a tax paid by those who disliked their families more than they distrusted the Inland Revenue. It might not be considered to be wholly inappropriate to advise partners living in a long-term relationship (not being married to each other) that on death of one of them, even if they have bequeathed their whole estates to each other, inheritance tax might fall to be suffered because the "spouse exemption" would not apply. In a fairly recent English case, an old gentleman (who knew that his time was limited) married a very much younger lady. The old gentleman was wealthy. He made a will providing that his estate should pass to his new wife. On his death, she inherited free of inheritance tax because of the spouse exemption. The Inland Revenue challenged the arrangement on the basis that it was a "sham", purely intended to avoid inheritance tax, which would otherwise have been due. However, the Revenue's claim was thrown out by the court.

---

[22] 1962 S.C. 43.
[23] *Couper's Judicial Factor v Valentine*, 1976 S.L.T. 83.

FORGOTTEN, BUT NOT GONE

4–23 Under Scottish law, a widow has a right to claim temporary aliment after her husband's death. Similarly, a surviving spouse may claim continuing aliment out of the estate of the pre-deceasing spouse. There are no cases in which a widower has been allowed to claim interim aliment. As Clive points out that the obligation of aliment between spouses is reciprocal, there would appear in theory to be no reason why a widower could not make the claim.[24] Clive also makes the point that the law on temporary aliment out of a deceased's estate is archaic and has become obsolete in practice; in 1990, the Scottish Law Commission recommended abolition of the right to claim temporary aliment out of a deceased's estate—it does, however, appear that the right still exists.

The right to claim temporary aliment and continuing aliment out of the estate of a pre-deceasing spouse is of particular importance where a client has never divorced his or her spouse and is now living in a different, long-term relationship with another party. Where one spouse may not have been provided for (as the other spouse has bequeathed his or her whole estate to a third party), it has long been recognised that a surviving spouse will have a claim for aliment, either against the trustees or executors if the estate has not been already disbursed,[25] or indeed against the beneficiary receiving the estate which has already been distributed.[26]

A claim has been recognised in cases where either the surviving spouse (although estranged) has received nothing, or a plainly inadequate provision from the deceased's estate. In cases where the surviving spouse is perceived to have received a reasonable or fair share from the estate of the deceased (by way of prior rights, legal rights or otherwise), Clive makes the point that the claim is unlikely to be recognised. As with legal rights, a claim is not a right of succession, but rather a debt due by the estate which needs to be met out of capital if the income produced by the estate is insufficient.[27] Where aliment is payable, this may be during the surviving spouse's life so long as circumstances require it.[28]

LEGAL RIGHTS OF CHILDREN

4–24 As a first point, whenever a will is made for a client, a client should be advised of the existence of legal rights, in relation to spouses who have not been divorced, as also those representing children who have pre-deceased the client. Failure to advise the client may at the very least lead to a suggestion that, had the client known about the problem of legal rights, he or she might have been able to "do something about them" before his or her death.

Problematic scenarios

4–25 Legal rights can be problematical for clients where:

---

[24] *The Law of Husband and Wife in Scotland*, cited above, p.604.
[25] *Blake v Bates* (1840) 3 D. 317.
[26] *Hobbs v Baird* (1845) 7 D. 492.
[27] *Anderson v Grant* (1899) 1 Fraser 484.
[28] See *Hobbs v Baird*, cited above.

- The client's spouse, who has never been divorced, is still alive and the client is now living in another long-term relationship.
- There are one or more "black sheep" children.
- A client is in a second marriage or long-term relationship, with children of his earlier marriage/relationship, but wishes above all to protect the financial position of the "new" spouse or partner. It can sometimes happen that the children and client become alienated, perhaps because of the remarriage or the parent taking up with a new partner.

Defeating legal rights

It is sometimes suggested that legal rights are indefeasible. This is not **4–26** the case, although, to all practical intents and purposes, defeating legal rights may be virtually impossible for particular clients. Steps which might be suggested to a client may be wholly impractical or unacceptable to that client for one reason or another. However, there are various possibilities:

- *Legal rights can only be claimed against the moveable estate of the client as at his or her date of death.* Thus, a client might consider converting all of his or her property into heritage or heritable bonds. This may be impractical for various reasons, including:
  - (a) Such a course of action can deprive the testator of a degree of flexibility. For example, a heritable property is not readily realisable in an emergency, and if an "investment" heritable property was required to be sold, the capital gains tax implications would need to be explained to the client.
  - (b) Such a course of action would in any event not defeat entitlement of a widow to claim aliment out of the estate (see above).
  - (c) A client could consider gifting his or her moveable property prior to death. However, once again, practicality may militate against this suggestion. The capital gains tax implications would also need to be borne in mind. The transfer needs to be "genuine", and a deliberate, sham transaction is likely to be struck out by the courts as not defeating legal rights.[29] Similarly, the institutional writers suggest that such a lifetime transfer must be irrevocable. However, this suggestion was not upheld in the case of *Huttons Trustees v Huttons Trustees*.[30] In the Hutton case, revocable but unrevoked gifts by a husband to his wife did not fall to being included in the husband's estate in order to calculate the amount of the legitim fund available to children. The rationale of the court was that although revocable, gifts had been unrevoked, and therefore formed part of the estate of the spouse on death of her husband.

---

[29] *Buchanan v Buchanan* (1876) 3 R. 556.
[30] 1916 S.C. 680.

In the case of *Buchanan v Buchanan*,[31] a father gave
£1,000 to his son. The son then in the context of one
document wrote out IOUs in favour of all of his brothers
and sisters, except one "black sheep". The document was
handed to the brothers and sisters in turn and then back to
the father who had kept it until his death some months
later. Although the court felt that there had been delivery,
it took the view that the transaction was a sham, and
therefore did not defeat the entitlement of the black sheep
to claim legitim:

> "The transaction was a mere bit of acting . . . the old
> man intended to retain control of the money himself
> and that his children should not have it until after his
> death."

A sham transfer does, however, need to be distinguished
from the case where there is a transfer with a benefit
reserved. In *Collie v Pirie's Trustees*,[32] transfer of property
under express reservation of a life-rent was considered by
the court to be effective in defeating legal rights. Similarly,
in *Rowley v Rowley*,[33] the husband set up a trust and
transferred shares in a company to the trustees. However,
no dividends were paid on the shareholdings owing to the
fact that the husband's salary exhausted excess profits from
which dividends might be paid. It was argued that the
husband had continued to enjoy the income of the property transferred and that the value of the shares should still
be taken into account when calculating the wife's entitlement to legal rights. However, the Court felt that he had
irrevocably divested himself of the shares, and that their
value should not be taken into account in calculating the
wife's entitlement.

- *A client could consider setting up a lifetime trust for administration with the client and/or the beneficiary.* Following the rationale
  in the *Rowley* case above, this might help to substantially defeat
  a claim to legal rights, but the client has to weigh up the
  element of loss of control, and the attendant costs of administering a trust would need to be borne in mind. Such a trust
  would, because of retention benefit, be wholly ineffective from
  the point of view of IHT mitigation, *i.e.* it would not be a
  potentially exempt transfer for IHT purposes.
- *Remain intestate.* The final strategy which a client might consider to defeat the legal rights of children is one which has
  worked in the past, but which has inherent dangers. Thus, if the
  whole estate falls within the limits detailed in sections 8 and 9
  of the 1964 Act, and given that prior rights rank and are paid
  before legal rights, and the surviving spouse will take every-

[31] *Buchanan v Buchanan* (1876) 3 R. 556, cited above.
[32] (1851) 13 D. 506.
[33] [1971] S.L.P. 16.

thing, the client might take the deliberate decision to remain intestate. The attendant additional costs and complications of an intestate's estate should be pointed out to the client, who also needs to be reminded that if his or her estate increases greatly in size, then children might once again come into line of succession. The case of Kerr[34] is of relevance here. Mr Kerr had left everything in his will to his wife, with no over destination in favour of children. Mrs Kerr renounced her entitlement under the will, which meant that the whole estate became intestate. As it fell within the limits which then applied under sections 8 and 9 of the 1964 Act, she was found to be entitled to take the whole estate on intestacy, thereby defeating the children's claims to legal rights. However, if a client were to wish to actively consider this course, then very careful drafting is required—see the cautionary note introduced by Barr, etc.[35]

Voluntary discharge of legal rights

A spouse or child can of course voluntarily discharge his or her **4–27** entitlement to legal rights. This will not amount to a transfer of value for inheritance tax purposes. A style of discharge of legal rights is produced in the Appendix of Styles.

The Unmarried Client with or without Dependants

It may be thought that the easiest will of all to make is for a client who **4–28** has never been married, and has no children or other dependants. However, it is just in this situation where difficult points can arise:

1. An unmarried client who has no children or other dependants may feel that there is little or no point in making a will. However, in such circumstances, it is appropriate to point out to the client the rules of intestate succession as set out under the 1964 Act. The client may recoil in horror when he or she realises that distant relatives whom he/she does not like, or may not even know, will succeed. In such circumstances, the client may quickly change his or her mind and decide that friends, other relatives, or indeed worthy charities should benefit under their will. It is important to bear in mind at all times that a will is an expression of the personal wishes of the client. Whilst the solicitor framing the will should always be prepared to discuss issues with the client and offer advice, at the end of the day, the solicitor must remember that the will belongs to the client.

2. Often, an unmarried client with no dependants will wish to leave legacies to friends, with the residue or main benefit under the will going to charities. Some charities are extremely proactive, if not aggressive, in marketing themselves.

---

[34] 1968 S.L.T. (Sh. Ct.) 61.

[35] Barr, etc., *The Drafting of Wills in Scotland*, (Butterworths/Law Scoiety of Scotland, 1994) para.6.31.

Points to consider

- Bear in mind that where a client's estate is liable to IHT, charities are exempt beneficiaries. Although of more relevance to the actual winding up of the client's estate, in calculating the final division as between beneficiaries of an exempt/non-exempt nature, the charities should not even indirectly bear any part of the inheritance tax payable in respect of the estate. This is an important point, and auditors acting for charities often come across final accounts in terms of which the calculation of the share of residue due to the two different types of beneficiary has been wrongly made.[36]

- As indicated, charities can be very proactive in pursuing benefits under a deceased client's will. It is important that the will should be framed to avoid confusion arising. Where a charity is involved, the will should contain a specific declaration to cover the situation where the charity in question may have changed its name or amalgamated with, or transferred its assets to, another charity, or indeed been wrongly designed (see below).

- It is submitted that where the testator wishes to leave a bequest to a charity, the draftsman should ensure that the testator gives clear instructions as to which charity should receive the relevant benefit. Clients often confuse charities and, where necessary, it might be advisable to "lend" to the testator one of the several "charity compendiums" which are now available. It may in fact be advisable to refer to the relevant charity not only by name, but also by reference to its registered charity number and present registered or chief office. Particular care needs to be taken with regard to charities involved in cancer research. Many major charities (including those involved in such research) subscribe to a bequest notification service which will inform the charities when probate or confirmation has been granted on an estate in which they have, or might have, an interest. In many older wills (particularly in England), the testator may have left a legacy for the purposes of "cancer research" without specifying a particular charity. In England, in such circumstances, the normal rule is that such bequests must be directed either by Royal Sign Manual Direction, or by the Charity Commission (*i.e.* the latter will decide which charity should benefit). It is understood that these particular provisions do not, however, apply in Scotland. In the author's view, such a system in Scotland might be of assistance—it might avoid needless litigation between charities in a difficult case—and it might also prevent the "losing" charity from seeking to call the draftsman of the relevant will to account!

---

[36] See Re *Benham's Will Trusts* [1995] S.T.C. 210; and Re *Ratcliffe* [1994] S.T.C. 262.

3. A similar related question arises where the client has a substantial estate which will be liable for IHT, in relation to the incidence of inheritance tax (see below).

4. An unmarried client, having no children of his or her own, may decide to leave substantial legacies to nephews or nieces. This could raise the question of whether or not the *conditio si institutus sine liberis decesserit* might apply. To avoid any doubt here then the *conditio* can be positively negated by the addition of a simple phrase—for example "but expressly excluding his or her issue in the event of him or her pre-deceasing me". The *conditio* only applies to pecuniary legacies, not to specific bequests (see below).

Further, the client should be encouraged to consider the relevant ages of such beneficiaries. Where it is possible that a child or children who are still young and vulnerable will succeed, then a simple accumulation and maintenance trust (see *infra*) can be incorporated within the will to avoid vesting until a chosen age.

Bear in mind that it is equally possible that whilst the client may never have been married, he or she may have one or more children. If the client has never had any contact with the child or children in question, he or she may not be inclined to bequeath anything to them. Again, a warning regarding the effects of legal rights must be given. The foregoing would not, however, be the normal situation, but again consideration should be given to protection of young and vulnerable individuals from their own financial naïvety. Unless a will states otherwise, children have a vested right at age 16. Whilst postponement of payment of a bequest may be deferred until age 16 is attained, an attempt to extend the payment period beyond 16 will fail unless vesting is also postponed. That being so, it is normal to suggest an accumulation and maintenance trust to the client (see below).

CONDITIOS

Types of *Conditios*

There are two *conditios* of which every will maker must be aware. These **4–29** are:

- *Conditio si testator sine liberis decesserit*; and
- The *conditio si institutus sine liberis decesserit*.

The *conditio si testator* can operate so as to revoke a will, whereas the *conditio si institutus* can apply so as to carry a pecuniary bequest to children of a pre-deceasing legatee in certain circumstances.

The *conditio si institutus sine liberis decesserit*

This presumption does not operate to revoke the will, but rather **4–30** extend the range of beneficiaries who may take thereunder. In certain circumstances, where a testamentary bequest has been left to a particular legatee without reference to his or her children, the presumption will operate so as to carry the legacy to the children of the legatee in the event of the latter pre-deceasing the testator.[37]

The *conditio* does not apply to:

- step children;
- others outwith the family circle; or
- brothers and sisters.

The *conditio* does apply to:

- descendants (including grandchildren)[38];
- great grandchildren[39] and indeed to any direct descendant however far removed from the testator; and
- nephews and nieces where the testator had placed himself *in loco parentis* to them. However, this does not require that the testator should have demonstrated any special interest, financial or otherwise, in nephews and nieces during their lifetime.[40]

Rebuttal of the presumption

4–31   Rebuttal can be achieved if it can be shown that the relevant bequest was made, not through relationship, but simply owing to personal regard for the legatee.[41] However, it will be considered to be conclusive of a relevant bequest arising through relationship if legatees are described as a class by reference to the relationship (for example "my children", or "my nephews and nieces". It is irrelevant that members of the class are not named.[42] Where the bequest refers to members of a particular class alive at a certain time, this will not exclude pre-deceasing members of that class in raising the presumption.

It should be noted that where the conditio applies, the issue will take only their pre-deceasing parent's original share, and is not entitled to any increase in their benefit by accretion which would otherwise have operated had their parent survived.[43]

How to avoid the *conditio*

4–32   Again, this is important to avoid other members of the class raising a complaint that they were deprived a higher share of the relevant bequest through accretion as, if the conditio applies, it will carry the share of the pre-deceasing legatee (but only his or her original share as detailed above) to his or her issue. Avoiding the effect of the *conditio* is straightforward; if the testator makes it clear that there should be no "over destination" to the issue of the relevant descendant of a nephew and niece, then the *conditio* is excluded. For example, a testator might leave a bequest in the following terms:

---

[37] *McGregor's Trustees v Gray*, 1969 S.L.T. 355.
[38] *Gwendolen Beatrice Thomson Trustees*, 1963 S.C. 141.
[39] *Grant v Brooke* (1882) 10 R. 92.
[40] *Bogie's Trustees v Christie* (1882) 9 R 453.
[41] *Traver's Trustees v Macintyre*, 1934 S.C. 520.
[42] *Allan v Thomson's Trustees* (1893) 20 R 733.
[43] *Campbell's Trustee v Dick*, 1915 S.C. 100.

"I bequeath the sum of THIRTY THOUSAND POUNDS (£30,000) STERLING equally between such of my nephews and nieces as shall survive me."

As drafted, the foregoing bequest might well raise the question of whether or not the conditio applies in the event of, for example, a nephew pre-deceasing the testator. However, the effect of the conditio can be easily excluded by simply adding to the end of the above clause ". . . but expressly excluding their issue".

Finally, the conditio applies only to a monetary bequest. It does not apply to a specific bequest, for example, an item of furniture or jewellery.

THE RIGHT TO REVOKE

We have already touched on the question of the freedom of a testator to   **4–33**
revoke an existing will, even if this means that the testator will be left intestate. The right to revoke can be exercised right up to the point of death. The right to revoke applies even where a testator has in fact delivered his will to a beneficiary—see *Clark's Executor v Clark*.[44] It is of course quite different if the deed delivered is an *inter vivos* conveyance. In the case of a will, death is generally considered to be equivalent to delivery in relation to an *inter vivos* deed, but until that moment (*i.e.* of death), the testator can revoke as he or she sees fit. As we have seen, even the inclusion of a statement in a will declaring that it is irrevocable is not binding on the testator.[45]

However, there may be a situation where an individual binds himself not to revoke a will. The institutional writers recognised that a testator can enter into an enforceable contract not to revoke his or her will, thereby depriving himself/herself of the power to do so, with the result that any attempted revocation of the will thereafter will be ineffective. This indicates an important strategy which may find favour with clients who wish to protect their present partners, and at the same time also seek to protect their natural children's spes successionis.

Although probably truly in respect of an *inter vivos* gift, in the case of *Curdy v Boyd*,[46] in return for an undertaking that Boyd would maintain him all the days of his life, Mr Curdy conveyed his property to the former. Three years later, however, Curdy purported to revoke the disposition. The court held that the disposition was onerous and thus irrevocable in the absence of any fraud. In the case of *Paterson v Paterson*,[47] Mrs Paterson had entered into a formal agreement with her son. The agreement bound him to make various payments to Mrs Paterson and her husband. She for her part was taken bound to execute a will of her whole property in favour of the son in question. Mrs Paterson did make the will required by the agreement, but on her death

---

[44] 1943 S.C. 216.
[45] See *Dougall's Trustees v Dougall*, cited above.
[46] 1775 Mor. 15946.
[47] (1893) 20 R. 484.

it transpired that she had made a later will purporting to revoke the
earlier one, and making a quite different disposal of her estate. The
contracting son sought to reduce the second will. The action was
successful on the ground that the onerous contract entered into by his
mother was binding upon her not only to make the will in his favour, but
also not to subsequently revoke the same.

4–34   The case of *McLachlan v Seton's Trustees*[48] is also of interest. In 1911,
Mrs Seton made a codicil to her then will, bequeathing the sum of
£6,000 equally among three beneficiaries, two of whom were relatives of
the deceased's husband. The bequest seems to have been made under
some duress and, in return for the same and on delivery of the codicil to
them, the beneficiaries undertook in writing not to call into question the
good faith of Mrs Seton's husband in connection with his management,
as trustee, of their late father's estate. Mrs Seton irrevocably bound
herself in 1911 in respect of the bequest. However, she subsequently
made a series of later wills, each containing a general clause of
revocation and a repetition of the £6,000 bequest in the same terms,
including a will of 1935. This differed slightly from the codicil of 1911 in
that she directed that certain legacies, including the one at issue, would
not carry interest.

On her death, the three beneficiaries in question brought an action
against her trustees, maintaining that Mrs Seton had no power to revoke
the codicil of 1911, and that accordingly they were entitled to payment of
the legacy under the codicil of 1911, as well as to the legacy of the 1935
will.

The court found that whilst Mrs Seton had irrevocably bound herself
in 1911 to bequeath £6,000 to the pursuers, she was entitled to revoke
the 1911 codicil and to substitute a similar bequest in a later testamentary writing. She had effectively done so in all of her later wills, and the
beneficiaries were therefore entitled to only one bite at the cherry. It
would therefore seem that it is possible for the testator to enter into a
contractual arrangement to make a will in certain terms, or not to alter
an existing will or a provision thereof. This might well offer scope or at
least some comfort to parties who wish to protect the financial position
of their partners without leaving it to trust that their own children will
not subsequently be disinherited. One point which I would make in
relation to the cases quoted above is that there is no doubt but that a
contractual obligation was undertaken for some consideration (although,
as we have seen, Clive is of the view that in relation to ante-nuptial
marriage contracts, consideration is irrelevant in Scotland).

As with any proposed solution, there are downsides:

- Even if there is a valid contract not to alter a will, normal rules
  of ademption will apply. If the testator dissipates his or her
  estate prior to death, then the contractual obligation may be of
  little value. For example, if a spouse has entered into such an
  obligation and then passes on, the surviving spouse could gift
  the estate to his or her children during lifetime whilst not
  altering the will, in terms of which the residue of his or her
  estate fall to be divided equally between the two families.

---

[48] 1937 S.C. 206.

- As the assets or property in question will remain within the estate of the surviving spouse, if he or she remarries those assets could be subject to a claim for legal rights at the instance of the "new spouse".
- From the point of view of IHT mitigation, obviously the fact that the whole estate is passing to the survivor means that the relevant spouse is effectively giving one nil-rate band back to the Inland Revenue.

THE FUTURE

Same sex couples and proposed changes in law

Manchester was the first city in England, outside London, to set up a **4–35** "Partnership Registration Scheme". The Registry Office in Manchester was the first in the country to perform a "commitment ceremony" in April 2002.

At present, the Manchester Partnership Registration Scheme has no particular legal status. It does, however, reflect the lead given by the Liberal Democrats in 2000 when they made it party policy to give same sex couples the same right as heterosexuals over inheritance, adoption and property.

The Westminster Government has now proposed a Registration Scheme which would have various effects in law. It is proposed that the scheme should come into effect in 2010, and it should be noted that Oliver Letwin, the Conservative Shadow Home Secretary (at the time of writing), has acknowledged that both same sex and unmarried couples should have "many of the rights of married couples".

The present position

At present, both in Scotland and England, cohabiting couples do not **4–36** get the same tax breaks or entitlements which married couples enjoy, such as access to a partner's pension. A number of test cases are underway to obtain recognition of same sex relationships under the Human Rights Act. However, it is also fair to point out that various organisations have begun to examine the position of same sex couples and are considering allowing them the same pension rights and staff discounts as are afforded to married couples. The Inland Revenue Application Form for Children's Tax Credit (replacing the Married Couples' Allowance) refers to spouses as "partners", and not "husbands" or "wives". There would appear to be a culture change in our society, although various campaign groups are pressing the Government to introduce their proposals earlier than 2010.

What are the proposals?

It should be noted that the following proposals only apply in England **4–37** and Wales. However, the Scottish Executive has now indicated that it will give effect to identical provisions in Scotland (see below). The proposals include the following:

- Same sex couples will be able to sign a document at a registry office in front of the registrar and two witnesses, although this will not be an official ceremony, and the word "marriage" will not be used. They will receive a certificate and be able to call themselves "registered civil partners", obliged to "support each other financially and emotionally throughout their lives".

- Partners upon registration will gain rights over property, social security benefits and pensions, both state and private.
- Again, upon registration the partners will gain parental responsibility for each other's children, with contact rights and child support obligations if the partnership fails and is dissolved.
- Same sex partners will be able to act as each other's "next of kin" in any medical situation.
- Same sex partners will receive the same protection against domestic violence as married couples, and will not be compelled to testify against each other in court.
- For the first time, if one partner dies, the other will be able to register the death, play a role in the funeral arrangements, claim a survivor's pension, and receive bereavement benefits or compensation for fatal accidents or criminal injury.
- The surviving partner will be recognised as a beneficiary if their partner dies without leaving a will.
- Surviving partners will be exempt from inheritance tax (which to date has forced many surviving partners to sell their homes).
- Same sex partners will not be expected to have lived together for two years before one partner can move with the other to Britain. However, once in the UK, there will be the same two-year probationary period which applies to heterosexual couples.
- There will be a court-based process for dissolution of a partnership in which the couple would have to show that the relationship had broken down irretrievably. Financial legal aid will be available.
- Couples will be able to officially register 15 days after putting in an application. There are to be limitations on partnerships between those with close blood ties, mirroring the incest laws for heterosexual marriage. There will be a new offence of perjury, reflecting the offence of bigamy in "straight" marriages.

Whilst the proposals have been welcomed, as indicated above, various campaign groups wish them to be introduced earlier than 2010. The charity, Stonewall, have indicated that they anticipate that at least 10,000 same sex couples will register their partnerships within the first 5 to 10 years of the proposals coming into effect. It is estimated that the total annual cost to the Government of implementing the proposals in 2010 will be around £75 million, including state pension, public service pension and dissolution costs. The annual cost to private employers could be £20 million per annum. There has, however, been some criticism—the proposals apply to same sex relationships only, thus leading some to complain that the Government has ignored one quarter of the heterosexual population under 60 who currently co-habit in Britain.

The position in Scotland

On September 30, 2003, the Scottish Executive published a consulta- **4–38** tion paper on the devolved aspects of a Civil Partnership Registration Scheme for same sex couples—*"Civil Partnership Registration. A Legal Status for Committed Same Sex Couples in Scotland"*. The Scottish consultation paper substantially follows the proposals of the Westminster Government, reflecting a promise made by the Scottish Executive that it would follow Westminster's lead in this area.

Part II—Drafting the Will

CHAPTER 5

THE ISLAMIC WILL

The Moslem community in Scotland adds not only to the cultural **5–01** diversity of our society, but also plays an important part in Scottish business and commerce. Moslem clients make great use of the services of the Scottish profession. Many have been loyal and valued clients of particular legal firms for a long number of years. However, and just like the majority of Scots, Moslem clients do not, for the most part, avail themselves of the services of will-drafting solicitors. This may be due to the fact that the Islamic faith has its own, longstanding testamentary code of succession, which is every bit as complicated as Scottish common law or the Rules of Succession set out under the 1964 Act.

THE ISLAMIC CODE OF SUCCESSION

The Qur'an (literally translated as "the Recitation" and also known, **5–02** perhaps more widely, as "the Koran") clearly recognises human mortality and that each individual should accept the fact of his or her own mortality.[1]

The Qur'an was the latest and last Revelation from Allah to mankind, being revealed to the Prophet Muhammed through the angel Gabriel over a period of 23 years, of which the first 13 were spent in Mecca, and the last 10 in Medina. Although originally committed to memory, it was first fully compiled in writing by the first Caliph, Abu Bakar.

THE OBLIGATION TO TEST

The prophet Muhammed said that, "It is the duty of a Moslem who has **5–03** something to be given as a bequest not to spend two nights without making a Will about it". The instruction to the individual to make a will has a force not only based in faith and religious instruction, but also in the Shari'a law of the Moslem faith. The Shari'a is a legal and social path to be followed by a people based on the revelation of their prophet. The Shari'a sets out rules which effectively govern the settlement/distribution of the estate of a deceased individual.

ISLAMIC RULES—ORDER OF PRIORITY

(i) On death, the first charge against the deceased's estate is a sum **5–04** necessary for shrouding and burying the individual in accordance with the provisions of the Qur'an.

---

[1] "Every self will taste death"—Aya 3.185 (an Aya is a verse of the Qur'an of which there are 6,666 in the Qur'an itself).

(ii) The debts of the individual then fall to be settled, prior to any other considerations, including beneficial succession.

(iii) Thereafter the individual can test/bequeath up to one-third of his or her estate.

(iv) The remainder or residue is divided into shares in accordance with the Shari'a, for distribution in accordance with detailed rules as set out in the Shari'a.

These rules obviously have a similarity and resonance with some of the legal rules which govern the Law of Succession (both testate and intestate) in Scotland, particularly in relation to the priority afforded to funeral expenses, etc.

Funeral expenses

5–05   The Qur'an contains very detailed rules for preparation of the dead for burial. The washing and shrouding of the dead for burial is regarded by many Moslems as a *fard kifaya,* which is a duty which must be fulfilled. It is something which is owed to the honour and dignity of every believer when he or she leaves this world. The Qur'an contains detailed rules regarding the funeral procession and the funeral prayers. It is interesting that again certain rules have a resonance with traditional practice in Scotland. For example, it is regarded as being appropriate to prepare food for the family after the deceased's funeral, and it is considered by the Qur'an to be *haram* (*i.e.* forbidden) to decorate the grave just for the sake of adornment, or to erect a building over it—this has a resonance with certain older Scottish cases where detailed instructions to expend large sums of money on, for example, a mausoleum, were considered to be excessive and unenforceable.

Debts

5–06   For Moslems, it is of paramount importance that they should pass from this world to the next without being in debt. The prophet Muhammed said that, "The soul of the believer is detained by his debts". Under the teaching of Muhammed, an individual cannot enter paradise until his or her debts have been settled. Under the Shari'a, if an individual dies in debt and his or her estate is insufficient to meet the liabilities in question, then, if not obligatory, it is an act of kindness for his or her relatives to pay off a deceased's debt on his behalf.

Bequests

5–07   Under the Shari'a, a Moslem can bequeath only one-third of his or her estate. Bequests can be made to relatives—including children—who are not entitled to a fixed share of the estate under the Shari'a; for charitable purposes; for the maintenance of places of worship; and for the upkeep of animals (under Scottish law, an animal is not "a person" and therefore cannot be a direct beneficiary under a deceased person's will). Bequests can be made by a Moslem to a non-Moslem. For example, if a Moslem dies survived by a non-Moslem wife, she is not entitled to a fixed share under the Shari'a; but she can be left a bequest under her husband's will. Interestingly, it would appear that a bequest cannot be made in favour of a relative who is already entitled to a fixed share in accordance with the Shari'a. This may be one reason why Moslem clients find it difficult to make a Scottish will.

Similarly, where an individual bequeaths more than a third of his or her estate in his or her will, then the bequests abate proportionately so that they no longer exceed a third of his estate in total, unless those heirs who are entitled to a fixed share of the residue in accordance with the Shari'a agree to accept lesser shares.

The residue

Under the Shari'a, there are five categories of relationship which may   **5–08** lead to entitlement to a share of a deceased person's estate. These relationships are provided by:

1. Kinship
2. Marriage
3. Emancipation
4. Slavedom
5. Where there is no living person entitled to succeed, the House of Wealth (the *Bayt al-Mal*, being akin to a Central Treasury where the estate of individuals who die intestate or without living relatives is ingathered for redistribution for charitable or other purposes, such as the alleviation of poverty).

There are very detailed rules as to which relatives are entitled to a fixed share. Without going into great detail, there are 15 different types of male relatives and 10 different types of female relatives who are entitled.

Heirs who are entitled to inherit do so either because they have been assigned a fixed share in terms of the Qur'an/Shari'a or by virtue of male kinship. Such residuary beneficiaries are entitled to take his or her share only and no more than this. Again, under the Qur'an/Shari'a there are very detailed rules as to the heirs who are entitled to inherit a fixed share. Individuals who inherit a fixed share under the Qur'an and by virtue of male kinship appear to be in a favoured position, although there are only two categories of heir who take in terms of the combined "tests". These are the father and the grandfather, who each will inherit his fixed share, and if there is any residue after other fixed shares have been apportioned, each is entitled to a share of the residue by virtue of male kinship.

Calculation of the shares

It is not the case that each individual entitled to succeed will   **5–09** necessarily receive an equal share, and there are certain circumstances in which those entitled to a share of the residue will find their entitlements being reduced. For example, under the Qur'an a bequest to a *mawla* or a *mudabbar* (either a freed slave or a slave contracted to be freed after his master's death or in some cases even a former master) is given priority even over payment of the Zakat[2] unpaid by the testator during his

---

[2] An annual wealth tax obligatory on Moslems, usually payable in the form of one fortieth of surplus wealth.

lifetime, but with instructions to be paid on his death. Zakat (unpaid during lifetime) is paid from the one-third share of the estate on which a Moslem can test, and if what remains of that one-third of the estate is insufficient to settle such bequests, then those entitled to the residue receive a reduced share in proportion.

With regard to the position of husbands and wives, in certain circumstances, where a husband survives a wife who has no living children or grandchildren, he will be entitled to one half of her estate. If the pre-deceasing wife is survived by children or grandchildren, then the husband's share will be one-quarter. In the reverse situation, the entitlement of a wife where the husband has no living children or grandchildren is one-quarter. Where the pre-deceasing husband is survived by children or grandchildren, then the wife's share will be one-eighth.

Whilst the rules of division appear to be very complicated, they are perceived in Islam to provide absolute certainty, and to achieve equity amongst whatever permutation of relatives shall survive the deceased.

Similarities and differences to Scottish law

5–10   There are various similarities/resonances between the Shari'a and the Law of Succession in Scotland. There are equally important differences between Islamic Rules of Succession and those which apply in Scotland.

Similarities

5–11   1. The rules under the Islamic Code regarding priority of payment of debts appear to be very close to those which apply in Scotland.
2. Under the Shari'a, there is freedom to test only in respect of one-third of the estate of the individual. This is not dissimilar to Scottish law (the dead's part) when one takes into account legal rights which apply where a deceased is survived by both a spouse and children.
3. The provisions of the Qur'an regarding adornment of a grave find resonance (as indicated above) with various Scottish cases. Scottish courts have long been prepared to strike down provisions of a will where they provide no benefit to any living party or existing concern, but merely represent extravagance or self glorification on the part of the testator. Lord President Clyde indicated that the Court would intervene where:

    > "The Testator's act may be regarded as going beyond the right of *testamenti factio* . . . the directions [*i.e.* those of the testator] reach a certain pitch of grotesqueness, of extravagance, of wastefulness or of futility."[3]

4. Where a Moslem man dies leaving a wife who is pregnant, his estate cannot be settled until either the child is born or there is a miscarriage or stillbirth. When one of the foregoing events has occurred distribution can take place, with a child born after

---

[3] *McKintosh's Judicial Factor v The Lord Advocate*, 1935 S.C. 406.

death receiving his or her share in accordance with the Shari'a. This is not dissimilar to the position of a child *in utero* in Scotland.

Similarly, in the well known *McCaig* cases, the court was prepared to intervene to strike down self-gratifying legacies contained in the wills of the McCaig brother and sister.

Mr McCaig (who was responsible for the building of the "folly" in Oban) had directed his executors to expend the revenue from his estate in perpetuity for the purpose of erecting various structures, statues, etc. of himself and of his family on his estate. Whilst the purpose of this was to encourage Scottish artists, the court intervened to strike the legacies down.[4]

In the sister's will, there were similar provisions, with no beneficial interest being conferred on anyone. The court was not prepared to permit implementation of a bequest which reflected Miss McCaig's vanity.[5]

Dissimilarities

1. Under the Shari'a a will can either be verbal or written, **5–12** although in either case, there must be two witnesses to it. Whilst a nuncupative will was recognised in old Scottish law, to all intents and purposes this recognition has now fallen into desuetude, and been removed by the Requirements of Writing (Scotland) Act, 1995.
2. The group of relatives who are entitled to succeed on intestacy under the Shari'a is much wider than under the Succession (Scotland) Act, 1964 Rules of Succession. The Islamic Rules of division bear little relationship to the Scottish Rules of Division.
3. Scottish law does not allow for the possibility of an individual having more than one spouse at the time of his or her death. The Shari'a does, however, make testamentary provision for up to four wives.
4. If a Moslem has recently divorced and then dies, the surviving spouse may still be entitled to a fixed share in accordance with the Shari'a, in certain defined circumstances.
5. Under the Shari'a, a child can directly inherit property once he or she has reached puberty. Where a child inherits before reaching puberty, the estate inherited will be looked after by a guardian informally appointed amongst the relatives or close friends of the deceased.

It may be that Islamic clients feel that the Rules of Succession under the Shari'a are such that it would not be possible for a Scottish solicitor to make a will which would fully comply with the complete rules of the Shari'a. Equally, it is submitted that most Scottish solicitors, having little

[4] *McCaig v University of Glasgow*, 1907 S.C. 231.
[5] *McCaig's Trustees v Lismore Kirk Session*, 1915 S.C. 426.

or no knowledge of Islamic Rules of Succession, would be unwilling to commit themselves to seeking to make a will which was wholly "Shari'a compliant". This does, of course, raise the question as to what happens where an Islamic client passes on, possibly intestate, and confirmation is required. It is likely that many Islamic clients will seek to order their affairs during their lifetime (just as many Scots will do), in such a fashion so that on death they have substantially achieved the succession which would otherwise have been the outcome under Shari'a law. It also raises the question as to whether such clients are unwittingly incurring potential (and perhaps large) capital gains tax liabilities when making such lifetime disposals. If such a practice were to be followed, then of course transfers within seven years of the relevant date of death would be at least partially failed potentially exempt transfers. It may be that a Scottish draftsman having an interest in this field will find that following the *Patak* case[6] might provide some guidance as to what practical approach might be adopted. The Patak family are not Moslem, they are of Indian origin. The will of the father (and figurehead of the Patak food empire) is being challenged by two daughters. They claim that during their father's lifetime, they came under pressure from him and acceded to his request that their shareholdings in the family company be transferred to their mother (Mr Patak's wife). On their father's death, instead of returning the shares to them (which is the understanding alleged by the two daughters), Mrs Patak made the combined shareholdings over to the eldest son of the family. It will be interesting to see how this case develops.

It may be that if an estate is distributed in an Islamic family in accordance with Scottish law, those who receive more than that to which they are entitled under Islamic rules will informally pass on part of their inheritance to others who are not necessarily entitled under Scottish law, but are so entitled under the Shari'a. This will of course again raise difficult questions in relation to unforeseen capital gains tax and inheritance tax consequences.

CONCLUSION

5–13 From one viewpoint, making a will for a Moslem client which complies with the Qu'ran and also Shari'a law may appear to be virtually impossible. It should, at all times, be borne in mind that difficult questions of domicile can arise, and the draftsman should never lose sight of this factor (see Chapter 6). However, especially for those generations of Islamic families who have been born, and have lived all of their lives in Scotland, then the question has to be posed whether it would be beyond the skill of a Scottish draftsman to draw up a will which would meet the requirements of an Islamic client wishing his estate to devolve in terms of the Shari'a. Obviously, Islamic draftsmen are capable of drawing up such a will and, at least in theory, there is no reason why their Scottish counterparts should not be able to do so.

Possible dangers

5–14 The danger areas for the draftsman can be summarised as follows:

---

[6] At the time of writing, this case is in the High Court in England.

- Domicile (as indicated above) and choice of law.
- The treatment of moveable and immoveable property situated abroad. Islamic clients may well own property in both Scotland and in another country.
- The draftsman would need to make it clear to the Islamic client that whilst the will had been drawn in accordance with the tenets of the Shari'a, etc. as advised by the client, where the client is a domiciled Islamic Scot, the will would fall to be interpreted in accordance with Scottish law.
- The question of legal rights. Whilst the Shari'a and Scottish law both contain provisions effectively to prevent disinheritance, an Islamic client would need to understand clearly that if he is domiciled in Scotland, then this opens to his family the right to claim legal rights, notwithstanding the terms of a will otherwise made in accordance with the terms of the Shari'a. Nonetheless, there is no imperative or obligation upon a Scottish spouse or child to claim his or her entitlement to legal rights, and it may be that all one can do in relation thereto is to advise Islamic clients of the entitlement (as the adviser should in any event do in relation to any client), leaving it to the client to assess whether his family will regard the tenets of the Shari'a and observance of their relative's expressed wishes as being more fundamentally important to them than a Kafir inheritance.[7]
- It is acknowledged that Scottish draftsmen may be reluctant to endeavour to incorporate the terms of the Shari'a code if this is taken by the testator (and indeed by his beneficiaries) to represent some claim to expertise in that field on the part of the draftsman. However, within the limits recognised in Scottish law, a testator is free to choose his beneficiaries. That being so, there is no reason why an Islamic client should not "choose" as legatees or residuary beneficiaries under his will those who would in any event have been entitled in terms of the Shari'a.
- Care would need to be taken that the will observed Islamic strictures regarding payment of interest.
- There is likely to be a conflict between Scottish and Islamic Rules of Succession as to questions such as survivorship, destinations over, etc. These issues would need to be properly explained to the client, as again for the client domiciled in Scotland, Scottish law will apply.

The purpose of this Chapter is largely an academic one, intended, if nothing more, to stimulate the interest of Scottish draftsmen, and perhaps a debate on how best to serve the needs of an important section of our clientele. However, as suggested above, if Islamic draftsmen can set down in writing for their clients wills which comply with Islamic Rules of Succession, is it beyond the capabilities of Scottish draftsmen to do the same, albeit that Islamic clients would need to accept in all cases that, at the end of the day, Scottish law would apply to the proper interpretation of such a will ?

---

[7] In Arabic, "kafir" denotes a person who rejects the word of Allah.

CHAPTER 6

CAPACITY AND DOMICILE

CAPACITY

Essential features

6–01   In order to make a valid will, the maker of that will needs to have capacity. As with the exercise of other similar rights, capacity in so far as a will is concerned has two essential features:

1. *That the maker of the will is of full age.* Scottish law has recognised for many years the ability of a minor to test in respect of his or her moveable property.[1] The present law is set out in section 2(2) of the Age of Legal Capacity (Scotland) Act 1991 which states that "a person of or over 12 years shall have testamentary capacity including legal capacity to exercise by testamentary writing any power of appointment". This section "standardised" the age of 12, as previously the ages of attainment of majority between male and female were different (14 for a male, 12 for a female). Where the child is of non age, then there is no argument but that any will made by that child is *null ab initio*.[2]

2. *The testator must also be of sound mind.* Whilst in respect of age, the situation is relatively straightforward, a quite different situation applies in respect of whether or not the testator is of sound mind. Our legal system has over a number of years found it difficult to define capacity. In their book, *Mental Handicap and the Law*, Ashton and Ward stated that there has been:

   "Little research into the skills and abilities needed to determine legal capacity. Assessment is not a medical or psychiatric diagnostic art but rests on judgement of the type that an informed lay person may make using a relatively simple checklist".

   It is noteworthy that section 1(6) of the Adults with Incapacity (Scotland) Act 2000 did not in fact seek to define capacity, but stated that, for the purposes of that Act, and unless the context otherwise required, "adult" means a person who has attained the age of 16 years, and "incapable" means incapable of:

---

[1] *Stevenson v Allan* (1680) Mor. 849.
[2] Erskine Institute 17–33.

(a) acting; or

(b) making decisions; or

(c) communicating decisions; or

(d) understanding decisions; or

(e) retaining the memory of decisions

as mentioned in any provision of the Act by reason of mental disorder or of inability to communicate because of physical disability. But a person shall not fall within this definition by reason only of a lack or deficiency in a faculty of communication, if that lack or deficiency can be made good by human or mechanical aid (whether of an interpretative nature or otherwise); and "incapacity" shall be construed accordingly.

Thus, the drafters of the 2000 Act did not seek to define capacity as such, but rather they preferred to define incapacity.

Who decides?

It is often thought that the assessment and final judgment on whether **6–02** or not capacity exists lies with the medical profession. This viewpoint may have arisen because if a lawyer is faced with a client and a doubt arises as to that client's capacity, it has always been considered to be good practice to take the view of a suitably qualified medical practitioner. However, even if you have a qualified medical practitioner's opinion as to capacity or otherwise, it will not be final. The opinion of a suitably qualified medical person may be of considerable weight in the eventual decision. However, it has been settled for many years that capacity is a quality which can ultimately be judged only in legal proceedings, with the judge in question acting not as a medical expert, but as a lay person called upon to deliberate on the basis of personal observation and evidence presented to him. As such, capacity is therefore always a legal rather than a medical quality.[3]

Ashton and Ward comment favourably on the English tests of testamentary capacity which are detailed in the case of *Banks v Goodfellow*[4]:

- that the testator must understand the nature of the act and its effects;
- he/she must understand the extent (as opposed to the value) of the property of which he is disposing; and
- appreciate the claims to which he or she ought to give effect, that is the nature and extent of obligations which he may have to relatives and others.

In the Banks' case, the fact that Mr Banks was suffering from an insane delusion was held to have no effect on the manner in which he had drawn up his will.

It can be seen from the foregoing that eccentricity, idiosyncrasy or, indeed, a degree of mental illness will not necessarily lead to the

---

[3] *Birkin v Wynne* (1880) 63 L.T. 80. In this case, the judgment of a solicitor who had taken instructions against the wishes of the doctor was preferred by the court.

[4] (1870) L.R. 5 Q.B. 549.

conclusion that the testator was incapax. In the case of *Nisbet's Trustees v Nisbet*,[5] the testator's will was upheld by the court notwithstanding the fact that he had been confined for many years in a mental institution. On the basis of the evidence presented to it, the court accepted that the testator had, at the time of the execution of his will, recovered from his previous state of general insanity so as to be of sufficiently sound mind to make a will. The question of insanity is considered in more detail below.

Legal capacity therefore depends on understanding rather than intelligence or wisdom. The quality of a decision is irrelevant as long as the individual in question understood what he was deciding. Thus, even a patently foolish decision can be upheld, provided the court is satisfied as to the capacity of the maker of that decision.

Similarly, a will which is validly made will not lose its validity if the maker subsequently loses capacity. Again, subject to retaining the necessary capacity so to do, the testator may revoke his or her will by destruction, or subsequent testamentary instruction. The level of understanding required to make a will is in fact higher than that required to carry out other activities or to enter into other transactions. In the English case of *Re Beaney* (deceased), the English Court recognised that in some circumstances, a different (*i.e.* lesser) degree of capacity was required to make a gift as opposed to making a will. Mrs Beaney was a 64 year old widow with 3 children. She owned and occupied a 3 bedroom semi-detached house. Her older daughter, Valerie, lived with her. Mrs Beaney suffered from advanced dementia and in May 1973 was admitted as an in-patient to hospital. Shortly after being admitted, she purported to execute a deed of gift transferring the house to Valerie. She died intestate in June 1974. Her estate amounted to approximately £1,150 whereas the house had a value of £14,000. Her other children applied to the court for a declaration that the transfer was void because their mother lacked capacity when she signed it. In the particular circumstances of this case, the court held that the degree of understanding required was as high as that required for a will. The judge found that if the subject-matter and value of the gift were trivial in relation to the donor's other assets, a low degree of understanding would suffice. However, as in this case the effect was to dispose of the donor's only asset of value, and thus for practical purposes to pre-empt the devolution of the donor's estate under will or intestacy, the judge found in favour of the applicant children.

Practical advice

6–03 The question of capacity will continue to be a difficult one for solicitors, particularly those who make wills. As human longevity increases, the likelihood is that solicitors will increasingly find themselves being asked to make wills for clients of advanced age, and who are perhaps already in a care home. It is important that the techniques for determining capacity are known to solicitors engaged in this field, as otherwise clients may be deprived of the opportunity of making a valid will. This a fundamental right and should not be lightly denied.

---

[5] (1871) 9 M. 937.

It is of great importance that the solicitor should not wrongly decide that a particular client does not retain capacity and therefore cannot properly instruct completion of a new will. The draftsman's decision here may be called into question by those parties who would otherwise have stood to benefit had the relevant will been made. A negligent decision not to make a will for a particular client is just as likely to be called into question as negligence in relation to the actual drafting of the will itself, or the timescale for completion of execution of the same. That being so the following practical advice maybe of assistance:

- The draftsman should be able to demonstrate familiarity with, for example, the definition of incapacity in the 2000 Act as also in relation to the tests outlined above in the case of *Banks v Goodfellow*. A draftsman who is not familiar with those tests may find some difficulty in justifying his decision (without seeking further advice, not to proceed with the drafting of the relevant will).
- In cases of doubt, the draftsman should seek the opinion of a suitably qualified medical person. The opinion should be in writing, carefully documented and retained by the draftsman.
- The draftsman should never make a peremptory decision (of incapacity) as this may be depriving the client of what is unarguably fundamental freedom—the right to make the will which the individual chooses.

The draftsman should avoid relying on assurances from unqualified third parties as to the capacity of the testator, particularly if those third parties are likely to benefit (even indirectly) from the making of a new will. For example, a typical scenario would be that the solicitor is contacted by a longstanding (and trusted) client who indicates that his old uncle is in a care home and wishes to make a new will (in terms of which the nephew may be a beneficiary) The draftsman should immediately be on his guard. Whilst it would be appropriate to ask the nephew about the capacity of the uncle, the draftsman should not simply reply on an assurance that the uncle is "fine". This scenario raises various different issues. As a first point, the Code of Conduct for Scottish solicitors recognises that, in the first instance, instructions maybe passed on by a third party. However, the draftsman needs to ensure that:

(i) he personally meets the older relative to confirm the instructions, at the same time endeavouring to assess the capacity of the "new" client.

(ii) where necessary (as a matter of practice, it may be that, owing to fear of challenge to the propriety of the solicitor's actings, this will become standard practice in every such case) he seeks appropriate and independent suitably qualified medical advice as to the capacity of the uncle. If medical advice is received to the effect that the uncle retains capacity, then it is submitted that the draftsman should ensure that, at the time of actual signature of the will, the uncle was not suffering from some short term fugue or loss of capacity. This would include seeking the contemporaneous opinion of the relevant medical practitioner that, at the time in question, the uncle retained capacity to sign the will. Where possible, the "certifying" practitioner should be invited to act as witness.

The author recognises that the foregoing represents a "counsel of perfection". However, if the foregoing recommendations are followed, then the draftsman will have placed himself in a position where his actings should be free from criticism, fair or unfair.

Intention to make a will

6–04   The fact that an individual is of full age and has capacity will not itself lead to the conclusion that a document granted by that individual is a valid will and disposition of his or her property, unless it is clear that it was indeed intended to be a will, demonstrating an intention to test. Scottish law requires no particular wording or language to demonstrate such an intention, although the relevant document must be capable of being fully construed as a will bequeathing all or part of the testator's estate. It is also irrelevant that the writing does not amount to a universal settlement, *i.e.* it does not deal with the whole of the testator's estate. In one case, the deceased had made use of a printed will form wherein the blanks had been filled in by the deceased in his own writing. The will form had been subscribed by the deceased, but had not been witnessed and had not been adopted as holograph. The handwritten passages set out a list of names each preceded by the word "to", with sums of money written after the names and the words "residue divided in four equal parts to" followed by another list of names. The court held that the writ was a valid testamentary writing and both the Lord President and Lord Guthrie commented that the use of the word "residue" had shown a testamentary intention.[6] In the case of *Ayrshire Hospice, Petitioners*,[7] an envelope upon which was printed "Will of [   ]" and "For the use of testator's domiciled in Scotland" was found amongst the papers of the deceased. Within that envelope was contained a document headed "Will of [   ]", one consisting of three pages, all in the handwriting of the deceased, all signed and dated by her. A handwritten document contained a list of relatives and friends, each prefaced by the word "to". The third page began, "The remainder to be divided into equal shares amongst the following charities". There followed a list of charities, including the petitioners who sought confirmation in the estate of the deceased as executors nominate. Sheriff Gow, in reaching his decision, stated that there were a number of points against the view that the document was valid testamentary writing. He pointed out that:

- Nowhere in the document was it described as the will of the testator.
- No formal words of bequest were used in any context.
- There was no appointment of executors or trustees.

---

[6] *Gillies v Glasgow Royal Infirmary*, 1960 S.C. 439.
[7] 1992 S.L.T. (Sh. Ct.) 75.

On the other hand, the sheriff found the following points to be favourable:

- The document was found in an envelope on which was printed "Will of [   ]", although no other writing was on the envelope.
- The whole document was holograph of the deceased, signed and dated by her.
- The document purported to dispose of the whole known estate of the deceased.
- Generally, therefore, the document conformed to what was conventionally accepted as being a will, with there being a clear and appropriate division of the remainder of the estate.

The validity of the document as a will was upheld. **6–05**

However, if the court finds that the writings of the deceased were merely informal jottings or notes, then the writing will not be held to be a will.

The best advice is that clients should refrain from endeavouring to create their own home-made wills. A client may fail to demonstrate a testamentary intention and do no more than precipitate a dispute amongst his or her family—those wishing to uphold the writing arrayed against those who would otherwise benefit on intestacy. The dislike of the legal profession for home-made wills is well known, and justified. Lay people are generally not skilled in drafting documents and doubts may arise as to whether or not the words that they have used are intended to amount to a valid testamentary document, or merely to be jottings which could be interpreted as instructions to a solicitor for preparation of a will.[8] A common difficulty is that clients do not appreciate that a will, properly made, should normally involve universality, *i.e.* a will should deal on a comprehensive basis with the totality of the client's estate. For example, a home-made will bequeathing "my insurance policies to my children" will mean that[9] the residue of the client's estate (other than insurance policies) will fall into intestacy.

Grounds for reduction of a will

A will which on the face of it would otherwise appear to be valid can **6–06** be reduced on the following grounds:

Non-age

As hereinbefore indicated, a will made by a person of non-age is void **6–07** *ab initio.*

Insanity

If, at the time of making the will, the testator was incapable of **6–08** understanding the nature and effect of the document granted by him or her (*i.e.* that it was a will), or just what the results of making a will would

---

[8] *Munro v Coutts* (1813) 1 Dow 437.
[9] Erskine Institute 17–33.

be, then it will be invalid.[10] As indicated earlier, however, eccentricity
and even delusion will not themselves invalidate a will. Suicidal depres-
sion was discounted in a case where it did not otherwise affect the will.[11]
The question is simply whether or not the maker of the will understood
that he was making a will, and what the consequences of that will might
be.[12]

DOMICILE

General

6–09   The question of domicile of the testator has wide and important
implications for the will-making solicitor, which may not be immediately
or readily apparent to the draftsman. In fact, the question of domicile is
one which may require detailed examination unless the testator:

- is domiciled and resident in Scotland;
- is making a will in normal Scottish form; and
- possesses only assets situated in Scotland.

As the wealth of Scottish society increases, many Scots now own assets
(and in particular heritable properties) situated abroad. That fact
emphasises the necessity of carrying out a proper, thorough information-
gathering process (see below). If the draftsman assumes that a ready
answer to an awkward question of domicile is simply to incorporate in
the testator's will a "Scottish choice of domicile", then the draftsman
may well be in danger.

Types of domicile

6–10   There are different types of domicile of which the draftsman must be
aware in deciding whether (if at all) and to what extent the draftsman
can safely make a will for the relevant client. The types of domicile are
as follows:

> *Domicile of origin*—this is acquired at birth, although it is not
> necessarily the place in which the individual is actually born. An
> individual's domicile of origin normally arises from his father or
> his mother (for example, where the child is illegitimate or
> posthumous to his father).
> *Domicile of choice*—Scottish law recognises that an individual
> can change his domicile of origin to that of a domicile of
> choice, although there can be evidential difficulties in that
> regard. If an individual has actual residence in a country
> different from the domicile of origin, there must also be
> evidence of a certain intention on the part of the individual to
> have a domicile of choice in that country.[13] In relation to a

---

[10] *Sivewright v Sivewright's Trustees*, 1920 S.C. (H.L.) 63.
[11] *Smith v Smith's Trustees*, 1972 S.L.T. (Notes) 81.
[12] *Nisbet's Trustees v Nisbet*, cited above.
[13] See *IRC v Bulloch*, 1976 3 E.A.R. 353.

married woman, the domicile of origin may be changed to that of a domicile of choice through the wife having acquired the same domicile as that of her husband. Again, however, this is a matter of fact and, since 1974, is not automatic.[14] In Scotland, a child is capable of acquiring a domicile of choice on attaining 16 years of age.[15]

Deemed domicile—this is, in fact, a taxation concept which allows the Inland Revenue to regard an individual resident within the United Kingdom in 17 out of the last 20 years, or who has been in the United Kingdom less than three years before the date of death despite having moved abroad, as still being resident and domiciled in the United Kingdom for IHT purposes.

The relevance of domicile

The question of deemed domicile under section 267 of the Inheritance **6–11** Tax Act 1984 is not relevant to the difficult questions which can arise under private international law, as to which system of law would order the succession to the testator's estate, and also:

1. govern the form in which the will requires to be made;
2. specify the formalities of execution of a particular will;
3. govern the rules of administration of the testator's estate (*i.e.* where it should be wound up);
4. determine the question of IHT liability in the United Kingdom.

Succession to the estate

Generally, in Scottish law the question of the proper law governing the **6–12** succession to a particular estate will be regulated by domicile of the deceased, other than the application of the *lex situs* in relation to immoveable property (generally heritage). That is, the law applicable to succession to moveable estate will, under Scottish law, be determined by the question of "domicile".

Formal validity

The Wills Act 1963 gave effect to The Hague Convention on the **6–13** conflicts of laws relating to the form of testamentary dispositions (1961). Section 1 provides that a will is formally valid if properly executed in accordance with the laws of either:

- The country in which the testator was domiciled or habitually resident, either at date of signature of the will, or at date of death; or
- The country in which the will was executed, even if that is neither the domicile or habitual residence of the testator.

In terms of section 2(1)(b) of the Act, it is provided that if the will disposed of immoveable property, then provided it conforms to the requirements of the *lex situs*, it is properly executed.

---

[14] Domicile and Matrimonial Proceedings Act 1973, ss.(3) and (4).
[15] Age of Capacity (Scotland) Act 1991, s.7.

The 1963 Act deals only with questions of formal validity—essential validity is quite another matter.

Essential validity

6–14   Even if a will is regarded as being valid on a formal basis, the question will still arise as to whether or not other jurisdictions will recognise and give effect to the terms of the same. More often than not this will turn on the question of succession to heritable property, in respect of which the position of Scottish law is that the *lex situs* will apply.

In one case,[16] the question of essential validity was considered in relation to the notarial execution of a will. The Conveyancing (Scotland) Act 1924 provided for notarial execution to be done by a solicitor/notary public, etc. The rules applying to such notarial execution were extremely strict (and some felt draconian). The solicitor, etc. was required to have no interest whatsoever in the will either as trustee, legatee or beneficiary. If the requirements regarding independence were transgressed, then the will itself, although on the face of it validly executed, would be void.[17] However, in the relevant case, the will of a domiciled Scot was notarially executed in Carlisle by a solicitor who was also nominated as executor, with power to charge for his services. Had that will been executed in Scotland, it would have been invalid. However, the court took the view that the execution was valid by English law (*i.e.* that the lex loci actus applied).

Where the will deals with immoveable property, then its essential validity will be regulated by the *lex situs*. Where the will deals with moveable property, then its essential validity is regulated by the law of the testator's domicile as at date of death.

The administration of the estate

6–15   As this question is not immediately relevant to the actual drafting of the will itself, the reader is referred to *Currie on Confirmation*[18] for the consideration of the relevant factors and points of law.

Practical considerations and difficulties

6–16   The offering of appropriate advice to a client in relation to the question of domicile is of great importance.

The question of domicile is one of fact, taking into account the whole circumstances of a particular case. Whilst, therefore, a declaration of domicile in a will may be of assistance to the court, it is not absolute. Such declaration by itself cannot change the existing domicile of the testator. A recent example is the case of Mr Riach[19] who had his domicile of origin in Scotland. This case considered, *inter alia*, whether legal rights of children could be claimed. He spent a considerable time abroad (including in Australia) following his career as a marine engi-

---

[16] *Irving v Snow*, 1956 S.C. 257.
[17] *Ferrie v Ferrie's Trustees* (1863) 1 M. 29.
[18] *Currie on Confirmation*, pp.238–247 and pp.258–273. See also A.E. Anton, *Private International Law* (W. Green 1967).
[19] *Reddington v Riach's Executor*, 2002 G.W.D. 7–214.

neer. On his retirement in 1964, he and his wife retired to Falkirk. However, they moved in 1978 to Bournemouth. Mrs Riach had relatives there. She died in Bournemouth in 1987 and was buried there.

Mr Riach died, also in Bournemouth, in 1999. His will of February 1996 had been made by his Scottish solicitors and included a declaration to the effect that Mr Riach had a Scottish domicile. He left assets in both Scotland and England.

The court had to decide the testator's intention. It found that Mr Riach had intended his home in Bournemouth to be his permanent one, and that being so, and notwithstanding the declaration as to domicile in the 1996 will, the court also held that Mr Riach had acquired a domicile of choice in England.

The draftsman, therefore, needs to carefully consider the client's position as to how his actual domicile should be viewed. A long period of residence, without the intention to be domiciled in a particular country, is not of itself sufficient. The draftsman should never, without examining the whole facts and circumstances, insert a choice of Scottish domicile in a will without properly discussing this with the client. The fact that such a discussion in detail has taken place, and the outcome of the same, may have evidential quality in deciding whether or not a declaration of domicile was appropriate in the first place. However, if the draftsman simply inserts such a choice of domicile without any discussion with his client, then this will be of no evidential help whatsoever. The message is simple—because style books include such a declaration, slavish adherence to the same, without proper discussion with the client and an examination of the position, might well lead to a claim against the draftsman.

Client with Scottish domicile but owning heritable property abroad

If the draftsman simply prepares a will in the nature of a universal **6–17** settlement (no matter where the property might be situated), then again difficulties may arise. In so far as it relates to immoveable property, the Scottish will may not be recognised by a foreign country in which the heritage is situated; for example, if it does not comply with the rules and format prescribed by the law of the country in which immoveable property lies. In such a case, the client should be advised to take advice, and, where appropriate, make a separate will in the country in which the property in question is situated. This itself raises other considerations.

The client is obviously currently domiciled in Scotland and wishes to make a new Scottish will. He already has an existing Scottish will, he owns property abroad and quite sensibly has made a will in relation to that property in the relevant country. The draftsman needs to consider the question of the revocation of both the earlier Scottish will and also the earlier foreign will and, quite apart from that, the possibility could arise that the earlier foreign will contains terms which might conflict with the new will to be made in Scotland. If that is the case, the draftsman will need to consider the terms of a translation of the foreign will. Advice from a lawyer in a foreign country might also be required on this point. A normal universal clause of revocation in a Scottish will could be quite inappropriate. An argument could arise that this would also revoke the earlier foreign will which should of course have remained in force. A suggested style of revocation clause in such circumstances would be:

"I revoke all prior Wills and testamentary writings made or granted by me, specifically excepting from such revocation my will dated [   ] so far as disposing of any heritable property owned by me as at my date of death and situated in Spain (or other country where the property might be situated)."

If it is clear that the Scottish will is only to deal with the Scottish estate, then a simple amendment to the Scottish will makes the position clear. For example:

"I. . . residing at . . . in order to settle the succession to my means and Estate situated solely within the United Kingdom upon my death do provide as follows . . . ".

Note the reference to the UK—careless reference to Scotland alone could arguably result in partial intestacy in that it could be argued that the terms of the will would not cover estate in the Channel Islands or indeed England.

Again, care will be required as to the terms of the clause of revocation to be utilised in the Scottish will, to ensure that it does not unintentionally revoke a pre-existing foreign will.

Where the client is clearly domiciled in another jurisdiction, then the draftsman should consider at the outset whether or not it is appropriate for him to make a will for the client in the first place. However, the client, even if clearly domiciled abroad, may still wish to make a will in Scotland which governs his succession to Scottish heritable property.[20] For a consideration of the issues here, see Barr, etc.[21]

Summary

6–18   Proper enquiry must always be made as to the question of domicile— in particular, a declaration as to domicile should not be inserted in the will without the issue being properly discussed with the client and considered by the draftsman.

Where the client, although domiciled in Scotland, has in particular an immoveable property situated abroad, then the client must be advised to take advice in the relevant jurisdiction as to whether or not a will is required there.

If the client has both Scottish and foreign wills then they should be checked to ensure that they are not mutually incompatible. In particular, the terms of any revocation clause should be carefully considered and amended as required.

A Scottish solicitor should never seek to give advice on the nature and effect of existing or proposed foreign wills. The client should always be advised to take advice in the appropriate country. For example, in relation to heritable property, France has rules (effectively of "forced heirship") which severely limit the client's freedom to direct disposal of heritable property in terms of his will.

---

[20] *Liverpool Royal Infirmary v Ramsay*, 1930 S.C. (H.L.) 83.
[21] Barr, etc., *The Drafting of Wills in Scotland* (Butterworths/Law Society of Scotland, 1994).

In case of any doubt, where a foreign element is involved then the draftsman must advise a patently Scottish client that advice from a lawyer in the relevant jurisdiction be obtained as to the requirements in that country.

In particular, Scottish draftsmen should never seek to advise on foreign taxation. This, in itself, is a difficult area and again advice in each of the relevant jurisdictions is required. It is never to be assumed that there is a double taxation agreement in every case.

Scottish law reform

The inflexibility of the law in this area has long been recognised, and **6–19** has not been free from justified criticism. In 1987, The Scottish Law Commission Report on the Law of Domicile recommended (in conjunction with the English Law Commission) wide changes to the Law of Domicile. For the present, however, once again the recommendations appear to be no more than an interesting historical footnote, as they have yet to see the light of statutory day.

The Report to the Commission of the EU Directorate General for Justice in Home Affairs was published in November 2002. The Report is effectively a study of comparative law governing conflict of laws and jurisdictions in relation to wills and succession in the Member States of the EU. The Report commented that there should be harmonisation in relation to the law of wills and succession. In particular, it is recommended that the concept of "domicile" should be effectively abandoned, and that the ruling law should be that of the deceased's last "habitual residence" in relation to his whole estate. Helpfully (in the view of the author), it is also recommended that a testator should be able to choose whether the law of his nationality or of his habitual residence should govern the succession to his estate. Adoption of these recommendations would assist in surmounting the type of difficulty occasioned in the *Reddington* case.

The Report also deals with the question of administration of estates, and proposes that there should be a common European Certificate of Inheritance (the equivalent of confirmation or probate). The Directorate General proposed that such Certificate of Inheritance should be granted by the Probate Court of the deceased's last permanent residence, and that its validity should be accepted in all EU Member States. The proposals certainly appear to move away from the older concepts of "domicile", with reference to the importance of "permanent" or "habitual" residence. For any solicitor who has assisted in dealing with foreign estate, implementation of the proposals would be a godsend. It would reduce stress levels considerably!

Final warning note

For an examination of the real difficulties which can arise in relation **6–20** to this particular area, it is submitted that one need only look at the case of *Scottish National Orchestra Limited v Thomson's Executor*.[22] This

---

[22] 1969 S.L.T. 325.

involved the case of a testatrix born in Scotland in 1892. In 1922, she married a Canadian (thereby acquiring his domicile). She lived with her husband until 1934 when she separated from him. Thereafter, she moved to Stockholm where (being pre-deceased by her husband in 1959) she continued to reside until her death in 1962. Following the death of her husband, the testatrix was, of course, free to choose her own domicile of choice. In 1951, she had executed a will which was registered in the Books of Council and Session, and upon which confirmation was granted from the Commissariot of Edinburgh in 1963. By far the greater proportion of the deceased's estate was moveable property in Scotland, but there were also moveable assets in Canada and Sweden. According to Swedish law she was regarded as permanently resident in Sweden, and the Swedish Court appointed an administrator on her estate. The executors obtained both confirmation in Scotland and probate in England, and thereafter proceeded to administer the estate in terms of the will, including pecuniary legacies "all free of Government duties" to legatees, three of whom resided in Sweden. Estate duty was paid on the property situated in Great Britain.

After settlement of all debts and administration expenses and pecuniary legacies in Great Britain, the sum of £16,000 was remitted to the Swedish administrator to "enable him to meet Swedish death duties". The residuary legatees (two British musical societies) raised an action against the surviving executor, contending that the executor was in breach of trust in paying the sum of £16,000 to the Swedish administrator. It was admitted that the deceased was, at the date of her death, domiciled in Sweden. It was held that, in accordance with the law of Sweden, where a person is permanently resided in that country at date of death, the whole estate had to be returned in a Swedish inventory and subject to Swedish inheritance tax. It was also held that if a Swedish administrator held money to pay Swedish legatees, and inheritance tax levied on the estate remained unpaid, his legal duty was to pay the tax before the legacies. It was held that the executor had acted properly in remitting to the Swedish administrator.

CHAPTER 7

INTERPRETATION

GENERAL RULES

The ordinary rule of interpretation is to give effect to the terms of a will **7–01** without resorting to intrinsic evidence. In *Borthwick's Trustees v Borthwick*,[1] Lord Justice-Clerk Thomson said:

"We must find the intention of testatrix within the four corners of the deed which she has legally executed. We are, undoubtedly, to look at the whole deed; and . . . if there be any doubt in the terms, we are to take into consideration the circumstances under which the deed was executed. . . it is only if the terms of the deed appear to be in themselves doubtful in their import or legal construction that is either necessary or legitimate to affect or explain them by extraneous circumstances."

The general rules may be expressed as follows:

- As indicated by Lord Justice-Clerk Thomson, the will must be read as a whole with words being given their ordinary meaning.
- Where parts of the will (including codicils, etc.) conflict, then the court should endeavour to reconcile the same. If the court finds itself unable to do so, then the most recent provision will receive effect (*i.e.* where clauses in a will and subsequent codicils conflict and it is impossible to reconcile the same, then the provision in the codicil will rule).

A court will normally seek to construe the will in a manner which will avoid intestacy, *i.e.* the court will assume that the testator did not intend to grant a testamentary writing which had no meaning and which still resulted in a intestacy—what would be the point in making the will in the first place? Again, following the tests set out by Lord Justice-Clerk Thomson, extrinsic evidence can only be allowed where the will (as a whole) is unclear, and application of the above rules fails to provide an acceptable solution. Where the court allows extrinsic evidence, then it will endeavour to put itself in the shoes of the testator at the time of making the will.[2] In acting in that fashion, the court's purpose is to give meaning to the will as expressed, not to rewrite the same.

---

[1] 1955 S.C. 227.
[2] *Hay v Duthie's Trustees*, 1956 S.C. 511.

EXTRINSIC EVIDENCE

7–02 Macdonald[3] gives examples of six areas, some of which may coincide, where extrinsic evidence may be admitted. An examination of the cases cited by Macdonald provides many examples of the difficulties which can arise where a will, as drafted, even where interpreted in accordance with the ordinary rules, cannot provide evidence of the testator's intention. In many of the cases, the difficulties of interpretation arose not because of any fault on the part of the draftsman, but because of some error of understanding on the part of the testator:

- A legacy to "my grand-nephew Robert Oftner" was found to be due to an individual named Richard Ofner, it being clear from the terms of correspondence from the testator to his solicitors that the testator had himself (wrongly) believed that Richard Ofner was properly named Robert Oftner.[4]
- A testator had referred to a beneficiary as "Mrs Boden" when, in fact, the beneficiary in question was a Mrs Bouine; the court accepted extrinsic evidence to the effect that "Boden" had been the maiden name of the beneficiary in question.[5]

PRACTICAL ADVICE

7–03 Where a client is operating under a fundamental error as to the name of a particular beneficiary, there is perhaps little which the draftsman can do—the testator himself is operating under a fundamental misapprehension and is likely to give no clue to the draftsman that this is so. However, there are certain basic rules, outlined below, which, if followed, can avoid resort to litigation after the testator's death in order to ascertain his true intention.

The draftsman should use clear language on the basis that the words used will be given their ordinary meaning. Where a word may have more than one ordinary meaning, then the draftsman should clarify with the testator which of the two meanings the latter intends (and should make clear in his drafting which of the two meanings has been preferred by the testator).

The testator may come from a particular professional trade or artistic background. Where the testator gives instructions using technical terms, then again the draftsman should check with the testator just exactly what the latter intends by use of a particular technical term (and it may be better to endeavour to express the same in plain English). See the case of *Goblet v Beechey*,[6] where the court had to interpret the will made by a sculptor in relation to the use of the word "mode" therein.

If conditions are to be attached to particular bequests, then these must be intelligible—the testator should be clear in his mind as to the

---

[3] D.R MacDonald, *An Introduction to the Scots Law of Succession*, (W. Green, 1990) pp.103—106.
[4] *Samuel v Ofner*, 1909 1 Ch. 60 CA.
[5] *Lee Pain* (1845) 4 Hare 201.
[6] (1829) 3 Sim. 24.

circumstances in which a particular condition will or will not be fulfilled, and this should be properly stated in the will.

The draftsman should, where possible, seek to clarify the relationship of individual beneficiaries to the testator, and state this appropriately in the will. For example, a testator may wish to leave a "class" bequest to his nephews and nieces. Although less common nowadays, some older clients will still regard, for example, the children of an old friend as being "courtesy" nephews, etc. However, such "courtesy" nephews would not come within the class bequest hereinbefore detailed. In such circumstances the draftsman should be careful to establish the exact intentions of the testator.

The draftsman should always take care to establish that the testator is **7–04** aware of the difference between *per stirpes* and *per capita* division. (See the Appendix of Styles)

Where possible, addresses of relevant beneficiaries at the time the will is made should be fully stated. This might avoid the difficulties in the *Keiller* case,[7] where the testator left a legacy to "William Keiller, confectioner, Dundee". The court found that the legacy was in fact due to a James Keiller, confectioner, Dundee. There was a William Keiller, confectioner of Montrose, but no such William Keiller in Dundee. The insertion of an exact address for a particular beneficiary may enable the true intention of the testator to be established. A similar consideration applies to charities—testators are more than capable of confusing two charities. This can be avoided by referring the testator to a charity source book and by inviting him or her to identify the chosen charity/charities. The charity should then be referred to by its current name at the time the will is made, its charity number and the address of its registered or main office. Even then it would not be inappropriate to incorporate an appropriate provision, which would allow the executor latitude where the charity has transferred its assets to, or amalgamated with, another, or indeed has been improperly designed in the first place..

Care needs to be taken where a testator may wish to bequeath a particular item to a specified beneficiary. However, the testator may own two or more items which are substantially similar. The classic example is jewellery. A bequest of "my diamond ring to my niece, Josephina Bloggs, residing at One Brown Street, Anytown", could cause great difficulty where, at the time of making the will, the testator had two or more diamond rings. In such circumstances, the draftsman should take specific care to properly identify which ring was intended; for example: "My three-stone diamond cluster ring set in white gold and in-subscribed to 'my loving wife'".

Careless drafting, even in respect of small bequests, should be avoided. The misuse of one very simple word can cause great difficulty; for example, "I bequeath a diamond ring to my niece, Josephina Bloggs". In such a case, the draftsman should immediately establish that the testator does in fact own a diamond ring, and it should be referred to in the will as "*my* diamond ring". The testator should be warned that if she owns, or is likely to own, more than one diamond ring as at her date of death, then difficulties can arise. If at the time the will was made the

---

[7] *Keiller v Thomson's Trustees* (1826) 4 S. 724.

testator owned no diamond ring, then the awkward question of whether or not a *legatum rei alienae* will arise. This is a bequest of property not owned by the testator. The normal presumption will be that the testator had made a mistake, and if so, the legacy will fail. If, however, it can be shown that the testator was aware that he or she did not own the item in question, then the bequest will be interpreted as an instruction to his executor either to acquire the item for the particular beneficiary, or, failing such acquisition being possible, to pay the value of the same to the beneficiary.

Proper and accurate record keeping

7–05   Even where the draftsman exercises due and proper care, it may be impossible to avoid difficulties of interpretation arising. Where, after applying the ordinary tests, the court cannot find an appropriate meaning for the testator's intentions, bearing this possibility in mind (with no fault being attributable to the draftsman), such extrinsic evidence as may be produced may be of great importance in deciding the true intention of the testator. That being so, the notes kept by the draftsman of meetings, etc., and also the terms of correspondence passing between the draftsman and his client may be of great importance in establishing the testator's true intentions. Proper and accurate record keeping is therefore vital, not only to be of assistance in a difficult case in establishing the testator's true intentions, but also on a self- defensive basis to avoid a possible claim by an otherwise disappointed legatee. In the author's view, will making by telephone should, as far as possible, be avoided.

CHAPTER 8

ESSENTIAL FORMALITIES OF EXECUTION

BACKGROUND

Scottish law has always required that certain basic formalities be **8–01** observed in order that a will should be regarded as being valid. The essential reason for this was to protect against fraud.

Significant changes were made to the law of execution of wills by the Requirements of Writing (Scotland) Act, 1995, which came into force on August 1, 1995. The provisions of that Act are not, however, retrospective, and its terms only apply to documents executed after August 1, 1995.[1] The foregoing being so, for many years to come advisers will need to be aware of both the pre- and post-Act formalities.[2]

PRE AUGUST 1, 1995

Prior to the relevant date, a valid will could be made in one of four ways: **8–02**

1. *Attested.* A will made in this fashion was required to be signed on each page by the granter before two witnesses, who were also required to sign on the final page only.
2. *Holograph.* A will would be valid if it was written out in the granter's own handwriting and subscribed by him.
3. *Adopted as holograph.* Such a will would be valid even if typed or handwritten by another, provided it was signed and "adopted as holograph" by the testator.
4. *A verbal will.* Scottish law would recognise a verbal will as the bequests of moveable estate not exceeding £100 Scots. The author makes mention of this solely as a historical footnote, as even prior to August 1, 1995 such a will was hardly likely to be encountered. It should be noted that the common law *testamentum militare* was not of itself recognised in Scottish law. Roman military authorities and jurists recognised that many legionnaires were illiterate, but nonetheless were afforded the privilege of making verbal wills on the eve of battle. Such verbal wills could be upheld if the legionnare lost his life in the following battle.

---

[1] s.8.14 (3).

[2] For a discussion on this point, see *McEleveen v McQuillan's Exor* 1997 S.L.T. (Sh. Ct) 46.

Attestation

8–03   This could either be by notarial execution (see below), or a signature of the will on every page by the testator, the testator's signature on the final page of the will being witnessed by two witnesses also signing. It should be noted that both before and after commencement of the 1995 Act, it was not a requirement that the witnesses should be allowed to read over the document in question, or indeed to know of or be advised of its contents. Although an essential formality, the witnesses' only role was to attest the signature of the testator as valid. A will executed in this fashion would be regarded as being probative. A probative document will be presumed to have been validly executed if that *ex facie* appears to be the case. Although a probative document can be reduced, compelling evidence is required to overturn its apparent validity.

On occasions, clients have found some difficulty with particular witnesses, who, if only for their own self protection, have demanded sight of the document. This is neither the function nor the right of the witness. The protection for any witness is to write the word "witness" after his signature. This clearly denotes the capacity in which that individual signed, and that is not as a principal.

Where a will has been attested, it is regarded as being probative, thereby proving its authenticity. Wills which are either holograph or "adopted as holograph" are not of themselves probative. In such cases, the Commissary Office will require that intrinsic evidence be produced (for example, affidavits of hand writing and signature). However, once confirmation has been issued on the basis of such documents, they are afforded the quality of probative status in terms of section 2 of the Succession (Scotland) Act 1964.

The granter's signature

8–04   It is essential that the testator should subscribe each page of the will.[3] It will be fatal to the validity of the will should the testator fail to subscribe.[4]

In terms of the Deeds Act 1896, the testator's signature, along with those of the witnesses and the testing clause, should appear on the last proper or operative page of the will. This meant that the signature of the testator and his witnesses were required to appear on the final page of the will which contained operative text for the will, *i.e.* if the testing clause and the final signature by the testator and witnesses appeared on the final page on which no part of the will itself appeared, then this was a failure to comply with the relevant provisions.[5]

Section 39 of the Conveyancing (Scotland) Act 1874

8–05   Section 39 provided a remedy in respect of deflective subscription.

Form of signature

8–06   It should be noted that the following comments are likely to apply whether the will in question was executed prior to, or after August 1, 1995.

---

[3] Conveyancing & Feudal Reform (Scotland) Act 1970, s.44(2).
[4] *Robbie v Carr*, 1959 S.L.T. (Notes) 16.
[5] *Baird's Trustees v Baird*, 1955 S.C. 286.

- An attorney cannot sign a will on behalf of his principal, even if the power of attorney authorises this. This is a reflection of the requirement that, in relation to a will, the signature must be the testator's own, voluntary act.
- General rule—it has been held that the signature by the testator was invalid if the testator's hand had been guided by another person (however well meaning).[6]
- In a later case, the court found that the signature was valid, even though the testator's wrist had been supported by another whilst he completed the signature.[7]
- An incomplete signature has been held to be invalid, even though it was witnessed by two independent witnesses.[8]
- The testator should not have signed using initials alone, and signature by mark is not acceptable, thus a cyclostyle or rubber stamp of his signature would be invalid.
- The signature does not need to be legible. The signature does not need to represent the full name of the testator nor the forenames or indeed middle names need to be represented in the signature (although in that case this should be detailed in the testing clause). A signature comprising simply the initials of the forenames of the testator, coupled with his full surname, will be acceptable.

Signature of will by third party

As noted above, even where a power of attorney specifically authorises **8–07** this, an attorney does not have valid power to sign a will on behalf of his principal. In Scotland, the third party cannot make a will on behalf of another party. However, such a power exists in England under the Mental Health Act 1983, in relation to an individual who is incapax and who does not already have a will.

Notarial execution

It should be noted that notarial execution does not amount to a third **8–08** party making a will for the testator. It was a facility provided under the Conveyancing (Scotland) Act 1924 to allow a notary or other suitably qualified person to execute a will on behalf of a testator who was blind or otherwise unable to sign. Again, given that the rules for such signature introduced in terms of the Requirements of Writing (Scotland) Act 1995 apply only after August 1, 1995, it should be borne in mind that very strict rules regarding interest, etc. will still apply in relation to a will which has been notarially executed prior to the commencement date of the Act.

Under the 1924 Act, notarial execution could be carried out by a solicitor, notary public, justice of the peace or Church of Scotland minister (or his assistant) acting within his own parish. The rules required that the notary must be absolutely independent, having no personal interest in the relevant will.

---

[6] *Moncrieff v Monypenny* (1710) Mor. 15936.
[7] *Noble v Noble* (1875) 3 R 74.
[8] *Donald v McGregor*, 1926 S.L.T. 103.

- The notary should not act if, in terms of the will, he was a legatee.
- The notary should not act if he or a partner was appointed as executor or trustee under the will with power to charge fees for professional services (and in particular where the notary's firm was likely to act in the winding up of the estate in question).[9]
- The notary should not act in relation to a codicil which related to a will in terms of which he might obtain a benefit.

The rules regarding interest were extremely strict and the penalty for infringing the same had the result that the whole will or codicil would be invalid. Such a result would of course effectively cause loss of benefit to all other beneficiaries in the will or under the codicil. Fortunately, this outcome has been addressed in terms of the 1995 Act (see below).

Failure to observe the requirements of the 1924 Act, not only in respect of interest, but also as to methodology of execution, would also invalidate the will. Such failures could not be cured by resort to section 39 of the 1874 Act.

Why should the penalties be so draconian? It is submitted that strict observance both as to interest and methodology were required in order to avoid any fraud being perpetrated upon the granter, this consideration outweighing the urgent need to make a particular will for a testator. Interestingly, it has never been part of Scottish law that a blind person cannot sign his own will.[10] The procedure authorised in terms of the 1924 Act was essentially optional, being essentially designed to protect blind persons, etc. from fraud or undue influence, etc. The facility provided by both the 1924 Act and in terms of section 9 of the 1995 Act[11] applied solely in relation to granters who suffered from some physical condition which made it either impossible or inadvisable for them to seek to sign their own wills—the relevant provisions at no time authorised notarial execution on behalf of a granter who was incapax.

Deletions, erasures and alterations

8–09   The responsibility of the draftsman goes beyond a simple compliance with the instructions of the testator, ensuring that the will made properly reflects the testator's wishes. The draftsman's responsibility extends to ensuring that the will in question is signed within a reasonable timescale from issuing instructions, but more than this, also to ensure that the will has been properly executed. These obligations apply with even more force following the decision in *Holmes v Bank of Scotland*.[12] For a consideration of how the draftsman should deal with corrections, deletions, erasures or alterations made prior to signature of the will, see Barr, etc.[13]

---

[9] *Finlay v Finlay's Trustees*, 1948 S.C. 16.
[10] *Duff v Earl of Fife* (1823) 1 Sh.App. 498.
[11] Requirements of Writing (Scotland) Act 1995, s.9.
[12] 2002 S.L.T. 544; and 2002 S.C.L.R. 481 (cited above in Chapter 2).
[13] Barr, etc., *The Drafting of Wills in Scotland*, (Butterworths/Law Society of Scotland, 1994), 2.442.48.

The role of the witness

Witnesses either had to see the signature by the testator, or have the **8–10**
signature acknowledged to them by the testator. Both witnesses[14] did not
need to be present at the time of signature of the document. Where a
testator signed in the presence of one witness and subsequently acknowledged signature to the other, this was thought to be sufficient, as was
the testator signing subsequently, acknowledging his signature of the two
witnesses but at different times.[15] Notwithstanding the foregoing, best
practice has always been that signature by the testator and its attestation
should take place as one legal act. The dangers of not following such
best practice can be seen in the leading case of *Walker v Whitwell*.[16] In
this case the testatrix subscribed her will in the presence of both her son
and a nurse, the latter subscribing as witness immediately. The son did
not sign at that point and his mother died six days later. Thereafter the
son added his signature to the will as witness. The House of Lords took
the view that the will was not valid as the mother was no longer able
(owing to her death) to consent to the signature of her will by her son as
witness. Her implied consent could no longer apply as it lapsed with her
death.

In *MacDougall v MacDougall's Executors*[17] a question arose as to
whether a will had been validly executed. Evidence was led that the
testator, Alexander MacDougall, had signed his will in his bedroom in
the presence of one witness. That witness confirmed to the testator that
another witness would be required. He left the bedroom and met the
second witness on the landing of the house. In the hearing of the
testator, the first witness explained that the will needed to be witnessed.
He asked one of the third parties (Malcolm MacLean) to sign the will as
witness. Mr MacLean readily agreed to do so and observed the
signatures of the testator and the first witness on the will. Mr MacLean
signed the will in the living room as a witness. The first witness
thereafter showed the will to Alexander MacDougall, the testator, and
indicated that the matter had been completed. Mr MacLean heard the
testator acknowledging that he had heard the first witness indicate
completion of the matter. It was submitted that this could not amount to
attestation in accordance with the legal requirements. However, Lord
Cameron of Lochbroom, in reciting the relevant requirements[18] indicated that the granter's acknowledgement might be made to the witness
by a combination of acts and words such as to leave no doubt in the
mind of the witness that the granter of the deed was acknowledging his
signature. Circumstances may be such that the silence of the granter may
suffice.[19] Lord Cameron also pointed out that the acknowledgement by

---

[14] Subscription of Deeds Act 1861; see also *Hogg v Campbell* (1864) 2 M. 848; *Walker v Whitwell*, 1916 S.C. (H.L.) 75; *MacDougall v MacDougall's Executor's*, 1994 S.L.T. 1178 (O.H.).

[15] *MacDougall, ibid.*, at 1181. See also *Hynd's Executor v Hynd's Trustees*, 1955 S.L.T. 105; 1955 S.C. (H.L.) 1.

[16] 1916 S.C. (H.L.) 75.

[17] *MacDougall v MacDougall's Executor's*, 1994 S.L.T. 1178 (O.H.).

[18] *ibid.*, at 1181.

[19] *ibid.*, at 1181. See also *Cumming v Skeoch's Trustees* (1879) 6 R. 63; *Bell on the Attestation of Deeds*, Ch.8.

the granter of the deed and subscription of the witness must both take place as parts of a continuous process.[20] "So long as the whole proceeding is transacted in a reasonable sense, *unico contextu*, the subscription of the witness need not be written in the presence of the granter or immediately the acknowledgement is received."[21]

Capacity of the witness

8–11   An individual under the age of 16 cannot act as a witness, lacking the necessary testamentary capacity.[22] An individual who is incapax, blind or unable to write cannot act as a witness.

REQUIREMENTS POST AUGUST 1, 1995

8–12   The common law methods for the granting of a formal writing outlined above were replaced by new rules contained in, effectively, sections 1, 2 and 3 of the 1995 Act.

In terms of section 1, a written document complying with section 2 of the Act is required for the making of any will, testamentary trust disposition and settlement or codicil.[23]

Section 2, when read along with section 11(3)(b), abolished the special status for documents which were either holograph or "adopted as holograph". Under section 2, a document is formally valid if subscribed by the granter.

Section 3(2) provides that where a testamentary document consists of more than one sheet, it shall not be presumed to have been subscribed by a granter as mentioned in section 1 unless, in addition to it bearing to have been subscribed by him and otherwise complying with that subsection, it bears to have been signed by him on every sheet.

Section 3 is of great importance in relation to the formal validity of wills and other testamentary documents. Section 3 amended the pre-existing law so that attestation by only one witness is now required. In the author's view, this might fall to be regarded as a retrograde step, increasing the possibility for fraud or undue influence.

Section 3 in subsections (1), (2) and (3) set out the current requirements in order for the presumption of valid execution to apply. These requirements are that:

- The granter has subscribed the document.
- A witness has signed.
- The name and address of the witness (which need not be written by the witness himself) is given in the deed or testing clause.
- The name and address was added before the deed was founded upon in legal proceedings, or registered for preservation in the Books of Council and Session; and

---

[20] *MacDougall* at 1181.
[21] *ibid.*, at 1181.
[22] Age of Capacity (Scotland) Act 1991, s.59.
[23] s.1(1)(c).

- Nothing in the deed or testing clause gives an indication that the document was not subscribed by the granter, or was not validly witnessed (see below).
- In the case of a will or other testamentary writing extending to more than one sheet, the granter signed on every sheet. Note the reference is to "sheet" and not to "page". This appears to leave open the previous law that a sheet folded into more than one page would be regarded as a valid will, validly executed, if it was signed on the last page only.[24]

To a large extent the above requirements restated the earlier law. **8-13** Section 7(2) sets out three methods of signature by a granter:

(a) A granter may sign with the full name by which he is identified in the document or in any testing clause or its equivalent; or
(b) With his surname, preceeded by at least one forename (or an initial or abbreviation or familiar form of a forename); or
(c) Except for the purposes of section 3(1) to (7) of the Act, with a name (not in accordance with paras (a) or (b) above) or description or initial or mark if it is established that the name, description, initial or mark was:

  (i) His usual method of signing or his usual method of signing documents or alterations of the type in question; or
  (ii) Intended by him as his signature of the document or alteration.

However, note that alternative (c) cannot be used for attested deeds (which benefit from the presumption of valid execution under section 3). Section 7(5) deals with the method of signature by which a witness may sign:

(a) With the full name by which he is identified in the document or in any testing clause or its equivalent; or
(b) With his surname, preceded by at least one forename (or an initial or abbreviation or familiar form of a forename).

Section 7 deals only with the methodology of signature—it presupposes that both the granter and witness have capacity. If they do not, and even if the document has been otherwise validly executed, it will be invalid.

Section 5 of the Act deals with alterations to documents. "Alteration" is defined in section 12(1) to include interlineation, marginal addition, deletion, substitution, erasure, or anything written on erasure. The approach of section 5 is to split alterations into those which are effected pre subscription and those that are effected post subscription. It is submitted that nowadays, given the immediate printing technologies available to most draftsmen, there is hardly any need for the granter to effect such alterations to his will prior to subscription. However, section 5(5) deals with the methodology for dealing with pre-subscription alterations.

---

[24] *Baird's Trustees v Baird*, 1955 S.C. 286.

The alteration should be stated "in the document" or in a testing clause or its equivalent to have been made before the document was subscribed.

Practical advice

8–14   Since the introduction of the 1995 Act, it is submitted that following the provisions of the same have not proved unduly burdensome or greatly changed practice in relation to the execution of wills. Many clients still find it convenient to have the wills sent out to them for signature accompanied by appropriate directions/instructions for proper execution. Where a will is sent out by post for signature, then upon its return the draftsman should:

- Check that the will has been signed as required by the granter on each page.
- Check that the methodology or signature complies with the provisions of section 7(2) of the 1995 Act.
- Ensure that the witness has signed properly, again in accordance with the provisions of section 7(5). Checking not only the signature of the granter but also that of the witness is of considerable importance. Although dealing with the pre-1995 Act law, the case of *Williamson v Williamson*[25] is of interest. In April 1988, the testatrix, Rachel Williamson, signed her will in the presence of two witnesses, one being a solicitor, David C.R. Wilson. Inadvertently, Mr Wilson signed "D.C.R. Williamson". After his mother's death and confirmation had been granted, the son of the testatrix sought reduction of the will on the basis of the above defect in execution. The executors tried to cure the "informality of execution" under section 39 of the Conveyancing (Scotland) Act, 1874. However, the court held that section 39 of the 1874 Act could not be brought into play. In the opinion of the court, before section 39 could take effect at all there had to be valid subscriptions of the granter and of two witnesses, which had to be determined objectively and not by the presence or absence of a testing clause. On that approach, the witness had failed to adhibit his normal signature or any customary equivalent. It is submitted that the same outcome (*i.e.* that the signature was invalid) would occur under section 7(5) of the 1995 Act (and it should be noted that following the passing of the 1995 Act, section 39 of the 1874 Act was repealed).
- The details of execution should be checked to ensure that they comply with the minimum requirements of the 1995 Act for construction of an appropriate testing clause. A similar consideration applies where the draftsman has adopted a "pre printed" format for insertion of the execution details.

As hereinbefore noted, the responsibility of the draftsman extends to more than just producing the will required by his client—the draftsman

---

[25] 1997 S.L.T. 1044.

also has to ensure proper execution of the will, and the consequences of failing to do so can be dire.

The new "notarial" execution

Section 9 of the 1995 Act replaced section 18 and Schedule 1 of the **8–15** Conveyancing (Scotland) Act, 1924. Section 9 and Schedule 3 of the 1995 Act authorise subscription by a "relevant person" on behalf of a granter who is blind or unable to write. The relevant person is defined in section 9(6) as a solicitor, an advocate, a justice of the peace or a sheriff clerk, and in relation to the execution of documents outwith Scotland includes a notary public or any other person with official authority under the law of the place of execution to execute documents on behalf of persons who are blind or unable to write. As with the pre-existing law, section 9 of the 1995 Act does not authorise a third party to execute a deed on behalf of a granter lacking mental (as opposed to physical) capacity. Similarly, section 9(7) continues the previous recognition that there is no legal bar to a blind person choosing to sign on his own behalf (although prudence would normally otherwise indicate).

Execution of a will in terms of Section 9

In order that the will can be self evidencing under section 3 of the **8–16** 1995 Act, a witness is required. The process to be followed under section 9 is as follows:

- The relevant person, the granter and the witness should meet.
- The granter needs to declare that he is blind or that he is unable to write, in the presence of both the relevant person and the witness.
- The relevant person will read over the will to the granter unless the granter makes a declaration that he does not wish the will to be read over to him.
- The granter will authorise the relevant person to subscribe (in terms of section 12(1) "authorised" means "expressly or impliedly authorised"—the Act gives no guidance as to what might amount to implied authorisation).
- The relevant person will then subscribe every sheet of the will.
- The witness must sign immediately.

All of the above stages should be carried out unico contextu. with all three parties (granter, relevant person and witness) being present throughout. The testing clause may be added at a subsequent stage.

Disqualification of relevant person

Under the provisions of the 1924 Act, the notary must have no interest **8–17** of any nature in the deed. As noted elsewhere in this text, the penalty was draconian, *i.e.* the will or codicil would be wholly invalid, thereby prejudicing the interests of third parties who would otherwise have benefited in terms of the will or codicil in question. This inequitable outcome was thankfully addressed in terms of section 9(4) of the 1995 Act, which provided that where a document subscribed by a relevant person conferred on the relevant person or his spouse, son or daughter a benefit in money or monies worth (whether directly or indirectly), then the document would be invalid to the extent, but only to the extent, that it conferred such a benefit. This would of course preserve the validity of the remaining parts of the will or codicil so that other beneficiaries would not suffer owing to the relevant person having a direct or indirect interest. This raises an interesting point—would the child of a draftsman who (hopefully inadvertently) infringed the rules, causing his child to lose a perhaps valuable bequest, have a good claim against the poor draftsman?

Practical advice

8–18   The relevant person needs to bear in mind that both the client and the witness may never have encountered execution under section 9 before. It is recommended that when a granter, the relevant person and the witness have assembled, the relevant person should explain the purpose of the procedure and outline what is to take place, explaining the roles of each of the "participants". Taking time to explain the procedure can put both the granter and the witness at their ease. Thereafter:

- It is essential that the process be carried out *unico contextu*. A failure to adhere to the requirements of section 9 will vitiate the proceedings and therefore the will itself. In those circumstances, where the relevant person is also the draftsman of the will, he may face enquiry at the instance of disappointed beneficiaries.
- It is submitted that where the granter is blind (and although section 9 offers alternatives) it is preferable for the document to be read over to the granter. However, against this has to be balanced a client's possible wishes that the contents of the document should not be made known to the witness. This does, however, predicate that prior to commencement of the formal procedure, a client has been advised in detail of the contents of the document.
- Always be aware of the possibility that the relevant person will have at least an indirect interest in the deed. This could occur where a partner of the relevant person is appointed an executor or trustee with power to charge for his services.

Chapter 9

REVOCATION OF A WILL

Background

This has proved to be a fruitful area of litigation in the past. This is **9–01** particularly so as Scottish law does not regard the *animus revocandi* (intention to revoke) as being absolute, even where it is expressed in clear terms in a will.

Methods

In brief terms, an existing Scottish will can be revoked by: **9–02**

- Deliberate intention (for example by making up a new will which expressly revokes earlier wills).
- By implication (for example, where a later will which does not expressly revoke an earlier will is totally inconsistent with the earlier document).
- A presumption of law.

The categories detailed above are not mutually exclusive. Examination of the case law in this area shows that there appears to be an overlap between the categories detailed above. For example, destruction of a later will may be deemed (*i.e.* by implication) to revive an earlier will, even though the later will contained an express clause of revocation of earlier testamentary documents (see below).

Drafting

As a starting point, when approaching the drafting of a new will, the **9–03** adviser should always:

(a) Make it clear to the client that the new will should be comprehensive and all encompassing of existing provisions which are required to remain in force. This includes provisions not only of earlier wills but, most importantly, also of codicils thereto and informal writings made under earlier wills.
(b) Advise destruction of earlier wills, codicils and informal writings once the new will has been fully and validly executed.

Traditionally, the revocation clause of a will appeared at the end of the will, being the last clause. Modern practice is that the revocation clause is the first provision of the will. This is perhaps to emphasise the effect of the new will.

The draftsman should take care to establish not only what wills may have been granted previously in Scotland, but also abroad. This is of particular importance. Some countries will not recognise wills made abroad in so far as they purport to relate to heritable/moveable property within that particular country (for example, Spain). As the wealth base of our society has increased, it has become more common for individuals to purchase properties in Spain and elsewhere. Whilst the question of domicile is considered separately (see Chapter 6), the question of revocation is one where particular care has to be taken. For example, a will made in Scotland which has the nature of a universal settlement, and containing a clause of revocation of all earlier wills, may have the effect of revoking a will made in a foreign domicile where, in truth, this was not the intention of the client. It is for this reason that the "fact finding" process in relation to a client is of particular importance. Equally, it should not be assumed that such a will made in Scotland would necessarily revoke a will made abroad (even if the latter result were the testator's intention). Difficult questions can arise here—for example, does the country in which the earlier foreign will was made recognise revocation by a will made in our country?[1] In such circumstances, not only is careful drafting required, but, where appropriate, advice from an appropriate adviser in the relevant foreign country is also indicated. Failure to offer such advice could render the adviser liable to fall foul of *Holmes v Bank of Scotland* .[2]

However, subject to appropriate advice from a foreign adviser, an appropriate clause of revocation might be expressed as follows:

> I revoke all prior wills and testamentary writings made or granted by me with the exception of my will dated . . . in so far as relating to my property or assets in Spain.

It should be borne in mind that it is not necessary that a Scottish will deals with assets worldwide, and many high value clients will have detailed the succession to their estates in various parts of the world by means of wills granted in the relevant countries.

GENERAL CONSIDERATIONS

9–04 With certain limited exceptions (see below), a will can be revoked right up to the point of death. Up until that point, the will might be regarded as being ineffective.[3] Even a statement, *in gremio* of the relevant will, that the particular will is irrevocable, is ineffective.[4]

---

[1] See A.E. Anton, *Private and International Law*, (W. Green, 1956), pp.694 *et seq.*; and the Wills Act, 1963, s.2(1)(c).
[2] 2002 S.L.T. 544; and 2002 S.C.L.R. 481 (cited above in Ch.2).
[3] Erskine, Institutes III. ix.5.
[4] *Dougall's Trustees v Dougall* (1789) M. 159 49.

Another aspect is just when does a will become effective? A deed granted *inter vivos* will, upon delivery, be regarded as irrevocable. This is not the case in respect of a will or codicil—even if delivered to the beneficiary, the testator retains the right to revoke.[5]

CAPACITY TO REVOKE

Just as the right to make a will may be characterised as a fundamental **9–05** freedom, so is the right to revoke a will at any time up to the point of death. The same degree of capacity is required to revoke a will as to make a will. An individual who has lost that capacity will not be able to revoke.[6] The individual must also have (and be capable of having) an *animus revocandi*.

EXPRESS REVOCATION

Express revocation can be effected in one of two ways—a physical act of **9–06** destruction, or by a specific clause of revocation detailed in a subsequent validly executed testamentary deed.

Destruction

Actual, total destruction is not required. However, there must be **9–07** *animo et facto* coupled with a physical act. If a testator deliberately incinerates, tears up or shreds his will, then this might be seen to be a clear act of revocation. However, where destruction was accidental, the required intention to revoke is absent and the will shall not be revoked. In the case of *Cunningham v Mouat's Trustees*,[7] the court found that a will inadvertently destroyed by an agent who had no authority so to act, was not revoked. Destruction or cancellation whilst the testator was insane or otherwise incapax will not amount to revocation. In *Norman v Dick*,[8] the pursuers had claimed that the deceased had custody of her will which, after her death, could not be found. The pursuers also contended that at the time of her death, the testator was insane; thus, any destruction of that will by her would not amount to revocation of the will in question. Unfortunately, the pursuers were unable to prove that the testator was insane at the time of her death—had they been able to satisfy the court on this point, this would have left it open to them to "set up" the "missing" will.

Onus of proof

This lies with the party who founds upon the revocation. In *Pattison v* **9–08** *University of Edinburgh*,[9] Lord McLaren stated that:

---

[5] *Clark's Executor v Clark*, 1943 S.C. 216.
[6] *Norman v Dick* (1938) D. 59.
[7] (1851) 13 D. 1376.
[8] Cited above.
[9] (1888) 16 R. 73 at p.76.

"On proof that the cancellation was done by the testator himself . . . with the intention of revoking the will, the will is held to be revoked; otherwise it is to be treated as a subsisting will".

As indicated, an act of less than total destruction will suffice, provided sufficient animus can be shown. Where something less than total destruction has occurred, then very clear evidence of intention will be required. In the case of *Nasmyth v Hare's Trustees*,[9a] the testator had cut off a seal which he had appended to the will. The will itself was otherwise unaffected and remained *ex facie* probative (being holograph and signed by the testator). There was, however, clear evidence that the testator intended that the will should be revoked by the symbolical act of removing the seal—there was clear evidence of *animus*, and that being so, little by way of actual physical destruction or cancellation was considered to be necessary. On the other hand, much stronger evidence of physical cancellation will be necessary if the intention of the testator is less clear[10]—unauthenticated pencil marks on a copy of a will had no effect.

Destruction must be by testator or with his authority

9–09   Cancellation or destruction must be carried out either by the testator himself or with his specific authority. Destruction, etc. by a third party without sufficient authority does not revoke the will, as the document cannot be revoked without clear evidence of *animus* of the testator. If that intention exists then it does not matter that a third party acts upon the testator's instruction to destroy the will. The authority can be provided parole evidence.[11] Conversely, where instructions to destroy a will have been issued to a third party but not observed prior to death of the testator, revocation will be regarded as having occurred, on the basis that a testator had done all that he could to complete the revocation of the will.

In the case of *Bruce's Judicial Factor v The Lord Advocate*,[12] the court found that merely instructing a new will was not to imply authority to destroy the old. This case is important for other reasons (see below), but it is also noteworthy that the court did appear to accept that evidence of a solicitor who had failed to implement an instruction to destroy the old will would not militate against the court finding that there had been constructive revocation.

Loss of a will

9–10   The Bruce case referred to above involved the loss of a will which had been in the possession of the testator. In such cases, the presumption is that if a will cannot be found following the death of the testator, and given that it was in his custody, then it has been destroyed with the intention of revoking the same. The presumption is rebuttable.[13]

[9a] 1821 1 Sh.App. 65.
[10] *Manson v Edinburgh Royal Institution for Education of Deaf & Dumb Children*, 1948 S.L.T. 196 (O.H.)
[11] *Cullen's Executor v Elphinstone*, 1948 S.C. 662.
[12] 1969 S.C. 296.
[13] *Bonthrone v Ireland*, 1883 I.O.R. 779.

Revocation by express clause in later will

Save in certain limited circumstances (see the sections below regarding **9–11** mutual wills, etc.), an earlier will is revoked by an express clause to that effect in a later will. This is clear evidence of the *animus revocandi*.

The general requirements for an effective express clause of revocation are that:

- The revocation must be stated in a later deed executed in accordance with formalities which apply at the time the later deed is signed. There is no requirement of public policy in Scotland that the later deed itself requires to be a will. Even where the later deed does not set out full testamentary instructions, an express clause of revocation therein will be effective to revoke an earlier will in which the testator had set out a comprehensive, universal settlement of his estate.[14]
- No special wording or format of wording is required, as long as the *animus revocandi* can be reasonably inferred from the language used.

POSSIBLE PROBLEM AREAS

Where clients make a new will, they should be advised that the later **9–12** document should be a full and comprehensive statement of their testamentary requirements. A client should not, in an ideal world, resort to a new will which deliberately leaves part of an older will in force, although there is no reason why this should not be done, however inadvisable. The express clause of revocation should refer to all prior wills and testamentary writings; in that connection the following points are of relevance:

(a) The clause of revocation should not refer to prior wills by their dates of execution—this runs the risk of a mistype or indeed the draftsman being supplied with incorrect information. An example of an unfortunate situation which arose in such circumstances is the case of *Gordon's Executor v McQueen*.[15] Here, the testatrix expressly revoked "two Wills . . . which are recorded in the Books of Council and Session, Edinburgh". However, it seems that no such wills existed. The testatrix had, however, granted an earlier will which had not been so registered. In those circumstances, the court found that the pursuer had not discharged the onus of proof of revocation, and also that the will which had not been registered was not revoked.

(b) The difficulties which can arise where the testator chooses to revoke only certain parts of a prior will can be seen in the cases of *Stewart v Campbell's Trustees*[16] and *Clarke's Trustees v Clarke's Executors*.[17]

---

[14] *Kirkpatrick's Trustees v Kirkpatrick* (1874) 1 R. (H.L.) 37.
[15] 1907 S.C. 373.
[16] 1917 2 S.L.T. 259 (O.H.)
[17] 1943 S.L.T. 266.

(c) The express clause of revocation should refer not only to wills, but also to all other prior testamentary writings, as in Clark's *Executor v Clark*[18] it was also decided that the phrase "testamentary writings" had a wider meaning than "wills". In this case, a revocation of "all wills previously executed by me" was held not to revoke a specific legacy of a stamp collection already made over to the legatee. It is, however, considered that revocation of a will also has the effect of revoking codicils and informal writings which may depend upon the will for their authority/validity.

ALTERATIONS TO EXISTING WILLS

9–13 A differentiation requires to be made between alterations made prior to execution of the will and alterations made thereafter. In the former case, these can normally be authenticated by way of reference being made thereto in a testing clause (for example "under declaration that the word 'my' is interlined so as to be read between the words 'bequeath' and 'jewellery', where those words respectively appear in the fourth line from the top of page second hereof"). Such a reference will clear up any doubt as to whether or not the alteration was made prior to subscription of the will by the granter. This is of particular importance where there is a discrepancy between the name of the granter of the testamentary writing and his signature.

The leading case dealing with alterations, additions, erasures, etc. is *Pattison's Trustees v University of Edinburgh*[19] to which the reader is referred for an appropriate consideration of the same.[20]

IMPLIED REVOCATION

9–14 Under Scottish law a will is not revoked by the subsequent marriage of the testator (see Chapter 4). A will may be revoked by implication if a later will is made which contains no cause of revocation, but does have provisions which are inconsistent with those of the earlier will. Similarly, a will may be deemed to have been revoked if the *conditio si testator sine liberis decesserit* applies.

THE SUBSEQUENT, INCONSISTENT WILL

9–15 The first point which requires to be established is that the second will should properly be regarded as the later and most up-to-date expression of the individual's testamentary wishes. If two separate wills are executed or are deemed to be executed on the same date, then they will normally fall to be viewed as separate parts of the same document.[21] This is

---

[18] Cited above.
[19] (1886) 16 R. 73.
[20] See also Barr, etc., cited above in Ch.8, paras 2.44—49.
[21] McLaren, *Law of Wills and Succession as Administered in Scotland* (3rd ed.,1894), para.749.

perhaps a reflection of the fact that the Scottish courts attempt to read the documents together and, where conflict is found between the two documents, the later will will prevail. It should be borne in mind that some of the difficulties occasioned by the cases hereinafter detailed would not have arisen had the later will contained an express, universal clause of revocation. Where the later will has the character of a universal settlement, then the earlier document will be regarded as being wholly revoked. It is for the court to decide whether or not the later document does have the character of universality. In the case of *Clark's Executor v Clark*[22] (see above), the will, bequeathing the testator's "whole estate heritable and moveable" and expressly cancelling all previous wills, did not revoke an earlier bequest of a stamp collection in a previously excuted testamentary writing (re-emphasising that a clause of express revocation should refer to all prior wills and testamentary writings).

Difficulties arise if the subsequent will is not universal. In such a case, implied revocation of an earlier will only applies in so far as there is necessary inconsistency between the two documents.[23] However, if the court can find a meaning which allows both documents to stand together, then the court is likely to adopt that meaning, with the result that both provisions will survive.[24] The court will not adopt an unreasonable interpretation of the perceived wishes of the testator.[25] However, if no reasonable interpretation can be brought to bear, then the earlier, inconsistent provision will fail as being revoked.

REVOCATION BY APPLICATION OF THE *CONDITIO SI TESTATOR SINE LIBERIS DECESSERIT*

As the result of the possible operation of this clause, great care needs to **9–16** be taken when drafting a will. Whilst the Latin wording of the presumption seems to indicate that the *conditio* will apply where a testator dies without children, it is in fact quite the opposite. The *conditio* will apply where an individual leaves a will which contains no provision for children who may be born to the testator after date of execution of the relevant will. Where a will makes no provision for children born after its date, then the assumption arises that the testator would not have wished his will to have remained in effect in those changed circumstances. Failing rebuttal of the presumption, revocation of the will occurs by operation of law. If the presumption applies, intestacy may be the result, although obviously a child to whom the *conditio* applies might need to consider carefully whether or not to revoke the same, as revocation of the will resulting in intestacy might simply produce the effect of the whole estate passing to the surviving parent in satisfaction of his or her prior rights. The following points should also be noted.

- The *conditio* does not apply solely to posthumous children. It will also apply to children born after the making of the relevant will, but prior to death of the parent.

[22] 1943 S.L.T. 266.
[23] *Park's Trustees v Park*, 1890 27 S.L.R. 528.
[24] Again, see *Clark's Executor v Clark*, cited above.
[25] *Rutherford's Trustees v Dickie*, 1907 S.C. 80.

- It would appear that only the relevant child may seek to found on the condition.[26] Others who have been passed over (for example, provision has been made for them only in the event of failure of the spouse—who survives to take), but to whom the *conditio* does not apply, cannot however insist upon its application if the relevant child chooses not to invoke the same.
- The presumption is a strong one and is difficult to rebut. There are few examples of the presumption being successfully overturned. In the case of *Stuart-Gordon v Stuart-Gordon*[27] the mother's will made no provision for a child born after the will in question had been executed. However, the court considered evidence that the mother had been reviewing the terms of her will when the child had been born. There was also evidence that the mother was satisfied that the child would be reasonably provided for by other means. The court found that the presumption had been rebutted.
- In the case of *Milligan's Judicial Factor v Milligan*,[28] the court would not accept the argument that, in view of the length of time which had passed between the birth of the child and the actual death of the parent, the presumption should be rebutted. The court appeared to be of the view that no matter how long a testator had to consider the review of his or her testamentary provisions, effluxion of time by itself would not be sufficient to rebut the presumption.

Practical Application

9–17 In light of the changed position for Scottish solicitors following the *Holmes v Bank of Scotland* case,[29] it is vital that a draftsman should not fall in to what is a simple trap. Many clients, for personal reasons, wish their children to be specifically named in their wills. For example:

> ". . . in the event of my said spouse failing to survive as aforesaid then I bequeath the whole residue and remainder of my means and estate equally between my children, JOHN SMITH, ROBERT SMITH and MELISSA SMITH, equally between them or wholly to the survivor of them declaring that in the event of any of my said children predeceasing me leaving issue who shall survive me . . . ."

Let us say that the will containing the foregoing residuary provision was executed by Mr Smith on August 10, 1998. On February 23, 2001, a fourth child, Elizabeth, is born. If Mr Smith does not change his will, then in light of the foregoing terms of the same, on his death, Elizabeth would be entitled to invoke the presumption. To avoid this, the solution is simple:

---

[26] *Stevenson's Trustees v Stevenson*, 1932 S.C. 657.
[27] (1899) I F. 1005.
[28] 1909 2 S.L.T. 338.
[29] Cited above.

- Either you persuade the client that he should not specifically name the children but simply make reference to "such of my children as shall survive me"; or
- Alternatively, the addition (after the name of Melissa) of the phrase "and any other child of mine subsequently born to me" would suffice.

ANOMALOUS POSITION?

Practitioners should not lose sight of the decision in the case of *Bruce's* **9–18** *Judicial Factor v The Lord Advocate*.[30] Quite apart from being authority for the proposition that destruction of a will not authorised by the testator did not revoke that will, the case also dealt with what some may regard to be an anomalous position. The testator had made an earlier will which was revoked by an express clause of revocation in a later will, which the testator himself held in safe custody. Following his death, the later will could not be found. The presumption (which can be rebutted) arose that the testator had destroyed the later will *animus revocandi*. However, and notwithstanding the fact that the later will had expressly revoked the earlier will, the presumption was also to the effect that in such circumstances, the testator would be taken to have destroyed the later will with the intention of bringing back into force the earlier will. This case is often cited as a reason why earlier wills should be destroyed by, or on the specific instructions of, the testator. As indicated, evidence can be led to rebut this presumption.[31]

Where there is no earlier will, and the only valid will has been lost, it may be possible for the tenor of the document to be set up. It is necessary to establish the *casus amissionis*—it is not simply a question of establishing that the will has been destroyed or lost, but also that "its destruction or loss took place in such a manner as implied no extinction of the right of which it was the evidence".[32]

REVOCATION BY PRE-EXISTING CONTRACT

In terms of section 1(2) of the Requirements of Writing (Scotland) Act **9–19** 1995, a written document complying with section 2 of the Act is required for the constitution of:

(i) A contract or unilateral obligation for the creation, transfer, variation or extension of an interest in land; and
(ii) A gratuitous unilateral obligation except an obligation undertaken in the course of business.

The only unilateral obligation recognised in Scottish law is a "promise". It would appear that since August 1, 1995, a verbal promise to bequeath

---

[30] Cited above.
[31] See *Norman v Dick*, cited above.
[32] *Winchester v Smith* (1863) 1 M. 685. See also *Clyde v Clyde*, 1958 S.C. 343.

will be unenforceable, as it does not comply with section 2 of the Requirements of Writing (Scotland) Act 1995.

It has long been recognised in Scotland that an individual can enter into an *inter vivos* contract binding himself not to revoke a particular will or certain parts of that will.[33] Where one party, having entered into such a contract and in breach thereof, seeks to revoke the relevant will or the relevant part of his will, the other will be entitled to reduce the later will. The underlying principle behind this is that the right of the "innocent" party to the contract is effectively a debt in the testator's estate. As such, that party is a creditor and his rights take priority before those of the beneficiaries under the will. The right of that creditor will also transmit to his heirs should the creditor pre-decease the testator. In the case of *Paterson v Paterson*,[34] Mrs Paterson agreed that, in return for financial support from her son (including payment of rent), she would bequeath her whole property to her son on death. This agreement was embodied in a formal minute of agreement, executed by both parties. Mrs Paterson proceeded to make the will required in implement of her obligations. However, on her death, it was found that she had made a subsequent will, revoking the earlier "contractual" will, with different provisions for the disposal of the estate as had been set out in the minute of agreement. Her son raised an action of reduction. The son was successful and the later will struck down.

The existence of a contract not to revoke must be proved in the required fashion—failing this, in the absence of adequate proof as to existence of the alleged contract, the later will survived.[35] Similarly, where a unilateral or gratuitous promise was made to make a will of a particular format or in particular terms, proof was restricted to the writ or oath of the promiser.[36]

9–20   An example of the dangers which can arise here can be seen in the case of *McEleveen v McQuillan's Executor*.[37] This case should be of interest to practitioners who have acted for older clients purchasing their council houses and utilising funds provided by one or more adult children. McQuillan resided in an SSHA property of which he was the tenant. He discovered that he was entitled to purchase the property under the Tenants Rights, etc. (Scotland) Act 1980. Mr McQuillan was not himself able to fund the purchase. There appears to have been evidence that an approach for funding made to adult children living in Scotland was unsuccessful. However, his daughter, Mrs McEleveen (who lived in Canada), agreed to provide her father with the money to enable him to purchase the dwelling-house. It was agreed that Mr McQuillan would make a will bequeathing the house to Mrs McEleveen. That agreement was verbal and was not reduced to writing. Mr McQuillan made the will required of him on February 15, 1984. Perhaps realising her danger, his daughter subsequently endeavoured to persuade her father on several occasions to enter into a formal agreement. Whilst he

---

[33] Erskine Institute III, IX, VI; Bell Principles S. (1866).
[34] (1893) 20 R. 484.
[35] *Gray v Johnston*, 1928 S.C. 659.
[36] *Smith v Oliver*, 1911 S.C.103.
[37] 1997 S.L.T. (Sh. Ct) 46.

indicated a willingness to do so, no written agreement was ever completed and he died in 1995. It was then discovered that by a will granted in October 1993, he had revoked the 1984 will, had appointed another daughter to be executor, and had instructed the division of residue of his estate (including the dwelling-house) equally between that other daughter and another.

Mrs McEleveen raised an action to seek implementation of the agreement.

Whilst the court appeared to accept that there had been an agreement, it had not been in the form appropriate to securing a valid bequest of heritage. On appeal, the sheriff principal referred to Erskine[38]—"in the transmission of heritage which is justly accounted of the greatest importance to society, parties are not to be caught by rash expressions, but continue free until they have discovered their deliberate and final resolution concerning it by writing". Mrs McEleveen failed.

See Chapter 4 for the practical uses to which the ratio in the *Paterson* case might be utilised. A brief style minute of agreement is included in the Appendix of Styles.

In the foregoing connection, however, do not seek to rely on the inclusion of a declaration in the relevant will that it is irrevocable—such a statement is not binding upon the testator.[39] In the case of *McLachlan v Seton's Trustees*[40] Mrs Seton made a codicil to her will, bequeathing the sum of £6,000 equally between three beneficiaries. However, she subsequently made a series of later wills, each containing a clause of revocation, and each containing repetition of the legacy of £6,000 in the same terms. In her will of 1935, she directed payment of certain legacies, including the one at issue, but without interest. On her death, the three beneficiaries in question brought an action against her trustees. They maintained that Mrs Seton had no power to revoke the codicil of 1911, and accordingly they were entitled to payment both of the legacy under the 1911 codicil and under the 1935 will. However, the court found that she was entitled to revoke the 1911 codicil and to substitute a similar bequest in a later testamentary writing.

Cautionary note

Whilst clients might find the idea of entering into the type of minute of agreement envisaged above to have a certain attraction, there are "danger areas" which need to be recognised (and obviously to be explained to the clients). **9–21**

1. Even where there is a valid contract or minute of agreement in place, the normal rules of ademption will apply. If a contractual obligation applies to a specific asset, the party owning that asset can still deal with the same (and dispose of it) during his lifetime. If the asset is not within the estate of the testator as at his date of death, then it will be deemed to have adeemed.

---

[38] III, II, 2.
[39] *Dougall's Trustees v Dougall*, cited above.
[40] 1937 S.L.T. 211.

2. Similarly, the testator is quite entitled to deal with his estate during his lifetime. That estate could be dissipated, and therefore implementation of the "contractual will" might, with the benefit of hindsight, appear not to be adequate recompense for the other party. For example, take two spouses, both in their second marriages, having children by their first marriages. They agree that they will make wills in terms of which they will bequeath their respective estates to each other, and on death of the survivor, the latter will bequeath the same equally or in some other agreed fashion between the two sets of adult children. On death of one spouse, the other could simply dissipate his estate (by gifting it to his own children) so that when the "contractual will" comes to be implemented, there is virtually nothing left for the children of the predecessor spouse.
3. In the example given above, spouses may well be depriving each other of scope for some IHT mitigation on first death.
4. As indicated, the assets in question will remain within the estate of the relevant party, the "contractual" will only taking effect on death of the latter. The estate will therefore be subject to legal rights claims, thereby reducing the benefit to the other party to the original contract or to his intended beneficiaries.

MUTUAL WILLS

9–22 Mutual wills have caused so much litigation and so many problems over the years that their use has virtually fallen into desuetude, to the extent that in their Memorandum of 1986, the Scottish Law Commission did not recommend any reform in this area.

It is surprising how often, when a practitioner is consulted by clients who wish to make wills, the clients believe that their respective testamentary wishes will be incorporated within the context of one document. Such a document would of course be "a mutual will". Whilst such documents were not uncommon many years ago, they proved to be a source of such difficulty and litigation that the legal profession moved away from the same.

Most of the problems in relation to mutual wills arose out of the question of their revocability. If a mutual will allowed for revocability by either, then that power could be properly invoked. However, where the mutual will contained either an express or implicit agreement (making it contractual) that each party should dispose of their estates as stated in the will, then the will would be irrevocable unless both consented to such revocation. Thus, where a mutual will provided that it could only be revoked by both, the survivor could not do so by himself.[41]

9–23 In *Dewar's Trustees v Dewar's Trustees and Others*,[42] a husband and wife executed a mutual trust disposition and settlement, the principal effect of which was to leave the residue of their respective estates to the survivor in life rent and to the whole nephews and nieces of both parties

---

[41] *Corrance's Trustees v Glen* (1903) 5 F. 77.
[42] 1950 S.L.T. 191.

in fee. The document contained a clause reserving power to each party respectively to "alter, innovate or revoke the Will in all or in part" so far as regarding their respective estates. The husband died in 1938. His wife died in 1948, it then being discovered that she had made a will in Canada in 1939 which bore to be her last will, which contained a clause of revocation of all former wills and codicils, and in terms of which the beneficiaries were her own nephews and nieces, to the exclusion of those of her late husband. Her 1939 Canadian will was not a universal settlement. A special case was brought to establish whether the widow had been entitled after the death of her husband to revoke the mutual will and, if so, whether her last will and testament had effectively done so only in whole or in part. It was decided that, given that the mutual will had contained a right to revoke, her Canadian will of 1939 had effectively done so and completely, even although under the 1939 will a substantial part of her estate fell into intestacy.

English law also has a doctrine of mutual wills (which do not need to be embodied in one single document). The English doctrine applies when the mutuality of the provisions of the wills is accompanied by an agreement that all (or part) of the wills shall not be revoked. The doctrine does not actually prevent revocation, as a mutually irrevocable will can in fact be revoked at any time in normal fashion. However, the main thrust of the doctrine can be seen where the first testator dies without having gone back on the agreement, which then becomes binding upon the surviving testator, giving rise to an equitable obligation to give effect to the mutually agreed dispositions. That equitable obligation can be enforced against the surviving testator's personal representatives.[43] In England, it is not sufficient that the wills are executed simultaneously and in identical form. There must be an obvious contract at law, it being necessary to establish an agreement between the parties to make, and not to revoke mutual wills, an understanding or non-contractual arrangement being insufficient.[44]

---

[43] *Re Goodchild* 1996 1 All E.R. 670; see also *Re Cleaver*, 1981 2 All E.R. 1018.
[44] *Re Grieve v Perpetual Trustee Co Ltd* [1928] A.C. 391.

CHAPTER 10

EXECUTORS AND TRUSTEES

APPOINTMENT OF EXECUTORS

10–01 In a properly made will, one of the first causes thereof will be the appointment of executors nominate. Where the will nominates a specific person to act as executor nominate, then the latter is entitled to the office in preference to all others.[1] An express nomination is of course the most common way of appointing an executor nominate, although a right of appointment can be delegated by the testator to a third party (who is thereby empowered to appoint the executor nominate). In the author's view, this methodology is not to be recommended—the testator should exercise his own free will and choice and appoint an individual or individuals in whom the testator reposes faith and trust.

Appointment as executor nominate may also arise:

- *By implication*—where the testator has not expressly appointed an individual as his executor but has nonetheless conferred upon the latter powers of an Executor,[2] then that individual will be entitled to be confirmed as executor nominate.
- *By constructive appointment*—the testator may make a will in terms of which he either fails to nominate an executor in the first place or, for example, the sole executor so nominated had pre-deceased the testator, the latter failing to make any substitute or later appointment. In such circumstances, any general disponee, universal legatory or residuary legatee under the relevant will can be held to be executor nominate, and entitled to confirmation in that character under section 3 of the Executors (Scotland) Act, 1900.

The 1900 Act also confirmed the practice which had previously existed, regarding testamentary trustees as executors nominate unless a contrary intention was expressed in the will in question. The facility afford by section 3 is extremely useful and covers any situation where the executor nominated by the deceased was unable to act for any reason (not just prior death).

GRATUITOUS OFFICE

10–02 Unless the will specifically authorises the same, an executor (or indeed testamentary trustee) is not entitled to a remuneration for his services. There is no rule against an executor or trustee being a beneficiary. The

---

[1] *Tod* (1890) 18 R. 152.
[2] *Martin v Ferguson's Trustees* (1892) 19 R. 474.

executor/trustee is entitled to a refund of properly incurred expenses in the furtherance of his duties, but otherwise is at no time to be *auctor in rem suam* and may not transact with the estate, even where the estate might be seen to benefit from such a transaction,[3] unless specifically authorised to do so by the relevant will. The client will often wish to appoint his solicitor or accountant as an executor. In such cases, a will should specifically authorise an executor or trustee who is employed as a solicitor or agent in some other capacity to charge his normal professional remuneration. Failing such authority being granted by the will, such charges can be made by a "professional executor" only if all parties having an interest in the will agree to this. The latter situation can lead to obvious difficulties where one or more of the residuary beneficiaries may be minors.

Similarly, the testator may have been a business person/sole trader. Executors or trustees who assume responsibility for continuing to run the business (in the hope of selling the same as a going concern and not as an asset-stripping exercise) will not be entitled to any payment of remuneration for so acting unless specifically authorised by the will.

However, just as the office of executor/trustee is gratuitous, it is also not compellable, although an *ex officio* trustee may be obliged by the terms of his office or employment to accept office as trustee. That being so, so far as possible, clients should not "ambush" friends and relatives into appointment as executor. Apart from the other considerations detailed below, when a client is issuing instructions for preparation of a will, a recommendation should be given that the client checks with those whom he would wish to nominate as executors that they would be prepared to act. Some individuals would not wish to act as an executor, and they should be given the opportunity of politely declining.[4]

On occasions the client will wish to include a legacy in favour of an individual, provided that individual agrees to act as executor. Such a provision is perhaps a fair recognition of the fact that the duties of an executor can be onerous so far as the lay person is concerned, particularly where a deceased's estate is likely to be complex. However, it might be appropriate to point out to such an individual that if he accepts office on the basis of receiving in due course the conditional legacy, then that individual cannot resign as executor unless specifically permitted to do so in terms of the will. The unstated rationale for this is to prevent an individual accepting office, receiving his legacy and then immediately departing the scene.

Care might be required where an individual is nominated as an **10–03** executor and trustee and is also left a legacy without further comment (*i.e.* it is not expressed to be conditional). In such circumstances, it may be necessary for enquiry to be made whether there is any connection between the legacy and the office.[5]

A bequest to a testamentary trustee for his time and care given effect to the provisions of the relevant will is not payable to a trustee who refuses to act. In the case of *Henderson v Stuart*[6] a bequest was made to the

---

[3] *Hall's Trustees v McArthur*, 1918 S.C. 646; *Inglis v Inglis*, 1983 S.C. 8.
[4] See *Currie on Confirmation*, p.88, cited above in Ch.6.
[5] See Menzies, *The Law of Scotland Affecting Trustees*, (2nd ed, W. Green, 1913), p.96.
[6] (1825) 4 S. 306.

testamentary trustees of £500 each as a mark of friendship, with a further £105 to each trustee to purchase a hogshead of claret as recompense for their care and trouble as trustees. One individual declined to accept office as trustee. Whilst he was held entitled to the legacy of £500, he was not entitled to the hogshead of claret. The two legacies were regarded as having been granted for different motives, the former to reflect the personal friendship, the latter reward to accepting trustees for their management.

When a testator passes on, it is normal for the executry solicitor to make contact with those nominated to act as executors to confirm that they are willing so to act. Where one of a number of executors nominated indicates his or her unwillingness to accept office, then a letter of declinature of office will be required, as such letter of declinature will require to be produced to the Commissariat when application for Confirmation is made. Commissary clerks do not insist that such letters of declinature be witnessed, and there is no statutory format required. A suggested style would be as follows:

> *To Maxwell MacLaurin,Solicitors,*
> *100 West Regent Street,*
> *GLASGOW*
>
> *Or to whomsoever else it may concern*
> *Dear Sirs,*
>
> *JOHN SMITH (DECEASED)*
>
> *I, JOSEPH SMITH, residing at 1 Brown Street, Anytown, hereby confirm that I am aware that I have been nominated to act as executor nominate in terms of the will of the late John Smith, who resided latterly at 25 Black Street, Anytown, and who died on September 20, 2002 and dated said will June 14, 1998. I confirm that I do not wish to accept and hereby decline the said nomination as such executor, and I hereby confirm and declare these presents are freely granted by me and are irrevocable.*
>
> *Signed by me at Anytown this 30th day of September, 2002.*
>
> *Yours faithfully,*

Obviously, however, if the individual has been left a legacy on condition that he or she acts as executor, then it must be made clear (as a matter of fairness) to that individual that the legacy will lapse on his or her declining office.

There are no strict rules regarding acceptance of office—this may be verbal or in writing. Difficulties can sometime arise where a testator has nominated only one person to act as executor and that individual indicates that he or she wishes to decline. Formal practice in such circumstances would be to seek to persuade the individual to accept office simply for the purpose of assuming another party entitled to apply for the office of executor nominate, with the original appointee thereafter resigning. This operation is normally effected in terms of a legal document—a minute of assumption and resignation (see Appendix of Styles). Obviously, as with a letter of declinature, such a minute will require to be presented, duly docqueted to the Commissariat, along with the application for Confirmation and the will.

Capacity of Executor/Trustee

Individuals of full age[7] who are capax may act as executor or trustee, as **10–04** may a limited company. Bankruptcy of an individual does not debar the latter from accepting appointment as executor or trustee. Although doubts have been expressed in the past as to whether or not a partnership could act as an executor or trustee, it is now thought that such appointments should in theory be possible, although not necessarily advisable. For example, a client may appoint the legal partnership of Brown & Co as executor. If that firm then amalgamates with another firm and becomes Brown Black & Co, in strict terms a different partnership exists and the question might be raised as to whether or not Brown Black & Co are entitled to act as executor.

The Solicitor Executor/Trustee

On occasion, clients will wish to appoint their solicitor as executor, often **10–05** along with other members of the client's family. If that is so, and the client has no specific preference as to the order in which the appointments are made, it would be appropriate for the solicitor to be the first named executor. This is due to the fact that company registrars will correspond with the first named executor, and the fact that dividends, communications regarding bonus rights, etc. will be sent immediately to the solicitor executor can save time and expense. It is in any event possible under commissary practice to have the Confirmation in favour of the executors issued in different order from that appearing in the confirmation application. This is achieved by adding a crave to the declaration, requesting that the solicitor executor be shown in the Confirmation as first named.

On occasions, a client may feel constrained to appoint certain members of his family as executors, even though he anticipates that there may perhaps be friction or disagreement between them. When a client expresses such concern then he should be advised to consider the wisdom of appointing such family members in the first place. However, a client may feel obliged in some way or another to make those appointments. In such circumstances, the client may also wish to appoint his solicitor on the basis that the latter can act as an independent, "honest broker". If these circumstances apply, then some consideration should be given as to whether or not the solicitor should be appointed as executor or trustee *sine qua non*.[8]

Some clients have sought to ensure that their estates would be wound up by the firm of solicitors with whom the client has had a longstanding

---

[7] Sections 1(1) and 9(f) of the Age of Legal Capacity (Scotland) Act 1991.
[8] See below.

connection. Such testators have included in their wills a provision that a particular firm, and only that firm, should act in the winding up of their estate. Such a statement is not binding on the executors, who are free to instruct whichever firm they see fit to deal with the winding up of the testator's estate. Similarly, if the testator wishes to appoint his solicitor as executor, also leaving a legacy in favour of the solicitor as a condition for accepting office, care should be taken that such a legacy should be no more than a token. Such care applies whether it is the draftsman solicitor who is to be nominated or another of his partners. (See below).

NOMINATION OF A TRUSTEE COMPANY

10–06 For some time, many of the larger legal firms in Scotland have had their own trustee companies (with the partners being officers of the company) who can be nominated to act as executors or trustees. Appointment of a trustee corporation might not be favoured by a testator who wishes to choose individuals to be nominated as executors for very personal reasons, owing to family or other relationships which they have with the individuals in question, or because of particular worthy traits possessed by the individuals in question. However, the appointment of a trustee corporation can have certain benefits (which will of course need to be explained to most testators). These are:

- Unlike a human executor, a trustee corporation will not die or lose capacity, thus possibly interfering in an adverse way with the actual administration of the estate.
- Where the trustee corporation is the sole or first named executor, as with the solicitor executor, all dividends, etc. can be sent direct to the trustee corporation, thereby saving some time and possible expense.
- When the trustee corporation is owned by the relevant firm of solicitors and the partners in the firm are also company officers, then any partner can sign documents on behalf of the trustee corporation, and this can of course avoid the difficulties which might arise where an executor falls ill or goes abroad for a length of time on business or holiday.

Where, for example, a bank is to be appointed as executor, then the client should be clear as to the bank's scale of charges for so acting. Similarly, and where the bank is not to be the sole executor, they will normally insist on the appointment of the bank as an executor *sine qua non*. The effect of such an appointment should be explained to the client.

EXECUTORS AND TRUSTEES—CLARIFYING THE DIFFERENCE

10–07 Clients can often become confused as to the essential difference between an executor on the one hand and a trustee on the other. Whilst solicitors may be familiar with the difference between the two offices, clients are not. Normally, executors will be appointed where an estate is straightforward and the executors' task is merely the ingathering or realisation of the estate and its subsequent distribution to beneficiaries. However, if a more complex will is involved (for example where vesting in child beneficiaries is postponed until a certain age is attained, thereby involving a lengthy period of administration), trustees will be appointed. Whilst they will have the same initial responsibilities as executors, they will thereafter be responsible for administering the relevant estate in accordance with the trust provisions set out in the will.

If a will simply appoints testamentary trustees, then in terms of section 3 of the Executors (Scotland) Act 1900, they will be entitled also to act as executors. Executors nominate (in terms of section 2 of the 1900 Act) will have all of the "normal" powers of trustees unless the contrary intention appears in the will itself.

Whether those nominated should be appointed as executors, or as executors and trustees, should be readily apparent to the draftsman. If the will contains no trust provisions of any type then appointment of executors will suffice. However, if it is clear that a testamentary trust of some description will be set up under the terms of the will, then the appointment should be of executors and trustees. On first sight, even where a client makes a traditional will (for example, in favour of the surviving spouse whom failing equally between adult children, with the issue of any pre-deceasing child representing the deceased parent), then the view of the testator as to when vesting in any such issue should take place should be ascertained. If vesting is to be postponed beyond age 16 then it is possible that appointment as executors and trustees would be more appropriate.

Appointment of Executors and Different Trustees

It is quite possible for a testator to nominate executors for the purposes **10–08** of ingathering his estate, and to nominate a separate set of trustees for a quite distinct purpose. For example, a testator may have an incapax child and wish to set up a "disabled trust" in terms of section 89 of the Inheritance Tax Act, 1984. The testator may form the view that specific individuals or charities (for example, Enable) should be appointed for the specific purpose of administering such a trust and be quite distinct from the executors themselves. This arrangement would be entirely competent. The executors would obtain Confirmation, ingather the estate and distribute the same in accordance with the terms of the will. Where the will contains provision for a disabled or separate trust having distinct trustees, then the executors will complete their function by making over the relevant portion of the estate to those trustees. Such an arrangement in respect of an incapacitated child might be entirely appropriate where, for example, the relevant charity appointed to act as trustee will have special skills in that area which can be brought to bear on a long-term basis in the best interests of the incapacitated child.

In one case,[9] two persons were nominated to act as executors and a third as "trustee". It was held that all three were entitled to act as executors under the will.

---

[9] *Reid's Executors v Reid*, 1954 S.L.T. (Notes) 20 (O.H.).

Although most uncommon (and perhaps not advisable), it is possible for executors or trustees to be nominated to administer different parts of the testator's estate, for example, where the testator has assets in two or more countries (although perhaps the best advice would be for that individual to make separate wills in each country dealing solely with his or her estate in each country). It is also possible to appoint executors or trustees for a limited period of time. Again, this should be regarded as being inadvisable, particularly if the jurisdiction of the appointment is fixed by reference to effluxion of a specific period of time as opposed to the occurrence of a specific event (for example, the testator nominating his widow to act as executor for as long as she remains unmarried).

Perhaps the clearest example of an appointment having a possible limited duration is where an appointment *ex officio* is made. In such cases, personal traits of the executor are largely irrelevant, and he or she is appointed simply owing to the fact of holding a specific office. Once the individual loses or demits that office then the appointment of that person as executor/trustee also lapses.

Voting Rights and Disputes

10–09 The normal position is that executors and trustees will reach decisions by majority. In a sizeable or complex estate the possibility for reasoned disagreement should not be discounted. However, a testator should seek to avoid appointing as executors and trustees individuals known to the testator to be at loggerheads, and who might allow personal disaffection to colour their respective judgments. Unless the will specifies otherwise, the majority of the trustees accepting office and surviving the testator shall be a quorum.[10] For example, if five trustees are appointed and section 3(c) of the 1921 Act applies, then the majority will be three. However, a will can provide that a quorum will be formed by a specific number of executors and trustees in such circumstances, and if through death or resignation the total number of executors and trustees falls below the specified quorum, then the quorum provision itself lapses.[11]

Although in the normal case it might be considered to be inadvisable to appoint an executor or trustee who lives abroad or who is abroad on business for large periods of time, where such an executor or trustee has been appointed, then the quorum can be specifically restricted to the majority who shall be at any time within the United Kingdom.

Executor or Trustee *Sine Qua Non*

10–10 Where one executor or trustee is appointed *sine qua non*, then no act of administration can take place without the concurrence of that individual, who will have a right to overrule the majority and quorum of the others. Effectively, a *sine qua non* can veto acts or decisions of the others. The appointment will normally relate to all aspects of administration of the

[10] s.3(c) of the Trusts (Scotland) Act, 1921.
[11] *Scott v Lunn*, 1908 15 S.L.T. 1045.

estate, although it can be restricted to decisions in respect of a particular of the estate (for example how the deceased's business should be dealt with, or how a particular property should be handled). At one time it was thought that where a person nominated to act as trustee *sine qua non* declined to accept office or was unable to do so, the very existence of the trust might be imperilled. The preferred view appears to be that failure of the trustee *sine qua non* should not affect the existence of the trust.[12] The preferred view in Scotland therefore appears to be that the purposes and existence of the trust are of prime importance, and are not to be frustrated simply owing to inability or refusal of one party to accept office *sine qua non.*

POWERS OF EXECUTORS AND TRUSTEES

In terms of section 3 of the Trust (Scotland) Act 1921, an executor is a **10–11** trustee, and as such has the normal powers of a trustee unless contrary intention is expressed in the relevant will.

Resignation

This matter is considered in more detail later in this chapter. **10–12**

Practical considerations for making an appointment

There are various practical pointers which you can offer to clients: **10–13**

(a) Clients should appoint more than one executor/trustee. Some clients will wish to appoint their spouse alone to be executor. In such circumstances the client should be advised to appoint substitute executors. If both spouses are killed in a common calamity, then in the absence of any substitute appointment, reliance will require to be placed on section 3 of the Executors (Scotland) Act, 1900.

(b) If the client is elderly, they should be advised to avoid appointing executors of the same generation. Elderly nominees of the same generation may pre-decease the testator or can become incapax prior to the testator's death. In such circumstances it would be advisable to appoint at least one co-executor or substitute executor of a younger generation. For obvious reasons of difficulty of communication, etc., it is not advisable to appoint executors who live abroad.

(c) Clients should avoid appointing individuals who are known to be antipathetic to one another. Whilst such personal antipathy might not impact adversely on the administration of the client's estate, there remains the possibility that this could occur.

(d) Where the client's estate is large and/or complex, then the client should appoint as executors/trustees individuals who shall be able to cope. Where the client is a business person,

---

[12] See the discussion on this point and the authorities cited in at *Stair Memorial Encyclopaedia*, Vol.24, para.140.

appointing individuals who have no business experience might be unfair and might impact again adversely on the administration of the estate.

(e) Bear in mind a person of full age and capacity can act as executor. However, a client might be keen that his child should be appointed as an executor provided that a child has attained legal capacity at the date of the testator's death. Such a conditional appointment is entirely possible.

Debts and liabilities

10–14   The first duty of the executors is to settle debts and liabilities due by the deceased. In that respect, the executor stands *eadem personam cum defuncto*. The executor "stands in the shoes" of the deceased and must deal with the debts due by the deceased. There is a common misapprehension that an individual's debts die with him—this is not and never has been the case (either in the case of a testate or intestate estate). Traditionally, and in so far as will drafting is concerned, the importance of the executor dealing with the deceased's debts was reflected in the inclusion (normally immediately after the appointment of executors) of a direction to the executor to settle all funeral expenses and debts. Inclusion of such direction is in fact unnecessary (as reflected in the drafting of modern wills), although many advisers will choose to include such a direction if only to focus the mind of the executor.

It is therefore of great importance that the executors should properly ascertain the debts and liabilities of the deceased before they seek to address payment of any description (whether income or capital) to beneficiaries.[13] In many straightforward executries, the debts and liabilities of the deceased are readily ascertainable. However, where there is any doubt, then the executor should advertise for claims against the estate. If the executor has any doubt as to the validity of a debt claimed, then he may require the creditor to constitute the debt on a formal basis by obtaining decree.

There are certain straightforward rules which an executor should observe in order to avoid difficulty:

1. If it becomes clear to the executor (having accepted office) that the estate is insolvent, then he must seek within a reasonable time to have a trustee in bankruptcy or judicial factor appointed.[14]
2. Whilst in some circumstances it may be possible for an executor to deal with a testator's estate without obtaining Confirmation, failing to obtain confirmation could lead to the executor being liable as a vitious intromitter for all of the deceased's debts, even where these in total exceed the value of the deceased's estate. If the executor has obtained Confirmation, then his liability will be restricted to the value of the estate to which the executor has confirmed.

[13] *Heritable Securities Investment Association Ltd v Miller's Trustees* (1892) 20 R. 675.
[14] Bankruptcy (Scotland) Act 1985, s.8(4).

3. The executor should always seek to observe the "six month rule".[15] With certain exceptions, where debts are intimated to the executor within six months of the relevant date of death, they are regarded as having equal priority and the executor cannot be compelled to pay those debts until a period of six months from the date of death has expired. If he does so, then the executor can be made personally liable to other creditors if the estate under his charge turns out to be insufficient—this rule applies even where the executor is not also a beneficiary in the estate. After the passing of the six-month period, the executor may, provided he is satisfied that the estate is solvent, pay creditors in the order in which they have claimed. "Privileged debts" may be paid within the six-month period (for example deathbed and funeral expenses).

Practical considerations for the draftsman

Although the inclusion of a specific direction as to payment of debts is **10–15** not required in the drafting a will, the draftsman should not lose sight of the importance of this matter when preparing a will for a client. Just as it is now considered to be good practice for clients to put up lists of their assets of estate with their will, it is equally valid to suggest to a client that a list of ongoing obligations and debts be similarly recorded. It should not be assumed that the deceased's family will necessarily know of all of their relative's liabilities. For example:

- If the deceased had granted a guarantee or cautionary obligation, then death of the obligant will not terminate the liability.
- The testator may be divorced and may be paying periodical allowance. His estate will remain obligated to meet those payments although an executor could make application to the court for termination or reduction of the allowance in question.
- In particular, the testator requires to be advised that a general direction to settle debts does not amount to an instruction to settle the debts secured over a specific asset, particularly where the asset is specifically bequeathed. The general rule is that the party inheriting the relevant asset will take *cum onere, i.e.* subject to the debt.[16] The case of *Muir's Trustees v Muir*[17] indicated that a general direction to an executor to pay all "just and lawful debts" does not free the legatee who is bequeathed a heritable property of the liability to meet the debts secured over that property. The court indicated:

> "Express directions are not essential but the inference (*i.e.* that the property was to be conveyed free of debt) must be irresistible and the intention clear beyond all doubt."

Thus, if the testator wishes to bequeath a specific heritable property to a particular person free of any liability to inheritance tax as also of any

---

[15] Act of Sederunt, February 28, 1662.
[16] See *Stewart v Stewart* (1891) 19 R. 310.
[17] 1916 1 S.L.T. 372.

debts secured on that property, then the following format of words is suggested:

> I bequeath to A (design) my whole interest in 1 Brown Street, Anytown and that free of all government taxes and duties payable upon my death, and of any heritable charges, debts or securities over the same and also free of the expenses of transfer and conveyance.

A consideration of the question of incidence of tax is specified later in this Chapter.

It should also be noted that where a specific legatee is bequeathed the property subject to a mortgage or similar such heritable debt, the legatee is not entitled to the benefit of an endowment policy arranged by the testator to provide funds to meet the heritable debt in question.[18] If the legatee is to be so entitled, then this will require to be specified by the testator in precise terms.

INFORMAL WRITINGS

The Requirements of Writing (Scotland) Act, 1995

10–16   This Act came into force on August 1, 1995. The terms of the Act only apply to wills, etc. granted after the Act came into force. That being so, in considering the question of the nature and effect of informal writings, the date of execution of the latter is of considerable importance. This will remain the case as many clients will have granted wills and informal writings prior to August 1, 1995 and may not properly review or update the same prior to death. The adviser will therefore require to be familiar with the law both before and after the 1995 Act came into force.

The position prior to August 1, 1995

10–17   Most modern pre-1995 Act wills contain a clause authorising executors to give effect to informal writings, perhaps owing to a recognition on the part of the legal profession of the propensity of clients to seek to create their own testamentary documentation.[19] Where a properly executed will authorised the executors to give effect to informal writings, those writings did not themselves require to pass the tests required for formal validity, *i.e.* for a will itself. Where the will contained an informal writings clause, it could specifically adopt and authorise the executors to give effect to future writings, however informal they may be. The principle which applied is that of adoption (dispensation *ab ante*)— provided the document authorising adoption was formally valid and properly and clearly denoted the type of informal document which it validated, then the informal writing could be given effect.[20] The inclusion

---

[18] Gretton (1987) 32 J.L.S.S. 303, and also (1988) J.L.S.S. 141.

[19] For the type of difficulties which can arise in that connection, see *Davidson v Convy* 2003 S.L.T. 650.

[20] See *Stair Memorial Encyclopaedia*, Vol.25, p.727; and *Currie on Confirmation*, p.55, cited above.

of such a clause in a properly made will could therefore avoid many of the difficulties (and litigation) which have been generated when clients had sought to create their own testamentary documents.

Possible uses

Clients should never at any time regard a will as being written in a **10–18** tablet of stone. It is the responsibility of the testator to ensure that his will remains an accurate and up-to-date statement of his testamentary wishes. However, if only for reasons of avoiding expense, some clients still may not wish to entrust the amendment of their wills to their solicitors. In such cases, and provided the amendment or addition to the relevant will was straightforward, the client could make use of the facility afforded by an informal writings clause. For example:

- Some testators wished their wills to be in relatively straightforward terms, uncomplicated by a long list of small bequests of money, jewellery or furniture. In fact, many clients still may not have appreciated that their wills can deal with such *minutiae*. Such clients may still prefer to deal with bequests of jewellery, etc. in terms of informal writings.
- Ability to make an informal writing, to which can be given testamentary effect, allowed clients flexibility, particularly, where, at the time of making the will, they might not have reached a decision on matters of fine detail.
- The facility, properly utilised, was straightforward and avoided the expense of instructing a solicitor to prepare a codicil to the will. The flexibility afforded by an informal writings clause allowed the client the ability to consider his options—the flexibility also extends to amendments and alterations in the client's wishes in relation to disposal of personal effects, etc. An informal writing, if considered no longer appropriate, could easily be withdrawn and replaced by a more up-to-date statement of the client's wishes.

Possible dangers

In theory, an informal writings clause could validate virtually any **10–19** document, even one which had not been subscribed.[21] However, care had to be taken. A clause which was too wide in its terms could occasion difficulty for the executors. An appropriate form of wording, often used, was:

I direct my executors to give effect to any future writings subscribed by me however informal they may be provided that they are clearly expressive of my intentions, as to which my executors shall be the sole judges.

Important points in relation to the foregoing are:

---

[21] *Crosbie v Wilson* (1865) 3 M. 870.

1. The clause only validated future writings, *i.e.* it operates on the basis of express adoption in advance. In theory a will could also retrospectively adopt such writings. This, however, was inadvisable. Clients should always be encouraged to adopt a "blank sheet" approach, *i.e.* their will should be a full and comprehensive statement of the client's testamentary wishes at the time it is signed—if the client wished to keep the provisions of earlier informal writings in force then the terms of the same should have been incorporated within, and form part of the new will, *i.e.* the earlier writings, once replaced in that way, should be destroyed

2. An attempt to retrospectively validate existing informal writings could make the drafting of the will convoluted, and assuming that the will contained the normal express clause of revocation of prior wills and testamentary writings, then that clause would require to be carefully amended.

3. The authorising clause refers to "a writing"—there was no requirement that a writing be holograph of the testator (*i.e.* in his handwriting), and any type of writing might be given effect, provided that it fulfilled the "other tests".

4. The writing required to be subscribed. This was an extremely important control although the effect of that control required to be explained to the testator. In the case of *Waterson's Trustees v St Gillies Boys Club*,[22] Mrs Helen Waterson, who died on August 9, 1940 detailed in her trust disposition and settlement of May 1935 that her trustees should "give effect to any informal writing under my hand". It was discovered that she had left an unsubscribed holograph writing of subsequent date which began, "I, Helen Young Jackson or Waterson, wish" and concluded with the words "written by my own hand", followed by the date and place of writing. The Court of Session held that in the absence of any controlling context, the words "writing under my hand" could not be construed as including an unsubscribed writing, and accordingly that the unsubscribed writing was not a valid testamentary writing of Mrs Waterson. In many ways this may have been an unfortunate outcome—it is understandable that a lay person could have regarded a document written out by them in their own hand and dated as being an exact equivalent of "a writing under my own hand". In the author's view, the phrase "under my own hand" is old fashioned and to be avoided. The draftsman required to take care to explain to the testator, for example, that if an informal writing was prepared and signed and a postscript added thereto, then, to achieve testamentary effect, the postscript would also require to be subscribed.

5. The writing must be clearly expressive of the testator's intention. However, as this was also expressed to be a matter upon which the executors were the sole judges, this did give executors more latitude, although again this may not have relieved the

---

[22] 1943 S.C. 369.

executors in every case from having to litigate. The potential difficulties which can arise, even where there was an informal writings clause, can be seen in the case of *Jay's Trustees v Murray and Others*,[23] where the testator had left a will directing his trustees to pay such legacies as he might leave by any writings under his hand, however informal, provided they were clearly indicative of his intentions. After his death, two deposit receipts were found in his wallet. These had been endorsed (in one case partially) to third parties. The testator's will was dated March 26, 1965. Both endorsements were in the deceased's handwriting and were signed by him. However, as the deposit receipts had not been delivered in the deceased's lifetime, the court took the view that endorsation of the deposit receipts did not amount to a testamentary intention—and no *mortis causa* donation had been effected. It should be remembered that a third party, disgruntled by an executor's decision not to implement a specific informal writing, could always seek to challenge the same and to have the informal writing set up.

The position post August 1, 1995

The 1995 Act effectively swept away the "common law" methods of **10–20** formal execution which were:

- The deed was subscribed by the granter and attested by two witnesses; or
- The deed was in the handwriting of and subscribed by the granter (holograph) or the deed although not of itself in the handwriting of the granter was subscribed by him and "adopted as holograph".

The 1995 Act abolished these methods of execution and in terms of section 2 provided that a deed is formally valid if it is subscribed by the granter. This has occasioned some practitioners to query the value of an informal writings clause. Doubts were raised as to whether such clauses would be effective after August 1, 1995. It appears to be clear that such a clause would not, post August 1, 1995, allow adoption of an unsigned "informal writing". However, as the normal format of such clauses required subscription on the part of the granter, this in any event would probably validate such informal writings in terms of the relevant provisions of the 1995 Act. It would still appear to be general practice to include such clauses, but again this should be after discussion with the testator.

Practical advice for the draftsman

The inclusion of the informal writings clause still offers a valuable **10–21** facility to the testator. The flexibility and other pre-1995 Act reasons for making an informal writing apply equally in the post Act era. However,

---

[23] 1970 S.L.T. (Reports) 105.

inclusion of the same should be discussed with the testator at the time of taking instructions, *i.e.* its inclusion should not be automatic, as without a brief explanation the testator might fall into one of a number of traps. The advice to be offered should cover the following points:

(a) The facility to create a future informal writing should be restricted to simple matters only. An informal writing should not be utilised to change the whole thrust of an existing will and it is also inadvisable to seek to change appointment of executors or trustees in that fashion.

(b) Informal writings should be short and to the point, and preferably restricted to one single page. A four-page informal writing written on separate sheets, subscribed on the last page only may occasion the executors difficulty. The testator would be advised to have the informal writing vetted by their solicitor (although this may be seen as defeating the whole purpose of being able to utilise the facility in the first place). However, human nature is such that if there is any doubt as to what the testator intended, dispute will arise. Although not dealing with informal writings, the case of *Stalker's Executors, Petitioners* is of interest.[24] Mrs Stalker died in 1975 leaving a settlement dated June 30, 1972. In terms of clause (third) she had provided that, "I leave and bequeath to my step-daughter, Mrs Maisie Moffat and her husband James equally between them and to the survivor of them my dwellinghouse known as 17 Bank Avenue, Cumnock, together with the whole furniture and furnishings therein with the exception of the items contained in the specific legacies above and also all cash, bank notes, deposit receipts, certificates for securities, bonds, promissory notes and all other documents of debt and the like." Mr and Mrs Moffat contended that a proper interpretation of the will was that Mrs Stalker had bequeathed to them, "all cash, bank notes, deposit receipts, certificates for securities, promissory notes and all other documents of debt and the like." Residuary beneficiaries contended for the opposite interpretation. Lord Keith held that the items in question were not included in the bequest but formed part of the residue. This difficulty of interpretation arose in respect of a professionally prepared will. The scope for such difficulties arising in respect of an unvetted formal writing is surely much the greater.

(c) It should be emphasised that the clause should be restricted to future writings. That being so, a testator should be advised that any informal writing should be dated so as to clearly demonstrate that it postdates the will itself.

(d) Re-emphasise that to be valid in terms of the above clause, the informal writing requires to be subscribed. As indicated, this must apply to any postscript to the informal writing. Failure to subscribe will be fatal under section 2 of the 1995 Act.

---

[24] 1977 S.L.T., (Notes) 4.

(e) Once completed, the testator should be advised to place any informal writing with the relevant will. In many cases, the will in question will be held by the testator's solicitor who will thereby be given a reasonable opportunity to assess the terms of the relevant informal writing, and raise any perceived difficulties with the testator.

(f) If the client wishes to leave legacies bearing their own share of inheritance tax or carrying interest from date of death, then the informal writing will require to specify this. In any event, clients should not be encouraged to construct testamentary documents which deal with such complexities.

(g) Clients should not confuse informal writings with letters of expression of wish. The former is testamentary in effect and can be binding on the executors. A letter of expression of wish (see below) is merely an illustration of how the testator would wish the executors/trustees to operate, and should never be expressed to be binding upon the executors/trustees.

The important message to convey is that simplicity in the creation of an informal writing is always desirable. Clients should not be encouraged to assume that an agglomeration of various types of paper in an envelope addressed "to my executors" gives any proper indication of the testator's intentions, nor will the same necessarily receive effect as an informal writing if it is clear that the 1995 Act applies. The difficulty which could arise where a number of different pieces of paper are involved can be seen in the case of *Barker's Executors v Scottish Rights of Way Society Ltd*.[25] Although this case, involving pre-1995 Act issues, related more to whether or not an agglomeration of papers when taken together with other facts and circumstances amounted to a new will, revoking an earlier will, it demonstrates the type of difficulties which can arise where a client resorts to a "self-help approach" when dealing with his own testamentary affairs.

THE INCIDENCE OF TAX

Just as with an informal writings clause, modern practice has seen the **10–22** inclusion as commonplace of a clause dealing with the incidence of government taxes and duties on death (effectively specifying from which parts of the estate such duties will be met). A typical clause is:

> Unless otherwise indicated, any legacy granted by any writing shall vest on my death and shall be paid or made over after my death as soon as my executors consider to be practicable and that free of all government duties in respect of my death and of expenses of delivery or transfer but without interest thereon.

In a simple will, on the face of it, inclusion of the foregoing type of clause is not necessary as the general rule is that, where the will is silent,

---

[25] 1996 S.L.T. 1319.

then IHT due in respect of a non- exempt legacy will fall to be met out
of the residue.[26] However, just as with an informal writings clause, the
draftsman should not assume that inclusion of an incidence of tax, etc.
clause should be automatic and without discussion with the testator.
Where a will contains no more than bequests of residue, then the point
may be academic. However, where, for example, a client wishes to leave
heritable property to a non-exempt beneficiary by way of specific
bequest, then care requires to be taken that the client is made aware of
the possible distorting effect of leaving such a bequest free of IHT. For
example, a testator has an estate comprising a dwelling-house worth
£250,000, with the total of his other assets and investments being
£150,000 (*i.e.* a gross estate of £400,000). The testator directs that his
dwelling-house should be conveyed to a nephew free of tax. The residue
of the estate is left equally between four other nephews and nieces. After
deduction of the nil-rate band, the taxable estate is £137,000, giving an
IHT liability of £54,800. This however requires to be paid from the
residue, reducing the benefit to the residuary beneficiaries to £23,800
each. It may be that the testator would be content with that outcome, but
it is important that it should be explained to him in the first place. If it is
not, and it could be demonstrated that the testator would have intended
a different outcome, with his residuary beneficiaries obtaining a larger
share of the estate, then the draftsman of the relevant will may find
himself under challenge from the residuary beneficiaries.

A similar situation applies where the testator has an asset (for
example, a stamp collection) which has a significant value, and he wishes
to bequeath the same to a particular beneficiary. The testator will
require to decide whether or not the bequest should bear its rateable
proportion of the inheritance tax payable in respect of his estate as a
whole. If the testator takes the view that the beneficiary should bear the
relevant proportion of IHT, then this can be achieved by a simple
amendment to the relevant purpose:

> Declaring that the foregoing bequest shall bear its rateable propor-
> tion of the government duties payable in respect of my death.

10–23 The draftsman should always be aware of the likely reluctance of a
testator to leave a bequest which requires to bear its own rateable
proportion of inheritance tax. For many clients, such a provision will, in
their minds, lessen the bequest, the fear being that the legatee might not
welcome such a bequest. The draftsman requires to be able to explore
the question with the testator. The most important point to make clear
to the testator is the question of balance. Where a particularly valuable
item is bequeathed free of tax, then the liability will fall upon the
residue. The testator must appreciate that where he or she has a
particularly valuable item, many individuals would welcome the opportunity of acquiring the same at a discount of approximately 60 per cent
of the current market value of that item.

Various problems can arise where a testator unthinkingly specifies that
bequests should be implemented free of government duties.

[26] Inheritance Tax Act 1984, s.211—see also *Cowie's Trustees*, 1982 S.L.T. 326.

- Dangers can arise where there are bequests of residue to exempt and non-exempt beneficiaries.[27]
- The terms of sections 38 and 39 of the Inheritance Tax Act 1984 should not be overlooked. The "grossing up" provisions of those sections can lead to an unexpected liability, which would again fall upon the residue, even where the residuary beneficiary is an exempt beneficiary. This is a complex area where, depending on his experience and skill in this field, the draftsman may be well advised to seek separate specialist advice.
- Similarly, difficulties can arise where there have been chargeable lifetime gifts or "failed" potentially exempt transfers. In the foregoing circumstances, the inheritance tax liability on death will be increased, and this should be pointed out to the testator. A client may be comforted when he is advised that, in normal circumstances, the transferee of such a lifetime gift would normally require to bear the tax. However, it should also be pointed out to the client that if the transferee does not, or is unable to pay the tax, then the Revenue will look to the executors to settle the same. It is essential that the draftsman of the will should establish whether or not the testator has made any lifetime transfers, and also when such transfers were made. Whilst some testators might perceive enquiry in this area to be unnecessary and indeed intrusive, these concerns on the part of the testator might be allayed if the draftsman explains that:

> If the recipient of a "failed" potentially exempt transfer does not pay the inheritance tax due within 12 months from the end of the month of the testator's date of death, the executors become liable for the tax due including interest (which is payable 6 months after the date of death).[28] The tax will fall upon the residue of the estate and the executors have no right of indemnification against the recipient of the gift, unless the donor had taken a specific indemnity from the donee at the time of making the gift in question (this of course begs the question as to whether or not the donor had taken specialist advice before making the gift—if not then the likelihood of such an indemnity being available is minimal).

- Where the transfer in question amounts to a gift with reservation[29] and the recipient fails to pay the inheritance tax then again the residue of the testator's estate may suffer (although in this case the executors do have a statutory indemnity against the donee).[30]

If the draftsman fails to make enquiry on this point and the residue **10–24** eventually bears the brunt of the tax liability (through failure on the part

---

[27] For a consideration of the possibly complex calculations, see *Re Benham's Will Trusts* [1995] S.T.C. 210; and *Re Ratcliffe* [1999] S.T.C. 262.
[28] Inheritance Tax Act 1984, s.199(2) and 204(8).
[29] Section 102(3) of the Finance Act 1986.
[30] IHT Act 1984, s.311(3).

of the donee to settle the additional IHT liability), then again questions of negligence on the part of the draftsman may arise. Where the draftsman also finds himself in the position of executry solicitor, then his embarrassment may be compounded if he or she has failed to make due enquiry about potentially exempt transfers at the relevant stage (*i.e.* at the time of making the will) where a previously unknown potentially exempt transfer comes to light after the executors have obtained a clearance certificate, in such circumstances, the executors will have no protection owing to "failure to disclose material facts".[31] How does the draftsman and executry solicitor satisfy the executors on this point if, at the time of making the will for the testator, the draftsman asked no questions whatsoever about previous gifts?

By the same token, the testator may not wish there to be any question of a lifetime donee having to pay any inheritance tax on their gift, arising from the unexpected or untimely death of the testator. In those circumstances, the testator would require to decide whether or not he wishes to make some provision in his will which might cushion the effect on the lifetime transferee of having to pay an unexpected IHT liability. Obviously, this could be achieved by leaving a legacy to the lifetime transferee of the anticipated IHT liability on the lifetime gift. This is where careful drafting is required. Such a provision might be as follows:

> In respect that I have made a lifetime gift of (specify the relevant amount) to [   ], residing at [   ] in the event that I die so as to occasion said gift to be a chargeable transfer under the Inheritance Tax Act 1984 or any amendment or replacement therefor, then I bequeath to A that sum as will reimburse A for any liability to government tax or duty payable on such lifetime gift as a result of my death, my executors being sole judges as to the appropriate amount of such legacy.

Practical advice

10–25   The task of the draftsman is not just to deal with the question of distribution of the estate of the testator at the time the will has been made. The draftsman must always look backwards to establish whether or not there have been any gifts made during the testator's lifetime which could come back into account, and offer practical advice as to how any additional liability is to be addressed. The draftsman must not assume that the testator is aware that, in the first instance the donee will be liable, and as indicated above, the testator may be unhappy to discover that the value of a lifetime gift might be diluted by the donee having to pay tax (this assumes that the donee would at the relevant time be in a position to pay the tax in question). Where the donee is a beneficiary under the will, then the testator may be content that the executors would be entitled, on a failure by the lifetime donee to pay the relevant tax, to set the additional tax due against the benefit otherwise left to that donee in terms of the will.

Expenses

10–26   One of the most common misconceptions on the part of a client is that his estate will bear the costs of implementation of a bequest. In fact, where a will is silent, expenses of implementation fall to be borne by the

---

[31] IHT Act 1984, s.339(4).

legatee. Again, bearing in mind the *Holmes v Bank of Scotland*[32] decision, the draftsman must seek the client's views on this matter. Most clients will generally be happy that, in a straightforward case, their executors should be directed to give effect to bequests free of expense to the legatee (in which case the costs will be borne by the residue). However, the testator may wish to bequeath a large, heavy item of furniture to a beneficiary who lives many miles from the place where that item of furniture is situated at the testator's death. The costs incurred (including insurance, if the item is one of intrinsic value) could be quite large, and again the testator should be given the option as to whether those costs should be borne by the residue of his estate or by the legatee.[33]

INTEREST

The question of whether or not interest is or should be payable arises **10–27** really only in respect of pecuniary legacies. A bequest of an object which is not of itself income producing raises no implication of interest being payable.

This is again an important area where the draftsman needs to be wary of client misconceptions. Some clients will automatically assume (and consider it to be fair) that interest should be payable on a pecuniary legacy. Others may be content (and believe) that the legatee will receive the amount stated and no more than that.

Where a will is silent on the question of interest, then interest will be payable. There is no statutory rate and the rate itself will depend on the average rate yielded by the estate itself.[34] Where the estate itself produces no income, then, even where the right of interest on pecuniary legacies is not negatived, no interest on the legacy will be paid.[35]

Practical advice

At the time of taking instructions for the will and where the client **10–28** wishes to leave a pecuniary llegacy, instructions should be taken as to whether the pecuniary legacy is to bear interest, and if so at what rate. In the case of a special legacy (for example, a house subject to a tenancy and which is thereby yielding a rental) some care is required—inclusion of the general clause regarding incidence of tax, expenses and interest may prevent the beneficiary from entitlement to the rental income until the property has been made over to them on a formal basis. In the latter case, and if the rental is to be regarded as being due immediately to the relevant beneficiary from date of death, then this should be specifically stated.

If the client is content that no interest should be payable on the pecuniary legacy, then the inclusion of the general clause referred to above will suffice.

---

[32] 2002 S.L.T. 544; and 2002 S.C.L.R. 481 (cited above in Ch.2).
[33] See also the section on abatement of legacies in relation to the question of expenses of delivery, etc.
[34] *Waddell's Trustees v Crawford*, 1926 S.C. 654.
[35] *Greig v Merchant Company of Edinburgh*, 1921 S.C. 76.

If the client does wish to provide that interest will be payable on the pecuniary legacy, then instructions are required as to:

- The rate of interest to be paid.
- The date from which interest is to be payable.

In so far as the rate is concerned, clients should be encouraged to be realistic in their approach. An unrealistic rate of interest may erode the value of the residue (as the executors may be forced to look to income which would otherwise have fallen to the residue in order to meet an unduly high legacy rate). In so far as the date of payment is concerned, where the will is silent, interest will run from the date of death itself unless realisation of the estate was at that point impossible.

As most clients are unfamiliar with the intricacies and timescales involved in obtaining confirmation, it may be that a possible approach would be that interest at a specific rate will be payable from the date upon which confirmation was obtained (on the basis that until they have confirmation, executors would not in any event have been in a position to settle the pecuniary legacy in question). It might also be appropriate to remind the clients of the "six-month rule" (and the possible liabilities which executors might incur if they do not adhere thereto) when a client is reaching a decision as to whether or not, and from what date or point in time, interest should be payable on a pecuniary legacy.

EXECUTORS' AND TRUSTEES' POWERS

10–29 The granting of appropriate powers to executors and trustees, in order to ensure that they can most effectively carry out the wishes of the testator, is as important as properly interpreting the testator's wishes as to who should benefit from his estate. The draftsman requires to know when a simple powers clause will suffice and, on the other hand, when more detailed and very specific powers should be conferred by the will.

Where the administration of the estate is likely to be straightforward, with the executors simply uplifting and then distributing, then it is likely that common law and statutory powers conferred on the executors will be sufficient. However, with a more complex estate, and where the executors may require to hold funds for a considerable period of time (for example, pending vesting of beneficiaries), then it would be appropriate to provide the executors with more detailed powers, and also to limit the restrictions which might otherwise be imposed upon them by statutory powers.

Statutory powers

10–30 In the main, the powers available to trustees under statute can be found in sections 3 and 4 of the Trusts (Scotland) Act 1921. Section 3 of the 1921 Act states:

> "All trusts shall be held to include the following powers and provisions unless the contrary be expressed (that is to say):
>
> (a) Power to any trustee to resign the office of trustee;

(b) Power to the trustee, if there be only one, or to the trustees, if there be more than one, or to a quorum of the trustees, if there more than two, to assume new trustees;

(c) A provision that each trustee shall be liable for his own acts and intromissions and shall not be liable only for his own acts and intromissions and shall not be liable for the acts and intromissions of co-trustees and shall not be liable for omissions, provided that:

    (i) A sole trustee shall not be entitled to resign his office by virtue of this Act unless either (1) he has assumed new Trustees and they have declared their acceptance of office or (2) the court shall have appointed new trustees or a Judicial Factor as hereinafter in this Act provided; and

    (ii) A trustee who has accepted any legacy or bequest or annuity expressly given on condition of the recipient thereof accepting the office of trustee by virtue of this Act, unless otherwise expressly declared in the trust deed, nor shall any trustee appointed to the office of trustee on the footing of receiving remuneration for his services be entitled so to resign that office in absence of an express power to resign; but it shall be competent to the court, on the petition of any trustee to whom the foregoing provisions of this proviso apply, to grant authority to such trustee to resign the office of trustee on such conditions (if any) with respect to repayment or otherwise of his legacy as the court may think just; and

    (iii) A judicial factor shall not, by virtue of this Act, have the power of assumption, nor shall he have the power by virtue of this Act to resign his office without judicial authority.

Nothing in this section shall affect any liability incurred by any trustee prior to the date of any resignation or assumption under the provisions of this Act or of any Act repealed by this Act."

The formula provided under section 3 is that the relevant powers are **10–31** implied unless a contrary intention is stated in the trust deed. Section 4 of the 1921 Act enacts the following 17 general powers which may be exercised by trustees but only where such Acts are not at variance with the terms or purposes of the trust (section 4(1)). The general powers conferred (subject to the foregoing qualification) under section 4 are:

(1) to sell the trust estate or any part thereof, heritable as well as moveable;

(2) to grant feus of the heritable estate or any part thereof;

(3) to grant leases of any duration (including mineral leases) of the heritable estate or any part thereof and to remove tenants;

(4) to borrow money on the security of the trust estate or any part thereof, heritable as well as moveable;

(5) to excamb any part of the trust estate which is heritable;

(6) to acquire with funds of the trust estate any interest in residential accommodation (whether in Scotland or elsewhere)

reasonably required to enable the trustees to provide a suitable residence for occupation by any of the beneficiaries;

(7) to appoint factors and law agents and to pay them suitable remuneration;

(8) to discharge trustees who have resigned and the representatives of trustees who have died;

(9) to uplift, discharge, or assign debts due to the trust estate;

(10) to compromise or to submit and refer all claims connected with the trust estate;

(11) to refrain from doing diligence for the recovery of any debt due to the truster which the trustees may reasonably deem irrecoverable;

(12) to grant all deeds necessary for carrying into effect the powers vested in the trustees;

(13) to pay debts due by the truster or by the trust estate without requiring the creditors to constitute such debts where the trustees are satisfied that the debts are proper debts of the trust;

(14) to make abatement or reduction, either temporary or permanent, of the rent, lordship, royalty or other consideration stipulated in any lease of land, houses, tenements, minerals, metals or other subjects, and to accept renunciations of leases of any such subjects;

(15) to apply the whole or any part of trust funds which the trustees are empowered or directed by the trust deed to invest in the purchase of heritable property in the payment or redemption of any debt or burden affecting heritable property which may be destined to the same series of heirs and subject to the same conditions as are by the trust deed made applicable to heritable property directed to be purchased;

(16) to concur, in respect of any securities of a company (being securities comprised in the trust estate), in any scheme or arrangement:

   (a) for the reconstruction of the company,

   (b) for the sale of all or any part of the property and undertaking of the company to another company,

   (c) for the acquisition of the securities of the company, or of control thereof, by another company,

   (d) for the amalgamation of the company with another company, or

   (e) for the release, modification, or variation of any rights, privileges or liabilities attached to the securities or any of them, in like manner as if the trustees were entitled to such securities beneficially; to accept any securities of any denomination or description of the reconstructed or purchasing or new company in lieu of, or in exchange for, all or any of the first mentioned securities; and to retain any securities so accepted as aforesaid for any period for which the trustees could have properly retained the original securities;

(17) to exercise, to such extent as the trustees think fit, any conditional or preferential right to subscribe for any securities

in a company (being a right offered to them in respect of any holding in the company), to apply capital money of the trust estate in payment of the consideration, and to retain any such securities for which they have subscribed for any period for which they have power to retain the holding in respect of which the right to subscribe for the securities was offered (but subject to any conditions subject to which they have that power); to renounce, to such extent as they think fit, any such right; or to assign, to such extent as they think fit and for the best consideration that can reasonably be obtained, the benefit of such right or the title thereto to any person, including any beneficiary under the trust.

These general powers have been added to by applications under the *nobile officium*, petitions under sections 5 and 16 of the 1921 Act, and petitions for directions under the Court of Session Act 1988. The powers under the 1921 Act have also been expanded by later statutes.[36]

Powers granted by the court

Under section 5 of the 1921 Act, the trustees under any trust **10–32** (excluding a trust constituted by private or local act of parliament) may petition the court to grant authority to the trustees to carry out any of the acts detailed in section 4 notwithstanding that the proposed acts may be at variance with the terms or purposes of the trust. The court requires to be satisfied that the proposed Act is in all the circumstances expedient for the execution of the trust.

In terms of section 16 of the 1921 Act, the trustees may petition the court for authority to advance any part of the capital of a fund held either absolutely or contingently to beneficiaries, who at the date of the petition, are not of full age, if in the view of the trustees the income of the relevant fund may be insufficient (or not payable to such beneficiary), and also that advance is justified as being necessary for the maintenance or education of any such beneficiary. An advance of capital must not be prohibited by the trust deed, and where the right of such a beneficiary is contingent then this must be only upon his survivance.

Powers granted under the *nobile officium*

If trustees consider that an appropriate power is lacking, then they can **10–33** petition the Court of Session under the *nobile officium* of that court. A petition should be made only in a case of real expediency or necessity.[37] Such petitions have been used to afford the trustees wider powers of investment than are contained in the Trustee Investments Act 1961.[38] The *nobile officium* has also been used to authorise trustees to make payments of income for the maintenance and education of beneficiaries,[39] and also to obtain authorisation for advances which have already being made by the trustees.[40]

---

[36] Forrestry Act 1967, s.5(4), Sch.2, para.4(2); Countryside (Scotland) Act 1967, s.13(5); The Agriculture Act 1970, s.33(3); The Field Monuments Act 1972, s.1(4), Sch. para.2(2).
[37] *Gibsons Trustees* 1933 S.C. 190.
[38] See s.15 of the Act.
[39] Walker (1905) 13 S.L.T. 141 (O.H.).
[40] Christie's Trustees, 1932 S.C. 189.

Exercise of discretionary powers

10–34　　The powers afforded by a will may be expressed to be discretionary. If they are, then the trustees must exercise the same in good faith, reasonably and with care. Unless there are averments of bad faith, the court will not review the basis upon which trustees can exercise their discretion, although in *Train v Buchanan's Trustees*[41] it was indicated that the court would interfere if trustees took up "an impossible attitude" in respect of their refusal to exercise a discretion at all.

　　Where discretionary powers are granted, it is considered that care should be exercised in the drafting of the will to ensure that any assumed trustees will also share in that discretion.[42]

Short form of powers clause

10–35　　Where a will is, in very simple terms, vesting taking place at death (and not being postponed to a later date) but with no trust provisions, then a very simple executors' powers clause will suffice. The suggested wording is:

> My executors shall have the fullest powers of retention, realisation, investment, appropriation, transfer of property without realisation, and management of my estate as if they were the absolute beneficial owners thereof; and they shall have power to resign office and to appoint one or more of their own number to act as solicitor or agent in any other capacity and to allow him, her or them the same remuneration to which he, she or they would have been entitled if not an executor or executors.

Reference to the female form (*i.e.* "she", "her") is not essential. Reference to the male would include the female under the Interpretation Act 1978. It will be a matter of stylistic preference of the draftsman, although where one or more females are nominated to act as executor or executors, the draftsman may consider it appropriate not to raise feminine hackles by making deliberate omission of the female form.

　　The draftsman must be able to explain why a particular form of executors'/trustees' powers clause is to be, or has been, suggested. On occasions, when a power in favour of executors is expressed to enable the latter to deal with the testator's estate "as if they were absolute beneficial owners", this can cause concern to the testator who may misinterpret the same as giving the executors carte blanche in how the estate is distributed, notwithstanding the earlier beneficial terms of the will. Such concerns on the part of the testator can be allayed by the draftsman explaining at the outset that the powers are merely to enable executors to give full and proper effect (in the circumstances which they face at the relevant time) to the beneficial purposes of the will—the powers do not allow the executors to do as they wish with the beneficial purposes. Such concern, albeit misplaced, on the part of the testator is likely to be the more so where, in appropriate cases, the much longer form of executors'/trustees' powers clause is adopted.

---

[41] 1907 S.C. 517.
[42] *Laurie v Brown*, 1911 1 S.L.T. 84 (O.H.).

More extensive powers clause

As with the simple form of executors' powers, the draftsman should **10–36** take some care to avoid testator concern by explaining to the testator why such wide-ranging powers are being made available. Particularly if of a younger age, clients may have hopes and aspirations as to how their financial futures will develop, but at the end of the day cannot predict the same. That being so, the draftsman should explain to the testator that whilst it may transpire that some of the powers are not in fact required, it is better to be too expansive in the granting of powers than run the risk that trustees might find themselves to be hamstrung and require, for example, to resort to a petition to the Court of Session under the *nobile officium*

Many draftsmen prefer to incorporate the executors'/trustees' powers clause (however long) in the body of the will itself. Others will prefer to append a Schedule of Powers to the will. Whilst this can be convenient and save time, the following points need to be borne in mind if a Schedule of Powers is adopted.

The Schedule itself should be referred to in the main body of the will (section 8(1)(a))[43]— it should also be identified on its face as being the annexation referred to in the will (section 8(1)(b)).

For example:

"This is the Schedule of Powers referred to in the foregoing will by Joseph Bloggs."

There are two further points which require some thought in relation to the use of a Schedule of Powers.

(i) In some circumstances, the unthinking attachment of a Schedule of Powers might lead to the incorporation of a power which could be considered to be at variance with the purposes of the will itself. The will should state that the powers and the schedule are granted and available for use only in so far as they are not at variance with other purposes of the will.

(ii) The question of whether or not each page of the schedule should be subscribed (or indeed subscribed at all) needs to be considered. This is due to the fact that section 8(1) of the 1995 Act provides that, subject to the above two tests being met, any "annexation to a document shall be regarded as incorporated in the document . . . without the annexation having to be signed or subscribed". In the author's view this would be a dangerous course to follow in respect of the will, and to avoid any questions as to whether or not the schedule is properly part of the will, it is submitted that each page of the schedule should also be subscribed by the granter (to avoid falling foul of s.3 (2) of the Act).

A style of Schedule of Powers appears in the Appendix. A style of will incorporating the powers *in gremio* of the will has also been included in the Appendix.

---

[43] The Requirements of Writing (Scotland) Act 1995.

The following comments relate to the Schedule of Powers.

Condition

10–37

(a) Quorum—the question of an appropriate quorum has already been commented upon. In this particular case, the draftsman has taken account of the possibility that one or more of the executors may be abroad from time to time. The format of this particular quorum provision is therefore to ensure the smooth running of the executry whilst one or more executors are abroad, providing that the absent executor's power to act will be suspended during any period of absence from Great Britain. This is intended to elide the necessity of removal by the court of an executor who is absent from Great Britain continuously for a period of at least six months (and a similar provision applies in respect of an executor who has disappeared for the same length of time).[44]

(b) The purpose of this provision is to avoid the difficulties which can arise where executors/trustees are empowered to advance income or capital prior to the relevant vesting dates specified by the will and, having made such advances, the beneficiary in question dies before achieving the vesting age.

(c) Indemnity—this is a fairly standard clause. It does not offer absolute protection. In *Clark v Clark's Trustee*,[45] Lord President Clyde made it clear that an immunity clause could not be absolute when he said that:

> "It is difficult to imagine any clause of indemnity in a trust settlement could be capable of being construed to mean that the Trustees might with impunity neglect to exercise their duty as Trustees, in other words, that they were licensed to perform their duty with care."

The clause did, however, offer protection to trustees who in good faith have committed an error of judgment, but not if there has been a breach of the trust provisions.

(d) Discharge—the purpose of this provision is to prevent the difficulties which can arise where a charity has changed its name or may have amalgamated with or transferred its assets to another similar charity, or indeed may have been mis-designed in the first instance. Given that the executors are provided with a degree of discretion, this can avoid unnecessary litigation. English charities are required to ensure that they obtain all benefits bequeathed to them by will, and where there has been disastrous drafting, litigation might be required to resolve the issue. Conclusion of a provision of this type is designed to avoid that outcome. In the case of *Scottish Missionary Society v Home Mission Committee of the General Assembly of the Church of*

---

[44] Trusts (Scotland) Act 1921, s.23 as amended by the Law Reform (Miscellaneous Provisions) (Scotland) Act, 1980, s.13(b) applied to Executors by Executors (Scotland) Act 1900, s.2.
[45] 1925 S.C. 693.

Scotland,[46] the legacy was to "The Scottish Missionary Society of the Established Church". The court felt that the legacy was payable to the Scottish Missionary Society which had no specific connection with any Established Church (see also *Russell's Executor v Balden*[47]).

It is normal to provide that the receipt of an authorised official of a charity or similar such body will be a sufficient discharge to the executors in order to avoid confusion as to who is entitled or empowered to grant such a receipt to the executors.

General powers

The "lead in" section is very similar to the simple style referred to **10–38** above. However, specific powers are also granted so as to widen executors' powers or to ensure that they are not made subject to restrictions which would otherwise be implied at common law or at statute (for example, specific power to allow an executor to act as *auctor in rem suam*, which would otherwise be prohibited at common law).

Specific powers

Just as the shorter form of powers clause does not entitle the **10–39** executors to act at variance with the purposes of the will, a similar consideration applies to the longer form of clause containing specific and extended powers. These powers still require to be exercised in furtherance of the terms of the will. Where the more extended form of powers clause is adopted, the draftsman must be able to explain to the testator why specific powers are included. There are various explanations/reasons which can be brought to bear.

- No one can predict the future. That being so it is advisable not to hamstring trustees by refusing to grant powers which may be required in the future. For example, sometime after making his will, the client may be made redundant. At that point, he may decide to use his redundancy monies to open a business. In such circumstances, it would be necessary to include a specific power to enable a trustee to be paid to run that business on death of the client. In statistical terms, something like 87 per cent of sole trader businesses effectively "die" along with the sole trader. In these circumstances, executors will be left only to carry out an asset-stripping exercise, the value of which to the deceased's estate may be very much less than the executors being able to continue the business in the hope of selling the same on as a going concern.
- Just as the individual cannot predict his own future, the type of tax regime which might be brought into play after the testator's death cannot be foreseen. In some circumstances the trustees might wish to have power to move the trust abroad to escape what is perceived to be an unduly harsh regime of taxation.

---

[46] (1858) 20 D.634.
[47] 1989 S.L.T. 188.

- Clients should not assume that the executors have power to do as they like (and in fact many testators will be comforted to know that the executors will not have carte blanche). However, it should also be explained that unless specific powers are granted (such as to allow shares to be registered in the name of a nominee—this is a service now offered by all stockbrokers), then the power is not implied.
- In particular, there may be occasions where it would be appropriate to allow an executor to transact with the estate. However, unless specifically authorised to act as *auctor in rem suam*, then even a beneficial transaction with an executor will be prohibited (this would include power to pay a particular trustee for exercising his skills in running the business of a deceased's testator).
- Even beneficial transactions with third parties may not be possible unless the third parties are reassured that the trustees do indeed have the specific power to enter into the transaction in question.

Taking time and care to explain the foregoing to the testator can overcome what might be otherwise understandable "customer reluctance" in so far as the granting of wide powers are concerned.

10–40   Dealing with the powers in the style Schedule, the following are of note:

1.&2. Sale and purchase of executry estate. Taken together, these powers would allow executors to transact with the executry estate, particularly where this may be seen to be beneficial.

3. Retention—this is reasonably self evident. The trustees could also be granted a power to restrict or to withhold the payment. In *Whyte's Trustees v Whyte's Trustees*,[48] in exercise of a discretion of power to withhold from a sequestrated beneficiary income in excess of a reasonable allowance to maintain that beneficiary, trustees were held to have acted properly on the basis that the trustee in sequestration of the bankrupt beneficiary could only obtain from the trustees that to which the beneficiary in question was himself entitled.

4. Investment—the purpose of this clause is to free the trustees from the restrictions otherwise imposed by common law or by statute. For example, section 15 of the Trusts (Scotland) Act 1921 prohibits investment in Bearers Securities. Similarly, historically a "deposit" has not been considered as an investment as such. Notwithstanding the seemingly wide power granted in terms of this clause, however, the trustees must still bear in mind the interest of the beneficiary.

5. Nominees—this power has been mentioned above but is one which must be specifically granted, as otherwise, at common law, trustees are required to take command of the trust estate, including registration of investments, in their names as trustees.

---

[48] 1917 S.L.T. 272 (O.H.).

The ability to register securities in the name of nominees can save time. For example, where a shareholding is registered in the name of stockbroker nominees then a transaction with that shareholding will be relatively straightforward and can avoid the delays which can occur where a number of trustees are required to sign stock transfers, etc.

6. Borrowing—although there is a statutory power to borrow (see the reference to section 4 of the Trust (Scotland) Act 1921 above), this particular clause contains an element of discretion not otherwise available under the statutory power.

7. Policies of assurance—this gives the trustees very wide powers in relation not only to policies which might be considered to be investments, but also in relation to buildings, etc. insurances. The power gives the trustees greater flexibility to enable them to give effect to their general duty to preserve the trust estate.

8. Management of heritable property—this is a wider power than otherwise conferred by section 2(1) of the Trust (Scotland) Act 1921, and again gives the trustees a wider discretion than is available under statute.

9. Companies—again this reflects one of the powers contained in section 4 of the Trust (Scotland) Act 1921. However, it also allows executors to act in a manner which would otherwise be prohibited as contravening the principle *auctor in rem suam* (*i.e.* the right to retain emoluments paid to an "executor director").

10. Proxies—at common law, trustees should not delegate any of their powers. The convenience of being able to do so is demonstrated by this clause.

11. Compromise of claims—normally it is the duty of the executors to protect the executry estate by resort to litigation if necessary.[49]

12. Apportionment—it can be of great assistance to the trustees to be empowered to decide what is income and what is capital. This can be particularly valuable in enabling the trustees to decide on what expenses incurred should be charged against income, and what against capital. It can assist in avoiding disputes between beneficiaries and can avoid the necessity for complex calculations.

13. Loans to beneficiaries—at common law executors cannot lend, even to beneficiaries, without security. The ability to lend on an interest-free basis might also be of considerable assistance to a beneficiary who wishes to purchase a dwelling-house.

14. Accommodation—in terms of section 4(1)(e) of the 1921 Act, trustees do have power to provide a suitable residence for occupation by any of the beneficiaries.[50] The power is restricted to any beneficiary in the estate and cannot be extended to strangers. The power expressed goes beyond that detailed in section 4 by, for example, allowing the executor specific power to improve, decorate, reconstruct or add to (*i.e.* extend) such a

[49] *Martin v City of Edinburgh District Council*, 1988 S.L.T. 329.
[50] *Moss's Trustees v King*, 1952 S.C.S. 23.

dwelling-house. It should be noted that the power makes specific reference to "any dwelling-house". If the property in question is not "a dwelling-house" as normally defined then this purpose would require some amendment.

15. Appropriation of investments—there are various aspects to this power:

  - The trustees can appropriate specific investments or property to represent all or part of the share of the beneficiary. Thereafter the interest of that beneficiary will be tied to the assets appropriated notwithstanding how other assets within the trust may perform.
  - The trustees are empowered to determine the valuation at which specific assets are so appropriated. This enables the trustees to determine the value of awkward assets such as shares in a private limited company.
  - Exercise of power does not, however, allow the trustees to ignore the main provisions of the trust. For example, where a beneficiary has a prospective one-quarter share, the trustees would not be entitled to allocate one-half of the trust assets to that beneficiary—this would be at variance with the main trust purposes and would adversely affect the remaining beneficiaries.

16. Satisfaction of bequests in cash or in kind—unless specifically authorised to do so, trustees cannot settle beneficiaries' interest by transferring specific assets of the trust to the beneficiary. This power falls to be distinguished from the "appropriation" power—the former is utilised during "the running" of the trust whereas the "satisfaction" power is utilised to distribute assets of the trust to beneficiaries when they vest absolutely in the capital of the trust.

17. Resignation—this power is specifically included to cover the position of a trustee who has been paid for accepting appointment or as an agent of the trust. Without this power, such a trustee in resigning would still be held liable, notwithstanding such resignation, as if he were still a trustee. Many testators will still wish to recognise the time and trouble which a trustee is likely to expend by leaving to a trustee a legacy expressed to be conditional upon the latter accepting office. This clause would allow such a trustee to resign office.

18. Appointment of agents—the statutory power[51] to appoint agents and to pay them suitable remuneration does not extend to a trustee acting in a professional capacity in seeking to charge his normal fees. Without specific authorisation as indicated in this clause, this could be deemed to be the trustee acting as *auctor in rem sum*.

19. Payment of expenses—this clause is reasonably self-explanatory.

20. General—as previously noted, this general clause can, on occasions, occasion concern to the testator. It does *not* allow the executors to act at variance with the purposes of the will.

---

[51] Trust (Scotland) Act 1921, s.4(1)(f).

21. Business—without such a specific power being granted, trustees have, save for one possible exception, no power to continue a business. In *MacKechnie's Trustees v Mcadam*,[52] a court held that trustees could carry on a business but only for so long as was required to avoid having to sell the business at a loss. Whilst this particular power goes beyond mere continuance of an existing business (and allows participation in a new business), in most cases it is unlikely that trustees or executors would wish to involve themselves in the creation of a new business enterprise. The powers as granted are, however, vital if a continuing business is to be continued. The important aspects here are:

- It allows the trustees to seek to continue the business for such period of time as will allow the business to be realised at "best price" for the beneficiaries. Where the business is not continued, then, at least in theory, goodwill evaporates and all the trustees may be left to oversee is the sale off (effectively on an asset-stripping basis) of individual assets.
- The power recognises that the trustees themselves may not have the skills or time to engage fully in the running of the business. They are therefore empowered to engage and pay others having the appropriate skills to run and manage the business, pending sale at the best realisable price of the same. The immunity or obligation of relief granted to the trustees would not extend to gross negligence in running of the business. Where a trustee becomes involved in the running of the business then he will be allowed to retain any salary paid for those services—without this provision, the trustee could again fall foul of the normal prohibition against acting as *auctor in rem suam*.

22. Promotion of companies—this power is really a refinement of the foregoing power in relation to the running of a business. It may be considered appropriate where the business in question is in fact a limited company and the testator wishes to more specifically outline his trustee's powers in that connection.

Know your client

Completion of an appropriate "fact find" in respect of the client at the **10–41** outset is of importance. Having knowledge of the client's existing business and other activities will enable the draftsman to more readily explain the importance and value of many of the more detailed powers hereinbefore referred to. It is submitted that failure to include power to continue to operate a business might in fact be challenged in retrospect as professional negligence, unless of course the trustees can bring themselves within the provisions of *MacKechnie's Trustees v Mcadam*.[53]

---

[52] 1912 S.C. 1059.
[53] Cited above.

THE TRUSTEE ACT 2000

10–42 This Act applies to England and Wales only. It was introduced after wide consultation and a review of the Law of Trusts applying south of the border. The Society of Trust and Estate Practitioners played an important role in the consultation process and in the work required to prepare for the legislation in question. This role was acknowledged by both Parliament and the Law Commission.

The Act itself comprises five main parts:

- Part I—The Duty of Care
- Part II—Investment
- Part III—Acquisition of Land
- Part IV—Agents' Nominees and Custodians
- Part V—Remuneration.

Although some concerns have been expressed regarding the question of the duty of care, the investment powers conferred by the Act have been largely welcomed. In effect, trustees can make any type of investment (as if they had been the owners of the fund in question), with exception of the acquisition of land which is of course the subject of a separate part on its own. In that connection, Part III of the Act allows trustees a new power—to acquire freehold or leasehold land (which must be within the United Kingdom) for any purpose.

The general thrust of the Act is that trustees will have all of the powers allowed thereunder save in so far as these are inconsistent with the trust deed itself.

The Act has been generally welcomed, in particular to the "freeing up" of trustees' powers of investment. It would appear that English practitioners regard the Act as representing a major advance in this area, although, as indicated, concerns have been expressed regarding the question of the duty of care and indeed the possibility within the Act of excluding the same.

Position in Scotland

10–43 The 2000 Act does not apply in Scotland. Unfortunately, once again, we appear to be lagging behind England in relation to what has been conceived to be a welcome law reform. For example, the 2000 Act repeals large parts of the Trustee & Investment Act 1961, thereby "freeing up" investment (subject to the qualification hereinbefore detailed) in so far as trustees are concerned. However, Scottish practitioners presently still have to operate under the "old" regime. At the time of writing, it is understood that the Scottish Executive are examining this area with particular reference to the Report of the Scottish Law Commission on Trustees' Powers and Duties.[54]

General note

10–44 The draftsmen should bear in mind that trustees will only have the powers conferred by statute or at common law or specifically conferred in terms of the trust deed. However, it is submitted that, pending

---

[54] No. 172.

legislative change in Scotland, there is no reason why Scottish draftsmen should not specifically incorporate within Scottish wills, etc. the powers now afforded in England under the 2000 Act.

CHAPTER 11

LEGACIES

DRAFTING CONSIDERATIONS

11–01 The draftsman must bear in mind that, just as there are different types of legacies, the views of the testator as to the order of importance of different bequests which he leaves need to be taken into account. In fact, it is submitted that, historically, this is a matter in which the legal profession has not, as a general rule, offered succinct advice. The testator will, for the most part, direct the terms of his new will, taking into account his financial position at the time the will is made. The legal profession appears to have been comfortable that this should be the case. However, given the new climate in which draftsmen will need to operate, it may well be that it will become a standard practice to encourage a testator to consider what, if any priority, should be accorded to his bequests in the event of a financial disaster, causing the testator's estate to shrink in size. The general rules as to priority in satisfaction of settlement of different types of legacy need to be borne in mind by the draftsman when he is framing the will for his client.

PRIORITY OF DEBTS AND FUNERAL EXPENSES

11–02 Settlement of debts and funeral expenses always takes priority over the beneficial aspects of the will. That being so, if the debts, etc. exceed the value of the estate, all legacies will fail. A testator cannot avoid this result by simply stating in his will that certain legacies are to be met notwithstanding the debt burden effecting the testator's estate. Historically, the priority afforded to debts and funeral expenses was reflected in the drafting of a will by inclusion of a specific direction to the executors to settle debts and funeral expenses. This clause normally appeared after the appointment of executors/trustees, perhaps to focus the mind of the testator on this priority. More modern draftsmen often choose to omit any clause directing payments of debts and funeral expenses on the basis that, in strict terms, the inclusion of such a clause is not necessary—the executors stand *eadem personam cum defuncto* as the deceased testator, and therefore are bound to settle his debts.

TYPES OF LEGACY

11–03 Legacies can be classified as falling into one of the following four main types:

- Specific or special legacies;
- Demonstrative legacies;
- General legacies;
- Bequest of residue.

The order in which the above types of legacy has been set out is not accidental, as it reflects the priority afforded to the different types of legacy in implementing the terms of a will (see below).

Specific or special legacies

A specific or special legacy is one of a particular, identified item which **11–04** forms part of the testator's estate. A specific legacy can be of virtually any type of estate—heritable or moveable, corporeal or incorporeal. A specific or special legacy can be subject to ademption if the subject of the bequest no longer forms part of the estate of the testator as at his death. Where the will is silent on this point, a specific legacy will normally require to bear the expenses of delivery or implementation of the same. A specific legacy comes *first* in the order of priority of settlement, after payment of death and funeral expenses.

Demonstrative legacies

A demonstrative legacy is one which is payable out of a specific, **11–05** identified fund or other source. Most commonly, a demonstrative legacy is a pecuniary or monetary one. However, it need not be pecuniary—for example, it could be an entitlement on the part of the beneficiary to choose stamps to a certain value (as determined by the executor) from the existing larger stamp collection of the testator.

If the specified fund or source does not exist as at the testator's death (for example, if the stamp collection referred to above had been sold by the deceased prior to his death), then a demonstrative legacy from that source will adeem. However, unlike a general legacy, the demonstrative legacy will not abate.[1]

General legacies

A general legacy comes next in the order of priority of settlement. A **11–06** legacy of a specific sum of money is a general legacy (as noted above, if the sum in question falls to be paid from a specific source, such as a bank account, then the legacy will be demonstrative in nature). The main difference between a specific legacy and a general legacy is that a general legacy does not adeem.[2] However, where the residue is insufficient to enable general legacies to be settled in full, then general legacies will abate.

Legacy of residue

A bequest of the residue or share therein comes last in the order of **11–07** priority of settlement. The residue is what remains after settlement of all debts, funeral expenses and taxes as also satisfaction of all other types of

---

[1] *Douglas' Executors v Scott* (1869) 7 M. 504.
[2] *Wilmot v Jenkins* (1838) 1 D. 401.

legacy. As such, a residuary legatee has no right to any particular asset within the testator's estate.[3] A legacy of a share of the residue of the testator's estate will abate, but will not adeem (although the effect of abatement can mean that there is no residue left to satisfy any legacies of residue).

ADEMPTION

11–08 Ademption can arise in respect of specific legacies where the item in question is no longer owned by the testator at his death. Ademption can also affect demonstrative legacies where, similarly, the source from which the demonstrative legacy was to be settled is no longer within the ownership of the testator at death. In that regard, the intention of the testator is irrelevant. The only question which requires to be satisfied is whether or not the item in question remained part of his estate at death. However, the item in question does not require to remain in the exact or same form in which it had existed at the time the will was made. The question of whether or not ademption has applied can be a difficult problem:

- Where the item in question has been sold and title thereto has passed, ademption will apply. However, if title has not passed, ademption has been held not to apply. In *McArthur's Executors v Guild*[4] the testator had bequeathed a hotel to his daughter. However, prior to his death, the testator had entered into a contract of sale of the hotel. Title had not passed as the contract was conditional upon the hotel licence being transferred. This had not occurred as at the date of death and in deciding the matter, the court felt that the daughter was entitled to the sale price, the legacy not having adeemed.
- With regard to government stock, if the stock is compulsorily reacquired by the Treasury prior to the testator's death, then it has been held that ademption did not apply and the beneficiary was entitled to receive the compulsory acquisition price.[5] When a holding of government stock has been converted from one denomination to another, and where the latter is still held by the testator at death, then the beneficiary will be entitled to the latter—ademption has not applied.
- It should be noted that a holding of stock appears to be in a different situation from a holding of shares in a company. In *Westminster Bank Ltd v O'Conner*[6] it was held that a legacy of stock is a general (and not specific) one. Even though the testator did not in fact retain the stock as at his date of death, ademption did not apply to general legacies.
- A legacy of shares (as opposed to stock) is not, however, a general legacy and ademption may apply if no shares represent-

---

[3] *Cochrane's Executors v Inland Revenue*, 1974 S.C. 158.
[4] 1908 S.C. 743.
[5] *Borne, Re, Bailey v Bailey* [1944] Ch.190.
[6] 1948 C.H. 628

ing the original holding remain within the testator's ownership at death. However, it has been held that a shareholding which has been reorganised or converted into a different form of security will not adeem.[7]

- A legacy of a debt adeems if the debt has been repaid prior to death.

Practical problems and advice

As indicated in Chapter 1 (paragraph 1–18), the fact that a particular **11–09** item has been made the subject of a special bequest in no way disentitles the testator from selling or otherwise disposing of the item in question during his lifetime. After making the relevant will, the financial affairs of the testator may change for the worse. Sale of an item specifically bequeathed may be a necessary part of the testator's revised financial planning.

In relation to ademption, there is general advice which can be offered to the client and also specific drafting techniques which can be applied.

General advice

The draftsman should always be aware of client misconceptions.   **11–10**

- Some testators may genuinely believe that if they dispose of an item otherwise specifically bequeathed in their will then the legatee will still be entitled to the value of that item, to be paid out of the residue of their estate. The draftsman should therefore make it clear that whilst the testator remains free to deal with the item in question as he sees fit during his lifetime. If he does dispose of it then the testator will require to consider whether the bequest should be fulfilled in some other way (see below), as otherwise there will be no benefit for the legatee in question.
- In the case (albeit unusual) of a solicitor requiring to advise a client who is a creditor of the testator and who, rather than pressing for payment of the debt due, has agreed that the debt will be settled by the debtor bequeathing a specific item (normally more valuable than the debt itself) to the creditor in his will, then the solicitor needs to advise the creditor that his rights may be affected if the testator debtor has sold or otherwise disposed of the item in question during his lifetime. A possible solution might be for the creditor to insist that the debtor:
  - (i) enter into a written agreement regarding the debt in question (thereby making the same enforceable beyond doubt as against the executors).
  - (ii) provides that if the "promised" item is no longer owned by the testator debtor as at his date of death then the executors will otherwise pay a legacy of a specified amount to the creditor.

---

[7] *Mitchell's Trustees v Ferguson* (1889) 11 R. 902.

- It is appropriate (if not a necessity) to advise clients that they should regularly review their wills. Where this advice is followed, the client can for his own part (subject to any lapses of memory) identify whether or not a special legacy will need to be amended in some way to reflect the fact that the client has already disposed of the item in question. Having identified that the item in question has been disposed of, and the testator is satisfied that it should not be replaced in some shape or form, then it would be appropriate for the testator to place an informal writing with his will confirming effective and deliberate cancellation of the special legacy in question. Where the testator wishes to replace the item in question with another form of bequest, then this can be achieved by an informal writing or, preferably, a codicil to the will.

Drafting solutions

11–11   Generally speaking, a draftsman should be aware of the possibility of ademption arising where the testator wishes to bequeath any specific item of his estate. This applies to particular types of item which clients will often wish to make the subjects of a specific legacy, namely:

- Houses;
- Motor vehicles;
- Shareholdings or bank accounts.

The draftsman should take the specific instructions of the testator as to whether the bequest is to be restricted to that specific item alone, or whether in the event of the item having been disposed of or replaced with something different, the testator wishes to cover the latter possibility in his will. In the former case, the testator could make his wishes clear by adding appropriate wording to his will; for example:

> "and I direct that in the event that I have disposed of or no longer own the foregoing item as at my death then this legacy will be deemed to have adeemed and be of no further force and effect."

In many cases, however, when the possibility of ademption is pointed out to the testator, he will make it clear that the bequest is not to be restricted to the specific item in question, but rather should extend to any direct replacement therefor.

DWELLING-HOUSES

11–12 Clients often fail to look beyond the assets which they own at the time of making the relevant will. They have to be encouraged to adopt a wider viewpoint, thus a bequest of "my dwelling-house at 1 Brown Street, Anytown" will adeem if the testator has sold that dwelling-house and bought another prior to his death. The draftsman must always bear in mind that the client will look to the former to guide him. If, on issuing instructions, the draftsman does not query whether the bequest is to apply to a specific or any dwelling-house, then the testator is likely to operate on the basis of an assumption which is, in fact, incorrect. The draftsman must query whether a bequest of a dwelling-house is to be restricted to a particular property or whether the testator intends a wider interpretation. In most cases, when the point is highlighted to the testator, it is likely that he will indicate that he intends the dwelling-house which he owns as at his date of death.

Such a viewpoint should be covered by making it clear that the bequest of the testator's dwelling-house applies to the dwelling-house of the testator as at his date of death. For example:

> "my dwelling-house at 1 Brown Street, Anytown or such other dwelling-house as is owned and occupied by me as at my date of death."

Again, care in drafting is required. The testator may own two or more properties which at different times of the year are occupied as his dwelling-house. In such circumstances a simple bequest of "any dwelling-house owned by me as at my date of death" may have the distorting effect of carrying all of those properties to the beneficiary. Equally, and given that no one can predict the future, a bequest of "such heritable property as is owned and occupied by me as my dwelling-house as at my date of death" may result in the beneficiary receiving a property of a lesser value than the testator had intended. The draftsman has to be able to ensure that the testator considers the foregoing points and is clear as to his wishes.

Equally, the testator may make his will at a point in time where he **11–13** owns and occupies a sizeable dwelling-house and his health is generally good. However, as the years pass, it may be that the testator will need to enter a care home, with his dwelling-house being sold to fund the relevant costs of the same. If the failure in health also involves loss of capacity then it will be too late for the testator to change his will so as to provide some other, suitable alternative for the beneficiary. This could be covered at the time of the making of the will by the testator, for example, making an alternative provision. For example:

> "and in the event that I own no such dwelling-house as at my date of death then in place therefor, I bequeath to the said . . . a legacy of THIRTY THOUSAND POUNDS (£30,000) STERLING free of government taxes and duties payable upon my death but without interest to date of payment."

If a testator wishes to offer a replacement legacy equivalent to the value of the property at the time it was sold, then the legacy could be specifically of the sale price at the relevant time, although it might be prudent to add to the relevant clause a provision allowing the executors to decide the amount of that sale price. For example:

> "as to which my executors shall be the sole judges".

This will avoid a dispute as to whether or not the value to be paid was the gross price of the property, or the net price after deduction of estate agency, legal and other costs in connection with the sale.

MOTOR VEHICLES

11–14 Similar considerations will apply to a bequest of a motor vehicle as to that of a dwelling-house. When the matter is put to the client, the testator may feel that a clause bequeathing "any motor vehicle" owned by him as at his date of death should cover the awkward question of possible ademption. However, the draftsman should point out that if the testator owned two or more motor vehicles as at his date of death, then the bequest would carry all of the same to the beneficiary. This may be more than the testator would wish, in which case very specific wording will be required.

Where the testator only owns one motor vehicle which he wishes to bequeath, then to avoid ademption applying in the event of the testator replacing that vehicle with another prior to his death, a small addition to the relevant clause should suffice. For example:

> "or any replacement therefor which I own as at my date of death as to which my executors shall be the sole judges".

Again, the addition of the discretionary power on the part of the executors should be made so as to allow the executors flexibility. A provision (where required by the testator) to allow the legacy to apply to an appropriate replacement can of course be utilised in respect of any specific item of the testator's estate.

BANK ACCOUNTS AND SHAREHOLDINGS

11–15 In *Ballantyne's Trustees v Ballantyne's Trustees*,[8] the court decided that a specific bequest of a bank account adeemed where the bank account was moved from one branch of the bank to another, within the same bank. In recent years, many of the clearing banks have closed branches, forcing customers to move accounts to other branches. The dangers here for the client are obvious. If the testator wishes to bequeath a specific bank account, then, to avoid ademption, the relevant provision would require amendment so as to allow the executor to extend the bequest to any replacement account opened with the same bank, even at a different branch of that bank. For example:

> "or any replacement account with the Bank of Scotland (wheresoever held) as to all of which my executors shall be the sole judges."

There is in fact merit in raising with the testator why a bequest in such format (*i.e.* of a bank account) should be left. The same end could be achieved by leaving a pecuniary legacy (which, being of a general nature, does not adeem). The testator, however, may feel that a bequest of a sum at credit of a particular bank account will allow the testator flexibility in relation to the benefit which the particular legatee is to

---

[8] 1941 S.C. 35.

obtain. As the bequest will be of the sum at credit of the account as at the date of death, including accrued interest, the testator may feel that this format of bequest will enable him to control the likely level of benefit to the legatee in question. It is submitted that it is incumbent on the draftsman to point out that the testator may, for various reasons, not be able to exercise the control which he had anticipated. For example, the account in question may contain £100,000. The testator may recognise that this would be too large a sum to leave to the particular legatee, it being the intention of the testator that he will direct transfers from the account in order to bring the level of the same down to the type of level which the testator intended should amount to the benefit to the particular legatee. However, on the basis that "no man knows what the day may bring", this could be misguided planning. If, for example, the testator were to suffer a stroke which deprived him of capacity, then his prior planning may be totally frustrated, again with a wholly distorting effect on the thrust of his will.

A similar prudent attitude would apply in relation to a proposed **11–16** bequest of a shareholding in a quoted company. Unlike a holding of government stock, a shareholding in a quoted company is a special bequest and may be subject to ademption. Again, over recent years there have been recapitalisations, mergers, demergers, hivings-off, etc., all of which could cause difficulty with such a bequest (and this should be explained to the testator).

However, where the testator insists that he wishes to leave a specific bequest of a particular shareholding, then the relevant provision should be amended by the addition of wording as follows:

> "or such other shares or other security as may represent the same at the time of my death as a result of any change of name, amalgamation, takeover or a reorganisation of such company, as to all of which my executors shall be the sole judges."

The foregoing addition would not of course cover the situation where the shares, held as an investment, are sold and replaced with a holding of shares in a wholly different company. Where such transactions occur, then, unless the will makes a suitable provision, ademption will take place. It would be possible to try and cover this situation by the inclusion of the provision of additional wording, for example:

> "or of any shares, securities or stock acquired by me at any time in replacement for those shares, as to all of which my executors shall be the sole judges."

Similar considerations and difficulties can apply in relation to other "investment" assets belonging to the testator, such as personal equity plans, unit trusts, etc.

GENERAL DRAFTING ADVICE

The draftsman has to be aware not only of his responsibilities to the **11–17** testator, but also to the beneficiaries under the will. The possibility of ademption cannot be ignored. Where a testator wishes to leave specific bequests, then the draftsman should seek to follow the following course:

- ensure that the testator is aware of the nature and effect of ademption (obviously the draftsman properly recording the advice given).
- establish the attitude of the testator to the possibility that a specific bequest may adeem. If the testator would wish ademption to apply if the item is no longer owned by him, then, if only on a self-protective basis, there is no reason why the draftsman should not include a specific statement within the bequest itself to that effect.
- where a testator would not wish ademption to apply, incorporate suitable provisions which would, so far as possible, seek to avoid this outcome. However, the testator may need to be reminded that the value of the item in question may greatly increase between the execution of the will and his date of death.
- be unafraid (in relation to specific items such as bank accounts and shareholdings) to seek to examine in the first place the reasons of the testator for wishing to leave a bequest of those specific items. A brief explanation of the difficulties which might arise (even with careful drafting) may be sufficient to persuade the testator to adopt another approach. This may be, for example, to provide a legacy of the sale price of the item in question (sold prior to the testator's death), or some other provision to compensate the beneficiary (such as a pecuniary legacy).
- recognise that it may not be possible to cover every possibility—to attempt to do so could unduly convolute the will and cause confusion.
- advise the testator that he should regularly review his will, not only in relation to changes in his family or in his general financial position, but also on the question of whether or not the subject-matter of a particular bequest still exists. Even where the draftsman has sought to cover the possibility of ademption, it would be appropriate to advise the testator that at all times he should not be unwilling to seek further advice on whether a particular change in his asset base points to preparation of a codicil, or perhaps a new will.

The Legacy *Rei Alienae*

11–18 This is an area where the benefit in completing a comprehensive examination of the composition and value of a testator's estate is demonstrated. The *legatum rei alienae* arises where, in his will, the testator provides that a specific bequest is to be made over to a legatee of an item which the testator does not own at his date of death. If it is established that the testator was aware that he did not own the item in question, then the bequest will be interpreted as an instruction to the executors to buy the item for the legatee if possible, and if not possible, to pay over to the legatee the value of the item bequeathed. If it is demonstrated that the testator did not realise that the item did not belong to him, the legacy will fail. The onus of proof lies with the legatee seeking to uphold the legacy *rei alienae*—the court will not presume such knowledge on the part of the testator.[9]

For various reasons, it is submitted that the draftsman should seek to discourage a bequest of such a legacy.

- Litigation may be required to establish the true nature of the bequest.
- The executors may be put to some trouble and expense in securing a "difficult" asset, if it is established that a legacy *rei alienae* has been granted.
- Where the asset in question cannot be obtained, difficulties as to its true value (and the sum to be made over to the legatee in place therefor) may be the subject of dispute.
- It is possible that the asset in question will become much more valuable (and therefore more expensive) than the testator had envisaged at the time of making his will. This could have a wholly distorting effect on implementation of the remaining provisions of the will and, in particular, in regard to the residue (which will require to bear the brunt of the expense to be incurred in implementing a legacy *rei alienae*).
- The value of the testator's estate at death is likely also to be uncertain. The value of the estate, occasioned by stock market fluctuations or unforeseen financial difficulties encountered by the testator after the will has been made, could equally distort the eventual thrust of the testator's will, particularly if the executors have to satisfy an expensive legacy *rei alienae*.

If the draftsman has carried out a comprehensive information-building **11–19** process prior to the drafting of the will, this may enable the draftsman to identify whether or not problems with the ownership of the particular bequest may give rise to a legacy *rei alienae*. Equally, the draftsman's responsibilities to the intended beneficiary should be borne in mind. The beneficiary may not be best pleased to have to convince a court of the true state of the testator's knowledge. Thus, if a testator cannot be persuaded from bequeathing a deliberate legacy *rei alienae*, then the draftsman should ensure that the relevant provision makes it perfectly clear that a deliberate legacy *rei alienae* is intended. It is submitted that there is no reason why the bequest should not make it clear that the testator acknowledges that at the time of making the bequest he does not own the item in question, *i.e.* that the instruction is specifically that the executors should acquire the same for the intended beneficiary. Where the item in question cannot be obtained, then the testator should consider placing a maximum value on the funds otherwise to be made over to the beneficiary. As an alternative, the relevant provision could provide a "compensatory" legacy to the beneficiary, not necessarily of the value of the item which has otherwise proven impossible to acquire. Again, the drafting should be sufficiently constructed so as to make it clear that it is intended that if the specific item cannot be obtained, then the legacy to be paid in its place is not directly related to the value of the item in question. For example:

---

[9] *Meeres v Dowell's Executor*, 1923 S.L.T. 184 (O.H.).

"in the event that it shall not prove possible for my executors to acquire the said item (as to which my executors shall be the sole judges) within six months of my date of death then the foregoing bequest shall be of no further force and effect but in place therefor I direct my executors to pay to . . . a legacy of TEN THOUSAND POUNDS (£10,000) STERLING free of all government taxes and duties payable on my death but without interest to date of payment which legacy for the avoidance of doubt is not related to the value of the bequest hereinbefore detailed . . . "

It is important that again the executors should enjoy some degree of discretion as to the circumstances in which it would not prove possible to acquire the specified item within the time-limit imposed. Such circumstances would obviously include unwillingness of the present owner of the item to sell the same, or the inability of the executors to "source" the item within the relevant time-limit, as it might be that no such item is available for sale to the executors within the relevant time-limit.

Falsa Demonstratio Non Nocet

11–20 This principle operates to the effect that where a testator has wrongly described a bequest in his will, the court will not prevent the will from being given effect in relation to that bequest if it is clear that a bequest was properly intended by the testator, and the court can determine the nature of that bequest. In effect, the court will not hold the legacy as being void if it can divine the testator's intention, either as to the subject-matter of the bequest or regarding the proper identity of the person for whom it is intended. If the terms of the bequest are sufficient for the court to estimate the amount bequeathed, then the legacy will be upheld. However, if there are no criteria for ascertaining the amount or value of the bequest, then the legacy will be void from uncertainty.[10]

Abatement

11–21 Abatement will occur where the value of the testator's estate is, after settlement of debts and funeral expenses, insufficient to meet the beneficial provisions of the testator's will. It is here that the classification of a particular legacy is of importance, as the general rules regarding abatement are as follows:

- The residue will abate first of all before any reduction in the size of general legacies need to be made.
- General legacies abate next. Unless the will specifies otherwise, general legacies will abate proportionately.
- Demonstrative legacies will not abate if the fund from which they are to be settled exists as at the testator's death. However, in so far as demonstrative legacies may require to be met from

---

[10] *Dundee Magistrates v Morris* (1858) 3 Macq.134 (H.L.).

outwith that specified fund, then, to that extent they will abate along with general legacies.

- Specific or special legacies will not as a general rule abate unless there are insufficient funds or assets after the settlement of debts to meet special legacies in full (and again provided that no order of preference in settlement of such legacies is stated in the will).

Simple examples

Testator A dies leaving a will in terms of which he has left four **11–22** pecuniary (*i.e.* general) legacies of £50,000 each to B, C, D and E. The residue of his estate is bequeathed to F. After settlement of all debts, A's estate amounts to £200,000. The four legatees would each receive payment of the legacies left to them by A. F, the residuary beneficiary, would, however, receive nothing.

Let us assume in the foregoing example that after settlement of debts, A's estate had amounted to £160,000. Again, F would receive nothing and the general legacies in favour of B, C, D and E would abate so that they would each receive £40,000.

Let us assume that we have the same testator (A) who bequeaths legacies of £50,000 each to B and C, and legacies of £25,000 to D and E with F again being the residuary beneficiary. On death of A, and after settlement of his debts, A's estate amounts to £75,000. The general legacies would abate proportionately, with B and C each receiving £25,000, and D and E each receiving £12,500. Again, there would be nothing for F.

In each of the above examples, the testator had expressed no preferential order in which the general legacies should abate. That being so, and where the will is silent on this point, no presumption arises as to the order in which legacies should abate from the order in which they are listed or appear in the testator's will.[11]

The testator's preference

It is of course open to the testator to offer the normal rules of **11–23** abatement by making a special provision in his will.[12]

Government duties and expenses of implementation

Where a will provides that pecuniary legacies are to be paid free of **11–24** government taxes and duties, etc., but the residue proves insufficient to meet such duties, then, so far as not paid from the residue, the general legacies will need to abate in order that inheritance tax, etc. can be settled. Where the will contains both special and general legacies, but the residue is insufficient to meet the inheritance tax liability, then the general legacies will also need to be abated in order to meet IHT due in respect of the special legacies, but not settled out of residue. However, if the level of debts and IHT, etc. is such that it exceeds the remaining

---

[11] *McConnel v McConnel's Trustees*, 1931 S.N. 31 (H.L.).
[12] For suggested styles, see Barr, etc., paras 4.08 and 4.09, cited above in Ch.8.

value of the estate *other than* special legacies is insufficient then again the special legacies may need to abate. This will also be the outcome where the special bequest is made on the basis that it is to be free of the expenses of transfer/implementation. Where no other estate is available to meet those expenses then the liability will fall on the special legacy itself.

Practical drafting advice

11–25   If the draftsman has carried out a full and comprehensive fact-finding exercise, then early potential problems can be identified and brought to the attention of the testator. In all of the examples given above, the residuary beneficiary (F) received nothing. This may not, however, have been in line with what the testator would really have wanted. Thus, where a testator indicates that he has a gross estate of, say, £240,000, and wishes to leave legacies of £50,000 to each of four legatees, the draftsman can point out that this will not mean that F will receive £40,000 (as the residue requires to bear debts and expenses). In some cases, realisation of the latter may occasion the testator to be less generous to his legatees.

Again, the value of a client regularly reviewing his will (bearing in mind the value from time to time of his estate) can avoid abatement requiring to be applied, by allowing the testator to make such amendments as are required, so as to ensure what he considers to be a fair and equitable distribution of his estate as between legatees and the residuary beneficiary. In the light of the post *Holmes v Bank of Scotland*[13] climate, it is not beyond the bounds of possibility that residuary beneficiaries, finding that their inheritance has been abated into nothingness, might seek to examine the advice offered by the draftsman at the relevant time.

Equally, however, the testator may seek to alter the normal rules of abatement, and it should be borne in mind that such alterations can be effected not only as to the preference as between legacies of the same class, but between legacies of different classes:

- If the testator is seeking a balance as between the legatee of a special bequest and general legatees, then there is no reason why the testator should not seek to avoid general legacies abating in favour of the special bequest by attaching to the special bequest a debt.[14]
- Where a particular item has high value, then the testator could direct that the latter in question be offered for sale to a particular individual at a discounted price (the intention being that on payment of the discounted price this would be available to, for example, substantially meet general legacies or to endeavour to ensure that there is some residue left for the residuary beneficiaries).
- Another way of ensuring that there is some residue left would be to specifically depart from the general rule of abatement,

---

[13] Cited above in Ch.2.
[14] *Greig's Trustees v Beach* (1854) 16 D. 899.

and to provide that, for example, general legacies will abate proportionately so as to provide a residue of a minimum, specific amount for the residuary beneficiaries.

- The testator should be warned that, where he has altered the normal rules of abatement, then care may be required regarding the wording of any future informal writing or codicil, if only to avoid unintended revocation of the provision altering the normal rules of abatement.

SPECIFIC BEQUESTS

Many testators are content to make simple wills which do not include **11–26** any specific bequests. Other testators will have very specific requirements as to the beneficiaries who should succeed to specific items of their estate. Even where the specific bequests to be included appear, on the face of it, to be reasonably straightforward, care is still required on the part of the draftsman—there are certain issues which are common to all such bequests and upon which the testator's instructions will be required. These have already been considered elsewhere in this book, but would involve:

- Delivery expenses (including transportation, security and insurance).
- The incidence of inheritance tax and whether or not a particular specific bequest should bear its own reasonable proportion of government duties payable in respect of the testator's death.

Where the item specifically bequeathed has a significant value, particularly in relation to the remainder of the testator's estate, then the testator does need to consider whether or not the residue should also bear possibly high costs of delivery, etc., and also the inheritance tax payable in respect of the value of the item in question.

Furniture, plenishings and personal effects

Save in the case where spouses are making wills in terms of which they **11–27** are bequeathing their whole estates to each other, perhaps the most common specific bequest relates to furnishings, plenishings and personal effects of the testator's dwelling-house. Although, on the face of it, such a bequest is straightforward, there are still points in respect of which the draftsman should take care.

- It is not advisable to refer to "house contents". The dwelling-house will contain many items which are not furniture and which may have some significant value. Where that phrase is used, this may lead the legatee who is offered only the furnishings to dispute the executor's interpretation. The case of *Stalker's Executors, Petitioners*[15] is of interest. The testator had left a will including a number of specific bequests. The will

---

[15] 1977 S.L.T., (Notes) 4.

included a specific bequest in favour of the testator's step-daughter and her husband of "my dwelling-house known as 17 Bank Avenue, Cumnock together with whole furniture and furnishings therein with the exception of the items contained in the specific legacies above and also cash, bank notes, deposit receipts, certificates for securities, bonds, promissory notes and other documents of debt and the like". The step-daughter and her husband contended that the bequest was not only of the furniture and furnishings, but also "all cash, bank notes . . .". The residuary beneficiaries did not agree. Whilst this case did not refer to "house contents", it amply demonstrates the difficulties which can arise, and in deciding the matter on the basis that the bequest did not include "all cash, bank notes . . ., etc.", Lord Keith referred to section 8(6)(b) of the Succession (Scotland) Act 1964, which provides that the expression "furniture and plenishings" does not include money or securities for money. Owing to that provision, Lord Keith conceded that the matter was not entirely free from doubt. He also commented, however, that in relation to such incorporeal moveable property he would normally have expected the same to have been the subject of a separate bequest. The difficulties which can arise from loose drafting are clear.

- Where the testator wishes to specifically bequeath his dwelling-house, he should at least be invited to consider whether the bequest should also include all furniture, plenishings, etc., again, if only to avoid unnecessary dispute amongst benefici-aries. If it is the testator's wish that the bequest of the heritage should not include moveable contents, then this should be specifically stated. Those contents should be specifically bequeathed to the intended beneficiary. As an alternative, and again for the purposes of clarity, there is no reason why the testator should not state that the bequest does not include the furnishings, which should be stated as forming part of the residue of his estate.

- It is considered to be good advice to recommend that furniture, etc. not be placed into trust, but rather should be the subject of a specific bequest, or should otherwise be allowed to fall into the residue of the testator's estate. A life renter must not exhaust the subject of the bequest, but furniture by its very nature may become damaged (see Chapter 4 for the type of difficulty which might arise here).

- Care also needs to be taken where a testator has two or more dwelling-houses. An unqualified bequest of "all my furniture, plenishings and personal effects" in those circumstances may carry the plenishings, etc. of all of the houses in question.

- The draftsman should always be wary (and ready to intervene) when a client indicates that he has left separate instructions for disposal of his furnishings, etc. Such separate instructions will normally involve either:

   (a) Verbal instructions left by the testator to his family as to how his furniture, etc. should be divided; or

(b) An earlier list made up by the testator.

In the case of (a) the testator should be warned that such a verbal specific bequest will be invalid. In the case of (b), then unless the testator provides full details of the separate written list (including its date), and that list is specifically adopted in terms of the testator's will, the general clause of revocation appearing in the will shall also "catch" (and render nugatory) the informal list.

Modern practice

Modern draftsmen, when dealing with the specific bequest of furni- **11–28** ture, etc. have found favour with the following wording;

"All my articles of personal, domestic, household, garage, garden or leisure use, ornament or consumption."[16]

That phrase has also been adopted for use in certain of the style wills appearing in students' Private Client Manual for the Diploma in Legal Practice.[17]

In the author's view, the wording is appropriate, comprehensive and will normally encapsulate what the testator would take to be his house, furnishings and contents. The main aspects of the clause are:

- It is readily adaptable and in particular it does not refer to "contents". It is again submitted that the use of the word "contents" is dangerous. For example, what would be the position if a free standing garage contained a brand new Mercedes Benz? The author has been unable to find any specific Scottish authority on this point, but in an older Canadian case the court held that a bequest of house contents did not include a valuable motor car kept at the time of the testator's death in the free standing garage serving the dwelling-house. The wording also makes reference to "articles of consumption".
- In the writer's view the wording is of assistance to the testator, as it gives more ready guidance to him or her (*i.e.* it focuses his thinking on what is in fact to be carried by the bequest) than a simple reference to plenishings and personal effects.
- As noted, the phrase is adaptable. It could be expanded to include motor vehicles or other items, and it can be adapted so as to make it clear that its terms apply to the furniture, etc. situated only within one specific dwelling-house. Yet again, and unless specifically adapted, it will carry all of the effects in question (wherever they may be situated as at the testator's death) to the beneficiary in question. The testator's intention here must be clarified.

Again, the draftsman should be careful not simply to adopt the wording **11–29** in question without being sure as to the testator's intentions. For

---

[16] See Barr, etc., *Drafting of Wills in Scotland*, (Butterworths/Law Society of Scotland, 1994).
[17] Written by Donald Gordon, Douglas Sneddon and Peter Shepherd.

example, is a caravan owned by the testator in St Andrews an item of leisure use? If the testator does own large items which may come within that debateable category, then the testator should put the matter beyond doubt, for example by adding to the wording:

> "and for the avoidance of doubt, including my caravan at Kinkel Braes, St Andrews. . . "

Or alternatively by adding wording such as:

> "but specifically excluding my caravan at Kinkel Braes, St Andrews".

If such large items are not to be included in the general bequest and are also not to form the subject of a separate special bequest, then it does no harm to direct that the item will fall to the residue of the testator's estate.

Bequest of furniture to a number of beneficiaries

11–30   The testator may wish to bequeath his furniture, etc between a number of beneficiaries. This of course raises the problems as to who gets what, in order to effect an equitable division, and avoid there being a dispute between two or more of the relevant beneficiaries.

Practical advice

11–31
- The testator should be encouraged to consider whether his furniture, etc. includes specific items which he would wish to bequeath to particular beneficiaries. If so, then such items should be made subject of their own specific bequests.
- In the latter case, the testator should give as much detail as possible to enable his executors to identify items to be specifically bequeathed to individual beneficiaries. This is of particular importance where the testator may have two or more items which might both or all conform to a general description (for example *I bequeath my diamond ring to A*—however the testator, as at her death, has three such rings). The difficulties which can arise here are obvious. The draftsman should:
  - (i) Check whether or not in relation to any item which is to be specifically bequeathed to an individual legatee, the testator has any other items which might come within the same description.
  - (ii) If the testator does have two such items, then specific details will require to be given in order that the intended object of the bequest is properly identified.
- The testator may express the view that he will issue more detailed instructions in due course. If so, then the draftsman needs to consider whether he should advise the testator to make a codicil, giving more detail, or whether the testator's aim can be achieved by an informal writing. However, in the latter case, this runs the risk that the testator may omit to subscribe

the informal writing, thereby perhaps invalidating the same in terms of the Requirements of Writing (Scotland) Act, 1995.

- Obviously, if specific, individual items are to be bequeathed to particular beneficiaries, but the will contains a provision otherwise bequeathing remaining furniture, etc., then (whether or not the bequest is to a single beneficiary or to a number of beneficiaries) the relevant bequest should be slightly altered (although this may appear to be self evident) as follows:

  > "I bequeath my *remaining* items of a personal domestic household, etc."

- Failing contemporaneous instructions as to division, the testator needs to incorporate a formula which would enable his executors to decide as to the division of the items in question in the event of dispute. A form of wording would be:

  > I bequeath my whole items of a personal, domestic, household, garage, garden or leisure use, ornament or consumption so far as possible equally between A, B and C in a reasonable and fair manner as to which division my executors shall be the sole judges.

  To discourage disputation (notwithstanding the discretion expressed in favour of the executors), the testator might go so far as to incorporate a forfeiture clause by adding to the above bequest wording of the following type:

  > . . . in the event of any of the said beneficiaries challenging the executors' decision, then such beneficiary shall forfeit all right under this purpose as if such beneficiary had predeceased me.

- The testator should not lose sight of the possibility of family jealousy. If he appoints members of his family to be executors and also bequeaths furniture, etc. to be divided amongst his family by the executors (who may also be beneficiaries in relation to the bequest in question), then the possibility of unspoken favouritism may arise. In such circumstances it may be appropriate to nominate an independent, non-family executor, who in relation to this particular purpose would be given *sine qua non* power. This is a difficult area and the independent executor may find himself placed in an invidious position. This of course raises a general point—where executors are given discretion to decide disputes, for example in relation to furniture, should the testator also make them beneficiaries in terms of the same purpose? This is of course a difficult and personal area for testators, but it is one which should be discussed in appropriate terms with them.

Specific bequests of other items

With regard to any item of the testator's estate which is to be **11–32** specifically bequeathed, the general considerations already outlined in this work apply. For example:

- Should the residue or the legatee bear the costs of implementation?

- Should the bequest be free of government tax or should it bear its rateable proportion?
- If the item in question has been disposed of by the testator prior to death, should the legatee be entitled to some alternative?
- Has the item been properly defined so as to facilitate its identification?
- If the beneficiary does not want the item in question, should the will provide for some alternative in his favour?
- If the beneficiary in question pre-deceases the testator, should there be some over destination, or should the item simply fall into the residue?
- Does the testator actually own the item in question, or is he operating under some misapprehension (for example, a motor vehicle subject to hire purchase)?
- Is the subject of the bequest already "attached" by a debt, and if so, is the bequest to be implemented free of that debt or to carry the same with it?

These are general considerations which apply to any specific bequest.

Once again, it is the responsibility of the draftsman to check these points out. Whilst the author acknowledges that the responsibility upon the draftsman is weighty, perhaps the *quid pro quo* is that clients will have to accept that will making is no longer, from the point of view of cost, a "Cinderella service".

Problem subjects of bequests

11–33   The draftsman cannot simply adopt a "blunderbuss" approach. Where a client indicates that he wishes a specific item to be bequeathed to a particular individual, it is submitted that the onus upon the draftsman is to establish whether or not it is in fact open to the testator so to direct without qualification or further enquiry. For example:

- If the subject or the bequest is a motor vehicle, the draftsman should establish whether or not it is truly owned by the testator. If the vehicle has been purchased on a hire purchase contract then it is in fact not open to the testator to bequeath the vehicle freely. The draftsman will need to explore this issue with his client and, if the testator insists that the bequest should be made, then provision will need to be made in specific and clear terms that the balance of the hire purchase price will need to be paid off (effectively from the residue) in order to enable the executors to implement the bequest. In some cases, it may in fact be appropriate to advise the testator to desist from a bequest, particularly where the residue available is small. It should be borne in mind that we now live in a society where the incurring of debt is encouraged, and clients may not appreciate that a vehicle purchase subject to hire purchase does not belong to them.
- When a client wishes to bequeath shares in a private company, then the client should be reminded that the Memorandum and

Articles of the company may contain restrictions on transfer, and that it would be appropriate to check the Memorandum and articles of the relevant company in order to advise the client as to what restrictions may have been made on such transfer.

- Clients should always be reminded that, where they are partners in a firm, and unless the partnership agreement makes specific allowance for this (and this would be unusual), the testator cannot bequeath his partnership to beneficiaries. As has already been commented upon in this book, in the main, in so far as partnerships are concerned, the legacy will be simply of the value of the testator's share in the business, not of the right to act as a partner.

Practical advice

The draftsman has a weighty responsibility. The following submissions **11–34** are made:

- It is the responsibility of the draftsman to ensure that the client's wishes are implemented. This means that the draftsman will need to assess the particular subject of the bequest and to advise the client as to any "hints and wrinkles" in relation to the same.
- Where the draftsman does not assess whether or not a specific item can be transferred free of particular complication, then, unfortunately, *Holmes v Bank of Scotland*[18] might again come into play.
- There is no shame in the draftsman advising a particular client that he is unsure as to whether or not he has the particular skills to ensure that a particular bequest can be implemented free of complication. In such circumstances, the draftsman should strongly recommend that specialist advice be sought. Where the draftsman offers such advice (making his own limitations clear) and properly records the same, then it is submitted that, unless in the view of the draftsman the course adopted by his client is absolute folly but he fails so to indicate, the draftsman will escape the consequences which ensued in *John J. Smith & Co v Gordon & Smyth*.[19]

There is no draftsman who can claim to be "master o' a' the airts".[20]

LEGACIES FOR SPECIFIC PURPOSES

The bequest of a legacy will reflect not just the love or respect which the **11–35** testator has for the chosen legatee—the legacy may be granted also in a manner which will reflect specific concerns of the testator, or perhaps the

---

[18] Cited above.

[19] 2002 S.C.L.R. 481.

[20] For an excellent consideration of the matters which fall to be considered in relation to various types of assets and rights, see Barr, etc., paras 448 *et seq.*, cited above.

age, capacity or specific personality traits of the legatee. Once more, the draftsman needs to have the appropriate skills in order to seek to achieve the end sought by the testator.

Examples

11–36
(a) The testator may wish a given class of beneficiaries (for example, nephews and nieces) to benefit. However, he recognises that, in their own lives, some of the members of the class are "doing better than others". He recognises that the financial position of the various beneficiaries within the class may have changed, and that being so he does not wish to lay down any hard and fast lines at the time of granting the will. In such circumstances, the testator can leave discretion to his executors to decide to what extent each beneficiary within the class is to benefit. This can be readily achieved by leaving a discretionary legacy.

(b) A testator may have offered financial support to, for example, some but not all of his adult children during his lifetime. At the time of making his will, the testator recognises that differing levels of support may have been made to the adult children who benefited from such lifetime advances. The testator may wish to achieve fairness as between all of his children in respect of the division of his estate, *i.e.* to ensure that when he passes on, each child will more or less have received over the testator's lifetime, and following his death, approximately the same benefit from the testator. Again, by appropriate drafting of the will, that end result can be achieved for the testator.

(c) Another testator may own a valuable asset (for example, a stamp collection). He may wish the collection to go to a particular beneficiary, but not absolutely, as the testator fears that the bequest of that one asset might remove too much by way of value from his estate, thereby reducing the benefit to the remaining beneficiaries. The testator could seek to achieve his end by leaving a bequest of an option to purchase the stamp collection to the relevant beneficiary, possibly at a stated discount.

(d) Similarly, the testator may own an asset, for example, a dwelling-house, which again he would wish to bequeath to a particular individual. However, at the time of making the will there is still a substantial mortgage outstanding over the dwelling-house. The concern of the testator is that payment of that mortgage should not fall on the residue of his estate, as this would again diminish the benefit to the other beneficiaries. The solution in such circumstances is to leave a bequest of the house, subject to the debt in question.

(e) The testator wishes to leave a pecuniary bequest to a young person but is concerned that the individual may, through youth and financial naïvety, squander their bequest. The testator will therefore wish to leave the bequest subject to, for example, an accumulation and maintenance trust provision, specifying the ages at which the right to income and capital will vest in the beneficiary.

(f) Finally, the testator may wish to leave a bequest to a particular individual, but only if certain conditions are fulfilled. In these circumstances, the testator will leave a conditional legacy. Obviously, one of the most common conditions is that the legatee should survive the testator.

Discretionary legacies

There are two main types of discretionary legacy. The first (and **11–37** perhaps the simplest) is the "selective legacy", where the beneficiary is himself given discretion to choose one or more items from a specified source. An example would be:

> I bequeath to A (design) the right to take from the angling equipment owned by me as at my date of death two fishing rods of his choice.

Where the testator may wish to leave a selective legacy in respect of items having perhaps greater value, then he may wish to incorporate a time-limit for exercise of the relevant choice (failing which the bequest will lapse) in order to avoid undue delay in the overall administration of his estate.

The second and perhaps more common form of discretionary legacy is where the testator gives his executors a discretion or power of appointment as to who should benefit and in what manner. The benefit of such a power of appointment or discretionary legacy is simplicity coupled with flexibility. An example would be:

> I direct my executors to pay to such of my nephews and nieces as shall survive me the sum of TWENTY THOUSAND POUNDS (£20,000) STERLING to be divided in such proportions (which may be nothing or the whole) as my executors in their sole discretion may decide and, failing such division by my executors within six months of the date of my death to such nephews and nieces in equal shares.

The foregoing is an example of a "special" power of appointment in terms of which the relevant beneficiaries are chosen from a defined class. The other type of power of appointment is a general one which (in theory) provides the executors with an unlimited choice as to the donee.

Drafting considerations

- A special power of appointment or discretionary legacy is **11–38** entirely appropriate where a degree of immediacy and also simplicity is required by the testator. There is no requirement to interpose a discretionary trust.
- Great care should, however, be taken in relation to general powers of appointment. Scottish law does not allow a testator to effectively leave the choice of devolution of his estate to a third party; that being so the class of beneficiary from whom the executors can choose requires to be properly defined.
- It is submitted that the power of appointment should have a "time-limit"—see above. If the executors do not exercise the

power of appointment within the time-limit then the legacy will vest in equal shares, although again a degree of flexibility could be achieved here. Instead of providing for the legacy vesting in equal shares, the testator could provide that the legacy will vest as to, for example:

> Two-thirds to the children who shall survive me of my brother A, and one- third to the children who shall survive me of my sister B.[21]

- The power allows the executors to exclude certain members of the class completely. This is entirely valid and is not contrary to public policy.[22] Nonetheless, it is submitted that the entitlement of the holder of the power of appointment to so act should be properly specified so as to leave none of the potential beneficiaries in any doubt. This will avoid a disappointed beneficiary (who is excluded from any benefit) claiming that the executors acted *ultra vires*, thereby entitling them to challenge the exercise of the power in court.[23]
- If the executors are to have power to pay nothing to *any* of the given class or legatees then it is recommended that, again to avoid difficulties, the testator might include a destination over, if only to make it clear that the testator had clearly envisaged his executors deciding not to bestow a benefit on the given class. This could be achieved by addition of wording such as:

> ... declaring that it shall be in the discretion of my executors to pay no share of the foregoing legacy to any of my nephews and nieces who shall survive me and in the event of my executors so deciding that the legacy shall be paid to X (design).

- Where the testator has a large or more complex estate and requires to impose a degree of control over the same following his death, then the use of a full discretionary trust is indicated.

EQUALISATION OF BENEFIT, TAKING INTO ACCOUNT LIFETIME ADVANCES

11–39 Where lifetime advances have been made to some but not all children, then the testator may be concerned to achieve overall fairness as between his children, as opposed to necessarily taking into account the financial position of each child as at his death. In those circumstances the testator does need to make specific provision in his will. The rules as to collation *inter liberos* in relation to legal rights claimants have no application in relation to the implementation of a testamentary bequest.

There are various issues for the testator to consider here:

- The testator may need to be specific as to what advances are to be taken into account by his executors. The simplest way of

---

[21] Obviously care is required here—if the testator had another brother C who also had children then the instruction detailed could cause obviously difficulty.

[22] The Powers of Appointment Act, 1874.

[23] *Callander v Callander's Executor*, 1976 S.L.T. 10.

dealing with this matter is for the testator to record in his will the total of the advances to be taken account at that point, and to leave a legacy of that total sum to each of his other children. For example:

> In respect that prior to the date hereof I have made advances to my son A totalling TWENTY THOUSAND POUNDS (£20,000) STERLING and that I wish to ensure equality of division of my estate so far as possible between my children I direct my executors to pay to my sons, B and C, a legacy of TWENTY THOUSAND POUNDS (£20,000) STERLING each.

The above example does of course not take into account the possibility that after making the will, but prior to his death, the testator will make further advances to A. To cover this possibility the following wording could be utilised:-

> And in the event that I shall make any further advance to A prior to my death, then I direct my executors to increase the foregoing legacies to B and C by the amount of such further advances made to A as to all of which my executors shall be the sole judges.

It is important that the executors be given discretion here to avoid dispute with a possibly recalcitrant A who may unfairly see the increase in the legacies to his siblings as otherwise diminishing his interest in the residue. **11–40**

- The testator may not be happy with the simple formula outlined above. The testator may feel that the legacies to be left to B and C should also include interest at a specified rate. The rate could be tied to the Retail Prices Index or to Bank of England base rate. The decision for the testator will be as to the date from which interest is to run—is it to be from the date of the advance made to A or from the date of the will itself? It is here that both the testator and the draftsman can run into difficulties, particularly where a series of advances have been made to A. It may be virtually impossible to cover all the possibilities which the testator may consider, and it may well be that the testator will simply opt to provide that interest, according to the chosen formula, should be paid either from the date of signature of the will itself or from his date of death, at the same time empowering his executors to be sole judges of the total amount advanced to A at either date.
- The testator may be concerned that, in calculating advances to A, the executors may, for example, take into account birthday or other such traditional gifts. In such cases, the testator will need to give his executors some guidance. This could be covered either by a suitable declaration contained in the purpose in question, or alternatively in terms of an informal letter of expression of wish (bear in mind that such instructions are, however, not binding upon executors). The testator may prefer to endeavour to adjust the shares of residue otherwise payable to children. An appropriate wording might be:

And in so far as I have made advances totalling TWENTY THOUSAND POUNDS (£20,000.00) STERLING to my son A, I direct my executors to adjust in such manner as they shall deem appropriate the sums payable to each of my said children A, B and C by way of residue to take into account said advances to A and in so far as possible to equalise the position as between my said children, my executors being sole judges as to the calculations required to achieve the foregoing balance.

11–41   The formula hereinbefore outlined does not take account of the possible wish of the testator to ensure that not only are the capital sums equalised, but also the fact that A had had the benefit of a substantial sum of funds for perhaps some years prior to B and C. If interest is to be taken into account, then again the residue clause would need to be adjusted by inclusion of an appropriate formula.

- Since the introduction of the concept of the potentially exempt transfer for inheritance tax purposes,[24] there has been no requirement to report sizeable lifetime gifts to the Inland Revenue. Where the testator wishes to achieve a fair balance between the beneficiaries, but does not wish to complicate matters by adding interest, etc., then it would still be prudent for the draftsman to seek to establish when the advance or advances were made and to record this information in some form to be held with the will. When the testator passes on, this would be of considerable assistance in calculating whether or not there have been any "failed" potentially exempt transfers.
- One area of possible sensitivity arises here. In the given example, A has received a lifetime gift of £20,000. The testator may need to consider his position in the event of A predeceasing the latter. Whilst it is entirely possible to ensure that the lifetime gift to A continues to be "debited" against the interest of his issue in the testator's estate (so as to procure the fair balance desired by the testator), the testator may feel that this might be depriving A's children of a degree of financial support at a point in time where they may be in most need of the same. It is suggested that the draftsman can only point this out, leaving it to the testator to balance the various and difficult issues involved here.

True collation *inter liberos*

11–42   Collation (the bringing back into account of lifetime advances) arises only where there is more than one claimant of the same class in respect of legal rights. A child cannot claim collation where the other claimant is a surviving spouse and vice versa. Testamentary beneficiaries cannot claim collation in respect of any legal rights claim, and the executors

---

[24] The Inheritance Tax Act 1984, s.3A.

cannot take into account collation where, for example, there is only one claimant. However, the testator may feel that sufficient financial assistance has been provided to particular children during the testator's lifetime, to the extent that those children are excluded from any benefit under the will. It will be of assistance to the executors for this fact to be brought to their attention. Suitable wording might be:

> Considering that I have advanced to my sons, A and D, the sums respectively of FIFTEEN THOUSAND POUNDS (£15,000) STERLING and TWENTY THOUSAND POUNDS (£20,000) STERLING to assist them in purchasing flatted dwelling-houses, I declare that should either A or D claim legal rights in my estate, the foregoing sums are to be collated appropriately with the amount of my estate available to meet such claims and deducted from the sums otherwise payable by way of legal rights to A and D.

BEQUEST OF AN OPTION TO PURCHASE

Why would a testator leave such a bequest? Again, this is an area where **11–43** the value of a comprehensive fact find by the draftsman can help to highlight issues for the testator, and assist the latter in completing a will which takes account of issues which may not otherwise have occurred to the testator:

- The testator has an asset having a high value in relation to the remainder of his estate, but which he would wish to bequeath to one individual for a variety of reasons. The draftsman would need to point out the possible distorting effect of leaving such a large single bequest (particularly if it is to be free of inheritance tax). On realising the "distorting" effect that this might have on his estate, the testator may consider bequeathing an option to the relevant individual to buy the item from his estate at either market or some discounted value. In the latter case, it may well be that the legatee would be delighted to acquire a particularly valuable item at a discount on its true price.
- The testator may own absolutely an asset which has been used by the partnership of which he is a partner, or by the limited company of which he is a shareholder. The testator needs to bear in mind that his beneficiaries' principal concern will be to realise the value bequeathed to them by the testator. Thus they may not be unduly concerned at the possible effect on the business in question of losing the asset (for example, a commercial building), unless of course this is also likely to have a direct effect on the ability of the partnership to pay out the deceased partner/testator's interest to the estate or of the value of the testator's shares in the limited company in question.

Whilst the reasons for leaving such a bequest may therefore appear to be straightforward, there are important issues which the testator must consider.

How is the price to be fixed? If it is to be market value then who is to decide that value? If the price is to be discounted then is this to be according to a formula (for example "50 per cent of market value as at my date of death"), or is it to be at a discounted price, set in terms of the deceased's will? In the latter case, the draftsman should remind the testator that the asset in question may increase greatly in value between the date of the will and the testator's date of death.

Is any time-limit to be fixed for exercise of the option, and if so, how long should the "option legatee" be allowed to exercise the same? This is an aspect upon which the testator may need to give some detailed consideration. Guidance may be required from the draftsman. There is little point in attaching an unreasonable time-limit (after which the option will be stated to have lapsed) if an otherwise willing option legatee, partnership or company would not have any fair opportunity of raising the appropriate funding within the time-limit specified by the testator.

Over what time period and in what manner is the price to be fixed? If by instalments, is interest to be payable by the beneficiary on the decreasing balance?

11–44   The difficulties which can arise here can be seen from the case of *Shepherd's Executor Petitioner*.[25] In this case, Mr Shepherd had provided (in a mutual testamentary settlement along with his wife, who had pre-deceased him) that the family home should be offered for sale to the eldest of their three sons, and in the event of him not wishing to take it up, to the remaining two sons in their order. The will declared that it was a condition of the sale that the purchasing son should have "not less than five years to pay up the balance of the price". The executor wrote to the eldest son with an offer to sell, to which he replied, on the face of it accepting the offer, but indicating that he wished to make payment of the price by no later than five years from the date of conclusion of the missives. The executor replied that the purchase price was payable by 60 equal monthly instalments beginning on the date of entry. The eldest son rejected that suggestion, as a result of which the executor sought directions on whether:

(a) The purchasing son could defer payment of the whole price for at least five years notwithstanding that he might have taken entry.

(b) Whether the purchasing son was bound to pay interest on the unpaid price for such time as it remained unpaid.

(c) Whether the eldest son had in fact declined the offer to sell so that the executor was now bound to offer it to the other two sons in order. The other two sons argued that the declaration itself was void from uncertainty. They argued that the executor could not know what length of time he should specify for payment to the eldest son and that he was not in a position to frame an offer to any son which would satisfy the requirements for certainty of a contract of sale. It was further argued for the other two sons that the reference to "pay up the balance" in the absence of a reference to deposit or instalments made it impossible for the executor fulfilling his duties under the will to give effect to the declaration. Finally, the other sons argued

---

[25] 2003 S.L.T. 818.

that if a valid offer had been made by the executor, then the eldest son's reply held to be regarded as a declinature of the offer, with the result that the executor was now obliged to offer to the next son in line.

The court rejected the arguments for the two other sons. The court found that:

(a) The executor was vested with, *inter alia*, the power to fix how any payment of trust assets acquired by a purchaser should be made, and to make it a condition of sale that the purchase price be paid in full not later than expiry of five years, or within a reasonable period thereafter, and thereby fix a final date for payment.

(b) That reference to "pay up the balance of the price" did not render the declaration incapable of giving effect, since balance of the price would include the whole price where no earlier payments had been made.

(c) That the offer from the executor did not need to be capable of *de plano* acceptance.

(d) That the eldest son was not bound to pay interest on the unpaid price, provided that payment in full was made by the fifth anniversary on the date on which Missives were concluded. In the absence of express provision for interest, it was held that Mr Shepherd's intention was that interest was not payable.

(e) That by responding to the executor's offer in the manner indicated above, A had not declined the offer of sale as such, and the executor was not therefore obliged to offer to sell it to the next son in line.

What is to happen if the option legatee declines to exercise the **11–45** option? Is it simply to lapse (leaving the item in question to fall back into the residue of the testator's estate), or is it to be bequeathed to a substitute option legatee? Should the option legatee who has declined to exercise the option receive some alternative benefit, either by way of legacy or a share of residue?

Is the testator aware that if the asset in question is an instalment option property, exercise of the option will be regarded by the Inland Revenue as a sale, thus depriving the executors of paying up the IHT by instalments?

If the property is to be offered at open market valuation as at date of death, who is to effect the valuation? It is submitted that it is better to leave this matter open; confusion and difficulty might arise if the testator directs that the valuation is to be carried out by a particular firm of experts, only for it to transpire that the firm in question no longer exists as at the date of death. It is better to provide the executors with discretion as to suitable experts/valuators.

Has the testator adequately identified the asset or property in question? Although not dealing with the subject of an option legacy, the difficulties which can arise where the description of a particular asset is disputed can be seen in the case of *Fortunato's Judicial Factor v Fortunato*.[26] In terms of the deceased's will, he had bequeathed to two

---

[26] 1981 S.L.T. 277.

named individuals, equally between them and to the survivor of them, two public houses belonging to the testator and known respectively as the Westend Bar and the Bolag Bar, both in Brechin. The two legatees contended that the bequest covered not only the two licensed premises, but also the dwelling-houses above both of the same. The court decided against the claimants, declining to allow the introduction of parole evidence as to the true intention of the testator.

11–46   Subject to all of the above matters having been taken into consideration, an appropriate format of provision would be as follows:

> I direct my executors to sell my interest in the heritable property known as and forming 1 Brown Street, Anytown to A at a price equal to 60 per cent of the value of the said heritable property as independently estimated as at my date of death; declaring that such option must be exercised within six months of my date of death with the price as hereinbefore fixed to be paid within one year of that date otherwise this provision shall lapse and be of no further force and effect; further declaring that (i) if A accepts this offer, the expenses of transfer shall be borne by the residue of my estate and (ii) in the event that A declines said offer I direct my executors to make over to A the sum of THIRTY THOUSAND POUNDS (£30,000.00) STERLING.

The "alternative" legacy does of course not require to bear any relation to the anticipated estimated value of the property as at date of death (although the testator may wish to make it clear in terms of the relevant clause that this is indeed the case).

LEGACY SUBJECT TO A DEBT

11–47 Again, why might a testator leave a bequest in terms of which the legacy also has to bear a debt attached thereto? The main consideration here is once again concern on the part of the testator that unless the legacy of the asset passes with the debt attached, the residue of his estate will require to bear that debt. This again may distort the terms of the testator's will and be perceived to be unfair on other beneficiaries. Equally, the testator may be entirely happy that a particular bequest should be made subject to a debt, comforted in the knowledge that the legatee will be happy to obtain the asset in question at what, at the end of the day, amounts to a substantial discount on its true, open market value. The draftsman may need to assist the testator here, as the latter may be confused as to whether or not a particular liability is attached to a particular asset. In the case of heritable property subject to a mortgage, the attachment is clear. However, the testator may have purchased an asset, having arranged a personal loan to enable him to do so. That loan does not, however, specifically attach to the asset (for example, a motor vehicle purchased with a car loan). The draftsman may need to point out that unless the balance of the car loan is specifically attached to the motor vehicle in question, then the outstanding liability as at the testator's date of death will fall to be borne by the residue of his estate, not by the legatee receiving the motor vehicle.

General rules

1. If the subject of the legacy is to be passed free from any debt **11–48**
   attaching thereto, then the testator will need to make this clear
   in express terms in his will, or otherwise by clear implication
   from the terms of the same.[27]
2. With regard to heritable properties, a statement that the same
   are to be conveyed "free of expenses" will not free the bequests
   from any outstanding mortgage.
3. Similarly, a general instruction to executors to pay all debts and
   funeral expenses will not disencumber an asset of a debt which
   has been specifically attached thereto.
4. Where debts are not attached to a specific item then they will
   need to be borne from the residue.

Drafting considerations

The testator should specify whether or not an asset is to pass free of **11–49**
any particular debt (in which case the latter will be borne by the
residue), or whether the bequest is to carry the debt with it. In order to
avoid difficulty with beneficiaries at a later stage, it may be as well for
the testator's intention (that the legacy should pass subject to a
particular debt) to be specified by clear wording in the will.

- Even where an asset is not already attached by a particular
  debt, there is no reason why the testator should not make this
  the case. For example:

  > I bequeath to A the motor vehicle owned by me as at my
  > date of death subject to A being liable for payment of any
  > balance outstanding on any personal or car loan due by me
  > as at my date of death in connection with the purchase of
  > said motor vehicle, as to all of which my executors shall be
  > the sole judges.

  It is important that where the bequest is expressed in such
  general terms, the executors should be given the power to
  decide as to the balance of any debt which the legatee should
  require to bear.
- There is no requirement that the debt attached to a specific
  asset should bear any relationship thereto. There is no reason
  why the testator should not attach to a specific asset a wholly
  unrelated debt. The purpose of this would once again be to
  avoid distortion of the estate, although equally it would be
  relevant to establish whether or not, in the testator's view, the
  legatee would have the ability to settle the debt in question
  without having to resort to sale of the asset in question. This is
  of particular importance where, owing to the effects of
  depreciation and excessive use by a testator, the value of a
  particular motor vehicle may possibly be less at the date of
  death than the total outstanding on the relevant personal or car
  loan which had been arranged in relation to the same.

---

[27] *Muir's Trustees v Muir*, 1916 1 S.L.T. 372.

- In a case where there may be doubt but the testator does not wish the legacy in question to have to bear the relevant debt, then he should include in the clause in question a declaration to the effect that any debt affecting the bequest should be paid from the residue.

Warning note

11–50   Once more, full and accurate completion of the fact find in relation to a testator is essential. Thus, the fact find needs not only to fully examine the nature and composition of the testator's estate, but also the nature and value of his debts and whether or not they may arguably attach to a particular asset. If the draftsman does not ascertain the specific views of the testator in relation to the possible attachment or otherwise of particular debts to particular assets, then he may find a disappointed beneficiary querying his advice after the death of the testator.

YOUNG BENEFICIARIES

11–51   In a general sense, the issues here which may concern a testator are obvious. However, it remains the draftsman's responsibility to explore with the testator his attitude as to the age at which all (or perhaps only some) beneficiaries should vest absolutely. The normal vehicle for offering protection to young beneficiaries from their own financial naïvety is an accumulation and maintenance trust, the technicalities and main aspects of which are considered in Chapter 12.

LEGACIES DESIGNED TO ACHIEVE IHT MITIGATION

11–52   In this section, we are in the main dealing with married clients who, in one way or another, wish to ensure that, so far as possible (but also within the limits of financial prudence and practicability), they make at least some use of their respective nil-rate bands. The proposals of both the Westminster Parliament and the Scottish Executive (see Chapter 4) should be borne in mind. If, as it would appear, the spouse exemption for IHT is to be extended to same sex couples who have properly registered their partnerships as required by the relevant legislation, then it would seem that such "registered" partners may have the same scope for use of their nil-rate bands as presently extends to married couples. However, as with any legislation, the "devil" may lie in the detail in so far as such partners are concerned.

Traditionally, for many years and save for a small number of clients, the question of inheritance tax has not loomed large in will drafting in Scotland. That being so, the majority of practitioners in Scotland will find that their wills safe is replete with wills in terms of which spouses have simply bequeathed their respective estates to each other whom failing issue. Such wills will have been entirely appropriate for the great majority of clients at the time they were drafted, but may no longer remain so for a number of reasons:

- The great increase in the value of dwelling-houses over the past few years (see Chapter 3).

- The increase of individuals in "pension participation" and other forms of insurance protection.
- Owing to the burgeoning wealth of Scottish society over the past 50 years, the possibility, if not the likelihood, of clients receiving an inheritance from the older generation.

As already suggested in this book, the drafting of a will cannot be carried out in isolation—it is important that the will maker should have full details of the nature and composition of his client's estate and, where appropriate, demonstrate that at the very least, the question of possible IHT mitigation through will drafting (or otherwise) has been raised (See Chapter 2).

Client awareness

Where the testator has informed himself as to the various reliefs and **11–53** exemptions which apply, he can engage in simple and straightforward IHT mitigation during his lifetime. More often than not, however, clients are not aware of very straightforward planning opportunities, and it is submitted that it is a useful add-on to the draftsman's services to bring such reliefs and exemptions to the testator's attention. Some firms have reasonably short "information sheets" which outline the relief and exemptions in question and detail how use of the same can be made. On occasions, consideration by the client of such an information sheet can stimulate the client's interest, leading to further valuable business opportunities for the draftsman or his firm.

Simple steps

There is a common misapprehension amongst clients that use of the **11–54** nil-rate band is "all or nothing"—nothing could be further from the truth. A client should be advised that he can make as much use as he sees fit of his nil-rate band (provided always that he has not substantially used the same up prior to the drafting of his will). For example:

1. A and B are spouses and have two adult children. The combined estates of A and B would be liable to inheritance tax on the death of the survivor. The spouses make wills in terms of which they bequeath "first death legacies" to both of their adult children. Even if A and B do nothing else, on death of one of them, a total of £20,000 would be directed in the first instance to the adult children, thereby saving a total of £8,000 by way of IHT following the death of the surviving spouse.
2. Take the same married couple again with two adult children. If the first death legacies are increased to £50,000 to both adult children, this will re-channel £100,000 away from the surviving spouse on first death with an IHT saving of £40,000 on death of the survivor.

In essence, use of first death legacies by spouses is perhaps the simplest drafting technique available to mitigate IHT.

Further points

Given that clients often do not understand how IHT is assessed, it may **11–55** be worthwhile pointing out that mitigation can be effected on a "first death" basis by spouses not just leaving pecuniary legacies. A bequest of any item of value not required by the surviving spouse could be made. For example, one of the spouses may own an antique vehicle which is still in working order. The other spouse does not drive. Unless the spouses were to consider that the non-driving spouse would, on survival, need to sell the antique vehicle in order to ensure his or her financial position following the loss of the spouse, then the motor car in question could be specifically bequeathed to another non-exempt beneficiary.

The nil-rate band legacy

11–56   When a client wishes to incorporate a full nil-rate band legacy, then the draftsman needs to bear in mind that the intention of his client may at least be partially frustrated.

Dangers for the draftsman

11–57   At pain of labouring this matter, it is submitted that a will cannot be prepared for a client unless the draftsman has full details as to "what has gone before".

1. If the client has already set up a discretionary trust for an amount which exceeds his nil-rate band, then inclusion of a nil-rate band legacy within the client's will is meaningless.
2. The nil-rate band legacy can only be given effect to the extent that no chargeable lifetime gifts require to be brought back into account. For example, if the testator has made a gift of £100,000 two years prior to his death, then any nil-rate band legacy contained within his will shall only (at present rates) be effective to the extent of £163,000.
3. Where the client has an interest in possession in a trust, then this could further restrict the amount of the nil-rate band available.
4. Where the client has made a gift which "offends" against section 102 of the Finance Act 1986 (gift subject to reservation of benefit), then this will further restrict the available amount of the nil-rate band.
5. Whilst perhaps presently no danger to the draftsman of the will (incorporating the nil-rate band legacy), the draftsman of a subsequent codicil which includes legacies to non- exempt beneficiaries should point out to the client that this will restrict the available amount of the nil-rate band which can be effectively bequeathed in terms of the earlier will.

The author accepts that it might be suggested that the draftsman cannot be held responsible where the testator's intention to leave as much as possible of the nil-rate band to legatees is frustrated for one or more of the above reasons. However, an analogy might be useful here—increasingly, where medical negligence is alleged, the concept of "informed consent" has been brought into play. In the legal world, a draftsman who does not fully explore the above issues might stand accused of failing his client in this respect—had the possible restrictions outlined above in respect of the nil-rate band legacy been outlined to the client, he could have taken steps during his lifetime to address the same.

Whilst it remains to be seen whether or not such an argument would find favour, the draftsman who carries out the comprehensive examination of his client's past financial history is less likely to subject himself to the stress and strain of such a claim on the part of a disappointed beneficiary.

There are various styles of inheritance tax nil-rate band legacies in use at present. Some of the clauses in question are lengthy (and include specific arithmetic examples of how the testator intends the clause to operate). However, the style offered by Barr, etc.[28] is in the author's view concise and covers the features outlined above.

Further considerations

At the time of writing, the current Chancellor, etc. has indicated a willingness to attack not only complicated and expensive tax mitigation schemes, but also other tax mitigation routes. As the legislation presently stands, it is hard to conceive that any Chancellor could prohibit the use of nil-rate band (or even "first death") legacies. However, in the current climate, it would be as well for the draftsman instructed to incorporate a nil-rate band legacy to offer an appropriate health warning, *i.e.* that his drafting reflects the law and practice as it presently stands, and that he or she cannot accept any responsibility for subsequent legislative change (see Chapter 8 and the comments on "pre-owned" properties).   **11–58**

The draftsman should also advise the client (in properly recorded fashion) that there is no guarantee that the nil-rate band might not be reduced at some future point. After the election of the Labour Government in 1997, various erudite pundits predicted that, in his first financial statement, the Chancellor would in fact reduce the amount of the nil-rate band. Although the Chancellor confounded such pundits, it should never be assumed that the nil-rate band will increase (albeit fractionally) from time to time, or even remain at its previous level. That being so, a nil-rate band legacy clause should *never* refer to the current amount applicable under Schedule 1 to the 1984 Act. Such a course will leave the draftsman a hostage to legislative fortune, and may leave him or her with difficult questions to answer at a later stage.

On the opposite side of the coin, there remains the possibility that the nil-rate band might be substantially increased over a period of time, following the making of the will. Again, it is submitted that it is the draftsman's responsibility to make this clear to the testator. In the latter case, and whilst the testator (who has made no potentially chargeable lifetime gifts, etc.) may be comfortable that a sum of £255,000 should pass to his chosen beneficiaries, the view of the client may be entirely different if, for example, at the time of his death, the nil-rate band had been increased to, say, £400,000. In such circumstances (and where the residuary beneficiary is the surviving spouse), implementation of the nil-rate band legacy of that level could have a seriously prejudicial effect on the financial position of the surviving spouse. Failure on the part of the draftsman to contemplate such a development might occasion grounds for grievance on the part of the surviving spouse, who finds that he or

---

[28] Paragraphs 438 *et seq.*, cited above.

she is left to face a degree of financial uncertainty. The draftsman should in no sense be responsible for how the testator conducts investment of his estate once the will has been made. However, it would be appropriate for the draftsman to remind his client that:

- Mitigation of tax involves a difficult balancing act. The financial position of the surviving spouse (or partner if proposals of the Scottish Executive regarding same sex partnerships are implemented) should perhaps take primacy.
- If a client's estate diminishes in value owing to some financial disaster or substantial drop in the stock market (where the client is over exposed to equity investment), then the "continued" inclusion of a nil-rate band legacy within the succession planning of the client may well be wholly inappropriate.

Other strategies

11–59   Where the client is unmarried, it should not be assumed that he cannot effect inheritance tax mitigation in terms of his will. In so far as "chosen" beneficiaries are concerned, the client could direct his nil-rate band to the latter. Equally, however, such a client, having no dependants, could seek to mitigate (or indeed avoid) IHT by bequeathing part, or indeed the whole of his estate to an exempt beneficiary. This could be achieved by incorporating bequests to:

1. *Charities*—the testator (or perhaps the draftsman) needs to be sure that the intended beneficiary is indeed an entity approved by the Inland Revenue as a charity. However, where such approval exists, then bequests to that body will be exempt from inheritance tax.[29]
2. *Political parties*—this is not a blanket exemption, as an entity which claims to be political is not automatically entitled to exemption.[30] The testator (or again perhaps the draftsman) needs to be assured that the chosen institution qualifies for this particular exemption. A political party which has no representation in the House of Commons will not qualify.
3. National heritage bodies.[31]

Where a testator wishes to leave legacies to "exempt" beneficiaries, then he will need to be guided by the draftsman. If there is any doubt as to the relevant exemption applying as at the testator's date of death (which will be the ruling date, not the date upon which the will is made), then the testator may wish to make any such bequest conditional upon exemption from IHT applying, and where it does not, or has moved on, then the testator might wish to provide that the legacy in question will lapse, with the executors perhaps being given discretion to pay the relevant legacy to such other body as will still retain such exemption as at

[29] Inheritance Tax Act 1984, s.23.
[30] *ibid.*, s.24.
[31] *ibid.*, s.26.

the testator's date of death. Care will need to be taken that the discretion is not considered to be too wide, bearing in mind the reluctance of Scottish law to recognise testamentary provisions which effectively entitle executors to provide/pass on the testator's estate as they see fit.

Making use of existing exemptions

As indicated elsewhere in this book (See Chapter 3), it might be **11–60** considered that there is little point in bequeathing assets which already benefit from business property or agricultural property relief to an already exempt beneficiary. There is little point in bequeathing the testator's business to a spouse who has little interest therein, who would not be able to operate the same, and who is already financially secure.

CONDITIONAL LEGACIES

General

In one sense, every bequest detailed in a will is conditional—and that **11–61** is upon the survivance of the beneficiary. In every case survivance is a matter of proof, and where that proof fails, the legacy will lapse unless accretion or the *conditio si institutus sine liberis decesserit* applies. Where the legacy fails in such circumstances, it will fall back into the residue or into intestacy.[32]

The unfortunate results which can arise from application of the requirement of proof of survivors can be seen in the case of *Mitchell's Executrix v Gordon*.[33] This involved a tragic case—a husband, wife and their daughter were killed in an air crash. The husband and wife were survived by two other children and a grandson (the child of the daughter who died along with them). The grandson sought to claim by way of representation his mother's share in the husband's intestacy as also under the will of his grandmother (applying the above *conditio*). The grandson failed as he was unable to prove that his mother had pre-deceased her parents.

Scottish law sought to at least partially address the problems of rigid adherence to the rules of survivance in terms of section 31 of the Succession (Scotland) Act 1964. This provides:

- Where two persons die in circumstances which indicate that they died simultaneously, which render it uncertain as to which, if either, survived the other, then the younger is presumed to have survived the elder for all purposes of succession to property, legal and prior rights.[34]
- Where the two persons are husband and wife, it will be presumed that the neither survived the other.[35]

---

[32] *Drummonds Judicial Factor v Lord Advocate*, 1944 S.C. 298.
[33] 1953 S.C. 176.
[34] Section 31(1)(b).
[35] Section 31(1)(a).

- Where the elder has left a legacy in favour of the younger or (the younger failing to survive) to a third person, and the younger dies intestate, the elder is presumed for the purpose of that legacy to survive.
- In all other circumstances the general rule hereinbefore referred to will apply

Practical advice

11–62   Scottish law does not imply any period of survivance. That being so, survivance for a few minutes only shall, unless the will provides otherwise, carry the benefit to the relevant beneficiary. Where the beneficiary takes a vested interest, it will become part of his estate and be subject to either his will or, if none, the rules of intestacy as they apply to that person's estate. It is therefore important that the draftsman should, in appropriate cases, include a *commorientes* (or survivorship) provision. At its most basic level, failure to include such a clause when making wills for husband and wife may achieve the undesirable end of giving up one nil-rate band. It is highly unlikely that clients would object to a reasonable *commorientes* clause of, say, 30 days when the implications of failing to include the same are explained to them. A simple example would be:

I bequeath the residue of my estate to my spouse provided he/she shall survive me for thirty days from my date of death.

Danger area

11–63   A *commorientes* clause for spouses should not be used unthinkingly. It may be wholly appropriate when neither spouse has made lifetime gifts or transfers which would affect the entitlement of either spouse to the full nil-rate band. However, the dangers in not carrying out a proper fact find to establish not only the respective financial positions of the two spouses, but also whether or not they have effected any potentially liable lifetime transfers, can be seen from the following example.

A and B are married. A has made lifetime gifts which have effectively used up his nil-rate band available on death. He leaves an estate of £200,000 to B subject to her surviving for 30 days from his date of death. B has an estate of her own of £50,000 and has made no potentially chargeable lifetime gifts. A dies, but B dies three weeks later. Applying the *commorientes* clause, A's estate of £200,000 is taxable in full to IHT (as his nil-rate band had already been used up by lifetime gifts). Had A included no *commorientes* clause in his will, his estate would have passed to B, and on her death the combined estate (totalling £250,000) would have escaped any taxation to IHT.

The message is clear—check the financial "history" of the clients.

In theory, a *commorientes* or survivorship provision could be attached to any bequest. However, to do so might unduly convolute the terms of the will, and in any event many testators will be entirely happy that a legacy (lapsing through failure of the beneficiary to survive) should revert to the residue of the testator's estate.

Inheritance tax points

For calculation of inheritance tax

There are two important sections of the 1984 Act.   **11–64**

- Section 4(2) which provides that where it cannot be known which of two or more persons who have died survived the other or others, they shall be presumed to have died at the same instant. This can avoid a double charge to IHT (for example, where the provisions of section 31(1)(b) of the Succession (Scotland) Act 1964 apply). Under section 4(2) of the 1984 Act the estate of the younger will not be deemed to have been increased by death of the elder and therefore suffer possibly an increased IHT charge.
- Section 92 recognises a *commorientes* clause of up to six months from the date of death. This means that the "substitute" beneficiary will be deemed to have taken direct under the relevant will.

Freedom of testator to attach conditions

In general, a testator can attach such conditions as he sees fit to **11–65** legacies bequeathed in his will, unless the conditions are themselves unenforceable owing to:

- Impossibility or uncertainty;
- Illegality;
- Being contrary to public policy or morality.

Characterisation of conditions

A condition can either be casual or potestative. A casual condition is **11–66** one which is outwith the power of the executors/trustees or indeed the relevant beneficiary to control. A potestative condition is one which requires that the gift be dependent on performance of an act which it is within the power of the legatee to effect. Failure to comply with the condition, no matter how difficult, will cause the legacy to fail unless the condition is of itself in some way unenforceable. As Lord Sorn indicated:

> "This may not be a happy position for the legatee, but a testator may do what he wishes with his own and, if he chooses to qualify his bounty with troublesome conditions, the legatee, if he takes it at all, must take the bad with the good".[36]

Many bequests are in some way conditional without perhaps, at first sight, appearing to be so. For example, a bequest to children in terms of which vesting is delayed to the age of 18 or beyond is in truth conditional upon the relevant child attaining that age.[37]

---

[36] *Veitch's Executry v Veitch*, 1947 S.L.T. 17 at 19.
[37] For detailed consideration of conditional legacies, see Barr, etc., paras 5.37 *et seq.*, cited above.

Treatment of ineffective conditions

11–67   As indicated above, conditions attached to legacies can be void for a variety of reasons.

In Scottish law, the approach has been that where the condition is ineffective for some reason, the legacy will not fail, but it will pass absolutely to the legatee unencumbered with the ineffective or failing condition. Conditions in relation to marriage (or refraining therefrom), requirements to occupy particular property, requiring spouses to separate, etc. have been held to be void under one or more of the grounds detailed above.[38]

Drafting considerations
11–68   As a first point, a testator is, subject to the limits referred to above, entitled to attach conditions to his bequests. However, the draftsman should be able to guide the testator as to whether or not the latter is perhaps overstepping the mark or straying into an area where the condition, although seemingly reasonable from a testator's point of view, is likely to be struck down. There can be a difficult balance here, as the normal position is that a Scottish court will instruct that a condition should be given effect even if others might consider it to be objectionable or capricious. The case of *Balfour's Trustees v Johnston*[39] is of interest. Colonel Balfour had left estate for alimentary life use by his daughter, Mildred, "subject to the express condition that she will never hold any communication with, nor take any interest whatsoever in, a child known as Master Dennis", and failing her adhering to that condition, the alimentary life rent was to be held for another member of his family. "Master Dennis" was a foundling not in any way related to the Balfour family, although Mildred had taken an interest in the child (somewhat against her father's wishes). Mildred brought a special case shortly after her father's death to determine the validity and effect of the condition attached to the bequest in her favour. She argued that the condition was ineffectual, in respect that it was void from uncertainty, and also that it was *contra bonas mores* and capricious. Further, she argued that even if the condition were effectual, she had not yet incurred any forfeiture, but was entitled to a reasonable time after the decision of the court within which to comply therewith and, finally, that having initially complied with it, forfeiture could not afterwards operate or, in any event, could only operate during any period of non compliance on her part.

The court held as follows:

1. That the condition was neither too vague to receive effect nor contrary to public policy. The court went so far as to suggest that an allegation that a condition was "capricious" was in any event of no legal effect. The condition was valid.
2. That until validity of the condition had been determined, Mildred could not, by failing to have complied with it, have elected to incur forfeiture.

---

[38] For further more detailed consideration of case law in this area, see the Stair Memorial Encyclopaedia, Vol. 25, paras 864—875.
[39] *Balfour's Trustees v Johnston*, 1936 S.C. 137.

3. The validity of the condition having been upheld, any future non compliance would result in the bequest being finally forfeited.

The draftsman should:

- Not seek to impose his own view of morality upon the testator.
- Where a particular condition is suggested by the testator, discuss with him his reasons for seeking to impose such a condition. On occasions, a frank discussion with a trusted adviser might be sufficient to persuade the testator to drop, or at least ameliorate, a proposed, highly contentious condition.
- Where appropriate, be able to direct the testator to previous authorities wherein similar conditions have been rendered ineffective.
- Remind a testator that the imposition of a particular condition may do no more than precipitate litigation after the testator's death. Being aware that society changes, a condition which may have been upheld 60 years ago may meet with a different view now.
- Advise the testator that, in some circumstances, even where the condition is considered to be reasonable, a beneficiary may still succeed thereto without having fulfilled the condition. This can arise where the court takes the view that the legatee has done all he can to meet the condition.[40]

Where the testator does wish to leave a bequest subject to a potestative condition, then precise drafting may be required in order to avoid difficulty. For example, many of the conditions imposed involve residence or occupancy in a particular place, or occupancy of a particular property. In the case of residence in a particular place, the testator should be clear as to what he means by this, and the draftsman should seek to give effect to the testator's intention. Without such clarity then the true intention of the testator may be frustrated. For example, in *MacCallum v Coxen*,[41] a condition was imposed that the beneficiary should reside in a particular place. The beneficiary did not take up permanent residence in that place but visited the same from time to time. The Court found that this was sufficient to meet the test of residency. However, in *Pary-Jones v Hillman*[42] a condition that the beneficiary should "live and reside in" and "occupy" a particular house was held ineffective owing to uncertainty, and yet in another case the addition of the word "permanent" was held sufficient to clarify what was required by way of "residence".[43] These three cases show the difficulties which the draftsman can encounter, and emphasise the degree of clarification as to the testator's intention which may be required.

The draftsman should also be on his guard to query whether or not **11–69** use of a descriptive term in respect of a particular beneficiary implies some degree of conditionality.

---

[40] *Cummings' Trustees Petitioners*, 1960 S.L.T. (Notes) 96.
[41] 1948 S.L.T. 747.
[42] [1950] Ch. 520.
[43] *Sifton v Sifton* [1938] A.C. 656.

For example, a testator may direct as follows:

> I bequeath a legacy of FIVE THOUSAND POUNDS (£5,000) to my employee, X (design).

Is the use of the word "employee" merely descriptive, or alternatively does it imply a condition that the individual in question should remain in the employ of the testator as at the testator's date of death? Similar difficulties have been attached to the description of the beneficiary as being "my spouse". Is this merely a descriptive reference, or does it imply that the bequest should fall if the individual is not still the spouse of the testator as at death of the latter?[44]

The draftsman should also be prepared to discuss alternative solutions with the testator. For example, the testator may wish to leave a sum of money to a friend, provided the latter takes the testator's pet dog. On the face of it, it would seem that there could be no possible objection to such a potestative condition. However, the draftsman should put the following points to the testator:

- What is to happen to the legacy if the pet dog pre-deceases the testator? In such circumstances, the testator might still wish to leave a lesser bequest to his friend.
- The testator's wishes could be frustrated by the friend simply taking possession of the dog, collecting his legacy and thereafter having the animal put to sleep.
- One solution might be to consider the bequest of an annuity legacy, although this of itself might be unduly complicating an otherwise straightforward estate where there are no other continuing trust purposes. A similar comment would apply to the creation of a trust (the beneficiary of which could not of course be the pet).

Unenforceable Legacies

11–70 The unenforceable legacy requires to be contrasted with a legacy subject to conditions which are themselves unenforceable. In the latter case, where the condition is uncertain or otherwise offends against one of the "tests" outlined above, the condition itself will be unenforceable, leaving the legacy to vest absolutely in the legatee. However, an unenforceable legacy is one which lapses in its entirety. The *McCaig* cases (see Chapter 13) are classic examples. In both cases, the court took the view that the provisions left by the testators amounted to no more than grotesque self glorification without any substantial benefit being left to any other party. To that extent, the relevant instructions to the executors were deemed to be wholly unenforceable.

Practical advice

11–71 It is considered that it is unlikely nowadays for a testator to wish to indulge in obvious self glorification *post mortem*. It is, however, possible that the testator may wish to leave instructions regarding his funeral and

---

[44] *Pirie's Trustees v Pirie*, 1962 S.C. 43.

a suitable memorial, which the draftsman might consider to be excessive. What approach should the draftsman take?

- It would be worthwhile pointing out to the testator that the Inland Revenue will not allow excessive funeral expenses to be set off against the gross estate, thereby reducing the same for IHT purposes. In fact it has only been since the case of *Prentice v Chalmers*[45] that the Inland Revenue has regarded the reasonable cost of a tombstone as being a debt which can be set off for IHT purposes.
- The testator should be advised that excessive provisions are almost certain to be challenged by residuary beneficiaries.
- Where the testator persists, then this might raise a question as to his capacity in the first place.

Repugnancy

Provisions contained within a will may be rendered ineffective if they **11–72** are mutually inconsistent. This is known as "repugnancy" and occurs where the testator leaves a bequest which is absolute, but then tries to "fence in" the bequest with provisions which are inconsistent with absolute ownership. Three examples are:

1. Directions to retain a vested right to a person of full age.
2. Directions that a legacy is given for alimentary use; and
3. Directions to executors to buy an annuity.[46]

In *Miller's Trustees v Miller*,[47] Lord President Inglis said:

"Where . . . the fee of an estate . . . has vested in a beneficiary the court will always, if possible, relieve him of any trust management that is cumbrous, unnecessary or expensive. Where there are trust purposes to be served which cannot be secured without the retention of the vested estate or interest of the beneficiary in the hands of trustees, the rule cannot be applied, and the right of the beneficiary must be subordinated to the will of the testator."

Retention of a vested right

Provisions which offend against this principle are perhaps more **11–73** common than might be thought. An example would be:

I bequeath a legacy of FIVE THOUSAND POUNDS (£5,000) STERLING to A (design) but I direct my executors that payment of the said legacy shall be deferred until A shall attain the age of twenty one.

Such a direction to retain is ineffective not being coupled with any trust provision.

---

[45] 1985 S.L.T. 168.
[46] R.C. Henderson, *The Principles of Vesting in the Law of Succession* (2nd ed., 1938).
[47] (1890) 18 R. 301.

Bequest of a legacy for alimentary use

11–74   Where the legatee has already vested in a full right, any direction to executors, that the legacy should be used to aliment the legatee is ineffectual.

Legacy left to buy an annuity

11–75   Such a provision is repugnant for the reason that the legatee could immediately sell the annuity.[48]

Practical advice

11–76   Where the testator does not wish a beneficiary to vest at age 16,[49] then the bequest must be coupled with appropriate trust purposes, including a postponement of vesting (such as an accumulation and maintenance trust). An instruction simply to manage the property until a particular age has been attained will not prevent vesting and the legatee claiming payment. In the case of *Smith's Trustee v Michael*,[50] a statement that trustees should not make over capital to the beneficiary at age 21 unless they were satisfied that there was a good reason for so doing was held to be ineffectual in preventing the beneficiary from demanding immediate payment once that beneficiary had attained the age of 18 (being the relevant age of majority at the time under the Age of Majority (Scotland) Act, 1969).

- The testator could insert a provision that payment was not to be made until, for example, age 18. Such a statement would be wholly ineffective, but the testator may wish to take the chance that the legatee will not realise this. It is submitted that it would not be appropriate for a draftsman to advise this course—if vesting is to be postponed, then appropriate trust provisions and purposes should be included.
- There is no repugnancy if the instruction to the executors is to purchase an annuity in their name for the benefit of a particular person. Similarly, the granting of an alimentary life rent will be effectual, as the right to income subject to management by the executors is not repugnant (although it may not be advisable given that, once a benefit has been received, it cannot be varied in terms of section 142 of the Inheritance Tax Act, 1984).

Unless a testator is happy that there is a possibility that part of his estate should fall into intestacy, the draftsman should advise (in plain English terms) his client on the question of accretion. It is submitted that few testators going to the trouble of making a will shall happily accept that the devolution to at least part of their estate should be directed in terms of the provisions of the Succession (Scotland) Act 1964 as amended.

In advising clients, it should be noted that the question of whether or not accretion should apply differs in respect of pecuniary legacies and shares of residue.

---

[48] *Dempster's Trustees v Dempster*, 1921 S.C. 332.
[49] The Age of Legal Capacity (Scotland) Act 1991.
[50] 1972 S.L.T. 89.

Accretion is a principle of construction of a will. Where the principle **11–77** applies, the benefit which falls to a pre-deceasing beneficiary will carry over to a survivor/survivors. Where accretion does not apply, and the bequest is, for example, a pecuniary legacy, the benefit will fall into the residue of the testator's estate. However, where the bequest is of a share of residue and there is no accretion or destination over, then intestacy will be the outcome. Accretion therefore applies to both legacies and shares of residue. It will apply to both heritable and moveable property.

The application of the *conditio si institutus sine liberis decesserit*

The nature and effect of the conditio is considered in more detail in **11–78** Chapter 4. However, where the conditio applies, it can have a direct effect on the terms of the testator's will—the *conditio* may need to be given effect prior to a "direct" provision in favour of survivors. Thus, where the conditio does apply, this will interpose the issue of, for example, a pre-deceasing nephew before the survivors detailed in the will.

Example:

A testator leaves a sum of £60,000 to be divided between four nephews and the survivors of them. One of the nephews pre-deceases the testator survived by three children. Where the conditio applies, the children of the pre-deceasing nephew would each be interposed so as to receive a one-third share of their pre-deceasing father's interest in the legacy fund (*i.e.* each of the children of the pre-deceasing nephew would receive £5,000). The conditio has prevented the share of the pre-deceasing nephew carrying over to the three surviving nephews.

It is therefore of importance that the executors charged with giving effect to the will should consider whether or not the conditio has any application, before moving on to simply divide the legacy fund between, in the above example, the three surviving nephews.

Interestingly, and while the interposition of the conditio can prevent accretion applying, accretion does not apply itself to any share taken as a result of the conditio being brought into play, unless the testator so provides.[51]

Where the testator does not wish accretion to apply, then inclusion of a phrase such as ". . . but expressly excluding the issue of any of them" will operate so as to prevent the conditio taking effect.

Legacies

The position may be clear where the client wishes to bequeath a series **11–79** of legacies to unrelated beneficiaries. In such circumstances, the client may be more than content that if an individual legatee pre-deceases him, the legacy should fall back into the residue of his estate. However,

---

[51] *Andrew's Executors v Andrew's Trustees*, 1925 E.T.C. 844.

different considerations apply where the testator wishes to leave a legacy to relatives or another class of beneficiaries. Where the client wishes to leave the legacy to be divided between a group or class of beneficiaries, what is to happen where one of those beneficiaries pre-deceases? In the normal case, where a sum is left to a number of beneficiaries and one or more of them fail to survive, then the benefits due to the survivors will increase, the share due to the predecessor accrescing to the survivors.[52] For example, where a testator makes provision in the following format, then accretion will apply.

> I bequeath the sum of TEN THOUSAND POUNDS (£10,000) to A, B, C and D.

If all of the legatees survive, they will each receive £2,500. If, however, only two of them survive, then the survivors will both receive £5,000. If only one survives then he will take the whole bequest.

Such a result may well equate to what the testator would wish. However, he does have an alternative.

Where the testator would not wish such a legacy to accresce to the relevant survivors, then words of "severance" can be used. In the example, if the instruction had been to pay the sum of £10,000 "equally between" the beneficiaries, then accretion would not operate in the event of any beneficiary pre-deceasing the testator.[53] Severance can be achieved by use of words or phrases such as "equally", "equally between" or "share and share alike".

Class gifts

11–80   A gift to a class represents the one category where use of the words of severance will not itself prevent the application of accretion. Perhaps the best example of a class gift is "to my children" or "my issue". In *Bartholomew's Trustees v Bartholomew*[54] a gift to the testator's "unmarried daughters" was held to be a class gift. Similarly, the phrase "nieces and nephews" was also held to be a class gift.[55]

Drafting considerations

11–81   In the case of a gift to "my children", it may be the implicit intention of the testator that accretion should apply. However, the draftsman should never operate on assumption. The nature and effect of accretion should be explained to the testator who can then decide whether or not he wishes accretion to apply. If accretion is not to apply, then perhaps the simplest way of avoiding the same would be to avoid description of any class in the first place, *i.e.* simply name the beneficiaries without indicating their relationship to the testator. For example, a legacy to "A, B and C equally between them" will not result in accretion, even if A, B and C are children of the testator.[56] However, this drafting technique

---

[52] *Mair's Trustees v Mair*, 1936 S.L.T. 519.
[53] *Youngs Trustees v Young*, 1927 S.C. (H.L.) 6.
[54] 11 S.L.T. 608
[55] *Clow's Trustees v Bethune*, 1935 S.C. 754.
[56] *Graham's Trustees v Graham* (1899) 2 F. 232.

may not find favour with the testator, who may consider it to be strange that a will-making provision for his family omits any reference to the nature of the testator's relationship to beneficiaries named therein.

The choice of whether or not accretion should apply should always lie with the testator. Thus, where accretion is to apply this can be achieved fairly simply, for example:

"To such of my nephews and nieces A, B, C, D and E who shall survive me equally among them".

Where accretion is not to apply, then the following wording might be used (making no reference whatsoever to survivorship):

"In equal shares to each of my nephews and nieces A, B, C, D and E".

Extending the benefit

Most testators specify those who are to be their principal beneficiaries. **11–82** In many cases, the testator will not have looked beyond his wife and children. However, many testators are understandably reluctant to contemplate circumstances which do not follow the "natural order", (*i.e.* that a parent will pre-decease his children). It is difficult for many clients (particularly those of younger generations) to contemplate the possibility that one or more of their children will die before them. However, the draftsman needs to be able to discuss this possibility with his clients in a sensitive fashion. The misconceptions under which many clients operate may appear to the skilled draftsman to be almost inexplicable, but some of the most common are:

- When a child pre-deceases his parent, any benefit left to the child in the parents' will automatically passes to the surviving spouse of that child. This, of course, has never been the case under Scottish law and if that result is truly the wish of the testator then it will require to be detailed in the testator's will. Such an over-destination is not common in Scottish wills and the draftsman may feel that where such a proposal is made by his client, the following matters should be brought to the client's attention:

  (a) Is such an over-destination in favour of the surviving spouse to apply only if the spouse in question was still married to, and living with, the adult child at the latter's date of death?

  (b) Does the testator appreciate that such a bequest could have the effect of disinheriting his own grandchildren? For example, the surviving spouse of a pre-deceasing child may re-marry, and it cannot be assumed that he or she will make iron cast provision for his or her own children in such circumstances (see Chapter 4).

- Many clients may overlook grandchildren in the belief that the share which would otherwise have gone to a pre-deceasing adult child will pass proportionately or equally amongst the testator's surviving adult children. If this is the requirement of the testator, then the issue of a pre-deceasing child will need to be specifically excluded (with the client being advised of the possibility in those circumstances of the grandchildren claiming legal rights as representing their deceased parent). However, in most cases, when the position is fully and properly explained to the testator, he will probably accept that such a provision would be inappropriate, as he would be denying his own bloodline financial support perhaps at the time when they are most financially vulnerable, and require as much financial support as can be made available to them for their upkeep, maintenance or education.

The above misconceptions are perhaps one reason why clients should be discouraged from seeking to draw up their own wills. However, it is part of the draftsman's task to explore with his client how a bequest, which fails owing to failure of the beneficiary to survive, should be handled. As indicated, this can be a sensitive area for some clients, but nonetheless the draftsman should explore with the client his feelings in relation to that scenario. This is of particular importance in relation to bequests of residue. If no suitable formula is adopted in the testator's will, then one or more shares of residue could fall into intestacy—such an outcome would at least partially defeat the testator's purpose of making a will in the first place.

The testator's choice

11–83   Whether in relation to a legacy or a share of residue, the testator should make a conscious choice as to whether or not, and to what extent, the relevant bequest should transmit to others in the event of the chosen beneficiary failing to survive the testator.

Specific bequests

11–84   In many cases, the view of the testator will be that if the relevant beneficiary fails to survive, then the bequest should simply pass back into the residue of the testator's estate. If, however, the testator would wish the item in question to pass to a substitute beneficiary, then this requires to be stated.

PECUNIARY LEGACIES

11–85   The attitude of the testator is often largely determined by the underlying family situation. For example, a testator who wishes to leave legacies to friends, but otherwise to bequeath the residue of his estate to family, may be content that in the event of any legatee failing to survive, the relevant bequest should fall back into the residue, thereby increasing the benefit to his family. However, where the testator is single and has no immediate family, then a different approach may well be required by the client. The approach of such a client may often be to leave a long list of legacies to friends, etc., with the residue being bequeathed to charity.

The testator may take the view that if a legatee fails to survive, then the bequest should not fall back into the residue of his estate, but rather should be utilised so as to increase the benefit to surviving legatees. Further, it may well be that the testator would wish the "failed" legacy not to be distributed equally among all surviving legatees, but rather to be directed to particular legatees whom the testator might consider to be more deserving or necessitous.

Drafting considerations

- The testator should make it clear whether or not he is content **11–86** that a failed legacy should pass back into the residue of his estate. However, where this is the requirement of the client, the draftsman still needs to be aware of the *conditio si institutus sine liberis decesserit*.
- Where the *conditio* is not to apply, then issue of the legatee should be expressly excluded.
- Where the legacy is not to fall back to residue, the draftsman needs to ascertain to whom the legacy should transmit. Where the testator has opted for a list of legacies, then it is entirely possible that in the event of one legatee failing to survive, the legacy in question should pass to another specified individual. Some care is required here—if, on failure of a particular legatee to survive, the will is to carry the legacy to another individual, and the latter is already a legatee in his own right, then it would be prudent for the testator to make it absolutely clear that the individual in question is to be entitled to both his "original" legacy, and also the further legacy as "substitute" for the pre-deceasing legatee. This is of particular importance where the legacies are of the same amount—in order to avoid any difficulty, the testator should make it clear that the legacies are to be cumulative.
- Where the testator leaves a list of legacies of differing amounts and does not wish any of the legacies to fall back into the residue owing to a particular legatee failing to survive him, then he will need to direct whether the "failed" legacy is to be divided equally between surviving legatees or on a *pro rata* basis. The draftsman should never assume that the testator would wish the failed legacy to be divided equally.

Division of a Bequest Among Beneficiaries

The testator indicates he wishes to leave a legacy to a number of **11–87** beneficiaries. The draftsman needs to check whether the legacy is to be left to the beneficiaries in equal shares or subject to some inequality of division. If equality of division is desired, then this is simply achieved. For example:

"I bequeath the sum of FORTY THOUSAND POUNDS (£40,000) STERLING to A, B, C, D and E."

The presumption here is that equal shares are intended by the testator, even though there has been no specific reference to equality of division.

Thus, in the example given, each of the beneficiaries would receive £8,000.

However, if inequality of division is the desired end then this will need to be specified, although in such circumstances, rather than complicate matters, the testator should be encouraged simply to leave separate legacies of the desired amounts to the relevant beneficiaries. This, of course, may not be possible if the subject to the bequest is not money but is, for example, a dwelling-house. At first sight, this may appear to be straightforward. For example:

> "I bequeath free of all expenses of transfer, heritable debts, securities and other burdens affecting the same my dwelling-house at 1 Brown Street, Anytown as follows:
>
>> (a) a one-fifth *pro indiviso* share to A;
>> (b) a two-fifths *pro indiviso* share to B;
>> (c) a two-fifths *pro indiviso* share to C."

On the face of it the foregoing bequest would achieve the aims of the testator. However, what are the difficulties?

- What happens if one of the beneficiaries pre-deceases the testator? This could be addressed by making provision for substitute beneficiaries in each case. This, however, may not be what the testator would wish.
- As drafted, accretion would not apply and the relevant interest would pass back into the residue of the testator's estate or perhaps into intestacy.
- Even where the draftsman persuades the testator to nominate "substitute" beneficiaries, then the draftsman needs to bear in mind the presumption that, with regard to a bequest of heritage, the destination over results in substitution, not conditional institution.[57] The presumption can of course be overcome, but difficulties can arise if the draftsman simply makes reference to "A whom failing B". Careful drafting is required— for example:

> ". . . to A declaring that in the event of A pre-deceasing me then the said one-fifth *pro indiviso* share shall pass to D".

11–88 This area is not free from difficulty, and it might be worthwhile for the draftsman to explore whether the testator really wishes to bequeath shares in the heritable property itself, or rather the monetary values arising from those shares. In the latter case, the less complex course for the testator to follow would be to direct his executors to sell the property and to divide the net proceeds on sale on the unequal basis required by the testator. The testator may, however, have specific and (from the testator's point of view) justifiable reasons as to why he would wish to bequeath shares in the property to A, B and C, and perhaps no others.

---

[57] *Watson v Giffen* (1884) 11 R. 444.

In those circumstances then the relevant clause can be amended so as to provide for accretion, to apply as between A, B and C in the event of one of them pre-deceasing the testator. In that event, however, the testator will need to direct in what proportions such accretion should apply; or for example, the position might appear simple if A pre-deceased the testator. Where a pre-deceasing beneficiary's share is to accresce equally among the survivors, then B and C in the given example would each end up receiving a one half *pro indiviso* share. However, what happens if C is the one to pre-decease.? If the latter's share accresces equally to A and B, the latter would end up with a three-fifth *pro indiviso* share, with A receiving the remaining two-fifths. If the testator is content with this outcome, then accretion, applying on an equal basis, is likely to find ready acceptance. However, further difficulties arise if the testator wishes the share of the pre-deceasing beneficiary to accresce in differing proportions to the survivors. This would involve careful drafting which may appear to be cumbersome, but which nonetheless may be necessary to achieve the testator's desired end. Thus:

". . . and in the event of the said C pre-deceasing me then I direct that the two-fifths *pro indiviso* share to which he would have succeeded had he survived me shall be made over as to one-quarter thereof to A and the remaining three-quarters thereof to B".

In the event of C pre-deceasing the testator, A would receive a three-tenths share of the heritable property, with B receiving a seven-tenths share.

FAMILY DIVISION

This is an area where the misconceptions and the misunderstandings of **11–89** the client may require some care on the part of the draftsman. Where the client is elderly and perhaps has a fairly extensive family, he may require some guidance as to appropriate division of his estate in the event of, for example, one or more adult children pre-deceasing the testator. For clients of any age, such a discussion can be difficult—as has already been recognised, many individuals find it difficult and distressing to have to consider the possibility that one or more of his children may go before him. Nonetheless, the draftsman should encourage the testator to consider how the testator's estate should in fact be divided amongst the surviving members of his family. The draftsman should prepare a "family tree" and, making use of the same, demonstrate to the client how the division of his estate might operate in differing circumstances.

It is in this area that clients need to be advised of the difference between *per capita* and *per stirpes* division. The draftsman should never assume that the client understands the quite different results which can arise from one method being used as opposed to the other. In particular, the general rule is that unless a contrary intention is indicated in the will itself, *per capita* division will fall to be applied.[58]

---

[58] *Boyd's Trustee v Shaw*, 1958 S.C. 115.

Example of *per capita* division

11–90   A, a widower, passes on. He is survived by two adult children, B and C, and by three grandchildren, X, Y and Z, who are the children of a third child, D, who pre-deceased A. A's estate amounts to £120,000. There is no instruction in his will that the division should be on a *per stirpes* basis. A's will provides that his estate should be divided between his surviving children and the issue of any pre-deceasing child. The result is that his adult children, B and C, each received £24,000, with the three grandchildren, X, Y and Z, also receiving the same amount. This is likely to be viewed by the adult children as a distortion of what their father had truly intended, and may lead to the draftsman facing awkward questions from those children. In fairness, the possible distorting effect of *per capita* division should be pointed out to the testator. In the author's experience, such advice normally results in the client immediately opting for *per stirpes* succession.

Example of *per stirpes* division

11–91   Let us assume that we have the same family as in the above example. However, the testator does include clear provision within his will, calling for *per stirpes* division between generations. In this case the result would be that B and C would each receive £40,000, with the three grandchildren sharing the remaining £40,000 between them.

It is, of course, for the testator to decide upon the "generational" division of his estate. However, he can only do so if he is given clear advice from the draftsman as to the choices which are open to the testator, in order that the latter can take a demonstrably informed decision.

The foregoing examples relate to the residue of the testator's estate. The possibly distorting effects of *per capita* division can apply equally to, for example, a pecuniary legacy, for example the testator may wish to leave a legacy of £60,000.00 "to such of my grandchildren as shall survive me". At his death, he has two adult children, B and C. B has one child, X. C has four children, S, T, U and V. As *per capita* division would apply, X would receive £12,000.00. The four children of C would also each receive £12,000.00. Whilst such a division might seem to be entirely equitable, the scope for family jealousy remains with B (perhaps albeit unfairly), forming the view that his father favoured C's line more than his own. Such family jealousies cannot be discounted, but the draftsman will have properly served his client if he ensures that the client is absolutely clear as to how the relevant bequest is to be divided. It should be noted in the last mentioned example that an attempt to introduce a stirpital division of the legacy by merely adding the words *"per stirpes"* thereto would fail, as there is no indication as the point at which division *per stirpes* is to apply. In the foregoing example, if the testator would wish to achieve an effect equivalent to stirpital division in respect of the legacy, then he would have to provide that one-half of the legacy fund should be paid to X, with the remaining half divided equally between S, T, U and V.

Use of plain English

11–92   The legal profession has taken great strides to simplify the documentation it produces for clients. In particular, the phrase *per stirpes* has, over a number of years, proven to most clients to be the equivalent of "double Dutch". This has resulted in many draftsmen seeking to construct provisions which do not use the phrase *per stirpes*, but which nonetheless seek to achieve a stirpital division.[59] Many of the attempts to achieve stirpital division using plain English are undoubtedly successful. However, it is submitted that only those who are skilled in this area should seek to construct their own "plain English" version of a *per stirpes* division. A well meaning attempt might fail, with those beneficiaries who feel that they have "lost out" seeking to vindicate their position against the well meaning draftsman in the manner now opened up by the *Holmes v Bank of Scotland* case.[60]

Practical advice

- Where a testator is clearly creating what amounts to a family **11–93** will, obtain full details of his family.
- Create a family tree and discuss the methodology of division with the testator. Albeit that many testators find such discussions distasteful, the best practice would be to indicate to the testator how his estate might be divided against the background of different eventualities.
- Check whether a stirpital division is to apply to all descendants or whether, at some point, a line is to be drawn. For example, the testator may not wish to "look beyond" his grandchildren. This may of course raise implications as to whether or not the *conditio si institutus* will have any application.
- Beware of client misconception as to the meaning of the word "issue". Used in a will, "issue" means all direct lineal descendants.[61] However, it is not uncommon to find clients believing that "issue" extends only to children and not beyond. When in discussion with a client regarding the terms of his will, the true meaning of the word should be explained, and the client clear as to the possible effect of the same in a true stirpital division— and this of course is of importance if, at some point, the testator does wish to draw a line in his family tree so far as implementation of his will is concerned.
- If a testator does wish to make provision for *per capita* division, notwithstanding that there are likely to be beneficiaries from different generations and branches of his family involved, then the draftsman would be advised to ensure that the testator has taken on board the possibility for family jealousy arising between different branches of his family. For his own self protection, the draftsman would also be well advised to ensure that he records in writing to the client the fact that there has been a full discussion on the effect of *per capita* division before the relevant will was executed.

---

[59] Barr, etc., para.5(10) *et acq.*, cited above.
[60] Cited above.
[61] *Turner's Trustees v Turner* (1887) 24 R. 619.

CHAPTER 12

TRUSTS

12–01 It is fair to suggest that, as our society has become more complex, and with the greater spread of wealth, will draftsmen have made increasing use of different types of trust in order to assist clients to achieve the strategies which the testator would wish to see adopted following his or her death. It should be borne in mind that trusts are used not simply for the purposes of mitigation of tax. A testamentary trust can be used to enable the testator to seek to protect young, financially naive, or incapacitated beneficiaries (see later in this Chapter).

Trusts have a very valuable role to play in testamentary planning, and it should be part of the draftsman's responsibility and function to highlight to clients when, and in what circumstances, use of a particular trust provision might be made. Anecdotal evidence suggests that some clients, perhaps themselves querying whether or not use might be made of a trust, have been advised that they should not avail themselves of a trust provision within their wills, either because trust administration is too complex and very expensive, or owing to perceived tax "problems". Whilst there is no doubt that the administration of a trust proper does require time, effort and expense, these are only aspects which require to be weighed in the balance by the testator. It may be that over-emphasis on these "downsides", in truth, reflects lack of experience or confidence of the draftsman in his own knowledge and skills. It is therefore important that, when consulted by a client, the draftsman should not deny him or her the opportunity to at least consider appropriate will-drafting strategies, simply because of a lack of familiarity with the same. Where the adviser confronts such a situation, then there is no shame in passing the client on to someone who has the requisite skills and expertise—this is professional common sense and in any event is implicit in the Code of Conduct. A draftsman who does not adhere to that common-sense approach may well be offending against article 5 of the Code of Conduct for Scottish Solicitors 2002: "solicitors must provide adequate professional services".

TYPES OF TRUST

12–02 Will drafting can involve consideration of different types of trust.

The bare trust

12–03 The bare trust arises where trustees hold property for other individuals without there necessarily being any trust purposes to fulfil. Where the beneficiary is capax and of full age, he can demand that the trustees make the assets over to him. The creation of a bare trust is in fact quite commonplace (for example, where a stockbroker nominee company holds shares for a client who is the true owner). The creation of such a trust arises where a will makes no specific provision in respect of children under the age of 16 years. Where such children are beneficiaries under the will and no specific trust provisions are included, then they will vest in their benefits *a morte testatoris*. However, under the Age of Capacity (Scotland) Act 1991, Scottish children are not entitled to demand payment until they attain the age of 16 years. What therefore is to be done in the interim? In the circumstances, and unless executors pay over the funds to the guardian of the child, they will normally retain the funds until the child attains the age of 16 years. A direction that the funds should be retained and not paid over until a later age (often 18 or 21 years) is, without any further trust purposes requiring to be fulfilled, ineffective, and will not prevent a child from being able to claim payment as soon as the age of 16 years has been attained.

Provision of flexibility

Even where the will does not contain full trust purposes, it is still **12–04** possible, by means of appropriate drafting, to provide the executors with a degree of flexibility in relation to benefits held for a child under the age of 16 years. This can be achieved by inclusion of the following purpose:

"Where any part of my estate is held for a beneficiary who lacks full legal capacity, the executors shall have full power either to pay or to apply the whole or any part of the income or capital which falls to such a beneficiary for his or her benefit in such manner as my executors may in their sole discretion think proper, or to retain the same until such capacity has been attained, or to pay or make over the same to the legal guardian or the person for the time being having custody of such beneficiary, any receipt granted by such guardian or person being a sufficient discharge to my executors."

The features of such a clause are:

- To allow the executors flexibility. Without such a clause being included, it is thought that where executors hold funds which have already vested in a child under the age of 16 years, they may be bound to pay the income of the fund, so far as necessary, for the child's education or maintenance. The above purpose does not restrict intervention on the part of the executors to education or maintenance, but empowers them to intervene in any manner the executors shall think proper, and then to such extent as the executors may decide.
- The purpose refers to any part of the testator's estate. It would therefore apply to both pecuniary legacies and shares of residue.
- Where the executors consider it to be appropriate, payments, if they are to be made, can be made to the guardian or person having custody of the beneficiary. As a practical matter, however, executors should bear the following points in mind.

(a) The guardian should be made aware that the payment belongs to the child, not to the guardian.

(b) A consideration of the lifestyle or personality of the guardian may be required. It would be wholly inappropriate for executors to make payments over to a guardian who may have a drink or drug problem.

(c) The executors cannot be forced by the guardian or parent to make over the funds. A decision as to when and how any payments should be made is the responsibility of the executors.

(d) The property being administered has vested in the minor beneficiary. If he or she dies before attaining the age of 16 years then the bequest forms part of the child's estate and the executors may be required to pay over such of the bequest as they still hold to the executors of the child—it is not for the "holding executors" to decide who should benefit in the circumstances given that the property has already vested.

Taxation

Income tax

12–05   Although no income on the retained fund is paid to the child, it still belongs to him and will therefore form part of the child's income for income tax purposes. In the unlikely event of the child being a higher rate tax payer, then the income in question may result in an additional income tax liability. The more normal situation is that the child will not have a tax liability, but still has an entitlement to personal tax relief—an income tax repayment claim can be made (by the guardian) on the child's behalf.[1]

Capital gains tax

12–06   Given that the property has already vested in the child where there is a disposal, the child's capital gains tax position must be considered. The child's annual exemption for capital gains tax purposes can be brought into play.

Inheritance tax

12–07   Where the child has an estate in excess of the nil-rate band then inheritance tax is payable—funds still held by executors for the child pending attainment of the age of 16 require to be aggregated with the child's personal estate.

Life-rent trust

12–08   A life rent trust is an interest in possession trust. In its simplest form, one beneficiary (the life renter) is entitled to enjoy income generated by the trust (or occupation if the trust asset is a dwelling-house) with

---

[1] The "aggregation" provisions of s.663 of the Income and Corporation Tax Act 1998 do not apply even where the original testator was a parent of the child (this being due to the fact that aggregation does not apply where the parent is dead).

another beneficiary (the fiar) being entitled to the capital of the trust on termination of the life rent itself.

The responsibility for administering the life rented estate lies with the trustees. Life rent trusts were fairly common in the past, but in recent years have diminished in popularity when compared with accumulation and maintenance or discretionary trusts. A consideration of one of the possible uses of a life rent trust appears in Chapter 4.

Other possible uses are:

- The testator may have concerns regarding the financial prudence of a beneficiary. In such circumstances, the testator may not wish to make capital (or particular assets) over absolutely to the beneficiary. However, the testator still wishes to afford some degree of financial support to the beneficiary in question. This can be achieved by giving the beneficiary an interest in possession (*i.e.* a right to income).
- A life rent may be of interest to a testator who has "generational concerns" (*i.e.* he wishes to exercise a degree of control from beyond the grave to ensure that successive generations of his family benefit from his estate). That being so, a life rent trust (wherein the testator's children are the life renters and his grandchildren the fiars) would achieve that aim.
- Where a degree of flexibility is required, the trustees could be empowered to advance capital to the life renter, although this power would require to be balanced against the other aims of the testator (for example, equality of benefit, generational succession and possible protection of a financially naïve beneficiary).

Taxation

Income tax

Trustees are liable to income tax at the basic rate on trust income. **12–09** Where the trustees mandate income tax under Sch.A or Sch.D direct to the beneficiary, where a return is made by the trustees under the Taxes Management Act 1970 (section 13), the trustees will not be assessed on the income in question. Whilst Revenue expenses can be set off against trust income, in the first instance they require to be set off against dividend income before other types are brought into play.[2] Other expenses of administering the trust cannot be set off against income tax assessments made on the trustee.[3]

Capital gains tax

The trustees are entitled to an annual exemption. For trusts made **12–10** before June 7, 1978, the exemption limit is one-half of that for an individual. For trusts created on or after June 7, 1978, the exemption limit is still one-half of that to an individual, but this exemption falls to

---

[2] Finance Act 1993, s.79(3).
[3] *Inverclyde's Trustees v Millar*, 1924 S.L.T. 414.

be subdivided where more than one trust has been set up by the same settlor. The rate of tax is the "applicable rate".[4] For a life rent trust, the "applicable rate" is the same as to the basic rate of income tax (note, however, that this only applies to the situation where the "whole trust" is an interest in possession one). Where, within an accumulation and maintenance trust, a life rent fund has been created, then the rate will still be the "applicable rate" for an accumulation and maintenance trust (presently 34 per cent but it has been proposed that this be increased to 40 per cent).

On death of the life renter, the trust funds will be deemed to have vested in the fiars at the values which applied as at the life renter's date of death, with no gain being deemed to arise as a result of such uplift.

Inheritance tax

12–11   Under section 49(1) of the Inheritance Tax Act 1984 the life rented fund is treated as having belonged to a life renter, and thereby falls to be aggregated with the personal estate of the life renter for inheritance tax purposes. The inheritance tax liability as so calculated requires to be apportioned on the one hand to the personal estate of the life renter, and on the other to the life rent trust. The liability for payment of the inheritance tax charge as so calculated in respect of the life rented property falls upon the life rent trustees.

Where a life renter has a power to terminate the life rent during his lifetime and does so, then this will not trigger any immediate inheritance tax liability, but will be treated as a potentially exempt transfer by the life renter. The testator needs to take care that he does not unwittingly produce an unexpectedly larger IHT liability by use of a life rent trust, owing to the aggregation provisions on death of the life renter. He is, after all, only entitled to the income from the trust (but who on death is nonetheless treated as if he had owned the trust capital).

Accumulation and maintenance trust

12–12   This type of trust has great value for testators who are concerned to offer a degree of protection to the beneficiaries from their own inexperience or financial naïvety. This single feature or attribute of such a trust has made their use much more widespread. In fact, it is now commonplace to find testators who will, without prompting, ask the draftsman to incorporate provisions which will postpone vesting but still allow flexibility for appropriate financial intervention on the part of their trustees. This type of trust fits the bill. It is in fact a form of discretionary trust to which special treatment is afforded.

In order to be a "proper" accumulation and maintenance trust, and to obtain the special treatment referred to above, it needs to satisfy the requirements of section 71 of the Inheritance Tax Act 1984. These are:

   (i)   There must be no interest in possession in the trust capital.
   (ii) One or more of the qualifying beneficiaries will become beneficially entitled to the capital, or to an interest in possession therein, at latest by the age of 25 years; and

---

[4] Taxation of Chargeable Gains Act 1992, s.4(1AA).

(iii) Pending such interest in possession, any income which is not applied for the maintenance, education or benefit of a qualifying beneficiary is to be accumulated.

It is clear from the foregoing that this type of trust may be suitable only for young persons. In particular, in order to comply with the provisions of section 71, it is considered that:

- The qualifying beneficiaries must be children of a common grandparent; or
- Qualifying beneficiaries must be the children of a pre-deceasing child of the common grandparent; or
- The trust must be limited to a life of a maximum of 25 years, still fitting in with the "tests" outlined above.

Care in drafting is required, as if it seems possible for a beneficiary over the age of 25 years to benefit, then the trust will not qualify under section 71. Note that the requirement is that the beneficiary needs to obtain only an interest in possession in income by the time he is 25 years of age. It is not a requirement of section 71 that the beneficiary should obtain a vested interest in any part of the capital by age 25, or indeed at any subsequent date. The "careful drafting" referred to earlier in this paragraph therefore relates to the age of the beneficiary at the time the trust comes into operation. Where one of the beneficiaries is already over the age of 25 years then the "privileges" afforded by section 71 will not apply, and that being so, most draftsmen are careful to ensure that the accumulation and maintenance trust provisions created by them comply with the age limits hereinbefore detailed; where a testator has, for example, one grandchild who is already 25 years of age but all others are still relatively young, then the testator should consider treating the eldest grandchild in some separate, suitable fashion.

Positive aspects

- As stated, the testator can build in financial protection for young beneficiaries.   **12–13**
- The testator can build in an over-destination, carrying the relevant estate to other beneficiaries in the event of one of the principal beneficiaries not attaining the vesting age.
- The testator can allow his trustee to intervene financially in support of a young beneficiary for maintenance, education, etc..
- The testator can choose within the above limits the age at which each beneficiary will take a right to income from.
- Where the "tests" required by section 71 of the 1984 Act are met, there will be no periodic charge to inheritance tax every 10 years, and no "proportionate/exit charges" to IHT arise on distribution of the trust and in particular on vesting of capital in beneficiaries attaining the vesting age.

Accumulation restrictions

The draftsman should always bear in mind the restrictions on periods of accumulation.[5] That being so, it is usual to limit accumulation until the specified beneficiaries respectively attain the age of 21. The drafts-   **12–14**

---

[5] Wilson and Duncan, *Trust, Trustees and Executors*, (W. Green, 1975), pp.107 *et seq.*

man should bear in mind that where the testator is not concerned to secure the IHT benefits provided by section 71 of the 1984 Act, it is possible for a trust to be set up to meet other aims. For example, the testator may have an adult spendthrift child who is already aged 25 years or over. The testator may choose to nominate, for example, the age of 35 years for vesting of capital. The testator can set up such a trust provided that the draftsman warns him that it will not have the benefits (outlined above) in so far as inheritance tax is concerned.

Taxation

Income tax

12–15 Accumulation and maintenance trusts, being a species of discretionary trust, are taxed at the special trust rate applicable to a discretionary trust. Credit is given against such higher charge for tax already deducted at source. For Schedule F dividends, the higher rate of 25 per cent is applied. When a beneficiary vests in the right to income, then, to the extent of that beneficiary's share, the trust will cease to be one subject to the special trust rate. The trustees will remain liable at the special trust rate only on that part of that income which they continue to accumulate for beneficiaries who have not yet vested in the right to income.

Capital gains tax

12–16 The trust will have an annual exemption at half of the rate available to an individual. The rate of charge is 34 per cent (increasing to 40 per cent) for the whole trust and that whether or not there is a mix of beneficiaries, *i.e.* where there are some under the age at which income vests and others who have already acquired an interest in possession in income having attained the relevant vesting age.

Inheritance tax

12–17 Where the trust qualifies in terms of section 71 of the 1984 Act, it is not treated as a discretionary trust. The main feature of this is that where a beneficiary attains the age for the vesting of capital, there will be no exit charge due on inheritance tax on payment of that beneficiary. Where a beneficiary has not yet vested in the interest in possession, then on death of that beneficiary there is no charge to IHT in the trust, nor is there any aggregation with the deceased beneficiary's personal estate. If, however, the beneficiary has already taken a vested interest in income, then the relevant funds will be treated as belonging to the beneficiary and will be liable to inheritance tax on his death.[6]

Discretionary trust

12–18 Such trusts are suitable for both adults and children and, subject to consideration of the tax implications of setting up such a trust, may offer great flexibility to testators, as to:

[6] Inheritance Tax Act 1984, s.52.

- who should benefit
- when they benefit
- in what respect and to what extent they benefit.

In more specific terms (again subject to the tax considerations detailed below), the following points are of interest:

   (i) For the most part, an accumulation and maintenance trust is really designed for younger beneficiaries, and in many cases has a limited life span of 25 years. This does not apply in respect of the discretionary trust.

  (ii) In an accumulation and maintenance trust, the relevant beneficiaries will, at some time, vest absolutely. However, in the case of a discretionary trust, vesting only occurs where, in exercising the discretion, the trustees appoint property or funds to a beneficiary.

 (iii) In an accumulation and maintenance trust, a vesting age has to be specified. There is no such requirement in a discretionary trust.

 (iv) In a discretionary trust, there is no requirement for the testator to provide for an over-destination or for substitute beneficiaries. It simply nominates the class and leaves it to his trustees to choose, in the light of the financial circumstances of the class of potential beneficiaries, taking into account, where necessary, the relevant tax laws at the time (although it is possible for the accumulation and maintenance trust for trustees to have power to select which beneficiaries should be included).[7]

 (vi) The testator can exercise a degree of control from beyond the grave, at least in theory, for a much longer time than he can in relation to an accumulation and maintenance trust, which complies with section 71 of the 1984 Act. It is normal for the testator to grant a letter of expression of wish detailing how he would wish his trustees to operate, and in what circumstances. Whilst (as already recognised in this book) such letters are not binding on the trustees, the latter will so far as possible seek to follow the same.

IHT mitigation

Where the testator provides that the discretion applies only for a **12–19** period of two years from his date of death, this allows his trustees to act in the light of relevant circumstances, with a view to seeking to mitigate IHT (especially when making use of the nil-rate band so far as still available of the testator). However, where IHT mitigation is not a principal concern of the testator, the other "aims" of the testator can be readily achieved through this particular trust vehicle.

Taxation

Income tax

The same rates apply as with an accumulation and maintenance trust. **12–20**

---

[7] Barr, etc., paras 653 to 658 and 665 to 685, cited above in Ch.8.

Capital gains tax

12–21   Again, a discretionary trust will attract its own annual capital gains tax exemption at one-half of the level available to an individual. However, the full annual exemption will be available if the beneficiary is in receipt of attendance allowance or is permanently mentally disabled.[8]

Inheritance tax

12–22   The inheritance tax rules for a discretionary trust are complicated and not readily understood by the lay person (nor by every draftsman!). These "complications" are often blamed for a perceived lack of popularity of the discretionary trust proper. Basically, IHT is charged as follows:

- There will be a normal charge to inheritance tax on death of the testator.
- Thereafter there will be a charge of IHT every 10 years (but charged only at the rate of 6 per cent).
- Where a distribution of trust capital occurs, there is an exit or proportionate charge (and here the complications and complexities of the relevant calculation are most recognisable).

Warning note

12–23   The various tax profiles of the different types of trusts are of relevance to the testator. However, any perceived disadvantage from a particular tax profile or method of treatment must be weighed against the aim which the testator seeks to achieve. The draftsman must always remember that he can only advise against the background of the existing tax regime. The possibility of a harsher tax regime cannot be discounted. Just as financial advisers who in the past sold endowment policies are now being "castigated" for failing to make it clear that the value of the underlying investments could go down as well as up (thereby reducing returns on endowment policies), the draftsman should make it clear that his advice relates solely to the current tax regime, which may have changed out of all recognition by the date of the testator's death and the time at which the relevant trust falls to be brought into being.

Inter vivos **trusts**

12–24   Those advising clients who wish to make provision for succession to their estates must bear in mind that lifetime (or *inter vivos*) trusts may also have a valuable place in such planning. That being so, there may be circumstances in which a client would wish to create an *inter vivos* interest in possession, accumulation and maintenance or discretionary trust. Such vehicles can also have a very valuable place in succession planning.

TRUSTS AND THEIR VALUE IN SUCCESSION PLANNING

12–25 Planning for succession involves being able to offer advice not only in respect of the making of a will (and the incorporation therein, where

---

[8] Taxation of Chargeable Gains Act 1992, Sch.1, para.1 .

appropriate, of relevant trust provisions), but also requires that the draftsman is able to advise in respect of lifetime planning. It is often thought that trusts are used purely as tax mitigation devices, but this is not always the case. It may well be that a trust will be created with no thought of inheritance (or capital gains) tax mitigation.

Uses other than Tax Mitigation

A client may wish to create a trust (either *inter vivos* or on death) for a **12–26** variety of reasons, including to achieve:

- Fairness amongst members of the client's family or potential beneficiaries.
- Flexibility, to allow the trustees to deal with various different types of situations which may arise and which, at the time of creation of the trust, may not be readily predictable.
- Protection for young, incapacitated or financially untrustworthy beneficiaries.
- Protection of assets from creditors.

Traditionally, where a client has sought to secure a fair balance between different types of beneficiary, a life rent trust has been the chosen vehicle. Similarly, where flexibility is required a discretionary trust has been adopted. The issues in relation to both types of trust are considered elsewhere in this book. Similarly, the question of protection of young financially naïve beneficiaries is considered elsewhere in this book. (See Chapter 1, paragraph 1–07).

Protection of incapacitated beneficiaries

A client may have a child who is incapax, with no hope of ever **12–27** gaining or regaining capacity. In the main, the issues for such a client involve combining financial protection and support for the incapax child whilst at the same time, and so far as possible, not imperilling the entitlement of that child to very valuable social security benefits. The normal methodology for such a client is to set up a discretionary trust which complies with section 89 of the Inheritance Tax Act, 1989 and also Sch.1, para.2 to the Taxation of Chargeable Gains Act, 1992 (as amended). These statutory provisions provide valuable inheritance tax and capital gains tax relief for disabled persons, being persons unable to administer their property or manage their affairs by reason of a mental disorder in terms of the Mental Health Act, 1986, or who receive attendance allowance or a disability living allowance. The "qualifying" conditions for exemption from inheritance tax are:

1. That not less than half of the trust property what has been applied is applied for the disabled person; and
2. There is no interest in possession in the trust property.

Drafting considerations

- Some clients may consider that the requirement that not less **12–28** than half of the trust property appointed needs to be appointed for the disabled child may be an unfair distortion of their estate (in so far as other children are concerned). If that is so, then the client may need to consider setting aside an appropriate share of his estate or fund to be subject to the relevant trust.

- The trustees need to exercise care in relation to the distribution of income. If income from the trust is mandated to an incapax child, or the trustees otherwise follow a pattern of making regular payments of income on behalf of that child, then the Department of Social Security may argue that the child has a right to the income in question, thereby disentitling the child from valuable social security benefits. There is also a danger that the Inland Revenue might seek to argue that, notwithstanding the terms of the trust, the child truly has an interest in possession.
- Trustees under such a trust need to have very wide powers, including powers which would not normally be found in a more traditional trust. For example, it might well be appropriate or advisable to grant specific powers:
    (i) To pay for holidays for the incapacitated child and also a carer;
    (ii) To meet any costs required to meet "special needs" of the child, including paying for the costs at respite centres or special educational or care establishments;
    (iii) To enable the trustees to buy special equipment, or indeed more mundane items, such as television sets, etc., including power to allow the incapax child to make use of the same without liability for damage or destruction, and also power to repair, improve, renew or replace the same.

Protection from creditors

12–29   If the client is concerned to protect beneficiaries from creditors, then traditionally an alimentary life rent would be granted. One drawback to such an approach is that, in an alimentary life rent trust, if the beneficiary has taken any benefit under the trust, it will thereafter be impossible to enter into a deed of variation. Where the client might wish protection from his own creditors, then a trust for administration could be granted. Under such a trust, the client would normally:

- Grant a trust deed appointing trustees.
- Convey his whole estate into the trust.
- Reserve the right to income from the trust and empower his trustees to advance capital for his maintenance or benefit.
- Provide as to the ultimate devolution of the trust estate upon his death.

It should be borne in mind that such a trust will be quite ineffective for IHT mitigation purposes. Such trusts have recently been compared to being the equivalent to granting a continuing power of attorney, with the added advantages of protecting the settlor's estate from creditors.

Trusts for Tax Mitigation Purposes

12–30   In so far as lifetime planning is concerned, the creation of a discretionary trust can achieve capital gains tax deferral. Thus, where the client has assets pregnant with capital gains, he might seek to dispose of the same without incurring a capital gains tax liability by conveying the same into a discretionary trust. Similarly, with the exception of a discretionary trust, the creation of other types of trust will be potentially exempt transfers for IHT purposes. Thus, if a client creates a trust (other than a discretionary trust) and places assets into that trust, then provided the client is not a beneficiary under the trust and he survives for seven years from the date of creation of the trust, etc., the transfer in question will escape liability to IHT on death of the client. Similarly, growth in value of the relevant assets will also escape such taxation (although the question of capital gains tax will still be an issue for the trustees in question upon disposal of trust assets).

More specific trust formats for tax mitigation

In relation to will drafting, there are specific techniques which can be **12–31** adopted with a view to achieving IHT mitigation, coupled with other aims such as flexibility. In Chapter 11 we have already considered the use of first death legacies or indeed a nil-rate band legacy. The testator may not be prepared to commit himself absolutely in terms of his testamentary instructions, particularly where the financial position of the testator may be subject to fluctuation prior to death or, more particularly, where the testator may be unsure as to the comparative financial needs of his possible beneficiaries following his death. In such circumstances, a testator who is married may wish to make use of part, if not all, of his nil-rate band without committing the relevant funds absolutely to particular beneficiaries. In such circumstances the testator may choose to incorporate a discretionary legacy (whether or not of a nil-rate band) in his will. For an appropriate style of nil-rate band discretionary legacy, the reader is referred to Barr.[9]

Benefits of such an approach

- The amount placed into such a discretionary legacy trust will **12–32** pass out of the estate of the testator and not immediately into the estate of the surviving spouse. To that extent the testator can be assured that at least some use will be made of his nil-rate band, thereby effecting an ultimate IHT saving on death of the spouse.
- As indicated, it allows flexibility to the executors to examine the financial position of each of the potential beneficiaries and to appoint the income or capital where it may be most required at the relevant time.
- Not only immediate but long-term IHT mitigation might be achieved—where, for example, funds are appointed to children or grandchildren, this will achieve "generational" savings in inheritance tax.
- Where the executors are not satisfied that the financial position of the surviving spouse has been properly secured, then the funds, or the bulk of them, can be appointed to the surviving

---

[9] Barr, etc., p.478, cited above.

spouse (although this would not achieve the ultimate aim of IHT mitigation).

- As with use of a simple nil-rate band legacy, there is no requirement that the full amount of the nil-rate band be utilised. At the time of granting his will, the testator can direct that a sum, with which both he and his spouse are comfortable, be made subject to the discretionary legacy.

Downsides

12–33

- Income within the trust will be taxed at the special trust income tax rate.
- If the trust in question continues in the first 10 years following the death of the testator, then the discretionary fund may (subject to the value of the fund at the relevant time) be subject to a 10-year charge.
- Where trust property (not income) is distributed then a proportionate charge may arise.
- The rules for calculation of 10 years and exit charges are not uncomplicated, certainly in so far as any "lay" trustee might be concerned.
- The trust will require administration although, at the end of the day, the overall costs in administering the trust need to be set against both the IHT saving which might be achieved, and the degree of flexibility afforded thereby.
- The Inland Revenue generally accept that such trusts are effective, but provided always that there is evidence of proper and active trust administration. If not, then the Revenue may argue that the provision was no more than a "sham" (at the time of writing it is understood that the Capital Taxes Office are considering taking at least one test case before the commissioners on this particular basis).

A problem area—the client's dwelling-house

12–34   "Here be dragons". Where the testator proposes to transfer his interest (or a share thereof) in his dwelling-house to the discretionary trustees, difficulties might arise:

- Even where the surviving spouse is the owner of the other half share in the property (and thereby entitled to occupy the same), it is possible that the Inland Revenue will seek to argue that the surviving spouse had been granted an interest in possession in the share of the pre-deceasing spouse, even though it was stated to be subject to the discretionary trust.
- In any event, and at the very least, the Revenue will require evidence of active trust administration.
- If, on sale of the dwelling-house, exemption from capital gains tax is claimed under section 225 of the Taxation of Chargeable Gains Act, 1995, the Revenue may argue that this was evidence that there had been an interest in possession in favour of the surviving spouse (under section 225 trustees can claim exception from capital gains tax if the dwelling-house had, prior to

sale, been the main residence of a person entitled to occupy the same under the relevant settlement).

How then can the testator make use of his interest in the matrimonial home avoiding the above pitfalls?

The mortgage solution

The dangers in leaving a "simple discretionary trust" involving the **12–35** deceased testator's half share therein are obvious. However, at present, the Revenue appears to accept schemes, the essential features of which are:

- The testator directs that his one-half interest in the dwelling-house (or a proportionate share thereof not exceeding the nil-rate band) be held in a discretionary trust.
- The discretionary trust appoints a range of beneficiaries including the surviving spouse (who is likely to be the owner of the other one-half share).
- The trustees are specifically empowered either to sell to the surviving spouse the interest in the dwelling-house passing to them within the trust, or alternatively to convey that interest subject to the surviving spouse granting a "mortgage" in their favour over the dwelling-house itself.
- Again there must be some evidence of active trust administration.

On death of the surviving spouse, the amount secured in favour of the trustees of the pre-deceasing spouse will require to be repaid from the survivor's estate. At that point the discretionary trustees can distribute the same, in many cases avoiding any charge to IHT. The amount secured by the charge over the dwelling-house is a debt in the estate of the surviving spouse and can therefore be set against his or her estate to mitigate IHT therein.

Possible downsides

The provisions of section 103 of the Finance Act, 1986 need to be **12–36** borne in mind. This disallows deduction if the consideration for the debt incurred by the surviving spouse relates to property which originated from that spouse. This could relate to a dwelling-house where one spouse had been the original, sole owner but had gifted a half share to the other; in this case, if the donee spouse pre-deceases the donor, the provisions of section 103 may come into play. Similar situations can arise if the surviving spouse decides that he or she wishes to sell the relevant dwelling-house and purchase another. No problems arise if the amount secured by the charge over the original dwelling-house is repaid to the discretionary trustees of the pre-deceasing spouse. If, however, the surviving spouse makes application to the trustees for an advance to purchase a further dwelling-house, then the Revenue may raise a query again under section 103 of the 1986 Act.

- The costs in setting up this type of scheme are not inconsiderable. However, they again require to be considered as against the ultimate IHT mitigation which might be achieved.

- The scheme is complex and requires to be properly explained to the spouses. If not, then the complexities of the same may militate against the spouses availing themselves of the same. In particular, client resistance is likely to be found immediately when reference is made to a "mortgage" in favour of the discretionary trustees.

- It should be borne in mind that the planning outlined above cannot be brought into effect if the title to the relevant dwelling-house stands in the joint names of the relevant spouses and the survivor of them. In such circumstances, then the destination will require to be evacuated. There is currently a debate as to whether or not such a survivorship destination can be properly evacuated by means of anything other than a disposition by the spouses in favour of themselves to excise the survivorship destination. Again, if not properly explained to clients they may not be prepared to commit themselves to the expense of such a disposition. However, a disposition by the spouses in favour of themselves to evacuate a survivorship destination does not transfer any property. That being so, provided the position is properly explained to the keeper, he is presently prepared to record such dispositions, charging only the minimum recording/registration dues (presently £22) in respect of the same, *i.e.* it is not necessary to pay recording/registration dues commensurate to the value of the property itself.

Use of insurance and other products for IHT mitigation

12–37   The insurance industry has, over a period of years, been ingenious in introducing products and schemes to assist clients to legitimately avoid IHT. Many high value individuals have taken advantage of such products and schemes with a view to mitigating potentially substantial IHT liabilities. However, the adviser does have to take care. The Inland Revenue has shown an increased willingness to "take on" some of the schemes, and where the Revenue has failed by way of litigation, the Chancellor has been persuaded to legislate to close down such planning opportunities. This happened in both the *Lady Ingram* and the *Eversden* cases. In both cases, the Revenue having failed in Court, legislation ensued.

The *Eversden* case is of interest.[10] This case involved what was commonly known as a "spousal interest trust". At its most basic level, this type of trust involved the creation of a trust in terms of which the settlor's spouse was given an interest in possession, with the settlor being declared to be a potential beneficiary. In theory, there was no reservation of benefit as this did not apply to transfers between spouses. After a suitable period of time, the spouse having the interest in possession would renounce the same in favour of children. Provided he or she survived for seven years from the date of that renunciation there would be no charge to IHT arising. The trust was, however, set up so that the

---

[10] *IRC v Eversden* [2003] EWCA Civ 668; [2003] S.T.C. 822, CA.

settlor could derive the benefit therefrom. The Inland Revenue attacked this vehicle, the arguments involving whether or not the gift with reservation rules of section 102 of the Finance Act, 1982, applied. The Revenue lost both at first instance and before the Court of Appeal. However, rather than risk the implications of a further defeat before the House of Lords, the Chancellor intervened on a legislative basis.

In December 2003, the Chancellor announced that he was also proposing to legislate to effectively close off IHT mitigation vehicles involving the use of "pre-owned" property. At its basic level, it was understood that the type of vehicle under attack was where:

- Spouses had created a lifetime trust (not being a discretionary trust so that the creation of the trust could have of itself qualified as a potentially exempt transfer). The spouses then "sold" their dwelling-house to the trustees in return for which the spouses received an IOU for the price from the trustees. The dwelling-house at that point became an asset of the trust.
- The spouses would then assign the IOU to, for example, their children. Provided they survived for seven years from the date of assignation of the IOU, the value represented thereby would also be a potentially exempt transfer.
- The spouses would continue to reside in the dwelling-house rent-free.

The problem which arises here is section 103 of the Finance Act 1986. In its consultation paper issued after the Chancellor's statement in December 2003,[11] the Inland Revenue proposed that from April 6, 2005, where an individual had previously divested himself of an asset which he continues to enjoy in some manner then he will become liable to a charge to income tax. The only exemption to this proposed rule would seem to be where the asset has been sold at arms length to an unconnected third party. This will of course "attack" the type of trust vehicle outlined above. It is also proposed that the individual would be deemed to have obtained a benefit to the full market extent where heritable property is concerned, and otherwise of a specified percentage of the value of any other asset (and it is proposed that there should be an "official" rate of interest of five per cent). The individual is to be taxed with income tax on that sum. It would appear that the proposals could go well beyond the scope originally envisaged by pundits.

Bearing in mind the foregoing warning note, the prudent practitioner should always make it clear to clients that the advice offered is based on tax law and practice at the relevant time, and that no guarantee can be given in relation to future legislative or other changes.

Use of insurance policies in IHT mitigation

It is not necessary for a client to take out a new insurance policy to engage in IHT mitigation. For example, where a client has an existing term assurance policy, the potential proceeds of the same can be written **12–38**

---

[11] "The tax treatment of pre-owned assets".

in trust for beneficiaries. If the life assured dies whilst the policy remains in force, then the proceeds of that policy will fall outwith his estate and escape taxation to IHT. The downside to such an approach is that, unless the policy in question is unit linked or convertible, at the end of the relevant term the policy will cease and be of no further value. The assignation of a term assurance policy into trust is therefore really a "protective" measure having a limited lifespan (the life of the policy itself). An existing endowment assurance policy could be placed into trust. The value of the policy at the time the trust is created would be a potentially exempt transfer. If the life assured survives for a period of seven years from the creation of the trust, then not only the original value of the policy (at time of creation of the trust) but growth within the same will escape taxation to IHT (although care has to be taken that this does not trigger an unwelcome income tax liability as the assignation of even a "qualifying" policy into trust can in some circumstances be regarded as being a "chargeable event" for income tax purposes). Where the premiums on a term assurance or endowment policy written in trust continue to be paid by the life assured, then these will each either be potentially exempt transfers, or may be immediately exempt under the normal expenditure out of income rule.

Where a new policy is being arranged as an IHT mitigation vehicle, perhaps the most common type of policy is the joint whole of life second death policy. This is arranged on the basis that the proceeds of the policy will be payable only on second death. Such policies can be arranged on a single or regular premium basis. Where a single premium is paid and the policy written in trust at the outset, the amount of that premium will be a potentially exempt transfer. Where regular premiums are paid, each will be a potentially exempt transfer, unless of course they qualify for immediate relief from IHT under the normal expenditure rule referred to above.

It is of vital importance that such policies be written in trust. If they are not, then the proceeds on second death will come back into the estate of the survivor and will simply increase (and not mitigate) an IHT liability.

It should also be borne in mind that death benefits or death in service benefits under existing personal pension plans or occupational pension schemes can also be placed in trust or otherwise made subject to letters of expression of wish, thereby avoiding the monies in question reverting to the estate of the contributor/employee.

MORE COMPLICATED SCHEMES

12–39 As indicated, the insurance industry has over a period of time been in ingenious in bringing forward schemes to mitigate inheritance tax. This applies particularly to clients who may be capital rich but income poor. The problem for those owning high value properties (which are increasing in value all the time) is a real one.

- Between April 1997 and April 2003, the IHT nil-rate band increased by 18.6 per cent, compared with an average house price increase of 84 per cent over the same period (115 per cent in London).[12]

---

[12] *The Times*, April 2003.

- In January 2004, the Inland Revenue indicated that in estates found chargeable to inheritance tax, heritable property accounted for 40 per cent of the total asset value of those estates.
- There are now over 1.4 million homes throughout the UK worth in excess of £250,000.[13]

The difficulty for many clients is that they are reluctant to endeavour to make use of their family home as a vehicle for IHT mitigation. This applies particularly where there is likely to be a surviving spouse who will wish to continue to occupy that family home. At present, the two main "vehicles" which seek to make use of a client's other assets (*i.e.* not his dwelling-house) are the gift and loan inheritance trust and the IHT discounted gift scheme. Both seek to address the question of preserving income for the donor of the relevant assets, whilst at the same time achieving differing degrees of IHT mitigation, either immediately or through passage of time (making use of the existing relief available to the donor).

Gift and loan inheritance trust

This combines a potentially exempt transfer, a trust, two capital **12–40** investment bonds and the use of an allowance to draw out 5 per cent of the amount originally invested as "income".

Example

The client has £100,000 to invest. Generally the following would occur: **12–41**

- The client invests a small amount of money into a capital investment bond, the amount of the same being determined by the Life Office's minimum premium requirements (usually around £2,000).
- A trust is created by the client and the above capital investment bond is placed into the trust which provides that on death of the settlor, the "property" will pass to identified beneficiaries (often children or grandchildren).
- At the time of creation of the trust, additional trustees are appointed, normally being individuals who will be expected to survive the settlor.
- The settlor will then proceed to make a loan of a further sum (in this example £98,000) to the trustees. The loan is expressed to be interest free and repayable upon demand.
- The trustees will then elect to invest the loan funds into a second capital investment bond which is an asset of the trust itself.
- The settlor can retain the right of withdrawing each year 5 per cent of the amount invested in the second capital investment bond, such withdrawals being regarded as an annual partial

---

[13] Land Registry, January 2004.

repayment of the interest-free loan. In this example, the sum in question repaid to the settlor each month would be £408.33. The advantages of this scheme are as follows:

(a) The initial payment into the smaller capital investment bond will either be exempt under the client's annual exemption or, if this has already been utilised, it will amount to a potentially exempt transfer.

(b) All subsequent growth on both bonds lie within the trust. They do not form part of the personal estate of the settlor and will be free from IHT.

(c) As the interest-free loan to the trustees was repayable on demand, it is not regarded as being a gift. The 5 per cent withdrawals are regarded as repayment of the loan to the settlor and therefore the reservation of benefit rules do not apply.

(d) Where the settlor expends the 5 per cent withdrawals/ repayments, his IHT taxable estate will, hopefully, reduce further through a period of time.

Possible downsides

12–42   Tax planning is always a balance and it is important that the client should be made aware of the possible downsides to the above scheme:

- Unpaid loan amounts due as at date of death will fall to be regarded as being part of the testator's estate and will therefore not escape IHT liability.
- As the capital investment bonds are "non-qualifying policies", in some circumstances an unexpected additional personal income tax liability could be triggered in the hands of the settlor if a client exceeds the 5 per cent annual limit allowable under the Income & Corporation Taxes Act 1988, and occasions a "chargeable event" which, when the relevant chargeable gain is added back to the client's income, takes the client into higher rate income tax bracket.
- It will take 20 years for this type of arrangement to prove fully effective. Where the client does not exceed the 5 per cent annual allowance limit (as indicated above), any part of the loan not repaid as at the settlor's date of death will fall to be regarded as part of his estate for IHT purposes.
- The effect of inflation will erode the value of the 5 per cent annual withdrawals over the period.
- If the settlor has been withdrawing at the allowed rate of 5 per cent per annum then after 20 years he can derive no further benefit of any nature from the trust. The loan will be deemed to have been repaid in full, and thereafter remaining funds in the trust cannot be used for the client's benefit (as they will be held for the trust beneficiaries).

Notwithstanding the foregoing "downsides", such schemes are fairly popular, although again and as final warning notes, it is understood that the Inland Revenue may well seek to examine whether these schemes come within the "pre-owned property" rules hereinbefore referred to, and, at the time of writing, the Chancellor may be reconsidering the 5 per cent annual allowance. No guarantee can therefore be given that an annual allowance at that level will be available throughout the 20-year period of the scheme.

Discounted gift schemes

Unlike gift and loan inheritance trusts, these schemes can provide an **12–43** immediate saving in relation to a potential IHT liability. However, the income which can be derived from this type of scheme will apply during the client's lifetime and is therefore not confined to the 20-year period referred to above. Given the foregoing, these schemes have proven to be more popular than the earlier type of scheme.

The mechanics of the scheme

- The client makes a trust into which is placed an investment **12–44** (often a redemption bond).
- Investment is notionally split into two different parts—the grantee's fund and the residuary fund.
- The grantee's fund is immediately removed from the estate of the client, thereby effecting an immediate IHT saving.
- The residuary fund is a potentially exempt transfer.
- The income from the grantee's fund is payable to the client for life, or until exhaustion of the grantee's fund.

Such schemes require active actuarial calculation as to the value of the grantee's fund. The potentially exempt transfer is the residuary fund. The "gift with reservation" rules of section 102 of the Finance Act, 1986 do not apply to the grantee's fund. In the *Lady Ingram*[14] case, the House of Lords indicated that in general terms a gift, albeit with a reservation of benefit, would not arise if the donor precisely defined the interest of which the donor was divesting himself, and also the interest which he was retaining subject to it being essential that the settlor should not receive any benefit from the divested interest ("horizontal severance"). Horizontal severance applies where an asset is divided into a number of separate limited interests which take effect in succession to, or subject to, the others. Discounted gift schemes use this principle to create the right to "income" before the capital is gifted into the trust. Although the Chancellor legislated to "close off" the tax planning afforded by the *Lady Ingram* scheme, it is considered that the legislation relates solely to heritable property and not to moveable property. It should be noted that the Capital Taxes Office remains prepared to examine the actuarial assumptions which have been made in relation to the determination of the value of the grantee's fund at the outset, *i.e.* the Capital Taxes Office may still be prepared to challenge the amount of "discount" granted in determining the amount of the residuary fund to be treated as a potentially exempt transfer. For this reason, investors are normally

---

[14] 1999 S.T.C. 37.

required to undergo detailed medical underwriting. thereby reducing the possibility of challenge on the part of the Capital Taxes Office.

The future for such schemes

12–45 Any practitioner who advises in relation to such schemes should make it clear that the advice which he offers reflects tax law and practice at the relevant time. The Inland Revenue have reserved their position in respect of such schemes. Whilst, at present, the Revenue appears prepared to accept the discounted gift scheme outlined above (provided they have been properly set up at the outset), they have reserved the right to challenge the same on a case-by-case basis. Gift and loan schemes may well be subject to attack under the "pre-owned property rules". As with all such schemes, "past performance" is no guarantee for the future. The prudent adviser should bear this in mind and always make this clear to his client, again, fully and properly recording the advice given to the client.

From the author's point of view, it would appear that the Inland Revenue are now seeking to attack tax planning schemes which have previously been tolerated. In particular, it is understood that the Inland Revenue recently called in representatives of leading accountancy firms for consultations regarding the unhappiness of the Inland Revenue in relation to advisers who seek to take advantage of "loopholes". It is understood that the view of the Revenue is that taking advantage of such loopholes is not appropriate tax planning advice and that, where a loophole appears, they will close it off as soon as they can. Advisors should take note.

CHAPTER 13

FUNERAL INSTRUCTIONS, DONATION OF BODY, ETC

FUNERAL INSTRUCTIONS

Taking instructions

When taking instructions for the preparation of a will, it is normal **13–01** practice to enquire whether or not the client wishes to incorporate specific funeral instructions in the will. Solicitors often find that some clients have never given this matter any thought, or are relatively blasé regarding the eventual fate of their remains, being content to leave it to their family to make suitable arrangements. Equally, however, other clients will have very detailed requirements. These can include:

- The nature of the means of disposal of their remains.
- The nature of the service or other commemoration to be held at the time of their funeral.
- The question of purchase of a headstone or inscription of an existing headstone.

There is in fact no necessity for funeral instructions to be incorporated in the client's will, and in the author's view, clients should be warned that incorporation of instructions within their wills is not necessarily any guarantee of those instructions being put into effect. Many individuals are private and may not have discussed the funeral requirements with their family. No mention may have been made of the fact that their funeral instructions are contained in their will (in fact the client may not even have told his family where the will is to be found). Similarly, some families choose not to contact the solicitor who acted for their late relative until after the formalities of the funeral have taken place. In such circumstances, there is more than adequate scope for a family unwittingly to make arrangements which do not conform to the instructions left by the testator. Whilst no one (perhaps with the exception of the testator) might be blamed for such a state of affairs, discovery by the family that they have failed to observe the last wishes of their loved one can cause great upset.

To avoid this type of situation arising, a client should be advised to inform his family of his specific requirements. It is equally possible to set out funeral instructions in an informal writing; there is no reason why a client should not do so and send copies of the same to members of his family in order to ensure their adherence to his wishes.

Interment

If the client wishes to be interred then the following points are of **13–02** particular importance:

1. Does the client already have a lair? Entitlement to be interred in a particular lair cannot be assumed. The cemetery authority will normally regard the holder of the relevant lair certificate as being owner of the lair. If the client does not hold the lair certificate, then he should not assume that the individual holding the lair will allow his remains to be interred therein. If the lair certificate has been lost, an approach should be made to the cemetery authority in order to rectify this state of affairs.

2. Is there room in the lair? Even where ownership of a lair is clear, interment of another body therein may not be allowed if the cemetery authority considers that there is insufficient room. If there is any doubt, cemetery authorities are usually prepared to carry out a test to ascertain whether or not there is room for interment of another body. Often, even where there is not such room, the cemetery authorities allow interment of ashes in the lair, and this alternative could be put to the client.

   What should be clear from both of the foregoing points is that there is work for the client to do whilst he is still alive. It is also important that the testator indicates where his lair certificate might be held.

   Where there are no doubts of the above type, then an appropriate clause for inclusion in the will might be:

   I direct that my remains shall be interred in lair number X49 in Anytown Cemetery, Anytown and I hereby record that the relevant lair certificate is held in safe custody by the bank of Anytown, 24 High Street, Anytown.

   Obviously, if the testator moves the lair certificate to another place of safe custody then an appropriate note to this effect should be placed with his will and other important papers. Bear in mind that inclusion of the information in the will, might, for the reasons expressed above, not be going far enough.

3. The testator may not own a lair but may nonetheless still wish his remains to be interred in a suitable cemetery. An appropriate instruction might be:

   I wish my remains to be interred in Anytown Cemetery, Anytown. I hereby specifically authorise and empower my executor to purchase an appropriate lair in said cemetery for that purpose, the cost of the same being borne by my estate as a funeral expense.

It should be noted that at one time the validity of such a purpose was doubted (it being a general principle that such a trust purpose would be valid only if it conferred a beneficial interest on the person who had survived the deceased). However, in *McCaig v Glasgow University*[1] it was recognised that such a provision could be valid, on a customary and rational scale, to secure a burial place and suitable memorial to the memory of a deceased. The important words here are "customary and rational". Scots law has over a long period of time shown itself to be entirely willing to strike down provisions which were considered to be

---

[1] 1907 S.C. 231.

excessive. There is, however, no absolute scale to be applied here. What
is customary and rational depends on the facts and circumstances of each
case. In *Mackintosh's Judicial Factor v Lord Advocate*,[2] the court held
that the direction that the whole estate should be utilised in purchasing a
mausoleum could be struck down as being so extravagant as to offend
against public policy.[3] Another example of a Scottish court applying the
customary and rational test referred to above is seen in the case of *Glass
v Weir*.[4] The estate of the deceased amounted to approximately £300. Of
this, in the course of an extended wake, £8 was spent on providing drink
for the mourners. The court took the view that this was excessive and
restricted the allowable funeral mournings to £3.

Cremation

Cremation is the preference of many clients. In that case the direction **13–03**
is simple.

> I wish that upon my death my remains shall be cremated.

If the client would have preferred to have his remains interred but this is
not possible owing to the lair in question having insufficient space, then
provided there is no objection from the cemetery authority, the instruction would be:

> I wish that upon my death my remains are cremated and my ashes
> interred in lair number X49 in Anytown Cemetery, Anytown.

Some clients may express a wish that their remains be cremated and
thereafter scattered in a particular place. Care should be taken that the
owners of the particular locus will not raise objection to this.

There is now no doubt that the expenses of cremation are regarded as
proper funeral expenses.[5]

Other specific requests

Quite apart from questions of extravagance, clients should be dis- **13–04**
suaded from leaving funeral instructions which are no more than
"wishful thinking". For example: "I wish that my remains be interred
under the centre spot at Hampden Park".

Many clients will wish to leave instructions for a funeral of a non-
religious nature. There is no objection to this and an appropriate format
of wording might be:

> . . . and I record that it is my wish that my funeral service should be
> of a non-religious (or humanist) nature.

The client can similarly direct that his funeral service should be private,
that there should be no flowers, or even if of a religious nature, that

---

[2] 1935 S.C. 406.
[3] See the case of *McCaig v University of Glasgow*, cited above; and *McCaig's Trustees v Kirk Session of United Free Church of Lismore*, 1915 S.C. 426.
[4] (1821) 1 S. 163.
[5] Cremation Act 1902.

there should be no hymns (or conversely that the client would wish certain hymns to be sung).

In particular, the adviser should remember that the funeral of the client is likely to be a difficult and sad occasion for those who survive. Inappropriate levity in funeral directions is to be avoided. When there is any doubt then clients should be advised to issue instructions separately and to discuss the same with their families, etc. in order to avoid causing offence.

Disputes as to funeral arrangements

13–05   Even where there are no public policy or other objections to the funeral directions left in a testator's will, a dispute can arise within the deceased's family as to the nature and type of funeral to be arranged. There appears to be no precedent regarding such a dispute. A considered view is, however, that, at the end of the day, the final decision will rest with the executor who, standing *eadem personam cum defuncto* has the primary responsibility for settlement of the funeral expenses. Such a dispute will be a difficult matter for all concerned and will on occasions occur. A possible (but not absolute) way of pre-empting a dispute would be for a testator to pre-pay his funeral, leaving specific instructions with the funeral directors as to the nature and type of funeral to be arranged. Such an arrangement will take much of the pressure from the shoulders of the executor—on the basis that such an arrangement will be a contract and, if the executor declines to complete the contract, he or she could be subject to a claim on the part of the funeral directors. Again, if a client has entered into such an arrangement, then quite apart from recording the same in his will or with his solicitor, he should also inform his family.

DONATION OF BODY

General

13–06   In strict terms, an individual cannot specifically bequeath his remains. That being so, just as with funeral instructions, a clause in a will directing donation of an individual's remains for medical purposes, etc. is, in truth, no more than an expression of the testator's wish. A written expression of wish will so far as possible be given effect by the executors—it is not, however, legally binding upon them. Equally, an expression of wish on donation of one's body does not require to be expressed in a will. Any individual, during a last illness, can express the wish that his body be used for medical purposes. If effected in the presence of two witnesses, the person lawfully in possession of the body can authorise such use.

Similarly, and where a testator wishes to donate his remains for medical research or for transplantation purposes, the testator should ensure that members of their family (and others) are aware of their wishes and feelings in that regard. For example, the testator may be keen that certain parts of his body be utilised for transplantation purposes. If the only repository of that wish after a testator has died is his will, then owing to the time-critical aspects of being able to remove parts of the body for transplantation into a living recipient, the fact that a testator may not have made his wishes known to anyone else in any other fashion could result in the opportunity for transplantation being lost. Although the question of a body being donated for medical research might be regarded as being less time critical, the same considerations apply—the testator should make sure that his family are aware of his wishes in order that if, for example, a spouse or child has qualms, the concerns of the latter can be discussed and hopefully resolved with the testator, thereby perhaps avoiding difficulty when the testator is no longer in a position to discuss the same with his loved ones.

Practical aspects

Whilst a purpose directing donation of a body for medical research, etc. is normally fairly short, there are numerous points which the draftsman should discuss with the testator: **13–07**

1. The exact wishes of the client should be explored. The client may be relaxed that his remains should be utilised for medical research and education whilst at the same time be strongly opposed to parts of his body being used for transplantation purposes. Whilst this is a grisly subject for many people, the draftsman should clarify the exact intentions of his client. It is important that the draftsman himself is aware of the different ways in which the remains of a deceased client might be made use of, and adoption of a standard all-inclusive clause (the nuances of which the testator himself might not fully understand) should not be automatic.

    The type of all inclusive expression of wish indicated above is as follows:

    > It is my wish that upon my death my body or parts thereof should be offered to any hospital or University Faculty of Medicine for the purposes of medical education or research, anatomical examination, therapeutic or treatment purposes, or transplantation for the treatment of others.

    It is important that the client should understand the full range of possibilities which can flow from adoption of a wide ranging purpose. If the client would not wish any part of his body to be used for transplantation or therapeutic (*i.e.* treatment) purposes, then the clause should be amended to specifically negate that possibility. Equally, the client may be happy that his remains be used for medical education or research, but it should be pointed out that, whilst there is an overlap between the former and use for an anatomical purpose, the latter use has wider implications. The testator should understand that after an anatomical examination has been completed and if he has consented thereto, parts of his body may be stored for indefinite periods of time, under the Anatomy Regulations 1988. However, under section 6(3) of the Anatomy Act 1984, parts of the body may be retained beyond the statutory period of three years, providing authority has been given by the deceased and not withdrawn (obviously such authority is contained in the above style), or the surviving spouse or relatives do not object.

2. Bearing in mind the difficulties which can arise where the will is the only repository of the client's wishes, if, for example, the client would wish parts of his body to be used for transplant purposes then he should be advised to carry a donor card. This can be of great assistance to hospital authorities in deciding whether or not it would be appropriate to remove organs for transplantation purposes, particularly giving the limited window of opportunity available to them in that regard. Generally, the client should be advised to make contact with the medical or anatomy department of the local or the client's favoured university. Members of those departments have much greater expertise in this field than the will-making solicitor and can offer very valuable advice to a client, commence an appropriate record-keeping process, and offer advice as to the procedure to be followed on death of the testator.

3. There is no reason why the client should not include a brief note of how he would wish his remains to be finally disposed of once they have served their purpose for medical research, etc., or if his remains are in fact declined by the relevant authority. However, where a client donates his whole body for research, etc. purposes, normally the relevant medical authorities will arrange for a simple funeral at their expense upon expiry of the statutory period of three years referred to above. If the client does not wish his remains to be used for any of the above purposes then this of course can be recorded by inclusion of an appropriate direction in the testator's will. Again, where a client has such feelings, then they should be intimated by the client to the testator's family and his doctor, etc. If not, under the Anatomy Act and Human Tissues Legislation, a person "lawfully in possession" of a body can direct that the body or parts thereof may be used for medical purposes, provided that person has no reason to believe that the deceased had expressed any prior objection thereto, or that a surviving spouse or any surviving relatives had any objection.

Client sensitivity

13–08   One final point—this is an area where sensitivity is required on the part of the draftsman. The draftsman on occasions may need to disappoint a client; for example, in some cases where the client suffers from (and perhaps dies owing to) a particular disease or medical condition, some medical authorities may decline to accept the remains. Individuals who wish to donate their bodies to science have generally given this matter some considerable thought. They may have engaged in lengthy and difficult negotiations/discussions with their spouses and family and are generally committed to the advancement of medical science or education, etc. It is likely to be a bitter disappointment to them to discover that their wishes cannot be obtempered owing to a medical condition which "intervenes" after their will has been made.

CHAPTER 14

CODICILS, DEEDS OF VARIATION AND PRECATORY BEQUESTS

CODICILS

Usage

A codicil is utilised to alter or to add to an existing will. In relation to **14–01** the making of a will itself, the same considerations regarding capacity of the granter and the essentials of execution apply to a codicil. A codicil should be a fairly simple document and may not always be required. For example, as indicated in Chapter 1, a change of address (or indeed of the name of someone named in the will owing to marriage or remarriage) does not require the granting of a codicil. A similar position applies in respect of death of one of a number of executors or of a member of a class of beneficiaries (although again it would be convenient for an informal note to the foregoing effect to be placed with the will itself). There is of course no reason why such changes could not be recorded in a codicil if the document is otherwise required to make some substantial change to the effect of the will (for example, the nomination of a new executor, the revocation of the appointment of an existing executor, or the addition of new specific bequests or pecuniary legacies to the will).

Careless drafting issues

However, even though the change effected by a codicil is of a **14–02** straightforward nature, it is recommended that the will itself be carefully checked. Careless drafting of a seemingly straightforward codicil can cause difficulty. For example, a will might obtain a nomination of "A whom failing B" as executor. The subsequent codicil provides:

> I hereby revoke the appointment of B as executor under my will. I appoint as executor under my will C.

Is the appointment of C intended to be a replacement for B (*i.e.* merely as a substitute to A) or as co-executor along with A? Any doubts which might arise here could be resolved by more precise drafting, *i.e.*:

> I revoke the appointment of B as substitute executor under my will and I appoint C as substitute executor in the event of A predeceasing me, being incapacitated or otherwise declining to act.

Similar doubts can arise where the original will appoints individuals as both trustees and executors. If the codicil only refers to the appointment of a new executor, are they also to be trustees in terms of the will and the purposes thereof?

Advising clients

Series of codicils

14–03   Some clients are aware that, at least in theory, the preparation of a codicil would be cheaper than the granting of a new will. That being so, a solicitor may encounter a client in the habit of making regular changes to his will, and who instructs a series of codicils. There can be inherent dangers here.

This is particularly so where a series of codicils have been granted and subsequent codicils seek to make changes, perhaps not just to the original will itself but also to intervening codicils. In such circumstances, the client should be advised to make a new will, starting from scratch, on a blank sheet of paper.

Change in circumstances

14–04   It can be dangerous for the drafting solicitor if he operates on the assumption that the client's underlying circumstances have not changed since the will was made (perhaps many years beforehand). For example, a client's financial position may have changed dramatically in the intervening time. This may be simply due to a great rise in the value of the client's house or perhaps he has had success with a premium bond or lottery ticket, or indeed has succeeded to a reasonably substantial inheritance. Whilst the drafting solicitor may recall that at the time of making of the will, inheritance tax was not an issue in any shape or form for the client, no such similar assumption should be made in relation to the drafting of a codicil—the solicitor would be well advised to check with the client as to whether the latter's financial position has changed in any way since the will was made, perhaps justifying a more detailed examination of the client's inheritance tax profile (in fact, a new and comprehensive "client fact find" may be indicated).

Failure to make such an enquiry of the client might lead to a beneficiary querying why the testamentary instructions as represented by the will and codicil do not take into account what, albeit with the benefit of hindsight, may have been a reasonable opportunity for IHT mitigation, or at the very least an informed consideration of that opportunity.

Testamentary informal writing

14–05   Similarly, and given the position which the draftsman now faces following the decision in *Holmes v Bank of Scotland* (See Chapter 2), the draftsman of the codicil must certainly enquire as to whether or not a client has availed himself of the ability to make a testamentary informal writing in terms of a power contained in the original will to that effect. It should be borne in mind that clients do not always send informal writings into their solicitor to be held along with the will. Lack of enquiry on that point could again cause difficulty of proper interpretation. If an informal writing has been made then the solicitor drafting the codicil should view the same and, where necessary, take the opportunity to correct any points of difficulty in terms of the codicil (with the client being advised that the informal writing should be destroyed and therefore rendered null and void).

Interpretation

Quite apart from *obvious* difficulties of interpretation, a question might **14–06** arise where a will has been altered or extended by a number of codicils, as to the true date of the principal testamentary wishes of the testator. See section 1(6) of the Age of Majority (Scotland) 1969.

Confidentiality and the emotional aspects

A surprising number of clients do not realise that their will and all **14–07** valid codicils thereto will come into the public domain if registered in the Books of Council and Session, or when an application for confirmation is required. This raises an important practical point of which the client should be made aware. For example, a client may in his will make provision for legacies of £10,000 each to a number of friends. The client subsequently falls out with one of those friends and instructs a codicil revoking the legacy in favour of that particular person. The friend in question may not even realise that he or she has caused any offence. Normal relations with that person are subsequently restored, but the client omits to reinstate the legacy. The client then dies. With the will and codicil coming into the public domain, it is possible (if not likely) that the person in question will realise that at some point in time (perhaps without realising it) he or she caused some offence which occasioned (at that point) the friend to take "testamentary action" against them. It should be remembered that it is not just the will which can be a lasting statement of love and affection.

Dangers in relation to past codicils and new wills

The draftsman may receive a letter from the client indicating that he **14–08** wishes certain stated changes to his existing will. Simple adherence to those instructions run the risk that possibly substantial amendments made by a subsequent codicil to the earlier will might be overlooked (it should not be assumed that the client has recalled the fact that he has made an earlier codicil to the will or indeed recalled the terms of the earlier codicil).

Drafting considerations

Various points arise here.   **14–09**

- In his will, the client may have left a legacy subject to a particular condition. He subsequently instructs his solicitor that the legacy should be increased in terms of the codicil. Is the condition attaching to the original legacy to apply to the increased legacy? This is a point which the draftsman should consider.
- The client instructs a codicil in terms of which a legacy of a particular sum is to be left to a particular individual. However, in terms of his existing will, there is already a legacy in favour

of that individual. The question which arises here is whether the legacy, instructed in terms of the codicil, is to be in substitution for the original bequest or in addition thereto. The draftsman must check the terms of the original will and to avoid any doubt, must check whether the legacy to be instructed in terms of the codicil is additional to that bequeathed in terms of the will. The presumption in this case (where the legacies appear in two different documents) is that the testator intends that both should be payable—in fact this may not be the case. Where the new legacy is in substitution for the original one, then this should be made clear. The original legacy should be revoked in clear terms. Where the "new" legacy is to be additional to any left in terms of the will, then again it is the draftsman's responsibility to ensure that this is reflected in terms of the codicil; for example, the following wording could be applied:

. . . and I hereby declare that the foregoing legacy is made by me in addition to (and not in substitution for) the legacy bequeathed by me to (A) in terms of my said will.

- Where the will bequeaths a "demonstrative" legacy, then notwithstanding the fact that the client may instruct a codicil for an entirely different purpose, it might be appropriate for the draftsman to check that the source from which the relevant demonstrative legacy is to be settled still exists.
- Where the will itself contains specific bequests, then it might be appropriate to check with the testator that he still owns the items in question—if not then the relevant bequest should be cancelled in terms of the codicil (even though instructed for an entirely different purpose).

The author accepts that the above recommendations may be seen by some practitioners to be "overkill". However, it remains to be seen what attitude Scottish courts will take to the role and responsibilities of the draftsman of the codicil following the "new" climate introduced by *Holmes v Bank of Scotland*.[1]

DEEDS OF VARIATION

Background

14–10 It has been possible for many years for the family/beneficiaries of a deceased individual to enter into a deed of variation, although it has only been since the 1970s that the "taxation advantages" referred to below have been allowed.[2] Initially, the preferred nomenclature for a deed of variation in Scotland was a deed of family arrangement. This description was, however, slightly misleading as the facility to enter into a deed of variation was not restricted to a family of a deceased testator (and in any

---

[1] Cited above.
[2] *Gray v Gray's Trustees* (1877) 4 R. 378.

event, a deed of variation can also be entered into in relation to an intestate estate; thus, it can vary not only the terms of a will but also the law of intestacy). In recent years, such documents have been called deeds of variation (although the Capital Taxes Office prefers the description "instruments of variation").

The ability of beneficiaries (both testate and intestate) to enter into such a deed has been a very valuable facility for a number of purposes, not just tax mitigation. However, on more than one occasion since 1989, the Chancellor for the time being has indicated that the right to enter into a deed of variation under section 142 of the Inheritance Tax Act 1984 might be withdrawn. Norman Lamont and successive Chancellors have all either mentioned this intention or hinted at this possibility. That being so, clients should not be encouraged to rely on the possibility of a deed of variation being entered into, after the death of that client, as being the principal reason for an individual not himself engaging in appropriate IHT mitigation, or at the very least considering his options.

Possible practical uses

There are various ways in which a deed of variation can be utilised, **14–11** although perhaps the principal justification for use of such a deed is in IHT planning or mitigation. However, a deed of variation is often used in the following circumstances:

  (i) If the estate is intestate—If the estate is sizeable a large sum by way of free estate may pass to, for example, adult children under the Rules of Succession. The adult children may be concerned that loss of control of the free estate by the surviving parent might prejudice the financial future of the surviving parent.

 (ii) A deed of variation might be utilised to put right perceived wrong. For example, the testator may have cancelled a legacy in favour of a friend or family member for no good or apparent reason. It would be possible for the other beneficiaries to effectively write the relevant legacy back into a deceased's will by means of a deed of variation.

(iii) Many clients find will making an unpleasant process and do not keep their wills up to date. A deceased individual may, however, have indicated that he or she wished to update an old will with a view to introducing new beneficiaries, etc. When a family are aware of this, they do at least have the option of putting the deceased relative's last wishes into effect by means of a deed of variation.

(iv) Again, a deed of variation could be used within a family to direct a greater share of the deceased's estate to more needy beneficiaries.[3] In the Appendix of Styles, the first style of deed of variation was intended to achieve this very aim. Adult children B and C are already fairly wealthy in their own right and consider that it would be more appropriate for the estate of

---

[3] *Gray v Gray's Trustees*, cited above.

the deceased parent to pass to child D, to whom life to date has not been quite so kind.

The foregoing examples do not delimit the circumstances in which a deed of variation may be put to a practical use. In the examples given, the same end could have been achieved in a different way without making use of a deed of variation. For example, if a legacy has been cancelled for no good or apparent reason, the other legatees could get together and, utilising funds received from the estate, make up and pass over the same amount of the original legacy to the individual in question. However, sums so gifted to the individual in question would be regarded as having been made over by the individuals themselves and would not have the benefit of being regarded as having been made under the deceased's will in terms of section 142. Such actings on the part of the kindly legatees could, if not achieved in terms of a valid deed of variation, start their own inheritance tax clocks ticking, and in some situations could result in an unexpected IHT liability arising in the estate of the "kindly" legatee.

Tax mitigation and planning

Common usage

14–12   The most common usage of a deed of variation is to enable a family to engage in tax planning and tax mitigation. This can be most commonly seen where spouses simply bequeath their whole estates to each other whom failing to children, etc. Such wills are still very common, and obviously under such a will neither spouse is making any use whatsoever of his or her nil-rate band. In such circumstances, a deed of variation can be utilised so as to make at least partial use of the nil-rate band of the first spouse to die and thereby minimise or restrict the estate of the survivor, which would otherwise be liable to be taxed in full after exhaustion of the nil-rate band of the survivor.

For example:

Husband (H) and wife (W) have assets of the values of respectively £300,000 and £150,000. They have wills in terms of which they simply bequeath their respective estates to each other whom failing to children, etc. Neither has made any lifetime gifts. H and W have two adult children, X and Y. H dies. The children decide not to claim their entitlement to legitim and his whole estate (£300,000) passes to W. No inheritance tax is payable because of the spouse exemption. W then dies. Her gross estate is £450,000. After deduction of her nil-rate band (£263,000), there remains an estate of £187,000 which is taxable to IHT at 40 per cent, *i.e.* inheritance tax bill of £74,800. This is effectively lost to the children, X and Y.

14–13   However, H and W could have sought to mitigate, if not wholly avoid, tax liability in question, by paying careful attention to the terms of their wills (although there are other considerations to be taken into account— see below). Thus, they could avoid any tax liability in the event of H pre-deceasing W. H could redraw his will leaving a legacy of £100,000 each to X and Y on his death with the residue (also £100,000) passing to W. On death of W, in this example, her estate would amount to £250,000. As this is below her nil-rate band, there would be no inheritance tax payable on the estate passing under her will to X and Y.

Again taking the same couple, W could alter her will to provide that in the event of her pre-deceasing H, her whole estate would pass not to H but equally between X and Y. On W dying first, her estate of £150,000 would be divided equally between X and Y. No tax would be payable as the estate is below the nil-rate threshold. On death of H leaving an estate of £300,000, after deduction of the nil-rate band the sum of £37,000 would be taxable at 40 per cent, *i.e.* an IHT bill of £14,800.

To wholly avoid a liability on either death, H and W could, during their lifetimes, equalise their respective estates and redraw their wills so as to ensure that the survivor of them would be left with an estate which would not exceed the survivor's nil-rate band.

In the first example given above (H and W having made no steps to mitigate IHT in terms of their wills), a deed of variation could be brought into play so as to pay an appropriate amount on first death to children or other beneficiaries, thereby making as much use as possible of the nil-rate band.

Other considerations

Clients require advice in relation to the proper structuring of their 14–14 wills, or, in respect of a deed of variation, for tax mitigation purposes at a future date. There is, however, one very important consideration of which the adviser must not lose sight—that is the financial position of the surviving spouse. Where relationships within a family are good, a surviving spouse can often be over generous in his or her initial approach to the amount which should be passed to family in terms of a deed of variation. At all times, the adviser must bear in mind the possible effect of passing too much out of the estate of the first to die, either by means of "first death legacies" in favour of adult children, etc. or in terms of a deed of variation. Human longevity is on the increase, and a widow aged 70 years may still have many years to live, during which she will need to support herself financially.

In the second style deed of variation in the Appendix, the surviving spouse has decided that he has sufficient assets and income of his own so that the sum of £75,000 can be passed from his deceased's wife's estate under the deed of variation to his three adult children. On the assumption that the surviving spouse's net estate would in any event exceed the nil-rate band, by entering into this deed of variation, the family have saved £30,000 in inheritance tax on death of the widow. This style also deals with an intestate estate.

Other aspects/possibilities

Consideration of the financial position of the surviving spouse is of 14–15 great importance. Where a spouse has died at a relatively young age, the surviving spouse might be uncertain as to what extent he or she could make use of a deed of variation to benefit adult children. If there is any doubt as to the financial position of the survivor, then this of itself may indicate that no deed of variation should be entered into, and that the surviving spouse should take prudent steps for his or her own part during his/her lifetime with a view to mitigating tax. As an alternative to that cautious approach, there is no reason why a deed of variation could not be used so as to create a discretionary trust. This would allow the executors great flexibility, and if it became obvious that the surviving spouse was not faring well on a financial basis, then the executors could intervene on his or her behalf. This latter approach would, however, allow some degree of tax mitigation as circumstances permitted. A deed of variation can also be brought into play, not just in relation to partial use of the nil-rate band, but also where the relevant estate is comprised of assets which attract business and/or agricultural relief (whether at the full rate or 50 per cent) for IHT purposes. If these assets have simply been bequeathed to the surviving spouse, then again some careful deliberation may be required as to whether or not the survivor actually requires the assets in question. If not, then a deed of variation could be utilised so as to transfer the assets to adult children, thereby taking advantage of current reliefs. As clients should not be encouraged to rely on the possibility of a deed of variation being entered into to rectify any failure in their planning after the fact, in the circumstances immediately hereinbefore outlined, the advisers should not lose sight of the possibility that at some point in the future there will be a reduction in the rates of relief available, or indeed the reliefs may be withdrawn. In such circumstances, simply leaving the assets to the survivor (on the assumption that business and/or agricultural property relief will be available on death of the survivor) will, admittedly with the benefit of hindsight, be seen to have been the wrong option.

Statutory requirements

14–16   Whilst deeds of variation have been with us for many years, the ability to utilise the same for tax mitigation only arose in the 1970s (section 47 of the Finance Act 1975 as amended/replaced by section 68 of the Finance Act 1978). Section 17(1) of the 1984 Act provides that a variation or disclaimer to which section 142(1) applies is not the transfer of value for IHT purposes. This has to be read in conjunction with section 142(1) which states that:

> "this applies as if the variation has been effected by the deceased or, as the case maybe, the disclaimed benefit had never been conferred".

These two provisions are of great importance for tax mitigation purposes when read in conjunction. The effect of the same permits, in terms of a deed of variation or disclaimer, an individual to give up an asset of value to a third party. This can allow for "long distance" tax planning. For example, an adult child who is already reasonably wealthy in his or her own right has an elderly parent who dies leaving an estate of £200,000. An adult child is the sole beneficiary. There is no inheritance tax payable in respect of a deceased's parent's estate as it is within the nil- rate band. However, the adult child is already independently wealthy and is aware that an influx of another £200,000 will simply, on the face of it, increase his potential IHT liability on death. Subject to the warning note detailed below, a deed of variation could be entered into, passing the £200,000 over to the adult child's own children. By so doing the adult child will avoid £80,000 inheritance tax on his death. Care does have to be taken with such a strategy. If the children to whom the estate is devolved are minors (for the purpose of section 663 of the Income and Corporation Taxes Act 1988, a child under the age of 18 years is regarded as a minor), then income from the property gifted by way of deed of variation will be aggregated with income of the parent who gave up the benefit under the will; this could lead to an unexpected, added income tax liability for the parent, and he is not allowed to mitigate that additional income tax liability by bringing his child's personal tax allowance into play.

Technical aspect

The technical requirements for an effective deed of variation under **14–17** section 142 of the 1984 Act are:

(1) That the deed be entered into and signed within two years of the relevant date of death.

(2) A deed of variation applies to the deceased's estate, both heritable and moveable. It can include "excluded property" such as a reversionary interest but, however, cannot include a property life-rented by the deceased under a trust section 142(5) or any property deemed to have been gifted subject to a reservation of benefit under section 102(3) of the Finance Act 1986.

(3) A deed of variation can apply to both testate and intestate estates.

(4) The instrument/deed requires to be in writing. There is, however, no statutory form of deed, although it must meet the requirements of section 142. The Inland Revenue Press Release of 1985 (May) made it clear that the Inland Revenue would accept a form of deed which identified the particular disposition of the will and did in fact vary the same.

(5) The deed should be entered into by those persons benefited or who would benefit. Those whose benefits are being affected need to enter into the deed. When a deed of variation was entered into prior to July 31, 2002, notice of the same required to be given to the Inland Revenue within six months from the date of the Instrument. Following the Finance Act 2002, the Inland Revenue announced[4] that with effect from August 2002, a deed of variation must contain an election as to whether or not it is to be treated as a disposal by the deceased for both inheritance tax and capital gains tax purposes.

(6) The elections can be made separately, for example, for IHT purposes but not for capital gains tax purposes.

(7) There must be no external financial consideration regarding the entering into of a deed of variation. For example, it will not

---

[4] IHT newsletter, April/May 2002.

apply on a sale of an asset, or when a financial inducement has been given by an individual for the deed to be entered into, or where the whole expenses of the document are paid by one individual by way of persuading the others to enter into the document.

Inland Revenue

14–18   Even though the above requirements may in fact be followed, the Inland Revenue have made it clear that deeds of variation have to exist "in the real world".[5] The Revenue indicated that where, on first death, a survivor is given a life interest in property, that interest will be extinguished on death of the survivor with the effect that, when in the "real world" those inheriting on second death come to consider a variation, there will be "nothing for the variation to bite on". The Revenue's view here was confirmed by a special commissioner in the case of *Soutter's Executry v IRC*.[6] Here, two ladies, Miss A and Miss B, lived together in a house owned by Miss A. On her death, Miss A bequeathed a life rent interest in her house to Miss B, who died less than a year later. The estate of Miss A was below the nil-rate band. However, the estate of Miss B exceeded the nil-rate band by "a considerable amount". A deed of variation was entered into which purported to remove the life rent provision in favour of Miss B in the will of Miss A. However, the deed was subsequently successfully challenged. The special commissioner took the view that there had been nothing to vary. Once Miss B had died, there was no property left. It should be noted that this decision has been queried on the basis that it was not, after all, the property which was being varied but the terms of the disposition (*i.e.* Miss A's will) in relation to the same.

The Inland Revenue adopt the view that section 142 of the 1984 Act offers only one opportunity for variation of a will, etc. The Inland Revenue will not accept a deed of variation which seeks to vary an earlier deed of variation, even if the provisions of section 142 regarding observance of time-limits, etc. are adhered to. Often the invariable position of the Inland Revenue is that the first deed of variation should be regarded as being irrevocable (and the styles adopted by many practitioners specifically state that the deed is irrevocable), and later amending deeds will not generally be accepted.[7]

The involvement of the executor

14–19   As noted above, it is not necessary that all persons involved in the estate should actually join in the deed of variation. If, for example, one of a number of residuary beneficiaries wishes to vary by giving up his or her share, then it may be that only the signature of that one person is required. In strict terms, the executors only need to be involved as parties to the deed, and the relevant election, if as a result of the granting of the deed, increases the IHT burden (section 142(2)).

---

[5] IHT newsletter, December 2001.
[6] S.T.C. (S.C.D.) 385.
[7] *Russell v IRC* [1988] S.T.C. 195.

However, it is considered that intimation of the terms of the deed to the executors may be required under common law in order to create a *ius quaesitum tertio* in favour of the party benefiting under the terms of the deed. In any event, the practice has developed of having executors join in the deed of variation even where it might not have been strictly necessary under section 142. Executors may decline to join in if they then hold insufficient assets to discharge any additional IHT liability (section 142(6)).

Stamp duty

Deeds of variation were and are exempt from stamp duty. For deeds **14–20** entered into prior to December 1, 2003, the exemption was applied provided the deed incorporated the appropriate certificate under the Stamp Duty (Exempt Instruments) Regulations 1987 (Category M to the schedule thereto). Under the new Stamp Duty Land Tax Rules, deeds varying the disposition under the will remain exempt, although an exemption form under the SDLT rules will be required.

Family home—a problem asset

Rises in house prices over recent years have caused many clients to **14–21** focus more particularly on the question of the value of a family dwelling-house. Some clients have mistakenly believed that the value of their home could be removed from the arena of IHT liability by the client taking the step of conveying the dwelling-house to their adult children, with the client continuing to reside in the same rent free. This is, of course, quite wrong—such a disposition will not be a potentially exempt transfer but will be deemed by the Revenue to be a property subject to a reservation of benefit (where the reservation still existed as a date of death) in terms of section 102(3) of the Finance Act 1986. However, where there is no survivorship destination, spouses may consider bequeathing their respective one-half shares in and to the property to adult children, thereby removing a sizeable asset from taxation on death of the survivor. Whilst such a course may have a seeming attraction to clients, there are dangers here (which must be pointed out to a client considering the same):

> (i) The surviving spouse will lose control of the dwelling-house and may become vulnerable where, for example, an adult child pre-deceases the surviving spouse or becomes bankrupt. The danger here may be seen in the English case of *Palmer v Brown*.[8] Here, the father lost his wife. He was grief stricken for some time and unable to cope with his loss. During that time he received great moral support from his daughter. To reflect the kindness and care which his daughter had given him, the father instructed his solicitor to convey his dwelling-house by way of gift to the daughter (and in fairness to the solicitor in question, there appears to have been clear evidence that the solicitor did warn

---

[8] [1997] EWCA Civ 2576.

the father of the possible consequences of taking this step). However, after a period of time, the father struck up a new relationship with another lady. They decided that they would sell their respective dwelling-houses and buy a new house together. Having approached his daughter, asking that she put the house on to the market for sale and make the proceeds on sale over to him, the father was rebuffed. He decided to vindicate his rights by means of litigation. The court found that the gift had been absolute without strings attached, and as the dwelling-house now belonged to the daughter, she was quite entitled to refuse to do anything at her father's behest regarding disposal or otherwise of the property.

(ii) If the will of the pre-deceasing spouse bequeaths his one-half interest to adult children subject to a life rent in favour of the survivor, this will in any event be wholly ineffective for inheritance tax mitigation purposes, as the value of the life rented estate would fall to be aggregated with that of the surviving spouse on her death. Even where the will remains silent, if the surviving spouse continues to reside in the property (enjoying the exclusive occupation of the same), then there is a possibility that the Inland Revenue might seek to argue that this amounted in truth to an interest in possession. This is likely to be more so if the testator includes in his will a provision to block a sale by the adult children whilst the surviving parent is still occupying the house.

(iii) In any event, the possibility of creating an unexpected capital gains tax liability in the hands of the adult children needs to be borne in mind. It is highly unlikely that the property will be the main or principal residence of any of the children, and they will lose the benefit of the uplift in value for CGT (on death of the survivor) in respect of the one- half (or other) interest conveyed to them following the granting of a deed of variation on death of the first parent to go.

Alimentary life-rents

14–22 Where a will provides for an alimentary life rent, if accepted, it cannot be renounced or varied, but if it has not been accepted then any benefit can be disclaimed.[9] Thus, where a will includes an alimentary life rent, the relevant beneficiary should take no benefit thereunder if there is any prospect of a variation being put in place.

Capital gains tax

14–23 Under section 62(6) of the Taxation of Chargeable Gains Act 1992, an election can be made in relation to a variation for capital gains tax purposes also. This applies even though the property may have risen in value by the time the variation is effected. If an election under section 62(6)(a) is made, then the party receiving the asset in question will be

---

[9] *Douglas v Hamilton*, 1961 S.C. 205.

deemed to acquire the same at the value pertaining to that asset as at the relevant date of death. This avoids there being a deemed disposal by the granter of the variation, having the result that the granter might unexpectedly incur a capital gains tax liability.

It is possible to elect for a variation under section 142 of the 1984 Act, but not to make an election under section 62(6). This would be appropriate where:

- The asset has dropped in value since the relevant date of death.
- Where the executor's annual exemption is available to utilise and cover any gain.
- Where the whole estate is in cash and there would in any event be no liability under existing capital gains tax rules.

Capacity

Parties to a deed of variation must, in accordance with the general **14–24** law, be capax, of full age and should consent to the deed.

Disclaimers/renunciations

The testator could, of course, build in a degree of flexibility for tax **14–25** planning by incorporating in his will a clause to specify what should happen in the event of a beneficiary renouncing his rights. The purpose will include a destination over to the effect that the renouncing beneficiary will be treated as having pre-deceased the testator with the benefit renounced passing to those beneficiaries deemed to have survived the testator. It is, however, possible to include a provision directing the relevant benefit to specific alternative beneficiaries in the event of the original beneficiary renouncing. In terms of sections 17(a) and 142(1) of the Inheritance Tax Act 1984, a renunciation is not by itself a "transfer of value", and IHT would be payable as if the benefit renounced had not been conferred in the first instance. A renunciation within the will may drafted as to allow a degree of flexibility, *i.e.* the beneficiary with the option of renouncing can assess his financial position at the relevant time and, if appropriate, renounce in favour of substitute beneficiaries. Inclusion of such a provision may offer some flexibility regarding IHT planning, particularly if the variation provisions (or at least the tax advantages thereof) of section 142 of the 1984 Act are in fact ever withdrawn by the Government.

Whilst it would appear that a partial renunciation or disclaimer is not possible in England, the Inland Revenue have no objections to partial renunciation in Scotland. It is also believed that a possible income tax trap, referred to above,[10] will not apply to renunciations. It is commonly held that the Pt XV Rules of the Finance Act 1988 will not apply to renunciations/disclaimers.

PRECATORY BEQUESTS

Background

Section 143 of the Inheritance Tax Act 1984 provides that: **14–26**

---

[10] Income & Corporation Taxes Act 1988, s.663.

"Where a testator expresses a wish that property bequeathed by his will shall be transferred by the legatee to other persons, and the legatee transfers any of the property in accordance with that wish within the period of two years after the death of the testator, this Act shall have effect as if the property transferred had been bequeathed by the will to the transferee".

Similarly, section 17(b) of the 1984 Act provides that a transfer to which section 143 applies is not a "transfer of value" for IHT purposes.

Section 143 of the 1984 Act offers further valuable tax planning possibilities.

Implementation

14–27   An example of a precatory bequest is:

I bequeath to A (design) the sum of TWENTY THOUSAND POUNDS, subject to it being my wish (without imposing any obligation upon A) that he should pay the said sum to B (Design) and that within two years of my date of death.

Why leave such a bequest?

14–28   The draftsman who is a professional sceptic may feel that such a bequest is pointless. However, this is not the case. The examination in more detail of the "style" bequest detailed above will, hopefully, illuminate the possible benefits of making use of a precatory legacy. Thus, let us assume that A is the adult child of the testator. B, already at university is the child of A. The testator has otherwise bequeathed the residue of his estate to his surviving spouse. The legacy is therefore "a first death" bequest. A may already be a person of some wealth. At the time of making his will, however, the testator may not be entirely sure as to whether or not they would require the relevant benefit. The testator is, in effect, entrusting A to assess his own financial position, and, where appropriate, pass the legacy to his child. In so doing, the testator may be allowing A to effect a degree of IHT mitigation in relation to his own estate, without the passing of the legacy to A's child being "counted against" A in so far as A's "IHT clock" is concerned.

Plus points

14–29   Whilst section 143 remains in force, it offers the following:

● Flexibility—for example, such bequests might be used as an alternative to a discretionary legacy. For example, where the surviving spouse is chosen as the "principal" beneficiary under such a bequest, with the amount of the same being restricted to the nil-rate band for the time being, this will allow the surviving spouse to assess his or her financial position and to take steps, within the relevant two-year period provided by section 143, to seek to mitigate IHT on his or her death while still allowing the surviving spouse to retain all or part of the bequest where there may be doubts as to the ongoing financial position of that spouse.

- Use of such bequests can avoid the necessity of entering into a deed of variation, and thereby avoid the attendant costs and complexities of such a deed.
- An appropriately drafted precatory bequest can avoid the difficulties which might arise where minor beneficiaries are involved.

Disadvantages

- A precatory bequest is no more than an expression of wish. **14–30** Thus, if the "principal" beneficiary chooses not to pass on the benefit within the two-year period indicated, then no sanction can be brought to bear. In effect, a precatory bequest is absolute, save in so far as the principal beneficiary chooses to act in accordance with the expression of wish detailed by the testator.
- There remains a possibility of legislative intervention. The threat to deeds of variation, first enunciated in 1989, also apply to section 143 of the 1984 Act. However, as with section 142, it remains the case that there has as yet been no legislative intervention. However, the possibility of the same cannot be discounted.
- The capital gains tax "advantages" attaching to deeds of variation under section 142 of the 1984 Act (as applied by section 62 of the Taxation of Chargeable Gains Act 1992) do not extend to section 143 precatory bequests. That being so, such bequests should be restricted to "cash".

Survivorship clauses

Under section 92 of the 1984 Act, a commorientes clause can apply **14–31** for a period up to six months from the testator's date of death. From a practical point of view, it may well be that a six month commorientes clause will cause concern to a surviving spouse, particularly if he or she is still relatively young at death of the testator.

Two-year discretionary trust will

Where the testator allows his executors/trustees a period of two years **14–32** from his date of death in which to assess the respective requirements of the potential beneficiary and to appoint funds in accordance with discretionary powers conferred upon them, then section 144 of the 1984 Act will apply, provided always that the relevant discretionary powers are exercised within two years of the date of death. In terms of section 144 where the executors/trustees exercise their discretion and appoint funds, there will be no further inheritance tax liability. Again, this provides great flexibility, particularly where, on "early death", the financial position of the surviving spouse may be uncertain. However, and as with section 143, there is no "mirror" capital gains tax relief under section 144 (subject to possibility of "roll over relief"). This needs to be taken into consideration and, again if the testator's estate is mainly in cash then, at present, such considerations are largely irrelevant. It should also be borne in mind that during the relevant two-year period and until an appointment has been made, income arising within the relevant fund will be subject to the special rate on trust income (40 per cent).

Disclaimer of certain property

14–33   Under section 93 of the 1984 Act, the fiar in a life rent trust can disclaim his interest. This will not be a transfer of value under the 1984 Act. Unlike section 142, there is no two-year (or indeed any) time-limit applied to such a disclaimer.

PART III—ADDITIONAL OPTIONS TO CONSIDER

CHAPTER 15

POWERS OF ATTORNEY, GUARDIANSHIPS AND LIVING WILLS

POWERS OF ATTORNEY

Background

In essence, a power of attorney is a written form of mandate or **15–01** agency. The ability to grant a power of attorney is of great value. That value has increasingly become known to the lay populace. For many years, however, the granting of a power of attorney did not loom large in the legal priorities of a client. Perhaps the main reason for this was that, prior to the passing of the Law Reform (Miscellaneous Provisions) (Scotland) Act 1990, a power of attorney was considered to have lapsed on supervening mental incapacity of the granter of the document.[1] The mental incapacity did have to be permanent.[2] The highly unfortunate result was that, just when a power of attorney could have been most appropriate and useful, it was denied effect, with families having to rely on having a "curator bonis" appointed.

Scottish law did, however, take a massive leap forward with effect from January 1, 1991 when section 71 of the Law Reform (Miscellaneous Provisions) (Scotland) Act 1990 came into force. Section 71 provided:

(i) Any rule of law by which a factory and commission or power of attorney ceases to have effect in the event of the mental incapacity of the granter shall not apply to a factory and commission or power of attorney granted on or after the date on which this section comes into force.

(ii) In subsection (i) above, "mental incapacity" means, in relation to a person, that he is incapable of managing his property and affairs by reason of mental disorder within the meaning of section 1 of the Mental Health (Scotland) Act 1984.

The section was not retrospective, but did not (as some had suggested) require that a power of attorney, granted after January 1, 1991, should specifically state that it would remain in force notwithstanding supervening mental incapacity. This is, however, a specific requirement in relation to a "continuing" power of attorney granted under section 15 of the Adults with Incapacity (Scotland) Act 2000 (see below). To a great

---

[1] *Dick Petitioner* (1901) 9 S.L.T. 177.
[2] *Wink v Mortimer* (1849) 11 D. 995.

extent, the passing of the 2000 Act galvanised this area of law. Strangely, for the complex society, prior to the 2000 Act coming into force, the body of law in relation to powers of attorney in Scotland was in fact relatively small. The 2000 Act saw a sea-change and we now have a great panoply of rules and regulations with which to contend.

The necessity of clarity

15–02   It was, and still is, essential that a power of attorney define with absolute clarity the powers to be granted:

> "The only safe footing is that the Attorney has no powers except those expressed. General expressions are not to be relied on. It might be said that a Power 'to manage the granter's affairs and to act for him therein as he could do himself' covers a great deal but it has been questioned whether it would cover even the uplifting of rents and interest."[3]

The rule to follow is "to ascertain what are the powers which will certainly or probably require to be exercised and confer these expressly and in such terms as will best cover the circumstances."[4] In *Goodall v Bilsland*,[5] a group of individuals wishing to object to an application for renewal of a public house licence granted a written mandate to a solicitor who otherwise did not himself have title to object. The mandate authorised the solicitor to lodge objections at the forthcoming Licensing Court and "to appear on our behalf in support of said objections". The solicitor lodged objections, appeared at the court and spoke to them. Unfortunately, the objections were repelled and the licence renewed. Without having specific authority to do so, the solicitor noted an appeal. At the appeal, his objections were upheld and renewal of the licence overturned. The disappointed licensee raised an action of reduction in respect of the decision of the Licensing Appeal Court. The Court of Session took the view that the solicitor had not had any authority to note the appeal, which was therefore void. Authority to appear before the Licensing Court did not extend to noting appeals before the Licensing Appeal Court—a different court.

The ability of a power of attorney to survive supervening mental incapacity on the part of a granter is a great boon. Increasing human longevity will itself increase the importance of individuals having suitably drafted powers of attorney in place.

The Code of Practice

15–03   In March 2001, the Scottish Parliament published a lengthy Code of Practice in relation to the actings of attorneys appointed under the 2000 Act. It is important that solicitors advising clients in relation to the granting of powers of attorney should be familiar with that Code of Practice. It is equally important that those acting as attorneys should be

---

[3] Bell, *Conveyancing*, p.448.
[4] Burns, *Conveyancing Practice* (4th ed. 1957, The Central Press, Aberdeen), p.49.
[5] 1909 S.C. 1152.

aware of the same. Although the actual legal standing of the Code of Practice is not entirely clear, an attorney who acts contrary to the spirit of that Code of Practice may find himself in some difficulty.

The draftsman's approach

In advising clients in relation to the granting of a power of attorney, **15–04** the following approach is recommended:

- Know the terms of the Code of Practice and advise both the granter of the document and his or her attorney of the existence of the Code. In some circumstances, knowing of the existence of the Code of Practice may be a reassurance to an elderly person. Prior to the 2000 Act coming into force, there was in fact no real practical means of policing the actions of an attorney. That fault has now been rectified.

- The draftsman should take care in some circumstances not to give the impression that he believes that the client is verging on incapacity. In fact, it should be emphasised to clients that a power of attorney must be granted when the client is in full charge of his or her affairs and faculties. Some clients may take offence if they feel that their abilities are being questioned and may baulk at granting a power of attorney.

- The draftsman should discuss the range of powers to be granted. It is better to grant a full range of wide powers from the outset rather than take the risk that a specific power may not be required further down the line. The draftsman should be able to explain the valid reasons for granting specific powers to the client. When points are properly explained to clients, they are more likely to appreciate the wisdom of granting very wide powers as opposed to a restricted range.

- A granter should not appoint another party as an attorney unless the granter reposes full faith and trust in that person. Whilst this may seem to be self-evident, a granter should make an appointment only after consideration of relevant issues. For example, a granter whose affairs are very complex should be advised not to appoint someone who "may not be up to it". This would be unfair on the attorney if he or she is likely to be overwhelmed by the extent and/or complexity of the estate and financial affairs of the granter.

- Similar considerations apply to the appointment of an attorney as to the appointment of an executor—an elderly granter should consider appointing as an attorney a member of a younger generation.

- Recommend to the granter that he appoint joint attorneys or a principal and substitute attorney. The whole purpose of granting the power of attorney might be defeated if the sole attorney pre-deceases the granter or becomes incapax him/herself. In that connection, para.2.25 of the Code of Practice states:

  "You and the granter should also discuss the question of whether he or she wishes to appoint more than one Attorney."

The granter may appoint:

(i) Separate attorneys to exercise functions in relation to property and financial affairs and in relation to personal welfare.

(ii) Joint attorneys with similar or different powers; for example, one person may be made the continuing attorney, with the other person being made the welfare attorney.

(iii) One or more substitute attorneys to take the place of an attorney who dies or resigns.

> "If you feel that it would be too much for you to be the sole attorney, or that you would like to exercise continuing powers but not welfare powers, or that you may not be able to exercise powers of attorney indefinitely, then you should discuss with the adult the possibility of appointing more than one attorney with different or similar powers; and/or one or more substitute attorneys."

In the foregoing connection, bear in mind the warning note introduced by Burns,[6] namely:

> "Attorneys in succession—in this case the Attorneys are so appointed that the second has no office until the first has ceased to be Attorney, though that need not be by death. In an appointment to A whom failing B, that is the result. It follows that, after A has accepted office, it is no reason for B acting that A is out of reach or that it is otherwise inconvenient to obtain A's signature. Until A has ceased to be Attorney, B has no standing."

• Do not appoint as attorneys two individuals who do not get on or are likely to be at loggerheads. This is a recipe for disaster, as there may be no effective short term formulae for resolving disputes between the joint attorneys.

15–05 Some clients, particularly of older generations, may baulk at granting a wide-ranging power of attorney. Older clients are individuals of wide life experience who rightly retain respect for their own capabilities and intellect. Tact, diplomacy and reasoned recommendations are required. It is no part of a solicitor's function to endeavour to persuade a client against his or her will to grant a wide-ranging power of attorney. However, if the draftsman can explain in reasoned and proper fashion the benefits which can flow from taking such a step, then the understandable resistance may decline. The draftsman needs to be able to explain that the alternatives to granting a continuing power of attorney—financial guardianship or intervention—are much less attractive, more expensive, complicated and will of necessity result in a much increased bureaucratic involvement. Many individuals have a mistrust of bureaucracy, and a carefully thought out argument detailing the benefits

---

[6] *Conveyancing Practice*, p.48, cited above.

of a continuing power of attorney will often win the day. Being armed with the appropriate arguments as to why a suitable power of attorney is advisable will often persuade clients as to the good sense in granting the appropriate document.

There are other specific matters which the draftsman should also be in a position to discuss with, and explain to, clients:

- As indicated above, the document should contain wide powers. However, even a properly drafted power of attorney with wide powers may not be able to cover every eventuality. This is recognised in the Code of Practice which, in para.5.95, recognises that, for example, an attorney may find that his or her powers are insufficient. The Code of Practice contains guidance in such circumstances and indicates that where appropriate, an attorney may need to consider applying to a sheriff for a financial guardianship.

- Clients should be encouraged to avoid nominating only one person to be attorney. The whole purpose of granting the power of attorney may be stymied if the sole appointee predeceases the granter, loses capacity or indeed declines (perhaps as an after thought) to act. A client should therefore be encouraged to consider appointing two attorneys or one whom failing another. Where a joint appointment is made, the client needs to issue instructions as to whether or not, although the appointment is joint, either attorney should be able to act on his or her own. To insist that both must act jointly would perhaps indicate a degree of lack of trust but could also cause difficulties, for example, if one attorney falls ill or goes abroad on business or on holiday. In discussing the question of joint attorneys, Burns[7] offers the following advice:

  "If they are to be Attorneys together, it will be made clear (1) whether the office is to fall if any of them should die or otherwise cease to hold office (2) whether both or all the acting Attorneys must concur in every act (3) or whether there is a quorum or (4) a *sine qua non* or (5) whether each of the Attorneys may act by himself alone. As a general rule, the Attorneys should be appointed jointly and severely, the Power, apart from recall, or other circumstances operating as recall, remaining in force so long as anyone survives and retains office, and each having full power to act independently of the others. Objections may be stated to this but a Power of Attorney implies trust between granter and grantee and also between joint grantees. Nor does it follow that, because these powers exist, they are to be acted on to the uttermost; rather, they are intended to smooth operations when it might be difficult to obtain the signatures of both or all the Attorneys."

The good sense in the latter statement is evident.[8] Whilst it is the author's view that where joint attorneys are appointed,

---

[7] *Conveyancing Practice*, cited above.
[8] See para.2.25 of the Code of Practice referred to above.

either/any one of them should be unable to act, the draftsman, again, needs to give some thought to his drafting. The possibility of a disagreement between the attorneys cannot be discounted—in such cases, the granter may wish to consider whether one or two (or more) attorneys should be appointed on a *sine qua non* basis. Similarly, if three joint attorneys are appointed (the author would recommend that this should be the maximum), then provision could be made that, in the vent of dispute, the decision of the majority will rule.

- It should be emphasised to the client that whilst he or she retains capacity, he or she remains in full control. The client may not be happy to grant a power of attorney which comes into effect immediately, and may wish to include a springing power in terms of which the attorney will only be able to act once the granter has become incapax. To reassure clients, they should be reminded that the attorney is after all no more than an agent. Powers granted can be removed (*i.e.* the client should be advised that whilst he or she retains capacity, it is always open for the granter to effectively sack an attorney). Clients should also be advised of the general supervisory powers of the public guardian.

Important clauses

15–06   It is important that, where a power of attorney is granted to enable the attorney to deal with all of the granter's affairs should incapacity intervene, then the document should contain the fullest range of powers necessary. Given that an attorney only has such powers as are granted specifically, the following matters are of note:

- Operation of bank accounts—a simple authority to operate on a bank account may not in fact be accepted by a bank. The concern of the bank is understandable. Where the account in question is a current account, it is possible that in drawing a cheque, the attorney may have inadvertently put the account in to debit. The bank does not wish to find itself in a situation where the granter then refuses to repay the amount overdrawn on the basis that the attorney had acted in breach of his or her authority.[9]

- Power to borrow—following on from the above comments, care needs to be taken in relation to the power to borrow. Burns[10] states that the power of borrowing conferred should:

  (a) Authorise the attorney to bind the constituent personally, and if there is to be power to bind him jointly and severally with others, that must be stated.
  (b) Authorise him to grant security over his estate.
  (c) Confer a power of sale on the creditor.

---

[9] See *Esmail v Bank of Scotland*, 1999 S.L.T. 1289 (O.H.).
[10] *Conveyancing Practice*, p.49.

In *Thomas v Walkers' Trustees*,[11] the power "in connection with my said business to make, draw, sign, accept or endorse" bills and notes was not accepted as a general power to borrow.

- The Inland Revenue will accept a tax return signed by an attorney only in certain circumstances, and then only if there is specific power for the attorney to make and sign tax returns. In any event, the Inland Revenue appear to be increasingly unwilling to accept tax returns signed by the attorney where the granter is still capax.[12] It is the view of the Board of the Inland Revenue that the signing of the declaration on a return falls within that class of statutory duties which cannot be delegated. The reason for this is that the Revenue take the view that the attorney might not have full details of the sources of income of the granter, and this could cause problems further down the line.

- Power to litigate—again a specific power requires to be granted. The case of *Goodall v Bilsland* above is of relevance here.

- A power to sign deeds is not the same as a power to sell heritable property. Both these powers must be specifically granted.

- The power to gift—see clause 16 of the style power of attorney in the Appendix of Styles. Again, from the Inland Revenue's point of view, this is a controversial clause. However, what appears to be clear is that the Capital Taxes Office will not recognise inheritance tax planning carried out by an attorney unless there is a specific power authorising the same. In a recent case,[13] The commissioners found in favour of the Capital Taxes Office on that very point. Further, the author understands that the Capital Taxes Office have at the very best queried whether or not power to gift will enable IHT mitigation planning to be carried out. At the time of writing, the Capital Taxes Office in Edinburgh have not yet had to consider a live case involving large scale gifting by an attorney (having specific power to so act) with a view to mitigating IHT (although the author understands that the Capital Taxes Office would probably not make an issue of small gifts made by the attorney having a specific power). The concern (and likely ground of challenge) on the part of the Capital Taxes Office is whether a granter can truly pass to his attorney the required *animus donandi*. It might be possible to argue this if the granter had himself been engaged in proper IHT mitigation—if the granter had never done so, then the Capital Taxes Office may well have a point— and that is a separate matter from whether or not such actings on the part of the attorney could be justified under the Principles/Code of Conduct (which itself is a very important issue). What is in any event clear is that unless you include a

---

[11] 1829 7.5 828.
[12] Section 42 of the Taxes Management Act 1970.
[13] *McDowall Executor's v IRC* [2004] S.T.C. (S.C.D.) 22; [2004] W.T.L.R. 221.

power of this type, then tax planning carried out by the attorney (however well intentioned and however much the granter might have supported the same) will be the subject of examination by the Capital Taxes Office and will be challenged.

- Remember always to include a charging clause. This is of great importance where a professional person has been appointed to act as attorney.

15–07 The following clauses are for the most part ineffective.

- Power to sign or alter a will—freedom to test (*i.e.* make a will) is a very personal right and cannot be delegated to another party; for example, a discretionary clause giving the executors power to virtually deal with the testators estate as they might see fit is likely to void from uncertainty.[14]
- Power to grant a matrimonial homes affidavit—in some cases, this clause might be of benefit, although in general terms, an attorney does not have power to grant an affidavit on behalf of the granter. However, in a conveyancing transaction where a matrimonial homes affidavit for the granter would normally have been required, the Keeper may be prepared to accept an affidavit by an attorney, provided that the Keeper had clear evidence as to the granter's incapacity, marital status, etc.
- Power (granted to the attorney) to appoint another attorney or a substitute attorney—the validity of such a clause has always been doubted on the basis of the principal *delegatus non potest delegare*. The Public Guardian has made it clear that he would not register a power of attorney containing such a power. This would enable the attorney to appoint someone else whose details had not been supplied to the Office of the Public Guardian. Interestingly, Burns[15] does appear to indicate that a granter can include power to appoint a factor for whom the attorney should not be responsible.
- In the case of *Toni, Petitioner*,[16] a debtor petitioned with concurrence of a creditor for the debtor's sequestration under setion 5(2)(a) of the Bankruptcy (Scotland) Act 1985. The petition was signed by the debtor's daughter under a power of attorney, the debtor being terminally ill and in the early stages of Alzheimer's disease. The daughter argued that the power of attorney gave her the required mandate to sign the petition. It was held that the power of attorney did not specifically give the petitioner's mandatory the required mandate and, strictly construed, did not extend to the surrendering control of the petitioner's affairs irrevocably, this being the inevitable consequence of sequestration. The sheriff expressed the opinion that it was doubtful whether a mandatory could even be specifically authorised to apply for sequestration of his principal. The petition was dismissed.

[14] *Bannerman's Trustees v Bannerman*, 1915 S.C. 398.
[15] *Conveyancing Practice*, p.51, cited above.
[16] S.L.T. 2002 (Sh. Ct.) 159.

- See the cautionary note expressed above regarding tax returns signed by the attorney.

Continuing and welfare powers of attorney

The 2000 Act introduced a wholly new regime including continuing **15–08** powers of attorney (section 15) and welfare powers of attorney (section 16). It should be noted that the 2000 Act was not intended to be a code which covered all powers of attorney. Powers of attorney for "one off" operations remain unaffected. For example:

- A power to sign documents whilst the granter is abroad.
- Power to negotiate missives.
- A "commissary power of attorney"—this is granted where, for example, a sole executor living abroad authorises an attorney to sign the inventory of the deceased person's estate on the executor's behalf.

If, however, an individual wishes to grant a continuing power of attorney which will remain in full force and effect after supervening incapacity or a welfare power of attorney, then the provisions of the Act have to be followed. In terms of section 15 of the Act, a continuing power of attorney shall be valid only if it is expressed in a written document which is:

(a) Subscribed by the granter.
(b) Incorporates a statement which clearly expresses the granter's intention that the power be a continuing power.
(c) Incorporates the Certificate in the prescribed form (see the style continuing and welfare power of attorney in the Appendix). Adherence to the terms of the certificates are required. Note that separate certificates are required and an attempt to make one certificate cover both situations will fail.

Before a continuing power of attorney can be exercised, it must be registered with the Office of the Public Guardian. This raises an interesting point. Should the power of attorney be registered immediately after its execution, or should it only be registered when it requires to be brought in to effect? Some solicitors will register continuing and welfare powers of attorney immediately. However, others take the view that, if only to save expense, the document should not be registered but should be retained in a safe place and presented to the Office of the Public Guardian for registration only as and when activation of the same is required. The view has been expressed that where a continuing power of attorney is granted but not immediately registered, then the attorney cannot utilise the powers thereunder in view of the provisions of s.19(1) of the 2000 Act, even where the granter of the power of attorney still retains full capacity. There is a real risk element in not registering a continuing or welfare power of attorney immediately. Let us say that it is decided to save some expense and simply to retain the unregistered document in a safe. Word then comes through that the granter of the power of attorney has become permanently incapax and the power of attorney is sent off to the Office of the Public Guardian. If the Office of the Public Guardian identifies a fundamental flaw in the document it may be impossible to correct the same, with the result that the whole purpose of the granting of the continuing power of attorney has been defeated.

Bear in mind that the protection of third parties is achieved in terms of section 19(4) of the Act—this gives official status to a copy of the power of attorney authenticated by the Office of the Public Guardian. Without such authentication, a continuing power of attorney may be rejected (as it is only when it is registered that the character of a continuing power of attorney after supervening incapacity is afforded) by a third party.

Welfare power of attorney

15–09   This was a wholly new concept introduced in to Scottish law by the 2000 Act. Medical/welfare powers of attorney have been in use in the United States for many years. The Act creates the ability to set up a welfare power of attorney (there is no reason why a power of attorney should not be a combined continuing and welfare power of attorney—see the style in the Appendix). This is an area of law which is still not much developed (although again see the detailed guidance offered in the Code of Practice in relation to welfare attorneys). The important aspect of a welfare power of attorney is that it does not come in to effect until incapacity has intervened. However, the provisions of the 2000 Act introduce a welcome facility which had not previously existed. Although many laypeople thought that being appointed a power of attorney did, for example, enable the attorney to place an old person in a nursing home—this was not the case—a "pre Act" power of attorney might have authorised the attorney to enter in to a contract with a nursing home, but not to take part in the decision-making process as to the appropriate care and treatment of the granter.

There is an important practical point. As a matter of proper professional practice, always discuss in detail with the client whether or not the client wishes to grant simply a continuing power of attorney, a welfare power of attorney or a combined continuing and welfare power of attorney. In that connection:

- Some clients will be entirely happy to appoint someone else as their continuing power of attorney and to have full control over the financial affairs of that client. However, it may be that they are less happy to grant welfare powers.
- If the client baulks at the granting of welfare powers then it is not a solicitor's responsibility to force a client to agree. However, the solicitor should endeavour patiently to explain the possible benefits of granting the welfare powers.
- Some solicitors, unfamiliar with welfare powers, appear not in fact to raise this question with clients. This is asking for trouble. Once the old person has lost capacity and an adult child with only continuing power of attorney finds that he or she is excluded from certain decision-making processes, the original draftsman may have an angry attorney with whom to contend.

Registration with the Office of the Public Guardian

It should be noted that the Office of the Public Guardian do not wish **15–10** individuals to be "ambushed" into acting. That being so, there is a specific section in the registration application form which needs to be signed and dated by the attorney indicating his or her consent to acting.

Avoiding difficulties in registration of a power of attorney with the Office of the Public Guardian

The figures for initial rejection of powers of attorney by the Office of **15–11** the Public Guardian are on the decrease, but they still represent a surprisingly high percentage of those powers of attorney which are submitted. Although completion of the registration application form should be reasonably straightforward, the Office of the Public Guardian has encountered problems here.

With thanks to the Office of the Public Guardian, the main reasons for rejection of powers of attorney on first submission are as follows:

- No certificate of any description is appended to the power of attorney.
- The certificate does not follow the prescribed form.
- Different names and addresses are specified in the power of attorney and in the registration application form.
- In respect of combined continuing and welfare powers of attorney, only one certificate is submitted or, alternatively, there has been a "failing" attempt to compose a joint certificate—it should be borne in mind that with a continuing and welfare power of attorney, separate "continuing" and "welfare" certificates (in prescribed form) are required.
- The interview date does not correspond with the relevant certificate (*i.e.* the date of interview on the certificate does not correspond with the date on which the power of attorney was signed). The date which appears in the testing clause should coincide with the date on which the appropriately qualified individual interviewed the grantee.
- The attorney has not signed the "consent section" in the registration application form.
- Amendments to the power of attorney have not been initialled by the granter.
- The power of attorney fails to specify either that there is to be a continuing power of attorney or a welfare power of attorney (or both in the case of a combined document) on the loss of capacity by the granter.

The above reasons for rejection should be noted—mistakes happen (we are all only human), but proper completion of the documentation at the first instance will save time and effort for both the profession and, more particularly, the Office of the Public Guardian. (Note, however, that failure to specify the date of birth of the granter will not normally lead to the public guardian refusing to register the power of attorney.)

Termination

Section 7, "Stopping being an Attorney", in the Code of Practice is of **15–12** importance here. In particular, note the "warnings" at the beginning of this section, namely:

- If you foresee that you will not be able to act as attorney, you should tell the granter straight away while he or she can still appoint someone else.
- If you find that you cannot act when the adult has lost incapacity, you should try to put alternative arrangements in place to manage the adult's affairs or make personal welfare decisions.
- Various other circumstances can bring your powers to an end, but if you are not aware of these and you continue to act in good faith you will not be liable.

  1. Resignation. It has always been possible for an attorney to resign. Bear in mind that the office is essentially one of agency. However, see para.7.6 of the Code of Practice which outlines the steps which a continuing or welfare power of attorney must take in relation to his or her resignation.
  2. Other circumstances that bring powers to an end—again I would refer you to the appropriate section of the Code of Practice (paras. 7.10 to 7.14).

Danger area

15–13   At the time of writing, it is understood that the Office of the Public Guardian has declined to accept certificates signed by "non-Scottish" solicitors. It is understood that this matter is under review. However, until resolved, no certificates should be signed by English etc., solicitors.

Springing power

15–14   It is possible to make a provision that the power of attorney should not be registered with the Office of the Public Guardian under section 19 of the 2000 Act until the incapacity of the granter has been certified by a medical practitioner. An example of such a clause is as follows:

> "This Continuing Power of Attorney shall not be registered by the Public Guardian in terms of Section 19 of the Adults with Incapacity (Scotland) Act 2000 unless and until a medical practitioner with knowledge of my medical condition has certified in writing that I am incapable to any extent as defined by the said Act."

There is a format of "springing power" which is designed to have the effect of "postponing" the powers granted under the power of attorney until incapacity (as defined by the Act) has occurred. A style of that "springing power" is detailed in the Appendix of Styles. The author should point out that the Office of the Public Guardian has, on at least one occasion, specifically queried the effect of the power, but after discussion indicated a willingness to proceed with registration of the document.

As a final point, this area almost overnight (from April 2, 2001) became very much more complex, involved and labour intensive in so far as solicitors are concerned. If a minimal fee is charged for a power of attorney, then whilst this may be being more than fair to the client, is the remuneration fair to the draftsman?

FINANCIAL GUARDIANSHIPS

The Adults with Incapacity (Scotland) Act 2000 saw what was an **15–15** effective "sea change" in relation to the management of the affairs of incapacitated individuals. How has the legal framework changed?

Prior to the 2000 Act

In his excellent book, *The Power to Act*,[17] Adrian Ward details the **15–16** history of Scottish law in relation to the management of the affairs of incapax or mentally handicapped individuals. Prior to the passing of the 2000 Act, the system of appointment of a suitable individual to manage the affairs of an incapacitated person was governed by law passed in the reign of Queen Victoria.[18]

Under the relevant legislation, the main function of the curator bonis was effectively the preservation of the estate of the incapax. Preservation also involves management, but it is now accepted that the ability of a curator bonis to manage was, for many years, unduly restricted. Frankly, it is submitted that in most cases solicitors would advise the appointment of a curator bonis only as a last resort.

Criticisms

Why should the appointment of a curator bonis be regarded as a **15–17** measure of a last resort? Some of the following criticisms were recognised by the Scottish Law Commission in its discussion paper No.94 issued in 1991.

1. Cost—The Scottish Law Commission was critical of the cost of setting up and "running" a curatory. The estate of the mentally disabled individual (generally known as "the ward") had to meet

   - The expenses of the court petition to appoint the curator in the first place, including the cost of the two medical certificates which needed to be submitted in support.
   - The cost of valuations of the ward's estate
   - The expense of the curator's ongoing remuneration for acting
   - Fees incurred to the accountant of court

   Where the ward's estate was large, such expenses could be absorbed. However, for smaller estates, the effect of the charges and expenses could be regressive. For example, it was only in 1989 that the Mental Welfare Commission raised from £10,000 to £50,000 the minimal level of the ward's estate at which, in the view of the Commission, appointment of a curator would be appropriate. In smaller estates, the outcome could be

---

[17] A. Ward, *The Power to Act*, (Scottish Society for the Mentally Handicapped, 1990).
[18] Judicial Factors Act 1849.

that the costs of setting up and running the curatory were such that that estate would be rapidly diminished. This led to criticisms that the very system which was designed to protect the estate of the ward was largely contributing to the denuding of that estate. Further, the effect of costs on the estate of the ward was believed to lead families and, indeed, professional advisers to shy away from seeking the appointment of a curator when, but for the expense involved, there may have been other valid grounds for seeking such an appointment.

2. Inflexibility—the Scottish Law Commission was also critical that the curator required to be focused on preservation of the estate of the ward, even though this might not objectively be considered to coincide with the best interest of the ward. In 1899, in the case of *Macqueen v Tod*,[19] the first division of the Court of Session held that it was the primary duty of a curator to preserve the estate of the ward, acting on the presumption that the ward would recover or, alternatively, if the ward failed to recover, for the ward's heirs. For many years, the decision of *Macqueen v Tod* was followed. This left the curator in a difficult position, particularly with the ward's family, who often failed to understand what they considered to be a wholly inflexible and uncaring approach to the ward. The perception (if not the reality) was that the duty to account for virtually every last penny and to produce detailed vouchers was at odds with the best interests of the ward in many cases.

3. Failure to meet the needs of the ward—the inability to encroach on capital for the benefit of the ward led to a perception that the system was not properly serving the needs of the ward. However, quite apart from concerns regarding the strict accounting procedures, the curatory system was seen as complex, hidebound by rules and regulation, and insensitive to the actual needs of the ward. This perhaps bespoke a fundamental misunderstanding on the part of the ward's family as to the role of the curator. Families often associated the appointment of a curator as being akin to the system putting in place an individual who was responsible for the personal welfare of the ward. Under the old system, however, the curator had no role whatsoever to play in relation to the welfare of the ward, and in fact had no obligation to meet with the ward or to consult with his family. This often led to the family of the ward concluding that the curator was remote and uncaring. This perhaps began to change as a result of the decision in *Broadfoot's Curatory*.[20] Although the court held that it was still outwith the curator's power to encroach on capital on his own, it did recommend that a new rule of court should be adopted, enabling the accountant of court to approve of encroachment on capital in circumstances where the accountant was satisfied

[19] 1899 1 F. 859.
[20] 1989 S.L.T. 567.

that the Act in question would be in the best interests of the ward.

4. Complexity—as has already been commented on, the curator was required to prepare audited accounts on a yearly basis. That and other requirements incumbent on a curator often led to professional advisors recommending to families that a member of the family should not put himself forward for appointment.

In fairness, the late 1980s and 1990s did see a welcome change. As a result of a deliberate effort on their part, the Accountant of Court's Department became much more "user friendly" and, indeed, following on the criticisms made by the Scottish Law Commission, it is submitted that his deliberate policy on the part of the Accountant of Court's Department was greatly helpful to families of mentally disabled individuals and contributed to a lessening of the possible friction between the curator on the one hand and the ward's family on the other.

The Adults with Incapacity (Scotland) Act 2000

This legislation which had its genesis in the Scottish Law Commission **15–18** Paper of 1991 was designed to remove some of the perceived rigidity and inflexibility in the appointment of suitable persons to act on behalf of incapacitated individuals. The provisions of the Act in relation to the granting of continuing and welfare powers of attorney are commented upon separately in this work.

Quite apart from seeking to create a new body of law in relation to the appointment of a suitable person or persons to intervene on behalf of mentally disabled individuals, one of the important aspects of the Act was that, in terms of section 13, they provided for the Scottish Ministers to have Codes of Practice prepared to contain guidance for:

(a) local authorities and their chief social work officers and mental health officers;
(b) continuing and welfare attorneys;
(c) persons authorised under intervention orders;
(d) guardians;
(e) withdrawers;
(f) managers of authorised establishments;
(g) supervisory bodies; and
(h) persons authorised to carry out medical treatment or research under Pt 5.

It is submitted that these Codes of Practice have great value, and practitioners involved in this area do need to have some familiarity, particularly with a Code of Practice in relation to continuing and welfare attorneys and guardians. The Codes of Practice are repositories of valuable guidance for both attorneys and guardians.

Main provisions of the Act

Given some of the justified criticisms which related to the appoint- **15–19** ment of a curator bonis, the Act allows for great flexibility. Bearing in mind the criticisms of the previous system (which on occasions amounted to "taking a sledgehammer to crack a nut"), the philosophy of the 2000 Act was to provide a range of remedies to meet particular circumstances. These remedies included the obtaining of :

- Authority to intromit with funds.
- An Intervention Order.
- A Guardianship Order.

The Act provides a range of possibilities, allowing for a minimalist approach where this is justified. This offers greater scope to those who have regard for the interests of an incapacitated individual, and allows them the possibility of choosing the best and least intrusive option. The philosophy of the Act and the Codes of Practice set out in terms of section 13 is intervention only where intervention is positively required. This is a welcome advance on the older system.

Authority to intromit with funds

15–20   This is governed by sections 25 to 33 of the 2000 Act. These sections allow:

- An individual (excluding an officer of the local authority or other body established under any enactment) to apply to the public guardian for authority to intromit with funds held by a "fund holder" on behalf of an incapable adult, in relation to decisions regarding the funds or safeguarding the interests of the adults in those funds. It applies only to an account of which the adult is the sole account holder. The application requires to be made in respect of a specific account.
- Under section 26 it is a requirement that the application for authority to intromit with the funds should state the purposes of the proposed intromission, setting out the specific sums relating to each purpose. Section 26 contains various safeguards.
- Section 28 details the purposes for which an application for intromission of funds may be granted. These include (in section 28(b)) the provision of subsistence, accommodation, fuel, clothing and related goods and services for the adult—this is a reflection of the ethos that the powers granted should be utilised in the best interests of the incapacitated adult. This is reflected in section 28(3) which provides that "any funds used by the withdrawers be applied only for the benefit of the adult". However, as at counterbalance, section 28(4) provides that where the withdrawer lives with the adult, he may to the extent authorised by the certificate (authorising withdrawal) apply any funds withdrawn into household expenses. This is a welcome recognition of the fact that those who provide primary care for the adult will enter costs in that regard. It might, however, be queried whether the restriction to "household expenses" will fully and properly indemnify the primary, resident carer. It may be that experience over a period of time will require some reassessment of this particular subsection.

- In terms of section 31, the authority to withdraw is valid only for a period of three years from the issuing of the relevant certificate by the public guardian. However, in terms of section 31(2) the public guardian may reduce or extend the period of validity of this certificate and that without limit of time.

The power to intromit in respect of a specific account is welcome. This may seek to address specific concerns and is entirely consistent with the minimalist approach already referred to. However, it is submitted that there may be dangers here. Whilst the minimalist approach is to be lauded, there may be temptations to apply for less than might be appropriate. This places an onus on the solicitor whose advice is sought. The solicitor will need to fully appraise himself of the position of the incapax and, where appropriate, advise that a greater degree of intervention is required. This will involve an assessment of many factors, including the age of the incapax, the complexity of his financial affairs, and a consideration of whether authority to operate on a particular account for a period of three years will sufficiently meet the needs and welfare of the incapax during and beyond that period of time. Again, sensitivity on the part of the adviser is required. The natural inclination of the spouse or family of the incapax will be to minimise legal expense. The adviser will therefore need to develop arguments and strategies which demonstrate to the spouse or family that, in some circumstances, a simple order to operate on an individual account will not serve the interests and welfare of the incapax.

Intervention order

The ability to apply for both an intervention and a guardianship order **15–21** are governed by Pt 6 of the Act. Application for intervention order is governed by sections 53—56 of the Act. In terms of section 53(1), any person (including the adult himself) showing an interest in the property, financial affairs or personal welfare of an adult can only apply for an intervention order. This is an intermediate form of authority. In terms of section 53(5), the intervention order may:

(a) Direct the taking of any action specified in the order.
(b) Authorise the person nominating the application to take such action or to make such decision in relation to the property, financial affairs or personal welfare of the adult as specified in the order. The application to the sheriff will normally require the applicant to find caution (section 73(7)).

There are specific provisions (section 56) regarding the registration of an intervention order which relates to heritable property.

An interesting provision of the 2000 Act is section 53(3) which, on the face of it, obliges a local authority to intervene where the adult is incapable and no application has been made or is likely to be made for an order under section 53, and the local authority considers that an intervention order is required for the protection of the property, financial affairs or personal welfare of the adult. This provision is most likely to be used where an elderly, incapax individual refuses to move into appropriate care accommodation. As a practical matter, when the solicitor is more likely to be consulted by the family of the elderly individual, it may be that there is a dispute regarding the requirement for care home accommodation. This is a difficult area. As a first point, the solicitor always needs to bear in mind the conflict of interest rules, *i.e.* who is the solicitor's client? Where the solicitor is satisfied that his client is the family member upset at the prospect of the granting of an intervention order, then he may also need to consider the motives of that client. Does the client have the welfare of the elderly relative in view, or is he simply thinking about diminution of the estate of the elderly incapax (thereby possibly reducing his inheritance) in relation to the payment of care home fees? Again, one of the considerations is as to whether or not an intervention order is sufficient to meet the interests of the incapax individual, or whether full guardianship should be applied for. This involves a detailed consideration of all of the issues involved. It is submitted that where the client is obviously motivated by reasons of self interest (*i.e.* maximisation of potential inheritance), the solicitor should give appropriate consideration to his own position.

As previously indicated, for some time prior to the passing of the Adults with Incapacity (Scotland) Act 2000, the law in this area had been undergoing modernisation; for example:

(a) The Law Reform (Miscellaneous Provisions) (Scotland) Act 1980. This Act:
  - allowed sheriffs to appoint curators regardless of the amount of the ward's estate.
  - afforded the accountant of court with power to approve of actings on the part of the curator which were at variance with the terms of the curator's appointment (basically for preservation of the ward's estate, *i.e.* the accountant of court could authorise sale of the ward's home).
(b) The Law Reform (Miscellaneous Provisions) (Scotland) Act 1990. This Act amended the longstanding section 5 of the Judicial Factor's Act 1849. Curators were empowered to place funds in any bank approved by the Banking Act 1987 and into a building society deposit (but not share) account.
(c) The Act of Sederunt (Rules of the Court of Session Amendment Number 1) (Miscellaneous) 1990. Following the recommendation made by the court in *Broadfoot's Curatory*,[21] this provision empowered to the accountant of court to approve of severe encroachment on the ward's capital, even where this was likely to result in the ward's estate being exhausted during his or her lifetime.
(d) The Act of Sederunt (Rules of Court of Session Amendment Number 8) Discharge of Judicial Factors 1991. This introduced another welcome provision, effectively the obtaining of the curator of an informal discharge without incurring the expense of the petition to the court for such discharge—particularly where the ward has died.

[21] Cited above.

The accountant of court, himself, had endeavoured to obtain an appropriate legislative amendment prior to the passing of the 2000 Act and played a major role in the consultative, etc. process. The accountant of court had proposed that in the event of a curator dying or becoming incapacitated or otherwise unable to act, the accountant would be able to have a new curator appointed without the necessity (and thereby the expense) of a new petition to court. It is understood that the accountant proposed that a new curator might be appointed following a report by the accountant himself, indicating the facts in relation to the particular curatory and nominating another appropriate curator. Although such a proposal was originally included in a Miscellaneous Provisions Bill, it did not see the light of legislative day.

Section 1 of the 2000 Act

Before going on to consider the detailed provisions of the 2000 Act in **15–22** relation to financial guardianships, it is worthwhile bearing in mind the fundamental principles which are contained in section 1 of the Act. These principles apply to any "intervenor". These are guiding principles which are designed to shape the conduct of not only guardians, but also those acting under a power of attorney. The principles are:

1. There shall be no intervention in the affairs of an adult unless the person responsible for authorising or effecting the intervention is satisfied that the intervention will benefit the adult and that such benefit cannot reasonably be achieved without the intervention.
2. Where it is determined that an intervention as mentioned in subs.(1) is to be made, such intervention shall be the least restrictive option in relation to the freedom of the adult, consistent with the purposes of the intervention.
3. In determining if an intervention is to be made, and if so, what intervention is to be made, account shall be taken of:

   (a) The present and past wishes and feelings of the adult so far as they can be ascertained by any means of communication, whether human or by a mechanical aid (whether of an interpretative nature or otherwise) appropriate to the adult.
   (b) The views of the nearest relative and primary carer of the adult in so far as it is reasonable and practicable to do so. The views of:

      (i) any guardian, continuing attorney or welfare attorney of the adult who has powers relating to the proposed intervention.
      (ii) any person whom the sheriff has directed to be consulted in so far as it is reasonable and practicable to do so.
      (iii) any other person appearing to the person responsible for authorising or effecting the intervention to have an interest in the welfare of the adult or in the proposed intervention, where views have been made

known to the person responsible, so far as is reasonable and practical to do so.

4. Any guardian, continuing attorney, welfare attorney or manager of an establishment exercising functions under the 2000 Act or under any order of the sheriff in relation to an adult shall, so far as it is reasonable and practicable to do so, encourage the adult to exercise whatever skills he has concerning his property, financial affairs or personal welfare as the case may be, and to develop such new skills.

It is submitted that the above principles are of more importance to guardians appointed under Pt 6 of the 2000 Act than to attorneys. Certainly, a guardian who does not observe the principles may find it difficult to justify himself to the public guardian or to the accountant of court (the latter still having appropriate jurisdiction where an existing curator bonis has become a financial guardian—this being automatic in terms of the 2000 Act). It is also submitted that these principles are a welcome recognition of the fact that the adult is still a person and should be treated as such. Again, in fairness, prior to the passing of the 2000 Act there was recognition on the part of the accountant of court that the curator was responsible for more than just the estate of the ward. More and more, the accountant of court encouraged curators to take a degree of responsibility for the person of the ward, including taking into account the views of the ward's family. Recognising that the ward was a human being, the accountant of court could authorise the ward to manage his own bank account. Again, the increasingly holistic view of the accountant of court is reflected in the principles outlined above and in the later provisions of the 2000 Act.

Part 6 of the 2000 Act—guardianship orders

15–23   The main provisions in relation to guardianship orders are contained within sections 57 to 79 of the Act.

In terms of section 57(1) of the Act:

> "an application may be made under this Section by any person (including the adult himself) claiming an interest in the property, financial affairs or personal welfare of an adult to the Sheriff for an order appointing an individual or office holder as Guardian in relation to the adult's property, financial affairs or personal welfare."

The terms of section 57(2) are of interest. They appear to place an obligation on the local authority to make an application for guardianship under section 57, where no other application has been made or is likely to be made, and a guardianship order is necessary for the protection of the property, financial affairs or personal welfare of the adult. It is the author's experience that local authorities seemed initially to be unwilling to undertake the duty which appeared to have been imposed on them by section 57(2), with the result that no intervention was made until another person presented himself to the court for appointment. Section 57 (3) specifies the types of report which needs to be lodged in support of the relevant summary application. Practitioners need to be familiar with these provisions, and in particular which reports are required and in what circumstances.

Section 58 of the Act deals with disposal of the application, details the matters to be taken into consideration by the sheriff dealing with the application, and his powers in relation thereto. In particular, in terms of section 58(3):

> "Where the Sheriff is satisfied that an intervention order would be sufficient. . . he may take the application under this Section as an application for intervention order under Section 53 and may make such order as appears to him to be appropriate."

Subsections (3) and (4) of section 59 reflect again the recognition of the fact that the adult is a person and should be treated as such. In particular, subs.(3) requires that the sheriff shall not appoint an individual as guardian to an adult unless he is satisfied that the individual is aware of:

(a) The adult's circumstances and condition, and of the needs arising from such circumstances and condition.
(b) The functions of a guardian.

Thus, the "old" viewpoint that the guardian need only concern himself with the preservation of the adult's estate is consigned to history (although in fairness the Accountant of Court's Office had been encouraging a much more enlightened view of the role of the curator bonis for some time prior to the passing of the 2000 Act).

Section 61 contains specific provisions in relation to the registration of a guardianship order relating to heritable property. Under section 61(3), the "Guardian shall, after finding caution if so required, forthwith apply to the Keeper of the Registers of Scotland for recording of the Interlocutor containing the order in the General Registers of Sasines or, as the case may be, registering of it in the Land Register of Scotland". This is an important provision of which the guardian should not lose sight, as the guardian is under obligation to exhibit evidence that he has complied with the provisions of section 61 in relation to the registration of the interlocutor in his favour with the keeper.

Two important innovations

Sections 62 and 63 allow for, respectively, the appointment of joint **15–24** guardians and a substitute guardian.

In terms of section 62(1)(a), an application may be made to the sheriff by two or more individuals seeking appointment as joint guardians or, under subs.(1) (b), an application may be made by an individual seeking appointment as a joint guardian with one or more existing guardians. Restrictions are, however, placed on such appointments as in terms of subs.(2). The sheriff should not appoint joint guardians to an adult unless:

(a) Individuals so appointed are parents, siblings or children of the adult; or

(b) The sheriff is satisfied that in the circumstances it is appropriate to appoint as joint guardians individuals who are not related to the adult first mentioned in para.(a).

Section 62 contains provisions regarding the liabilities of joint guardians and their duties to consult (or not) as the case may be.

In terms of section 62(8), where there is disagreement between joint guardians as to the exercise of their functions, either or both of them may apply to the sheriff for directions under section 3 of the Act.

Section 62 (9) contains provisions for protection of a third party acting in good faith with joint guardians or one of them.

Perhaps one of the most innovative provisions of the 2000 Act is contained in section 63, which allows the sheriff to appoint a substitute guardian in the event of the principal guardian becoming unable to act. Section 63 (8) requires that on:

"death or incapacity of the original Guardian, the substitute Guardian shall without undue delay notify the Public Guardian:-

(a) of the death or incapacity (and where the original Guardian has died, provide the Public Guardian with documentary evidence of the death) and,

(b) whether or not he is prepared to act as Guardian."

There was no similar provision under the pre-existing legislation, either for the appointment of joint curators or indeed a substitute curator. This is most definitely a progressive innovation which will allow:

- Members of families to become joint guardians and therefore remove a criticism that a curator bonis was remote and impersonal.
- The replacement of a deceased or incapax guardian without having to revert to court with a new summary application (and this reflects the frustrated attempt of the accountant of court to allow for a much less informal appointment of a replacement curator bonis as detailed above).

Functions and powers of guardians

15–25   These are detailed in section 4 of the Act. It should be noted that it will no longer be appropriate to make application for "the usual powers". Where specific powers are required these should be detailed in the summary application seeking appointment of the guardian. This is reflected in section 64(1)(a), which states that an order appointing a guardian may confer on him "power to deal with such particular matters in relation to the property, financial affairs or personal welfare of the adult as may be specified in the order".

Under subsection (1)(b), it was similarly specified that the order appointing a welfare guardian will confer on such a guardian power in respect of those aspects as may be specified in the order. However, in terms of subsection (2), the guardian may not:

(a) place the adult in hospital for treatment of mental disorder against his will; or

(b) consent on behalf of the adult to any form of treatment mentioned in section 48(1) or (2).

The power to gift

Section 66 contains powers to gift subject to authorisation by the **15–26** public guardian. This is a most useful power (see below).

Plus points and criticisms

As hereinbefore detailed, the provisions of the 2000 Act in relation to **15–27** the appointment of a financial guardian are very welcome, in the sense that they recognise the ongoing personality of the adult. In particular, a guardian cannot act on an impersonal basis when the principles detailed in section 1 of the Act are taken into account. A further recognition of the fact that the position of the adult cannot be ignored can be found in section 67(1) of the Act which, although depriving the adult of any capacity to enter into any transaction which is within the scope of the authority awarded by the court to the guardian, nonetheless does not affect the capacity of the adult in relation to other matters. This reflects the fact that there are different degrees of capacity required for different matters, and finds resonance with the previous practice of the accountant of court to allow, in suitable circumstances, the ward to operate his own bank account.

The provisions for appointment of joint and substitute guardians allow much greater flexibility than was possible under the "old" legislation.

There are, however, possible criticisms which can be levied:

- In terms of section 58(4), the appointment of the guardian is for a period of three years only. Whilst this may reflect an increasing recognition that it is possible that the adult may (owing to advances in medical skill or otherwise) improve or substantially regain capacity, it does raise the question of perhaps additional expenses on a regular basis. Again, it is understood that the accountant of court found no favour with the proposal that a guardianship required to be renewed after every period of three years. This reflected the view of the Accountant of Court's Office that less of the estate of the adult should be used in management expenses, not more.
- Under section 58 (6) of the Act, a guardian still needs to find caution. Whilst this may be appropriate, it is understood that originally it had been proposed that there should be a master policy. This proposal has not been followed up and leaves guardians with the difficulties of arranging what is essentially an indemnity policy against the background of recent world events and only a very limited number of companies prepared to offer caution.
- When an interim guardian is appointed, he is required to make monthly reports under section 64(a) to the public guardian (where he is a financial guardian) and to the chief social worker for the relevant area (where he is a welfare guardian). This again seems to be an undue bureaucratic burden on the guardian.

- Under the "old" practice, it was normal to seek appointment of a curator "with the usual powers". This is no longer possible, which means that great importance is laid on the drafting of the summary application. The applicant is thereby required at an early stage perhaps to second guess what powers may be required. This can be a difficult task where there is a degree of urgency in securing the appointment of a financial guardian, in particular, for example, where the hospital in which the adult may have been receiving treatment decides that the care of the adult would be better served in a care home. This can place pressure on those concerned with the welfare of the adult to make speedy progress in relation to the guardian's appointment, and can lead to powers being hurriedly "scrambled together", perhaps not properly taking into account the provisions of section 59(3) of the Act (see above). In that connection, it is submitted that the practitioner assisting with the drafting of the relevant petition does need to familiarise himself as much as possible with the particular requirements and needs of the adult. In that connection, reference to the "old" practice is useful. Consonant with the desire of the accountant of court from the 1980s onwards to place more emphasis on the welfare of the ward as opposed to preservation of his estate, the following powers were granted by the court after due investigation by and upon the recommendation of the accountant:
- Power to purchase reasonably expensive photographic equipment over a period of time where the ward had developed an interest in that hobby and was showing considerable improvement, (*i.e.* the hobby was regarded as therapeutic).
- Power to have the ward's pension paid to him direct (there being medical evidence to the effect that this would be in the ward's best interests).
- Power to pay for a visit to a foreign country so that the ward might see her closest relatives for the last time.
- Power to pay for the cost of extensive alteration to the house of the brother of the ward in order that the latter could reside with his brother.
- Power to build a suitably designed house (including a swimming pool) for the ward where it was considered not only that this would meet the needs of the ward, but would prove therapeutic for him.

The practitioner assisting a family/others in the drafting of a summary application for appointment of a guardianship should therefore not fall into the trap of adopting a standard style. The practitioner should, so far as possible, thoroughly brief himself as to the exact needs and requirements of the adult and seek to incorporate relevant/suitable powers in the application. There is of course no point in incorporating such powers unless they can be properly justified before the sheriff who hears the relevant application—thus, a degree of familiarity with, and knowledge of, the adult's needs is required.

POWERS OF ATTORNEY AND GUARDIANSHIPS—A COMPARISON

There can be no doubt that a power of attorney is a much better option **15-28** than requiring to resort to a financial guardianship. Although the following points may, to a certain extent, appear self evident, they are nonetheless valid.

- From the perspective of both the granter and the attorney, the setting up of a power of attorney is reasonably straightforward, fairly quick in execution and relatively inexpensive. The same cannot be said of a financial guardianship which, from the lay client's point of view, is complex and sometimes difficult to understand, a lengthy process and not inexpensive.
- The granter of the power of attorney can choose which powers are granted and which are not (although it is the author's view that a client should be encouraged to grant the widest powers possible, so as not to hamstring his attorney at a later date, particularly where the granter has lost capacity). A financial guardian only has the powers which are granted to him/her by the court.
- For the most part, unless the granter (still retaining capacity) revokes the power of attorney or the attorney is removed by a sheriff following a reference from the public guardian, a power of attorney, once granted, will last until the granter dies. As commented upon above, financial guardianship requires to be renewed from time to time.
- In many cases, it will be possible for a lay person to operate properly as attorney without any involved legal assistance. In the author's view, however, there are few lay people who, once appointed as a financial guardian, can operate without regular legal assistance. The requirements of The Adults with Incapacity (Scotland) Act 2000 which, *inter alia*, provides for preparation of management plans and regular accounts are probably beyond the ability and ken of most lay clients (who may find themselves encountering some difficulty with the Office of the Public Guardian by their failure to understand (and therefore comply with) the Statutory requirements).
- Subject to taking into account the provisions of the Code of Conduct, an attorney can resign—the same facility is not so readily available to a financial guardian.

Perhaps the above comparisons are unfair in the sense that a properly advised client would, it is suggested, not choose a financial guardianship before the granting of a power of attorney. However, this does raise an important point for the legal profession. Given increasing human longevity, should the profession not be more proactive in recommending to its clientele that they should consider granting "protective" powers of attorney so as to elide the necessity of the client's family having to seek appointment of the financial guardian? In the author's view it is, at least at present, neither professional negligence nor inadequate professional service not to take the step of advising clients in relation to powers of attorney. However, in an area where the legal profession is the subject of increasing levels of complaint, that balance might be partly redressed by demonstrating to clients that the profession can be proactive instead of so often appearing to be traditional, hidebound and reactive.

15–29   It is to be welcomed that there is clear evidence that the legal profession has realised the value of clients granting powers of attorney. The table of statistics below has been reproduced with the kind permission of the Office of the Public Guardian.

OFFICE OF THE PUBLIC GUARDIAN STATISTICS

		2001/2002	2002/03	2003/2004	TOTALS
1	Continuing Powers of Attorney Registered	3947	6382	7576	17905
2	Welfare Powers of Attorney Registered	197	468	1097	1762
3	Combined Powers of Attorney Registered	1448	3508	5820	10776
	Totals	5592	10358	14493	30443
4	Interested Parties Complaints	74	119	135	328
5	Referred to Sheriff-Removal of Attorney	0	0	0	0
6	Financial Guardianships Granted	0	50	200	250
	Welfare Guardianships Granted	0	210	273	483
	Combined Guardianships Granted	0	28	120	148
	Totals	288	593	881	
7	Financial Intervention Orders Granted	0	49	135	184
	Welfare Intervention Orders Granted	0	6	17	23
	Combined Intervention Orders Granted	0	1	15	16
	Totals	56	167	223	
8	Overall Total Percentage of Power of Attorneys Rejected	29%	22%	21%	

The author believes that given the great increase in the number of powers of attorney granted since inception of the 2000 Act, it is reasonable to at least suggest that the legal profession has clearly recognised the value of the granting of protective continuing and welfare powers of attorney. The author understands from the Office of the Public Guardian that it is anticipated that in the year 2004/2005, 16,000 will be registered with them. The Office of the Public Guardian have also indicated that the Registers of Scotland have advised that prior to the passing of the 2000 Act, a total of somewhere between 5,000 and 10,000 powers of attorney were registered in the Books of Council and Session. The message is getting through. The fact that in the first year no guardianships or intervention orders were granted is surprising. This may have been due to unfamiliarity of the legal profession with the new procedures. However, the statistics would appear to indicate that the legal profession is now more comfortable with the provisions of the Act and the procedures to be followed.

The above statistical table does not specifically refer to cases in which authority has been granted to operate on a specific bank account. The author does, however, understand that at least informally, the Office of the Public Guardian is surprised that more advantage has not been taken of the relevant provisions of the 2000 Act.

LIVING WILLS

A misnomer

The term "living will" is a misnomer, as such a document: **15–30**

- is not a will at all, having no effect after the death of the granter.
- does not take effect upon death but rather details how certain aspects of the last stages of the granter's physical (but not his business or financial) life should be regulated or managed.
- conveys or leaves no beneficial interest to any third party.

A living will should more properly be called an advance medical directive or declaration. It is a written record, setting out in advance the granter's wishes regarding the medical treatment(s) to be given (or not) in the event of the individual becoming incapable of communicating his wishes to the doctors and nurses treating him. It can set out the wishes of the granter in general terms, or be very detailed as to the granter's prospective refusal of specific (generally life prolonging) procedures or treatments.

Controversy

The subject of living wills has been a controversial one for some time, **15–31** particularly in the United Kingdom.

The United States appears to have taken the lead in recognition of such directives.[22] It is now commonplace in the United States for individuals granting "normal" powers of attorney for the administration of their business, etc. affairs at the same time to grant healthcare powers of attorney, setting out in advance the wishes of the individual regarding what treatments the individual should or should not receive or undergo

---

[22] The Patient Self Determination Act, 1990.

once the individual is no longer capable of communicating his wishes (whether this is due to incapacity or the medical condition of the individual).

In Europe, Holland has perhaps taken the lead in this area.

The Dutch experience is of interest. In 1990, the Dutch Government commissioned the "first" Remmelink Report. As a result, in early 1993 Holland introduced statutory provisions in terms of which doctors were to be protected from criminal prosecution in relation to the "mercy killing" of patients, provided that the guidelines of the legislation were followed. In the second Remmelink Report, it was reported that, in 1995, approximately 3,600 individuals died as a result of voluntary euthanasia or "physician assisted suicide". Of those dying after having received such assistance, the majority were suffering from incurable cancer. Interestingly, the report concluded that in 90 per cent of assisted deaths, life was shortened by one month or less, and in 42 per cent of those cases, life was shortened by less than a week. Much of the resistance to implementation of a living will often come from the family of an individual, who have either not been consulted in advance in relation to their relative's wishes or, at the appropriate time, have moral or other objections to implementation of the document. It is submitted that if a client expresses a wish to grant a living will, it would be appropriate to inform that client of the foregoing Dutch statistics in order that he, in his turn, can inform his family of those "statistics"— families sometimes retain hopes of a "miracle cure" or that a loved one may make some limited recovery, so as to be able to enjoy a few more months of worthwhile life. The Dutch statistics indicate that such hopes are for the most part forlorn and misplaced, and knowledge of the same may assist in persuading the granter's family not to object to implementation.

Following the Dutch model, Belgium carried out similar research.[23] The Belgian research indicated a much greater level of "non-voluntary euthanasia" (basically doctors taking steps to end the lives of their patients without the latter specifically requesting this) in Belgium than in Holland. A similar outcome was reached following an examination of the position in Australia.[24]

The Belgian research concluded that where there was no system of regulation, vulnerable patients could be put at risk unless the end of life decision-making process was regulated. As a result, the Belgian Government introduced provisions allowing "assisted dying", subject to certain safeguards.

15–32   In the UK, the idea of the legislation of euthanasia has been controversial for many years. Attempts to introduce permissive legislation have failed over a long period of time. As a result, at present, the legal status of an advance medical directive remains uncertain. At the time of writing, the best that can be said is that such directives remain no more than the expression of a person's wishes, although there have been

[23] "'End of Life Decisions' in Medical Practice in Flanders—Belgium a Nationwide Survey" *The Lancet* 356, pp.1806–1811.
[24] "'End of Life Decisions' in Australian Practice *Medical Journal of Australia* 166, pp.191–196.

various developments (particularly in England) in recent years which have afforded greater strength to the documents in question. Although no decision was taken on the status of advance directives in the tragic case of *Tony Bland*,[25] views generally supportive of the use of such directives were given in the House of Lords' judgment.

The background to the *Bland* case is well known. Tony Bland had entered a permanent vegetative state (PVS). He could not see, hear, smell or feel, had no cognitive function and was being kept alive through artificial feeding. The House of Lords, in reaching its decision, confirmed that where an adult is competent, he has the right to self-determination and can take decisions regarding his or her own treatment whether or not others might regard those decisions as being irrational. Where the adult has capacity, then the adult can decide whether or not they wish to undergo a specific therapy or treatment.

The question of capacity is not to be confused with intelligence. In a recent unreported case, a woman who was acknowledged as being highly intelligent also suffered from a delusion that her own blood was "evil". On several occasions, she had cut her own wrists. The issue for the court was whether or not the unfortunate woman had capacity, which would allow her to refuse blood transfusions (required to save her life). The court found, in the circumstances of this particular case, that the woman did not have capacity (and therefore was not competent to refuse the treatment).

Following the *Bland* decision, the practice has been adopted that:

- Where life supporting treatment might be withheld in a PVS case, the matter must be decided upon by the court.
- Where there is doubt or disagreement between doctors as to the treatment to be provided or as to the individual's capacity, then the matter must be decided by a court.
- Where the individual's family do not accept the decision/ opinion of doctors, the matter must be brought to court.

The Miss B case provoked much discussion. The issues in that case were, however, confused to a certain extent. Miss B was paralysed and wished to refuse treatment. It would appear that the medical team treating her refused to accept her denial of treatment on the basis that they queried her capacity. However, the court found that Miss B was an intelligent woman who retained capacity and was entitled to refuse treatment. In England, it has long been recognised that an individual with capacity has the right to refuse treatment. In the Miss B case, the High Court found that artificial ventilation amounted to treatment which Miss B, retaining capacity, was entitled to refuse, even though this would inevitably lead to her death. The issue in her case was one of capacity, not euthanasia.

Recent advances

In the British Medical Association's (BMA's) Code of Practice, **15–33** doctors and clinicians are advised that "where valid and applicable, advance medical directives" (refusals) must be followed. Even where the

---

[25] *Airedale NHS Trust v Bland*, 1993 1 All E.R. 281.

particular circumstances of a given case are not identical to those
described in the Code of Practice, doctors should still endeavour to
follow "the general spirit of the statement if this is evident". The Code
of Practice recommends that doctors should consult any person nominated by the patient and seek clarification (and this is why it is
commonplace in a living will to nominate a proxy). The BMA Code of
Practice indicates that if there is any doubt as to a patient's current
wishes, the decision (whether or not to give treatment) will rest with the
senior health care professional. The Royal College of Nursing (RCN)
has a similar approach in its advice to nurses regarding advance medical
directives, which perhaps goes slightly further than the Code issued by
the BMA, in that the RCN Code suggests that a treatment carried out
against the expressed wishes of the individual will represent a trespass
and may be assault. Perhaps not unreasonably, the BMA's view is that
whilst the patient has the right to grant such a directive, including the
right to decline specific treatments, care should be taken in the drafting
of a directive and, prior to completion of the documentation in question,
there should be appropriate discussions between the individual and his
doctor. The BMA also recognises that some doctors may have strong
religious, moral or ethical objections to such directives. Where this is the
case, the view of the BMA is that such doctors should move to one side
and pass management of the individual's care to another doctor.

Although the Voluntary Euthanasia Society (VES) maintains its
concerns that we are still lagging behind other countries in relation to
this field,[26] it would appear that we are moving towards acceptance of
the position that an individual should be able to direct what treatments
he should receive (or not) at the close of his life.

Both the Terence Higgins' Trust and the Voluntary Euthanasia
Society have produced very useful styles of advance medical directives.
Many individuals have taken advantage of these styles without reference
to their solicitors.

Practical advice for the legal adviser

15–34   An individual solicitor may have religious, moral or philosophical
difficulties in this area. If he does, then he should not seek to impose his
own moral, etc. viewpoint upon the client. He should, in the author's
view, and as suggested by the BMA, step aside and allow another
solicitor to advise. Further points are:

1. Obviously, the granter of an advance directive needs to be
   capax at the time of executing the same. If legal force is to be
   afforded to such documents, then there may be merit in
   introducing *mutatis mutandis* the provisions of sections 15 and
   16 of the Adults With Incapacity (Scotland) Act, 2000
   (although this might also be considered to be overkill). That is,
   such directives might require to be executed in the presence of
   a solicitor or other suitably qualified person who would certify
   that the granter fully understood the import and likely effect of

---

[26] VES Briefing, April 2003.

the document, and also that the person signing the certificate was satisfied as to the granter's capacity at the time the directive was signed. If a doubt arises as to the granter's capacity at the time of making the directive, it is unlikely that it will be given effect.

2. The client needs to be certain as to the circumstances in which treatment should or should not be applied. However, in most cases it will be clear to the client, whose main aim is not to be kept alive artificially and beyond a point in time where acceptable recovery is no longer possible.

3. The client should be advised to discuss the terms of the document with his family and also with his medical practitioner (it is to be hoped that medical practitioners with moral or religious objections to such directives should, as suggested by the BMA, stand to one side without seeking to influence the client). It should be borne in mind that the directive "belongs to" the client. Relatives may have objections and the client should indicate his feelings to those relatives so that this is at least a matter of record (to avoid relatives objecting to the implementation of the directive on the basis that they disagreed that it represented the true wishes of their relative).

4. Most suggested styles of advance medical directives include the provision for the appointment of a proxy. Whilst there remains doubt as to the actual legal position of the proxy, the client should discuss his wishes with the latter, and obviously he should not appoint a proxy whose views do not coincide with those of the granter of the directive. Similar (if not identical) considerations will apply to the appointment of a suitable proxy as with an executor under a will (for example, an elderly client should be recommended to appoint a younger proxy). There is no reason why a substitute proxy should not also be appointed. It should be noted that the BMA guidelines recommend that doctors should consult with a proxy in reaching decisions regarding treatment of the individual in question. As matters presently stand, however, doctors are not in strict terms legally obliged to consult with the proxy. It might also be advisable to nominate the proxy as "next of kin". The Terence Higgins' Trust recommends that the individual nominated as proxy should also be nominated as "next of kin". In England, the Mental Health Act of 1983 is the only legislation which clearly outlines the hierarchy of individuals to be consulted on treatment, "next of kin" being the first in line.

5. Until the legal status of advance medical directives has been finally settled, there remains a possible difficulty and an area of challenge in so far as the granter is concerned. Indeed, there might be an argument that a directive granted several years before a catastrophic failure in health on the part of the granter no longer represented the granter's true feelings. That being so, the client should be advised that from time to time he should indicate in writing the fact that an advance medical directive previously granted remains his up-to-date expression of wish. Such "updating" letters should be placed with the directive

itself and should also be copied to the client's doctors, family and proxies.

6. The client should be advised to carry with him at all times an indication that he has granted a living will and where it can be found. This may be of importance, for example, where the client is taken seriously ill whilst on holiday.

7. Free will is an essential feature of human life. The client, having granted a living will, may decide that it should no longer apply. In these circumstances, the living will should be withdrawn/destroyed and those previously consulted advised of the client's change of mind.

Welfare powers of attorney

15–35 It has been suggested that where a power of attorney is granted including welfare powers (incorporating power to decide as to the medical treatment, etc. of the granter), this is tantamount to a Scottish living will. In the opinion of the author, such a view should be regarded as being doubtful. The draftsmen of powers of attorney in Scotland which comply with the provisions of the 2000 Act are still "feeling their way" to a large extent. It may be that healthcare powers of attorney in the United States will increasingly be followed by Scottish practitioners. However, as matters presently stand, Scottish experience is that welfare powers of attorney tend to be fairly short documents. It is suggested by the author that a general power to "decide upon the medical care and attention" of the granter once the granter has lost capacity would not be regarded by the medical profession as an advance medical directive. Welfare powers only come into effect when the granter of the power of attorney has lost capacity. The power of attorney (containing welfare powers) may have been granted many years beforehand, and it might be doubted as to whether or not it would become established practice for the granter of a welfare power of attorney to have to continually indicate his ongoing consent thereto. For the present, it is the author's view that a welfare power of attorney should not be regarded as being a valid and foreshortened version of the format of the advance medical directive proposed by the Voluntary Euthanasia Society or the Terence Higgins' Trust.

Possible legislation

15–36 The government have shown little inclination to legislate in this field. In 1994, the House of Lords Select Committee on Medical Ethics considered a change in the law which would allow voluntary euthanasia. The Committee took the view that "it was virtually impossible to ensure that all acts of euthanasia were truly voluntary and that any liberalisation of the Law in the United Kingdom would not be abused". This of course begs the question as to the viewpoint and practice of the British medical profession (as the recent "do not resuscitate" controversy appears to indicate). The government attitude also does not appear to be reflected in the country at large, as over several years there appears to have been a large body of opinion that the law should be changed to allow voluntary euthanasia.

In 2003, Lord Joel Joffe (who at one time defended Nelson Mandela) introduced a Private Members Bill—the Patient (Assisted Dying) Bill—

into the House of Lords. The Bill passed its second reading on June 6, 2003, although most observers considered that it had little chance of becoming law. However, the provisions of the Bill are of interest:

- A competent adult who is either terminally ill or who has a serious incurable physical illness can make a written declaration that they wish to die.
- Two doctors, including a consultant, would need to confirm the diagnosis. The doctors would have to show that all alternatives had been considered, including palliative and hospice care.
- The written declaration by the patient would need to be witnessed by a solicitor.
- There would be a "waiting period" so that patients would be able to give their decision more consideration.
- The Bill contains provision for doctors to opt out if they feel unable to assist for reasons of conscience, etc.
- The Bill was backed by the Voluntary Euthanasia Society, but there was been considerable opposition, including the Archbishop of Canterbury, the Bishop of Oxford and Professor Robert Winstone.

Conclusion

This is a complex and difficult area, involving not just legal but moral **15–37** issues. It remains to be seen when and if enabling legislation will be enacted.

The proposals of the Scottish Executive[27] are of interest here. In paragraphs 6.46 and 6.47, the difficulties for same sex partners are recognised in respect of hospital visiting and medical treatment. In its paper, the Scottish Executive recognises that there is no legal definition of "next of kin" in Scotland in this particular context. The Scottish Executive recognises that:

"No person has the right to consent to medical treatment on behalf of another adult. If the patient is not in a position to give consent to a medical intervention, a married or unmarried partner, or others in a close relationship with a patient may be asked to advise on the patient's likely best interests, the decision ultimately rests with the doctors. However, we believe that the creation of the status of "the registered partner" will help to bring about a cultural change to remove the difficulties currently faced by some of the same sex couples when one partner becomes ill. We will ensure that, within our devolved responsibilities, guidance given to medical staff adequately addresses the situation."

---

[27] "A legal status for committed same sex couples in Scotland", September 10, 2003 .

CHAPTER 16

CARE HOMES

16–01 Just as will making has become, almost overnight, an area laden with risk for solicitors, this is another area where Scottish solicitors might find themselves increasingly subject to scrutiny. However, it is important that a solicitor should have the skills to advise clients in this area, not just on a self-defensive basis, but also arising from the fact that knowledge of the law in this area and the strategies which can be adopted offer scope for both increased profitability and added value to the client. Private client practitioners increasingly have to be able to look beyond the task with which they have been entrusted by their clients, and be aware of other opportunities to add value to their overall service to the client.[1]

Relevance to succession

16–02 Why is this particular area relevant to the subject-matter of this book? The simple reason is that much of the asset transferral which has gone on in the past within families has taken place with the principal aim of preserving an elderly relative's estate, so that as much as possible might pass to that person's family on their death and not (as the client and his family might perceive) be dissipated or eaten up in paying care home fees. In the author's view, it is not unreasonable to suggest that advice sought and given in this area is every bit as much about planning for succession as the drafting of a will. Throughout history, civilised society has recognised that the *spes successionis* ("hope of succeeding") is a legitimate aspiration between generations.

Many of the arguments which have arisen between the funding local authorities and families revolve around regulation 25 of the National Assistance (Assessment of Resources) Regulations 1992 as amended.[2]

Professional concern

16–03 This is an area in which clients have increasingly sought advice in recent years. It is also a subject which has troubled many practitioners, some of whom who have declined to offer advice in this area for fear that it might be perceived to be assisting the client to achieve what is tantamount to a benefit fraud. The question in essence is whether it is appropriate to offer advice which may amount to deprivation of capital (and thereby fall foul of the 1992 Regulations). Is it appropriate to

---

[1] 3 See *Yule v South Lanarkshire Council* 2000 S.L.T. 1249; and *Robertson v Fife Council* [2002] UKHL 35; 2002 S.C. (H.L.) 145, for an examination of the difficulties arising from transfer of capital followed by an application for assistance with care home fees.
[2] SI 1992/2977.

advise a client in relation to an area which might, if advice is given and followed, increase the burden on the body of tax payers in general? The counterpoint to this is that most solicitors with the appropriate level of skills can quite happily give advice to clients on legitimate mitigation of inheritance tax. For the latter, and whilst their advice may well increase the burden on the general body of taxpayers, no difficult, ethical questions are posed. The Law Society of Scotland has no specific guidelines in this area—the only formal guidance which a Scottish solicitor is likely to obtain falls under the more general conflict of interest rules.

When faced with a family seeking advice, the solicitor has to decide for whom he or she is acting—is it the parent (who fears that he may need to go into a care home at some point in the future) or is it the family (normally adult children), whose normally unstated concern may be that their *spes successionis* will be eroded, if not eradicated, by the effect of having to pay care home fees over a period of time? There is a potential conflict of interest here. The nature of the issues which can arise in such a circumstance are examined in the Court of Appeal in England in the case of *Brown v Palmer*.[3]

The importance of choice

When acting for an elderly parent, the solicitor should emphasise that, **16–04** if he gives away his assets, then he may have no choice as to what care home he enters. The right to choose is very important. The elderly parent may wish to choose a comfortable and conveniently located care home, close to his children. The solicitor has to be aware of the fact that the maximum sum which a local authority will pay by way of financial support to an elderly individual is not necessarily (and is usually less than) the contractual rate charged by many care homes.

Experience in England is that where the capital of the elderly client has been expended, a care home will not necessarily accept the lower "maximum" rate which the local authority will make available.

In these circumstances there are two stark choices:

- The elderly person's family must "top up" the difference between the local authority maximum rate and the contractual rate charged by the nursing home in question; or
- The elderly client has to move to a cheaper nursing home. In fact, there is some evidence that, where families have not agreed to top up, the care home in question has effectively evicted the elderly individual.

Effect on clients of moving care homes

To be evicted (effectively) would be upsetting for most people. **16–05** However, there appears to be evidence that, for those elderly individuals suffering from dementia, the consequences of such a move can be extreme. The University of Stirling recently carried out a study of the

---

[3] 1997 EW Civ 2576.

effects on care home residents of being moved from one home to another. In the case of those suffering from dementia, it was noted that the death rate was almost double that of those not suffering from that condition. The conclusions of the University of Stirling study appear to have found recognition with many local authority social work departments.

The position in England

16–06   The Law Society in England has had guidelines in this specific area for some time.[4] These guidelines were revised in March 2000. The English Law Society do appear to give comfort to solicitors advising in relation to possible deprivation of assets on p.28 of their guidelines, where it is stated that:

> "the solicitor has a duty to ensure that the client fully understands the nature, effect, benefits, risks and foreseeable consequences of making the gift. The solicitor has no obligation to advise the client on the wisdom or morality of the transaction unless the clients specifically request this.

The position in Scotland

16–07   Many solicitors have adopted the view that Lord Hope's leading opinion of the Law Lords in *Robertson v Fife Council*,[5] as decided in July 2002, offers absolute protection to individuals who wish to transfer assets with a view to preserving an inheritance for their family.

In fact, Lord Hope in his decision clearly indicated that in carrying out the financial assessments, local authorities could take into account "notional capital".

Insurance options

16–08   As might be expected, the insurance industry has been ingenious in providing products to meet perceived needs. These include:

- Long-term care bonds
- Immediate care plans.

In the author's view, the above products cannot be overlooked in an overall scheme of succession. The solicitor should be able to offer full and comprehensive advice on how a client is to structure his financial affairs so as to secure the best outcome for his intended beneficiaries, and any practitioner in this field needs to have some knowledge of the availability of these products and how they operate. In particular, it should not be assumed that, where a client has taken up permanent residence in a care home, there is little or nothing which can be done to avoid the client's assets being consumed over a period of time in meeting care home fees.

---

[4] "Gifts of Property: Implications for Future Liability to Pay for Long Term Care", (The Law Society of England and Wales, 1995 (revised 2000)).
[5] [2002] UKHL 35; 2002 145 H.L.

Long-term care bonds

These policies involve advance planning. They are usually arranged **16–09** several (if not, many) years in advance by an individual who fears that he/she may need to enter a residential or care home in their older age. They normally involve payment of regular premiums, the level of which are set in advance to take account of the likely commitment of the insurance company if the insured needs to enter a care home, but taking into account, always, the anticipated income of the insured. Usually there is a savings element involved in the policies in question—if the insured dies without needing to enter a care home or having been there only for a short time, there will be a return to his/her estate. As with any insurance products, the investment element can be written in trust as an effective means of IHT mitigation. Similarly, the question of "insurable interest" is of less importance in relation to such policies as they can, in fact, be arranged and paid for by an adult child on behalf of his/her parent. Whilst many advisers are aware of the existence of long-term care bonds, in the author's experience, a lesser number of advisers are aware of immediate care plans—for those advisers this *lacuna* represents a decided risk.

Immediate care plans

These plans are presently offered by five companies (including Nor- **16–10** wich Union PPP and BUPA). Where an elderly person has already gone into a care home or is about to take up residence there, the plans are very carefully underwritten, with medical assessments needing to be considered and detailed actuarial consideration brought to bear. Without going into the technicalities of the products in question, they can operate so as to at least partially protect a proportion of the client's capital, thereby ensuring that the client will have some capital left on death in order to provide his family with an inheritance.

Why recommend insurance options?

Ease financial pressures

The insurance "solutions" mentioned above do not find favour with **16–11** some individuals. However, they do offer freedom of choice and can avoid the possibility of being "evicted" from a particular care home (unless of course other financial pressures force the closure of a chosen care home).

Risk management

The author makes mention of the foregoing as this can be a distinct **16–12** danger area for solicitors who have clients already in, or about to go into care homes. It is the author's understanding that solicitors in England are now being sued on the grounds of professional negligence by disappointed beneficiaries.

A typical scenario is as follows:

A client goes into a care home. The client appoints his solicitor as attorney in order to deal with care home fees, etc. The solicitor, over a period of years, faithfully ekes out the capital of the client in meeting the home fees. The client passes on. The nephew or other relative or residuary beneficiary under the client's will arrives at the solicitor's office. The solicitor explains that although the client left a will, its terms are effectively meaningless as although the client's estate had been carefully shepherded, it was nonetheless expended over a period of years in meeting care home fees. The solicitor is then asked why he did not suggest an immediate care plan. If the answer to this is that the solicitor did not know of the existence of such a financial product, then on the basis of the principal set out in *White v Jones*[6] or, in Scotland, *Holmes v Bank of Scotland,*[7] the solicitor may just have a case to answer.

It is inevitable that as the population ages the insurance market will develop new products and those working with elderly clients or clients who are concerned about the provision of care in old age will need to keep abreast of changes. If not to avoid litigation then to ensure that they are providing their clients with the best advice in making what can be difficult and emotive decisions.

[6] [1995] 2 A.C. 207 (cited above in Ch.2).
[7] 2002 S.L.T. s.44; and 2002 S.C.L.R. 481 (cited above in Ch.2).

PART IV—STYLES

INDEX TO APPENDIX OF STYLES

294   *Drafting for Succession*

AUTHOR'S INTRODUCTION TO STYLES

The style bank of any solicitor is based on a combination of the following factors:

- Experience ("once bitten, twice shy")
- Personal preference ("I don't like the language used or the way that document has been set out")
- Original thinking ("Now here's a point, and I bet no one else has considered it")
- Adaptation (or less kindly put, plagiarism) ("That's a good style, let's scan it and adapt it")

The author makes it clear that the Appendix of Styles (with certain exceptions—for example, the Suggested Notes) are not "original thinking" and are based on adaptation of styles encountered over a period of years. In particular, the author acknowledges the sources of older Law Society styles, styles (or at least ideas) incorporated within a more recent Law Society Update series of Seminars, styles/materials presented to Diploma of Law Students (particularly those in use in the Glasgow Graduate School of Law ,wherein the author is a tutor), "Drafting Wills in Scotland" by A. R. Barr and others, styles/suggestions presented/made at the numerous seminars which the author has attended over the years and the "tweakings"/suggestions made by many other solicitors, practitioners and academics with whom the author has corresponded over a period of time. Nowadays, the pressure of business is such that there are few practitioners, working at the coal face, who can legitimately claim sole and true authorship of the documents which they produce. The author gratefully acknowledges the work and intellect of others in the styles represented in this book. To all of those mentioned (and to anyone else whom the author may have omitted), if you recognise wording or basic styles of which you were the original authors, the author extends his ready thanks and appreciation.

296 Drafting for Succession

AUTHOR'S INTRODUCTION TO SUGGESTED NOTES IN APPENDIX OF STYLES

The Appendix of Styles contains various suggested notes. Some readers may find the notes to be, perhaps, unnecessary or unduly "wordy". It is, however, the view of the author that, increasingly, our profession requires both to demonstrate that we are providing a quality service to our clients but also, and at the same time, practice in what might be regarded as being a "self-defensive" basis. The doctrine of "informed consent" has increasingly directed medical practice over a period of time. It is likely that the legal profession will face either claims or complaints in time to come on the basis that we failed to bring important and relevant information to the attention of the client—for example:

- *"If the lawyer had told my spouse about legal rights and given that we have a "black sheep" son, he could have done something about it—I have lost out"*
- *"If the lawyer had only told my father about the value of a power of attorney, my family wouldn't have had to undergo the stress, delay and expense of having a financial guardian appointed"*
- *"When I was appointed as attorney the law did not tell me about the principles/code of practice as also that in some circumstances, I might become personally liable—it was not explained to me that on each and every occasion I should indicate in advance that I was acting only as attorney and not as the principal"*
- *"When my father made his will the lawyer asked him nothing about the value of his assets and estate—he offered no advice in relation to inheritance tax. If he only had, my father would have done something about the large inheritance tax bill which the family now faces."*
- *"The lawyer had acted for my mother for 20 years—she assumed that he would write to her to review her will, from time to time particularly after mother won £500,000 on the Premium Bonds (and the lawyer was aware of this). My mother received no advice about review of her will which I think was wholly inappropriate given the change in her financial circumstances when she died"*

Some of these complaints/comments might be stretching a point. However, and frankly, others would, in appropriate circumstances, be entirely justified.

It is the author's view that sending appropriate Explanatory Notes to clients will not only demonstrate the quality of the service which the solicitors are providing but they also protect the latter from claims/ complaints further down the line. The stresses and pressures of current practice are such that it is almost impossible to write at great length to each and every client on such points. However, if a solicitor has standard "handout" which he can send to clients for consideration by the latter (and the file clearly demonstrates that this has been done—with a copy of the relevant note being placed on file) then it is the view of the author that the solicitor is not only demonstrating that he is providing a good service but will also have, hopefully, a ready answer to a complaint/claim based on lack of information/advice.

WILLS CONTAINING COMMON ERRORS AND MISTAKES

STYLE WILL NO.1

I, JOSEPH BROWN, residing at One Brown Street, Gourock, in order to settle the succession to my means and Estate upon my death do provide as follows:

ONE	I appoint as my executor, my wife, MRS JOAN BROWN, residing with me at One Brown Street, aforesaid (hereinafter referred to as "my executor")
TWO	I direct my executor to make payment of my lawful debts and funeral expenses and of the expenses of winding up my estate.
THREE	I direct my executor to give effect to any writings granted by me, however informal they may be provided they are signed by me, dated after the date hereof and are clearly expressive of my intention as to which my executor shall be the sole judge. Any bequests so made shall be free of interest, delivery expenses and government taxes unless otherwise stipulated.
FOUR	I bequeath a legacy of TEN THOUSAND POUNDS (£10,000) STERLING equally between my parents, HORACE BROWN, and MRS ELAINE BROWN, residing together at Twelve Montague Gardens, Hillhead, Glasgow or wholly to the survivor of them.
FIVE	I direct my executor to hold the whole residue and remainder of my means and estate to my said wife whom failing equally between my said parents or wholly to the survivor of them.
SIX	In the event that I am not survived by my said wife but that I am survived by any child of mine still in the minority as at my date of death I appoint my said parents and the survivor of them to be guardians or guardian to such children.
SEVEN	My executors shall have the fullest powers of retention, realisation, investment, appropriation, transfer of property without realisation and management of my estate as if she were absolute beneficial owner; and she shall have power to appoint herself or any other person to act as solicitor or agent in any other capacity and to allow her, him or them the same remuneration to which she, he or they would have been entitled if not an executor.
LASTLY	I revoke all prior wills and testamentary writings made or granted by me: IN WITNESS WHEREOF

STYLE WILL NO.2

I, ANDREW GORDON, residing at Fifteen James Watt Road, Milngavie, Glasgow, in order to settle the succession to my means and estate upon my death do provide as follows:

ONE	I appoint as my trustee, my father, WILLIAM GORDON, residing at Three Springbank Road, Hillfoot, Glasgow (hereinafter referred to as "my trustee").
TWO	I direct my trustee to make payment of my lawful debts and funeral expenses and of the expenses of winding up my estate.
THREE	I direct my trustee to give effect to any writings granted by me, however informal they may be provided they are signed by me, dated after the date hereof and are clearly expressive of my intention as to which my trustee shall be the sole judges. Any bequests so made shall be free of interest, delivery expenses and government taxes unless otherwise stipulated.
FOUR	I bequeath free of all government taxes and duties payable upon my death a legacy of TWENTY THOUSAND POUNDS (£20,000) STERLING to my nephew, IAN GORDON, residing with me.
FIVE	I bequeath the whole residue and remainder of my means and estate to my wife, MRS JOAN GORDON, residing with me provided she survives me for thirty clear days from the date of my death. In the event of my said wife predeceasing me or failing so to survive I bequeath the whole residue and remainder of my means and estate equally between my children, JOHN GORDON and ELEANOR GORDON, both residing with me equally between them or wholly to the survivor of them declaring that should either of my said children pre-decease me leaving issue who shall survive me then such issue shall take equally between or among them *per stirpes* the share original and accrescing which would have fallen to his, her or their parent had such parent survived me.
SIX	In the event of my said wife predeceasing and either of my said children being in minority as at the date of my death I appoint my said father to be guardian to such child.
SEVEN	My trustee shall have the fullest powers of retention, realisation, investment, appropriation, transfer of property without realisation and management of my estate as if he was absolute beneficial owner; and shall have power to resign office and appoint himself or any other person to act as solicitor or agent in any other capacity and to allow him, her or them the same remuneration to which he, she or they would have been entitled if not a trustee.
EIGHT	I direct that my body shall be interred in lair number 621 in the Western, Glasgow.

LASTLY   I hereby revoke and cancel all prior wills and testamentary writings made or granted by me: IN WITNESS
WHEREOF

STYLE WILL NO.3

I, MISS JOAN LEIGH, residing at One Ralston Road, Paisley in order to settle the succession to my means and estate upon my death do provide as follows:

ONE	I appoint as my executors FREDRICK GRABBIT and WILLIAM RUNN, both solicitors of One Town Square, Gourock (and hereinafter referred to as "my executors").
TWO	I direct my executors to make payment of my lawful debts and funeral expenses and of the expenses of winding up my estate.
THREE	I direct my executors to give effect to any writings granted by me, however informal they may be provided they are signed by me, dated after the date hereof and are clearly expressive of my intention as to which my executors shall be the sole judges. Any bequests so made shall be free of interest, delivery expenses and government taxes unless otherwise stipulated.
FOUR	I bequeath my painting "Sunflowers" by Vincent Van Gogh to my friend MRS LINDA CURRIE, residing at Ninety-eight Ralston Road, Paisley and that free of all government taxes and duties payable upon my death but without interest to date of payment.
FIVE	I bequeath, again free of all government taxes and duties payable upon my death but without interest due to payment such item of jewellery as my friend MRS LAURA DAVIES, residing at One Golf Road, Troon may chose.
SIX	I bequeath free of all government taxes and duties payable upon my death but without interest to date of payment the following pecuniary legacies namely:

    (a) to each of my nephews WILLIAM BRAXTON, JOHN BRAXTON and IAN ROBERT BRAXTON, all residing at Thirty-two Kilmuirs Road, Troon the sum of SEVENTY THOUSAND POUNDS (£70,000) STERLING; declaring that each of the said legacies shall not be paid to my nephews until they have each attained the age of twenty-five years;

    (b) to my niece, MISS WILMA JOHNSTON, residing at One St Andrews Drive, Girvan, the sum of SIXTY THOUSAND POUNDS (£60,000) STERLING; declaring that the said legacy shall not be paid to my said niece until she shall have attained the age of twenty-five;

    (c) to my friend, MRS JOAN BLACK, residing at Two Culloden Drive, Inverness, the sum of FIFTY THOUSAND POUNDS (£50,000) STERLING

SEVEN	I bequeath the whole residue and remainder of my means and estate equally between the following charitable beneficiaries namely;

(a) OXFAM;
(b) WFW;
(c) IMPERIAL CANCER RESEARCH MAC-MILLAN FUND.

EIGHT My executors shall have the fullest powers of retention, realisation, investment, appropriation, transfer of property without realisation and management of my estate as if they were absolute beneficial owners.

NINE I wish my body to be cremated.

LASTLY I hereby cancel and revoke my previous will dated Twenty-first December Nineteen hundred and Ninety-eight: IN WITNESS WHEREOF

302 Drafting for Succession

STYLE WILL NO.4

I, JOHN SMITH, residing at Fifteen Cowan Drive, Stirling in order to settle the succession to my means and estate upon my death do provide as follows, namely:

ONE	I appoint as my executors my uncle, JOSEPH SMITH, retired solicitor, residing at Fifteen Haymarket Road, Edinburgh and my brother, ROBERT SMITH, residing at One thousand and twelve Wilshire Boulevard, Santa Monica, California, United States of America (my said uncle and my said brother being hereinafter referred to as "my executors").
TWO	I direct my executors to make payment of my lawful debts and funeral expenses and of the expenses of winding up my estate.
THREE	I direct my executors to give effect to any writings granted by me, however informal they may be provided they are signed by me, dated after the date hereof and are clearly expressive of my intention as to which my Executors shall be the sole judges. Any bequests so made shall be free of interest, delivery expenses and government taxes unless otherwise stipulated.
FOUR	I bequeath free of all government taxes and duties upon my death but without interest to date of payment a legacy of TWO HUNDRED AND THIRTY ONE THOUSAND POUNDS (£231,000) STERLING equally between my children, JOAN SMITH, ROBERTA SMITH and DANIEL SMITH all presently residing at Seventeen The Beeches, Brookfield, Renfrewshire and the survivors of them or wholly to the survivor of them.
FIVE	I bequeath free of all government taxes and duties payable upon my death but without interest to date of payment a legal of TEN THOUSAND POUNDS (£10,000) STERLING to my nephew, IAN SMITH, residing at Seventeen Stirling Drive, Bearsden, Glasgow.
SIX	I direct my executors to effect a sale of my holiday home at One Braemar Glen, Dornoch, Sutherland and after deduction of all estate agency and other expenses properly incurred in such sale to make over the net free proceeds of such sale to my friend, WILLIAM SINCLAIR, residing at One Brown Street, Gourock.
SEVEN	I bequeath to my friend, JAMES STIRLING, residing at Three Firpark Terrace, Motherwell my sculpture by Monet "The Diligent Notaire".

EIGHT
I bequeath the whole residue and remainder of my means and estate to my wife, MRS SAMANTHA SMITH, residing at Seventeen The Beeches, aforesaid whom failing equally between my said children or wholly to the survivor of them. Declaring that it is my wish that my children and the survivors of them should not receive any benefit in terms of this purpose of my will until each of them has attained the eighteen.

NINE
I confer upon my executors the fullest powers available to gratuitous trustees under statute or at common law including (without prejudice to the foregoing generality):

(a) power to invest my estate as if they were the absolute owners of it and beneficially entitled thereto;

(b) power to settle any pecuniary legacies bequeathed by me either in cash or in kind or partly in cash and partly in kind;

(c) power to pay the whole or part of any testamentary provision payable to a beneficiary who has not attained the age of eighteen to either parent or to the guardian of such beneficiary or to any person who may be acting as guardian of such a beneficiary although not legally appointed, whose receipt shall be a sufficient discharge to my executors, or to retain the whole or part of such provision falling to any such beneficiary until he or she reaches that age and to apply the free income (or even the capital) for the maintenance, education or benefit of such beneficiary and except as so applied to re-invest the income for such beneficiary;

(d) power to appoint themselves or any other person to be agents or solicitors for carrying into effect the powers and purposes of this will and to allow such agents or solicitors their usual professional charges and remunerations.

TEN
I appoint my brother, the said ROBERT SMITH to be guardian of my children; in the event of my said brother predeceasing me then I direct that my said uncle shall have power to appoint a suitable guardian or guardians in his place.

LASTLY
I hereby revoke all prior wills and testamentary writings made or granted by me: IN WITNESS WHEREOF

STYLE CODICIL NO.1

I, MALCOLM SMITH, residing at Three Glenfinnan Drive, Summerston, Glasgow do hereby make the following codicil to my will dated First June Nineteen hundred and Ninety and codicils thereto dated Second July Nineteen hundred and Ninety-two, Seventh July Nineteen hundred and Ninety-three, Third October Nineteen hundred and Ninety-seven, Fifth December Nineteen hundred and Ninety-eight and First January Two thousand and One namely:

ONE   I hereby cancel the bequest of the residue detailed in my said will and earlier codicils.

TWO   I leave the residue of my estate to my executor ROBERT WILKINS, designed in my said will for my said executor to dispose of as he shall see fit.

Save as hereinbefore amended I hereby confirm and ratify the terms of my said will and earlier codicils: IN WITNESS WHEREOF

AUTHOR'S NOTE ON STYLE WILL No.1

- Mr Black is appointing his wife as his sole executor. Although not disastrous given the terms of section 3 of the Executors (Scotland) Act 1900, Mr Black would be well advised to appoint a substitute/substitutes in the event of his wife predeceasing him, dying in a common calamity or being incapax.
- Whilst it may be entirely appropriate to leave a legacy to Mr Black's parents (if Mr Black considers that they require financial support) the legacy is not stated to be free of interest. The adviser should check with Mr Black as to whether or not interest is to be payable.
- In purpose FIVE, the executor is directed "to hold" the residue for Mr Black's wife. What does this mean?
- The terms of purpose SIX are at variance with the remainder of the will. Mr Black at least seems to predicate that there may be minor children when both he and his wife die. However, there has been no bequest in favour of any such children anywhere in the will—this means that the will may be subject to challenge under the *conditio si testator sine liberis decesserit*. This is a major flaw.
- Purpose SEVEN contains some "sloppy" drafting (particularly the reference to "the executors").

Authors Note on Style Will No.2

- Mr Andrews has appointed his father as sole executor. This may not be sensible depending on the age of Mr Andrew's father. Clients are notorious for not keeping their wills up-to-date and Mr Andrew's will may lie in a solicitor's wills safe for 10 or more years without any amendment. At that time, it may no longer be appropriate for Mr William Andrew's to have been appointed in the first place. Similarly, there are no protective, additional or substitute executor appointments.
- Purpose FOUR leaves a legacy of £20,000 to the client's nephew who is stated to reside with him. As a first point, there is no "negative" of interest on the legacy, and also given that the nephew is residing with the testator the question of the *conditio si institutus* . . . must arise. This point should have been checked with the client and where the *conditio* is not to apply, the nephew's issue should have been expressly excluded.
- When purposes FIVE and SIX are read together, it is reasonable to assume that the testator has two children, John and Eleanor, who were still minors when the will was granted. Notwithstanding the client's protestations, it remains possible that there will be a further child or children. However, no provision has been made for any future children thus, again, running the risk that the *conditio si testator* . . . will be brought into play.
- Are the terms of purpose SEVEN adequate?
- Has the testator been advised of the fact that, if his children come into the line of succession, they will vest at the age of sixteen years? There is a risk that this will does not build in the requisite financial protections which many parents would desire for young and financially naïve or vulnerable children.
- The terms of purpose EIGHT are fairly commonplace. Whilst there may be no drafting error here, where the adviser is asked to prepare a clause to this effect, he should advise the client:

  (a) To check for the whereabouts of the relevant lair certificate
  (b) To leave a note with his will as to the whereabouts of that lair certificate (normally the *indicium* of ownership of the lair)
  (c) Even where the client holds the lair certificate, to ask the relevant Cemetery Authority to check that a further burial within the relevant lair is possible.

AUTHOR'S NOTE ON STYLE WILL NO.3

- The painting bequeathed in terms of Purpose FOUR is (if an original) extremely valuable. However, has the client been advised of the possible effect of bequeathing such a single valuable item, free of inheritance tax, to the beneficiary in question? The phrase " . . . but without interest to date of payment" is meaningless in the context of this purpose. There has probably been some "sloppy" cutting and pasting on a word processor. Whilst this might not be disastrous in the context of this clause, the message is clear—computer technology is wonderful but careless use of the same could, in some circumstances, lead to erroneous importation of wording which could seriously affect the true intent of the will.

- Purpose FIVE, again, contains "sloppy" drafting with reference to interest being meaningless in relation to a specific bequest. However, the wording of this clause could cause great difficulty—the prospect of a legacy *rei alienae* arises. If Miss Leigh intended that her friend should be able to choose an item from her collection of jewellery as at Miss Leigh's date of death, then the clause should have specified "such item of my jewellery" as her friend might choose. Again, if Miss Leigh has a particularly valuable collection of jewellery then the effect of the incidence of tax on the residue should be explained to the testator. This is re-enforced given the terms of purpose SIX

- Again, to exclude the possibility of the *condition si institutus*, issue should be expressly excluded in paragraphs (a) and (b). The terms of these two paragraphs also stipulate that the legacies have not to be paid to the relatives in question until they attain the age of twenty five years. However, in truth, as there has been no postponement of vesting, the particular direction is ineffective with the nephews and niece being entitled to demand payment of their legacies at age 16 years

- Bearing in mind that the residue has been bequeathed in terms of purpose EIGHT to exempt beneficiaries, the terms of this will will lead to "grossing up" for IHT purposes.

- The terms of paragraph (c) of purpose SEVEN are likely to cause serious difficulty to the executors—someone has not checked exactly which charity was intended by the testator. Similarly, the clause contains no declaration allowing the executors a degree of discretion if a charity is wound up or transfers its assets to another charity etc

- The terms of purpose EIGHT are a disaster. The executors are solicitors but have no "charging power"

- The terms of the final clause run the risk that there is an earlier will which is not specifically revoked and with the difficulties which that might entail

AUTHOR'S NOTE ON STYLE WILL NO.4

- The wisdom of appointment of an executor who lives abroad may be questioned.
- In terms of purposes FOUR and EIGHT it would appear that the testator is separated from his wife and children. Some enquiry as to the background is indicated, particularly if a divorce is in the offing (bearing in mind the recommendations of the Scottish Law Commission, relative to the effect of a divorce on testamentary provisions). Similarly, it would appear that the testator's children are minors. That being so, they will each vest on respectively attaining the age of sixteen years. Is this appropriate? Again, the question of the *conditio si institutus* arises. A similar consideration applies to purpose FIVE
- Given the terms of purposes FOUR, FIVE, SIX and SEVEN of the will, it would appear to be clear that inheritance tax will be payable in Mr Smith's Estate. The terms of purposes SIX and SEVEN say nothing about the incidence of IHT. In those circumstances, the IHT referable to the particular bequests will require to be met from the residue
- Has the client been made aware of this, particularly given the likely value of the bequest in purpose SEVEN
- Although the testator has specified that, where children come into line of succession in respect of the residue, they are not to receive their benefit until they respectively attain the age of eighteen years, he has failed to prevent vesting at age sixteen years
- The terms of paragraph (c) of purpose NINE will similarly not prevent vesting at age sixteen years. The question has to be raised whether or not there should not have been an accumulation and maintenance trust created not only in respect of the large legacy bequeathed to the children but also in respect of any residuary beneficiaries
- The terms of the appointment of Robert Smith, as guardian, under purpose TEN, will be ineffective if the testator is survived by his wife. Similarly, the testator has endeavoured to delegate the right to appoint a further guardian in his place— this is not valid

AUTHOR'S NOTE ON STYLE CODICIL NO.1

- As a first point, Mr Smith is obviously in the habit of making codicils to his will. His codicil represents the sixth such testamentary direction. This runs the risk of absolute confusion arising. Mr Smith should have been advised to make a wholly new will, incorporating the desired provisions of his existing will and the codicils thereto.
- The terms of purpose TWO may make the testator's testamentary provisions unworkable. Effectively, he is giving his executor absolute discretion to dispose of his estate—this goes beyond what Scots Law would normally accept as a discretionary legacy/provision in respect of residue—effectively, Mr Smith is delegating the powers to make a will (at least in respect of the residue of his estate) to a third party.

A SIMPLE WILL

I, KENNETH WALTERS, residing at Sixty Calderview, Rothesay, Isle of Bute in order to settle the succession to my means and estate upon my death do provide as follows, namely:

ONE
I appoint as my executors my wife, MRS DANI MYRA WALTERS. residing with me at Sixty Calderview, aforesaid and my brother-in-law, ROBERT AILTON, residing at Two Kirk Drive. Rothesay, aforesaid (my said wife and my said brother-in-law being hereinafter referred to as "my executors").

TWO
I direct my executors to make payment of my lawful debts and funeral expenses and of the expenses of winding up my estate.

THREE
I direct my executors to give effect to any writings granted by me, however informal they may be provided they are signed by me, dated after the date hereof and are clearly expressive of my intention as to which my. Executors shall be the sole judges. Any bequests so made shall be free of interest, delivery expenses and government taxes unless otherwise stipulated.

FOUR
I bequeath the whole residue and remainder of my means and estate to my wife, the said MRS DANI MYRA WALTERS, provided she survives me for Thirty clear days from the date of my death; in the event of my said wife failing so to survive then I bequeath the whole residue and remainder of my means and estate equally between or among any children of mine who shall survive me; declaring that in the event of any of my children predeceasing me leaving issue who shall survive me, then such issue shall take equally between or among them *per stirpes* if more than one the share to which his, her or their parent would have succeeded had such parent survived me but subject always to the provisions as to vesting et cetera hereinafter detailed in Purpose SIX of this my will.

FIVE
In the event that I am not survived as aforesaid by my said wife nor by any of my children nor by any of their issue, then I bequeath the whole residue and remainder of my means and estate as follows:

(a) one-half thereof to my sister, MRS LYNDA THOM, residing at Three Kenneth Muir Street, Falkirk whom failing in the event of my said sister also failing to survive me equally between or among such of her children as shall survive me; and

(b) the other one-half thereof to my mother-in-law, MRS ELY AILTON, residing at One Blackview Road, Gourock and in the event of my said mother-in-law failing to survive me then equally between my brother-in-law, the said Robert Ailton, my sister-in-law, MARION AILTON, residing at One Blackview Road, aforesaid and my brother-in-law, CHARLES AILTON. residing at Twenty Crow Road, Glasgow and the survivors of them or wholly to the survivor of them but declaring that in the event of any of my said brothers-in-law and sister-in-law predeceasing me leaving issue who shall survive me then such issue shall take equally between or among them *per stirpes* if more than one the share to which his, her or their parent would have succeeded had such parent survived me.

SIX

Where any benefit under this my will by way of residue or otherwise falls to a beneficiary who is under the age of twenty one years, then the benefit in question shall be held by my executors in trust for such beneficiary until he or she attains the age of twenty one years when the benefit will vest: income arising from such benefit shall be accumulated but my executors shall have power to apply all or part of the income or capital of such benefit for the education. maintenance or benefit of such beneficiary and if such beneficiary does not attain the age of twenty one years then the benefit with any accumulated income shall be held for the beneficiaries who would have been entitled had such beneficiary predeceased me.

SEVEN

If any part of my estate falls to a beneficiary who lacks full legal capacity my executors shall full power either to pay or apply the whole or any part of the income or capital falling to such beneficiary for his or her benefit in any manner as my executors may in their sole discretion think proper, to retain the same until such capacity is attained, accumulating income with capital, or to pay the same over to the legal guardian or person for the time being having the custody of such beneficiary whose receipt shall be a sufficient discharge to my executors.

EIGHT

My executors shall have the fullest powers of and in regard to retention, realisation, investment, appropriation, transfer of property without realisation and management of my estate as if my executors were absolute beneficial owners; and my executors shall have power to resign office and to appoint himself/herself or any other person to act as solicitor or agent in any other capacity until allow him, her or them the same remuneration to which he, she or they would have been entitled if not an executor or executors.

NINE

In the event that I am not survived as aforesaid by my said wife whilst any of my children are in minority I appoint as guardians or guardian thereto my said brother-in-law, Robert Ailton and his wife Mrs Theresa Ailton, residing with him or the survivor of them.

LASTLY   I hereby revoke and cancel all prior wills and testamen-
                tary writings made or granted by me: IN WITNESS
                WHEREOF

Author's Note Re: A Simple Will

Mr Walters is a fairly young man who is married but, as yet, has no children. He wishes to make a will which will protect his wife but also to provide for children born after the date of execution of the will (he and his wife intend to have children).

He is aware of the issues which fall to be considered even in a simple will, *i.e.*:

- The nomination of "substitute" beneficiaries in the event, for example, of he and his wife being killed in a mutual catastrophe.
- The advisability of postponing vesting in so far as young beneficiaries might be concerned purpose SIX of the will represents a "short form" accumulation and maintenance trust.
- Kenneth is aware that if he and his wife are both killed in the type of mutual catastrophe outlined above, some provision should be made for appointment of suitable guardians to minor children.
- Kenneth (in consultation with his wife) has made provision (in purpose FIVE) to cover the situation of both he and his wife being killed together in a mutual catastrophe when they have no children. Very sensibly, he has nominated "substitute" residuary beneficiaries.

It is, of course, envisaged that his wife, Dani, will make a "mirror image" will. The draftsman would be prudent to point out to the client that where one survives the other for more than thirty days, then the survivor could redirect his/her residue as he/she might see fit. Obviously, it would appear that Kenneth and Dani have agreed that the terms of purpose FIVE are, at least at this present time, an equitable division of their estate between their respective families (**see the author's comments on problems of revocation in such circumstances in the foregoing text**).

A WILL INCORPORATING A NIL-RATE BAND LEGACY AND A FULL ACCUMULATION AND MAINTENANCE TRUST FOR CHILDREN

I, JOHN McBRIDE, residing at Six Langton Drive, New Cumnock, Ayrshire in order to settle the succession to my means and estate upon my death do provide as follows, namely:

ONE   I appoint as my executors and trustees my wife, MRS JANET McBRIDE, residing with me at Six Langton Drive, aforesaid and my brothers, DREW McBRIDE, residing at The Lodge, Bogie Road, Kilmacolm and WILLIAM McBRIDE, residing at Twenty Yellowbrick Road, Glasgow (all being hereinafter referred to as "my trustees").

TWO   I direct my trustees to make payment of my lawful debts and funeral expenses and of the expenses of winding up my estate.

THREE   I direct my trustees to give effect to any writings granted by me, however informal they may be provided they are signed by me, dated after the date hereof and are clearly expressive of my intention as to which my trustees shall be the sole judges. Any bequests so made shall be free of interest, delivery expenses and government taxes unless otherwise stipulated.

FOUR   I direct my trustees to hold (subject to the provisions as to vesting etcetera hereinafter detailed in purpose FIVE of this my will as if the bequest immediately hereinafter detailed formed part of the residue of my estate) for the benefit of such of my children as shall survive me such sum (or property to such value) as will exhaust the nil-rate band of inheritance tax as set out in Schedule one to the Inheritance Tax Act 1984 and any similar statutory successor after taking into account:

(a) Lifetime gifts made by me which are for inheritance tax purposes aggregable with or deemed to be part of my executry estate.

(b) Legacies which are not exempt from inheritance tax.

(c) Funds in trust which are aggregable for inheritance tax purposes with my executry estate other than those exempt from inheritance tax.

(d) Any claims to legitim except those discharged without consideration after my death as to all of which my executors shall be the sole judges.

FIVE

I bequeath the whole residue and remainder of my means and estate to my wife, Mrs Janet McBride provided she survives me for thirty clear days from the date of my death; In the event that she shall predecease me or fail so to survive then I direct my trustees to hold the whole residue and remainder of my means and estate (hereinafter referred to as "the trust fund")equally for such of my children who shall survive me (hereinafter referred to as "the said children") or wholly for the survivor of them but subject always to the provisions as to vesting etcetera aftermentioned namely:

(a) for behoof of the said children equally among them contingently on their attaining a vested interest as after provided with the powers after specified in relation to payment of income to any beneficiary prospectively entitled to share in the trust fund;

(b) to accumulate the income arising from the trust fund and from any share thereof to which any of the said children is prospectively entitled by investing the surplus of such income and the resulting income therefrom until such income is paid or applied otherwise in accordance with paragraphs (a), (c), (d) or (e) hereof;

(c) for payment of the income or the share of the trust fund to which any of the said children is prospectively entitled to such child from the attainment by him or her of the age of twenty-one years until he or she attains a vested interest as provided for in the immediately succeeding paragraph;

(d) for payment of (1) an equal share of the capital of the trust fund and (2) the proportion of accumulated income referable to such share to each of the said children on their respectively attaining the age of twenty-five years complete and subject as aftermentioned the said capital and accumulated income shall not vest in any of the said children until the date for payment of his or her share;

(e) in the event of any of the said children failing to attain a vested interest by reason of his or her predeceasing leaving issue, such issue as survive and attain the age of twenty-five years complete shall be entitled equally amongst them if more than one to the share original and accrescing which his, her or their parent would have taken on survivance on the same terms and conditions as are herein provided with regard to such original share; And in the event of any of the said children failing to attain a vested interest as before provided for, leaving no issue who shall survive and attain the age of twenty-five, to hold the share of the trust fund and any income accumulated at the date of such failure for behoof of the survivors or survivor of the said children or the issue of any predeceasing child taking a vested interest as aforesaid as an accretion to their, his or her share or shares and subject to the same Trusts as are hereby declared concerning their, his or her original share or shares;

(f) declaring

(i) should any accumulation of income of the trust fund hereinbefore directed to be made be prohibited by law by reason of any event the income affected by such prohibition shall in that event be paid or applied to or for the maintenance, education or benefit of the said children or their issue for the time being presumptively entitled to the capital of the Trust Fund or that part thereof from which such income arose;

(ii) notwithstanding anything beforewritten the trustees shall have power in their discretion to apply for the maintenance, education or benefit of any beneficiary the income including accumulated income in whole or in part and any part up to the whole of the share of the capital of the trust fund of any child or the issue of any child prospectively entitled to such share of the capital of the trust fund and in that event of such application being made in the minority of said child or issue of such child the receipt of the parent or legal guardian of such child or issue of such child shall be sufficient discharge to the trustees and notwithstanding the foregoing provision in regard to vesting, such advances shall vest on payment; further declaring that in the event outlined in purpose EIGHT hereof and the guardian appointed in terms of said purpose requiring to act in respect of any of my children who shall be a minority at time of my death (my said wife having predeceased me) I hereby specifically empower my trustees to make such payments on such terms and conditions as they may consider appropriate to the guardian of such minor children including making payments absolutely to such guardian; where such payments are made absolutely to such guardian to support her in her care etcetera of such minor children then they shall be deemed to be payments made in terms hereof for the benefit of such minor children and shall be deemed to vest in such minor children as at the date of such payment to my guardian; further declaring that my trustees shall also have power to lend such part of the trust fund as they may consider appropriate to such guardian and on such terms and conditions as they consider reasonable in all the circumstances in order to secure, ensure or promote the maintenance, education or benefit of any such minor child.

(iii) there shall be no apportionment of revenue accruing from any part of y estate between income and capital on any occasion all revenue being deemed to have accrued on the date upon which it is payable.

SIX My trustees shall have the fullest powers of and in regard to retention, realisation, investment, appropriation, transfer of property without realisation, and management of my estate as if they were absolute beneficial owners; and shall have power to do everything they may consider necessary or expedient for the administration of the trust; and in particular and without prejudice to these general powers my trustees shall have power:

(a) to retain, sell, purchase, lease or hire the estate or any part thereof;

(b) to invest the whole or any part of the estate in heritable and leasehold property, investments, securities, insurance policies, deposits and other assets of whatever description, whether producing income or not, whether or not falling within the class of investments authorised for trust funds, whether or not payable to bearer, and wherever situated;

(c) to effect, maintain, renew and acquire policies of insurance of whatever description; and to insure any property on whatever terms they think fit including on a first loss basis;

(d) to administer and manage any heritable or real property forming part of the estate; to repair, maintain, renew and improve the same and to erect additional buildings and structures; to grant, vary and terminate lease and rights of tenancy or occupancy; to plant, thin and cut down timber; to work or let minerals; all as my trustees may think proper and as if they were absolute owners of the estate;

(e) to continue or to commence any business, whether alone or in conjunction or in partnership with any other persons, or through any companies, for such period as my trustees may think proper; to appoint or employ a trustee or any other person in any capacity in relation to such business and to pay to them suitable remuneration for services, including pension provisions for any employees or their dependants; and to delegate or entrust to any persons the control and management of such business to such extent as my trustees may think fit; and my trustees:

(i) may employ for the purposes of such business such part of the income or capital as they think proper;

(ii) shall exercise only such control or supervision of such business as they shall think fit;

(iii) shall be entitled to be relieved from the estate from all personal responsibility for any loss arising from such business operations; and

(iv) shall be entitled to retain personally any remuneration for their services;

(f) to borrow or lend with or without security; and to grant or continue any guarantee or indemnity for the benefit of any beneficiary actual or prospective;

(g) to lend or allow to be used the whole or any part of the estate at such rate of interest or rent as they may consider appropriate, or free of interest or rent, to or by any person who is for the time being entitled to payment of a share of the income of the estate or to whom or for whose benefit the income may be paid or applied in the exercise of a discretion then available to my trustees;

(h) to allow the estate or any part thereof to be registered in the names of or held or the documents of title to be held by any person, firm, corporation or other body as nominee of my trustees;

(i) revocably to delegate any power or powers of making, managing, realising or otherwise dealing with any investment or deposit comprised in the estate to any person or persons upon such terms as to remuneration or otherwise as my Trustees may think fit and no trustee shall be responsible for the default of any such agent if the trustee in question employed him in good faith;

(j) to accept as an addition to my estate any other property as may be made over to them;

(k) to decide what is capital and what is income and the proportion in which expenses are to be charged against capital and income respectively;

(l) to set apart and appropriate specific property of any description to represent the whole or part of the share, prospective or otherwise, of any beneficiary at such valuation as my trustees shall determine, so that thereafter the particular share or part shall have the full benefit and the whole risk of the appropriated investments of assets;

(m) to settle with any beneficiary entitled to any part of the estate by conveying to him or her in satisfaction thereof either specific property or money, or partly one and partly the other, as to my trustees shall seem proper and at such valuation as they shall determine and to compel acceptance accordingly;

(n) to enter into any transaction or do any act otherwise authorised by law or by this deed notwithstanding that any trustee is or might be acting as *auctor in rem suam* or with a conflict of interest between such trustee and himself as an individual or as trustee of any other trust or any partnership of which a trustee is a partner or any company of which a trustee is a shareholder or director or in relation to any combination of these capacities provided that the trustee or trustees with whom there is or may be any such conflict is or are not the sole trustee or trustees;

(o) to participate in the exercise of any discretion granted to my trustees notwithstanding that a trustee is or may be a or the sole beneficiary in whose favour the discretion is then exercised provided that there is at least one trustee not so favoured;

(p) to resign office notwithstanding any benefit hereunder;

(q) to appoint one or more of their own number to act as solicitor or agent in any other capacity and to allow him or them the same remuneration to which he or they would have been entitled if not a trustee or trustees;

(r) to appoint one or more trustees resident out of the United Kingdom and themselves to resign office;

(s) to carry on the administration of the trust hereby created in some place out of the United Kingdom;

(t) to renounce for themselves and their successors in office the power to exercise any of the foregoing powers in this purpose as if the same were vested in them beneficially and not as trustees.

SEVEN   My trustees shall not be liable for depreciation in value of the property in my estate, nor for omissions or errors in judgement, nor for neglect in management, nor for insolvency of debtors, nor for the acts, omissions, neglects or defaults of each other or of any agent employed by them.

EIGHT In the event of my said wife predeceasing me whilst any of my children are in minority, I appoint as Guardian to such of my children as are in minority as at my date of death my sister-in-law, HELEN COLCLOUGH, residing at Four Edzell Avenue, Glasgow.

NINE I declare that my domicile is Scottish.

LASTLY I hereby revoke and cancel all prior wills and testamentary writings made or granted by me: IN WITNESS WHEREOF

AUTHOR'S NOTE RE: FOREGOING WILL

This will is granted by a testator who is married, who has young children (and who may have more) and is sufficiently wealthy to make full use of his nil-rate band in the event of him pre-deceasing wife.
The following points should be noted:

- Purpose FOUR is a legacy of a nil-rate band to Mr McBride's children subject always to the full accumulation and maintenance trust provisions appearing later in the document.
- Mr McBride is obviously confident that whatever the nil-rate band might amount to, from time to time, removal of the same from the estate passing to his wife would not leave Mrs McBride in a difficult financial position. This is a point which should always be clarified with clients who wish to make use of a nil-rate legacy clause. Albeit unlikely, if the Chancellor were to increase the nil-rate band to £500,000, this could totally distort Mr and Mrs McBride's financial planning following Mr McBride's death.
- Purpose FIVE represents a full accumulation and maintenance trust with income vesting at the age of 21 years and capital vesting at the age of 25 years.
- Mr McBride has decided to appoint his sister-in-law as guardian to minor children in the event of he and his wife being killed in a mutual catastrophe. He has, however, quite sensibly recognised that being a guardian to minor children can be an expensive responsibility. He has therefore (in terms of purpose FIVE) empowered his trustees to offer financial support to the guardian.

A WILL INCORPORATING A DISCRETIONARY TRUST

I, MRS MARJORIE ANTON, residing at Flat 1/1, Nineteen Walton Street, Glasgow in order to settle the succession to my means and estate upon my death do provide as follows:

ONE   I appoint as my Trustees and Executors my husband, ANTONY ANTON, residing with me at Flat 1/1, Nineteen Walton Street, aforesaid and KERRY BLACK and PAUL DUFFUS, both solicitors of One hundred West Regent Street, Glasgow (all hereinafter referred to as "my trustees").

TWO   I direct my trustees to make payment of my lawful debts and funeral expenses and of the expenses of winding up my estate.

THREE   I direct my trustees to give effect to any writings granted by me, however informal they may be provided they are signed by me, dated after the date hereof and are clearly expressive of my intention as to which my trustees shall be the sole judges. Any bequests so made shall be free of interest, delivery expenses and government taxes unless otherwise stipulated.

FOUR   If my husband, the said Antony Anton, survives me for thirty clear days from the date of my death but in such event only, I direct my trustees to hold a sum or property (including my one half *pro indiviso* share in Flat 1/1, Nineteen Walton Street, aforesaid) to the value of TWO HUNDRED THOUSAND POUNDS (£200,000) (hereinafter referred to as "the Discretionary Fund") for such one or more of:

(a) My said husband;
(b) My issue (including adopted issue);
(c) Any Trust established by any person (including by my trustees) for the benefit, (whether of an income or a capital or discretionary nature) of any one or more of the foregoing persons (all of whom are referred to as "the beneficiaries") and in such shares or proportions as my trustees may by minute or minutes at any time or times within two years of my husband's death determine; declaring:
(i) that my trustees may by such minute or minutes grant legacies, shares of residue, interests in income or prospective or contingent interests of any kind in the whole or any part or parts of the discretionary fund subject to such provisions as they may determine, including but without prejudice to the foregoing generality provisions as to the accumulation of income, the vesting of capital in any beneficiary, the granting to any beneficiary or any other person of powers to

appoint rights to income or capital, and the continuation of their discretionary powers;

(ii) that my trustees may at any time before the death of my said husband lend the Discretionary Fund or any part thereof to him subject to their accepting in satisfaction thereof a personal obligation to repay such loan on demand by my trustees. Such personal obligation will include such other terms as my trustees see fit including without prejudice to the foregoing generality the provision of interest, index linking of the sum payable and a requirement to give such security including heritable security, as my trustees shall require. My trustees shall be under no obligation to demand repayment of the loan and may waive payment of any income or capital due in respect thereof. Further, my trustees shall not be liable if my said husband becomes unable to make any repayment or if any security which has been given for the loan becomes inadequate or for any other loss which may occur in the exercise of this power. The provisions of this sub-clause shall not be exercisable so as to give any person an interest in possession in the Discretionary Fund.

(iii) that my trustees may renounce for themselves and their successors in office the power to exercise any of the foregoing powers as if the same were vested in them beneficially and not as trustees;

(iv) that until the expiry of the period of two years from the date of my husband's death, or until the date or dates when any such determination or power to make a determination is renounced by them, my trustees shall pay and apply the whole of the income of the Discretionary Fund without any apportionment being made to or for behoof of any one or more of the beneficiaries in such shares or proportions and in such manner as they may determine with power during the said period or until the said date or dates, to accumulate the income for twenty one years; and

(v) that in the event of my trustees having failed to make a determination taking effect in relation to the whole or any part of the Discretionary Fund before the expiry of two years from the date of my husband's death or having renounced the power to make such a determination they shall on and from the expiry of the said period or the date of such renunciation hold the whole or such part of the Discretionary Fund as part of the residue of my estate as if my husband had pre-deceased me.

FIVE   I direct my Trustees to pay and make over a sum of TWENTY THOUSAND POUNDS (£20,000) Sterling and that free of government taxes and duties payable upon my death but without interest to date of payment equally between my daughters, JANE ANTON, residing at Twenty Five Crest Gardens, Inverness and KATE ANTON, residing at Four Baronsgate Street, Edinburgh or wholly to the survivor of them but declaring that in the event of either of my children predeceasing me leaving issue who shall survive me then such issue shall take equally between or among them *per stirpes* if more than one the share to which his, her or their parent would have succeeded had such parent survived me.

SIX   I bequeath free of all government taxes and duties payable upon my death but without interest to date of payment a legacy of ONE THOUSAND POUNDS (£1,000) STERLING to NSE SCOTLAND, (Charity Number SCO 23490), having the Chief Office in Scotland at Five Arneston Street, Glasgow; declaring that in the event of the said Charity changing its name, amalgamating, transferring its assets to another body or being misnamed or otherwise incorrectly designed, then I direct my trustees to make payment of the said legacy to such other body as in their sole discretion they shall consider to have the same or similar aims and objectives as the said charity, the receipt by the treasurer of the time being of any such body being a sufficient discharge to be trustees.

SEVEN   I bequeath the whole residue and remainder of my means and estate to my husband, the said Antony Anton, provided he survives me for thirty clear days from the date of my death; If my said husband fails to survive as aforesaid but in such event only I direct my trustees to make over the residue and remainder of my means and estate equally between my said daughters or wholly to the survivor of them but declaring that in the event of either of my said daughters predeceasing me leaving issue who shall survive me then such issue shall take equally between or among them *per stirpes* if more than one the share to which his, her or their parent would have succeeded had such parent survived me.

EIGHT   Declaring that if any part of the residue of my estate falls to a beneficiary who has not attained the age of twenty five years then my trustees shall hold the same in accordance with purpose NINE.

NINE   I direct my trustees to hold any part of my estate for a beneficiary under the age of twenty five years (which is referred to as "the trust fund") for the following purposes:

(a) for such beneficiaries contingently on their attaining a vested interest as after provided for;

(b) to accumulate the income arising from the trust fund by investing all surplus thereof and the resulting income therefrom in accordance with the powers hereafter conferred until such beneficiaries respectively attain the age of twenty-one years;

(c) for payment of the income of the share of the trust fund to which any of the beneficiaries is prospectively entitled to such beneficiary from the attainment by him or her of the age of twenty-one until he or she attains a vested interest as provided for in the immediately succeeding paragraph;

(d) for payment of an equal share of the capital of the trust fund and the income accumulated prior to his or her acquiring a vested interest in the income to such beneficiaries on their respectively attaining the age of twenty-five years and subject as aftermentioned the said capital and accumulated income shall not vest in any of such children or issue until the date of payment of his or her share;

(e) if any of such beneficiaries fail to attain a vested interest by reason of his or her predeceasing leaving issue (including adopted issue), each member of a generation of issue of such predeceasing beneficiary as survives and attains the age of twenty-five years shall share equally in the share of the trust fund, both original and accresced, which would have fallen to its parent if in life; and if any of such beneficiaries fail to attain a vested interest as before provided for leaving no issue who survive me and attain the age of twenty-five, to hold the share of the trust fund and any income accumulated at the date of such failure for behoof of the beneficiaries who would have been entitled if such beneficiary had never existed;

(f) if any accumulation of income of the fund is prohibited by law by reason of any event the income affected by such prohibition shall be paid or applied to or for such beneficiaries for the time being presumptively entitled to the capital of the trust fund or that part thereof from which such income arose;

(g) my trustees may apply for the maintenance, education or benefit of any beneficiary of a share of the trust fund (a) the income thereof including accumulated income in whole or in part and (b) the capital thereof in whole or in part, and such advances shall vest on payment or such application;

(h) my trustees may appoint at any time or times and in whole or in part that the age at which a beneficiary would otherwise become entitled to a

share of the capital of the trust fund or to a right
to the income thereof shall be advanced to such
earlier age as they may decide, and if any such
appointment is revocable it shall unless earlier
revoked become irrevocable when and to the
extent that it shall become operative;

(i)   my trustees shall have power, in relation to any
part of the trust fund of which a beneficiary is then
entitled to the income, to appoint that such part of
the trust fund or any part or parts of the income or
capital thereof shall be held for such trust purposes, together with such limitations, conditions
and provisions for accumulation, maintenance,
education and advancement for the benefit of such
beneficiary alone or of such beneficiary's issue or
the spouses of any of these person, or of any other
person or persons whom such beneficiary desires
to be included as beneficiaries, or of him or her
and them, and generally with such powers and
discretions exercisable by my trustees or by any
other person or persons and on such terms as my
trustees shall think fit;

(j)   there shall be no apportionment as between capital
and income on any occasion;

TEN   If any part of my estate is held for a beneficiary who
lacks full legal capacity my trustees shall have full power
either to pay or apply the whole or any part of the
income or capital falling to such beneficiary for his or
her behoof in any manner my trustees may think
proper, or to retain the same until such capacity is
attained accumulating income with capital, or to pay
over the same to the legal guardian or the person for
the time being having the custody of such beneficiary
whose receipt shall be a sufficient discharge to my
trustees;

ELEVEN   In the event of any benefit conferred by this will being
renounced in whole or in part the benefit or such part
or parts thereof shall pass to the beneficiary or beneficiaries who would have been entitled and on the terms
and conditions which would have applied had the
beneficiary so renouncing predeceased me;

TWELVE   My trustees shall have the fullest powers of and in
regard to retention, realisation, investment, appropriation, transfer of property without realisation, and management of my estate as if they were absolute beneficial
owners; and shall have power to do everything they may
consider necessary or expedient for the administration
of the trusts; and in particular and without prejudice to
these general powers my trustees shall have power;

(a) to retain, sell, purchase, lease or hire the estate or any part thereof;

(b) to invest the whole or any part of the estate in heritable and leasehold property, investments, securities, insurance policies, deposits and other assets of whatever description, whether producing income or not, whether or not falling within the class of investments authorised for trust funds, whether or not payable to bearer, and wherever situated;

(c) to effect, maintain and acquire policies of insurance of whatever description; and to insure any property on whatever terms they think fit including on a first loss basis;

(d) to administer and manage any heritable or real property forming part of the estate; to repair, maintain, renew and improve the same and to erect additional buildings and structures; to grant, vary and terminate lease and rights of tenancy or occupancy; to plant, thin and cut down timber; to work or let minerals; all as my trustees may think proper and as if they were absolute owners of the estate;

(e) to continue or to commence any business, whether alone or in conjunction or in partnership with any other persons, or through any companies, for such period as my trustees may think proper; to appoint or employ a trustee or any other person in any capacity in relation to such business and to pay to them suitable remuneration for services, including pension provisions for any employees or their dependants; and to delegate or entrust to any persons the control and management of such business to such extent as my trustees may think fit; and my trustees:

   (i) may apply for the purposes of such business such part of the income or capital as they think proper;

   (ii) shall exercise only such control or supervision of such business as they shall think fit;

   (iii) shall be entitled to be relieved from the estate from all personal responsibility for any loss arising from such business operations; and

   (iv) shall be entitled to retain personally any remuneration for their services;

(f) to borrow or lend with or without security; and to grant or continue any guarantee or indemnity for the benefit of any beneficiary actual or prospective;

(g) to lend or allow to be used the whole or any part of the estate at such rate of interest or rent as they may consider appropriate, or free of interest or rent, to or by any person who is for the time being entitled to payment of a share of the income of the estate or to whom or for whose benefit the income may be paid or applied in the exercise of a discretion then available to my trustees;

(h) to allow the estate or any part thereof to be registered in the names of or held or the documents of title to be held by any person, firm, corporation or other body as nominee of my trustees;

(i) revocably to delegate any power or powers of making, managing, realising or otherwise dealing with any investment or deposit comprised in the estate to any person or persons upon such terms as to remuneration or otherwise as my Trustees may think fit and no trustee shall be responsible for the default of any such agent if the trustee in question employed him in good faith;

(j) to accept as an addition to my estate any other property as may be made over to them;

(k) to decide what is capital and what is income and the proportion in which expenses are to be charged against capital and income respectively;

(l) to set apart and appropriate specific property of any description to represent the whole or part of the share, prospective or otherwise, of any beneficiary at such valuation as my trustees shall determine, so that thereafter the particular share or part shall have the full benefit and the whole risk of the appropriated investments of assets;

(m) to settle with any beneficiary entitled to any part of the estate by conveying to him or her in satisfaction thereof either specific property or money, or partly one and partly the other, as to my trustees shall seem proper and at such valuation as they shall determine and to compel acceptance accordingly;

(n) to enter into any transaction or do any act otherwise authorised by law or by this deed notwithstanding that any trustee is or might be acting as *auctor in rem suam* or with a conflict of interest between such trustee and himself as an individual or as trustee of any other trust or any partnership of which a trustee is a partner or any company of which a trustee is a shareholder or director or in relation to any combination of these capacities provided that the trustee or trustees with whom there is or may be any such conflict is or are not the sole trustee or trustees;

(o) to participate in the exercise of any discretion granted to my trustees notwithstanding that a trustee is or may be a or the sole beneficiary in

whose favour the discretion is then exercised provided that there is at least one trustee not so
favoured;

(p) to resign office notwithstanding any benefit
hereunder;

(q) to appoint one or more of their own number to act
as solicitor or agent in any other capacity and to
allow him or them the same remuneration to
which he or they would have been entitled if not a
trustee or trustees;

(r) to appoint one or more trustees resident out of the
United Kingdom and themselves to resign office;

(s) to carry on the administration of the trust hereby
created in some place out of the United Kingdom;

(t) to renounce for themselves and their successors in
office the power to exercise any of the foregoing
powers in this purpose as if the same were vested
in them beneficially and not as trustees.

THIRTEEN   My trustees shall not be liable for depreciation in value
of the property in my estate, nor for omissions or errors
in judgement, nor for neglect in management, nor for
insolvency of debtors, nor for the acts, omissions,
neglects or defaults of each other or of any agent
employed by them;

FOURTEEN   I declare that my domicile is Scottish.

LASTLY   I hereby revoke and cancel all prior wills and testamentary writings made or granted by me: IN WITNESS
WHEREOF

AUTHOR'S NOTE RE: FOREGOING STYLE

This will incorporates various features which require careful consideration:

- Purpose FOUR represents a degree of IHT planning but not to the extent of the full nil-rate band. The purpose creates a discretionary trust which offers a degree of IHT mitigation planning, making use of Mrs Anton's interest in the dwelling-house at Walton Street, Glasgow.
- The intention is, in truth, that Mrs Anton's one-half interest in the flat should pass into the discretionary trust. This should then be "sold" to her surviving husband for its market value as at her date of death. However, Mr Anton is not required to pay the cash price but rather, will grant a standard security in favour of Mrs Anton's trustees for the value of the property conveyed by them to Mr Anton.
- The normal format of a discretionary legacy has been amended so as to specifically empower the trustees to take the steps hereinbefore detailed.
- The strategy in question works only if the title to the property does not contain a "survivorship" destination. If clients wish to make use of this strategy, then the title to their heritable property will require to be checked and any existing "survivorship" destination evacuated. It is recommended that this be effected by means of conveyance by the clients in favour of themselves, excising any reference to "survivorship". Such a deed is not an alienation, and the keeper will (provided the effect of the deed is explained to him) record or register the same against payment of recording/registration dues of £22. The author would suggest that there is no point in framing a will of the type hereinbefore indicated unless the title has been checked and put into proper order. Failure to do so may amount to professional negligence.
- It should be emphasised to clients (owing to fears that what is being granted is a "traditional mortgage" requiring payment of interest or repayment of capital) that nothing need be paid by the surviving spouse until he/she has passed on. At that point, and on the reasonable basis that the dwellinghouse in question will be sold, the value secured by the standard security will be repaid to the trustees of the predecessor (who can then distribute the same to the true, intended, ultimate beneficiaries (normally adult children)) hopefully free of IHT. The debt secured by the standard security is, however, a heritable debt in the estate of the survivor and the value of that security can be deducted from the survivor's gross estate (without, in any way, affecting the right of the executors of the survivor also to claim the nil-rate band of the survivor) thereby reducing the estate of the survivor for IHT purposes.
- The strategy is very flexible. This is demonstrated by the terms of paragraph (b) of purpose FOUR.
- It is recommended that Mrs Anton should grant a letter of expression of wish detailing how she would like purpose FOUR

to be operated. This could be of some importance if the trustees (other than her surviving spouse) were wholly unfamiliar with this type of IHT planning.

- In this particular case, Mrs Anton is confident that 19 Walton Street will be her last property jointly owned with her husband. The draftsman has been persuaded by her assurances on that point. However, it is suggested that it might be more prudent to amend the clause to make reference to any other dwellinghouse jointly owned by Mr and Mrs Anton as their matrimonial home as at Mrs Anton's date of death.

Care has to be taken in the drafting of this clause. Some concern has been expressed as to whether or not a clause of this type would offend against the pre-owned assets of rules introduced by the Chancellor in The Finance Act of 2004. It is the view of the author that the clause does not offend against those rules particularly given the exemption in respect of spouses as indicated by the Inland Revenue. However, there is a possibility of conflict with the pre-owned assets rules in certain circumstances. Let us imagine that the procedure outlined in purpose FOUR has been carried through. Thereafter, after a few years, the surviving spouse indicates that it is too big for him. He wishes to purchase another, smaller, house but cannot do so if he is required by the trustees of the predeceasing spouse to fully repay the amount secured by the relevant standard security—he will have insufficient funds to purchase a new house

As indicated, care requires to be taken regarding the valuation of the one-half *pro indiviso* share of Mrs Anton's property as at her date of death. If house prices have increased to the extent that her one half interest exceeds the nil-rate band available to Mrs Anton as at her date of death then, obviously, the trustees could not make use of all of her one-half *pro indiviso* share in and to the property. If considered necessary, purpose FOUR could be amended to refer to "an appropriate part of my one-half *pro indiviso* share". Bear in mind that the value of an one half interest in a property is not the same as the value of the property divided by two—this is a viewpoint accepted by the Inland Revenue.

Subject as aforesaid, the terms of purpose FIVE amount to further IHT mitigation.

Purpose SIX is an example of "best practice" in relation to description of a charity. Where the charity is properly named (including reference being made to the exact charity number of the body in question) difficulties arising with description should be avoided.

Mrs Anton is also concerned that in the event of any young beneficiaries coming into line of succession, some protection should be built in against their own financial naivety. To achieve this, she has incorporated a full accumulation and maintenance trust.

A SIMPLE CODICIL

I, HARRY PRINCE, residing formerly at One Black Street, Gourock and now at Three Brownview Place there do hereby make the following codicil to my will dated Thirty first July, Two thousand and One, namely:

ONE
> I hereby cancel and revoke the legacy of FIVE THOUSAND POUNDS (£5,000) STERLING bequeathed in terms of purpose FIVE of my said will to JOHN SMITH, designed in my said will.

TWO
> With regard to the pecuniary legacies left to each of my nephews who shall survive me in terms of purpose SIX of my said will, I hereby direct that the issue of all such nephews is expressly excluded.

THREE
> I bequeath to SAINT LUKE'S CHURCH OF SCOTLAND, Church Street, Milngavie, a legacy of ONE THOUSAND POUNDS (£1,000) STERLING.

FOUR
> I hereby record that JOSEPH BLOGGS designed in purpose SIX of my said WILL now resides at 50 Muir Terrace, Gourock.

Save as hereinbefore amended I hereby confirm and ratify the terms of my said will: IN WITNESS WHEREOF

AUTHOR'S NOTE RE: FOREGOING SIMPLE CODICIL

Harry has changed address since granting his will. This is recorded in simple fashion in the codicil.

Harry has decided to cancel one of the legacies bequeathed in terms of his will. The draftsman should, of course, check to ensure that there was no over-destination regarding that legacy (as it may well be that Harry would still have wished the "substitute" legatee to have benefited).

The draftsman has noted that Harry has left legacies to his nephews in terms of his will. Having clarified Harry's wishes, the draftsman has taken the opportunity to negative the *conditio si institutu* by expressly excluding in each case the issue of the nephew.

Harry wishes to include a new legacy of £1,000 to his church. The following points should be noted:

- It is advisable to specify the denomination of the church and its exact address. The draftsman has also checked that the will contains a general clause "negativing" interest on a legacy left by any writing as also that the will contains a power in favour of the executors to take a receipt from any authorised official of the church.
- Although it is not necessary to make a codicil to record changes of address, Harry has conveniently recorded a change of address for one of the beneficiaries named in the will.
- Although not strictly necessary, in terms of the final paragraph of the codicil, Harry has confirmed that, save as amended by this document, the underlying will remains in full force and effect.

POWER OF ATTORNEY NO.1

(complying with the provisions of the Adults with Incapacity (Scotland) Act 2000)

I, [   ], residing at [   ] CONSIDERING that I am desirous of appointing a suitable person or persons to manage my affairs, and in the event of my being incapable in terms of the Act aftermentioned to take decisions about my personal welfare and having confidence in the persons afternamed DO HEREBY APPOINT [   ] whom failing in the event of the said pre-deceasing me, or having taken up office under these presents thereafter being unable to act in terms of these presents for any reason [   ] and the survivor of them or either of them alone as my continuing attorney and also as my welfare attorney (and all hereinafter referred to as "my attorney" the singular including the plural where the context so requires) in terms of sections 15 and 16 of the Adults With Incapacity (Scotland) Act 2000 (which Act and any subsequent amendment thereof is referred to as "the Act") and that with effect from the date of these presents and that on the following terms and conditions:

ONE   My attorney shall have the following powers ("the powers").

(a) To open, operate, overdraw and close any account in my name at any bank, building society or other institution, and to operate on, overdraw and close any existing such account in my name.

(b) To execute and deliver deeds and documents, including without prejudice to the said generality, dispositions, leases or standard securities in respect of any heritable property belonging to me.

(c) To maintain, and to pay any expense in connection with me and my property.

(d) To deposit for safe custody in any bank or other depository any property or document and to withdraw any property or document deposited by me or on my account.

(e) To effect, pay the premiums on, alter or surrender any insurance policy of any description, and to effect any new insurances of any description which my attorney may, in his sole discretion, consider appropriate.

(f) To take possession of, and complete my title to, any interest in property.

(g) To make, settle, compromise, discharge and refer to arbitration, and raise, defend, compromise and settle any court action and enforce any decree in respect of, any claim.

(h) To make tax returns and settle, adjust and compromise and claim for tax or any tax refund.

(i) To attend and vote, in person or by proxy, at any meeting of any company or corporation in respect of any investment and to exercise any right arising from it.

(j) To appoint a solicitor, accountant, stockbroker and other professional advisers.

(k) To buy, lease, sell and otherwise deal with any interest which I may have in property both heritable and moveable.

(l) To make, purchase, vary and dispose of investments (including any pension or life assurance policies held by me), whether stock exchange or unlisted investments or otherwise and to take up or refuse or renounce rights issues, to accept or reject offers and bids, to accept or renounce bonus issues and, without prejudice to the foregoing, generally to handle my investment portfolio, to arrange investment in or purchase of any insurance or product designed or intended to defray or to assist in defraying the costs of long term care for me.

(m) To have access to any information regarding my financial affairs and to have access to confidential information regarding the provisions of my will and/or any codicil thereto, any trust in which I am a settlor or one of the beneficiaries, and any information held on me under any statute and in respect of which I myself would have been entitled to require the release of such information.

(n) To borrow and grant security for any sum, binding me and my executors or personal representatives jointly and severally in that regard.

(o) To claim any social security or other benefits to which I may be entitled and to demand, sue for and recover all debts, claims and sums of money or property due or which may become due to me or be exigible by me on any account or in any manner of way and to give time for payment of any debt or claim and to grant receipts or discharges therefor; any persons paying money or transferring property to my attorney shall not be concerned with the application thereof by my attorney.

(p) To engage in inheritance tax planning on my behalf including without prejudice to the said generality to make gifts of my property and assets of whatever nature and wheresoever situated to my spouse or to any of my children or remoter issue, or to any charity or organisation to whom I may have made previous such gifts as also to any trust established for the administration of my affairs; to make gifts to disposals into any trust created by me or in which I am one of the settlors; to establish any trust (including a discretionary trust) for the benefit of any of the foregoing persons or bodies and where appropriate in the judgement of my attorney to pay any tax chargeable or arising in respect of any such gifts.

(q) To make payments of an alimentary nature to or on behalf of my spouse or to or on behalf of any of my children or remoter issue as my attorney in his or her sole discretion shall consider to be reasonable.

(r) Generally to do everything with regard to my estate and affairs which I could have done myself without limitation by reason of anything herein contained or any incapacity on my part, whether mental or physical, occurring after the date of the granting of these presents, it being my intention that the powers shall subsist and remain in full force and effect notwithstanding incapacity as defined by the Act on my part.

(s) (i) To decide what care and accommodation may be appropriate for me.

(ii) To consent to any medical treatment or procedure or therapy of whatever nature my Attorney may decide is for my benefit and may provide access for that, or may refuse such consent.

(iii) To make decisions about my dress, diet and personal appearance.

(iv) To make decisions regarding my taking part in educative or social activities, holidays, travel and other pastimes.

(v) To exercise any rights of access which I may have in relation to personal data and records.

(vi) To take any proceedings, legal or otherwise, on my behalf in relation to my personal welfare and the above matters hereinbefore detailed.

(vii) To pay for holidays for me and one or more of my carers so far as my attorney in his or her sole discretion may consider appropriate.

(viii) To pay for items (including a motor car) or service which, in the sole opinion of my attorney is for my benefit; the said power shall include power to pay for, repair, improve or replace any such item or service.

TWO   My attorney shall be entitled to exercise the powers until my attorney receives actual written notice of recall of his or her appointment in terms hereof; all powers hereby conferred maybe exercised by either of the said [   ] or the survivor of them alone.

THREE   All acts and deeds granted by my attorney in exercise of the powers shall be as binding upon me as if they were my acts or deeds granted by me.

FOUR My attorney shall not be personally liable for acts and omissions as attorney unless he or she is shown to have been wilfully and grossly negligent and in particular my attorney shall not be liable for depreciation of investments made in virtue of this power of attorney or in terms hereof.

FIVE My attorney (whether acting as continuing or welfare attorney or both) shall be bound by acceptance hereof to account to me for intromissions in virtue hereof and to make payment to me of whatever balance may be due to me after deduction of any remuneration for services including remuneration on the appropriate scale for any professional services rendered and all charges and expenses upon being relieved of all obligations and liabilities undertaken or incurred on my behalf; further declaring that my attorney shall incur no responsibility whatever on account of or in respect of the actings, intromissions and management of any bankers, brokers or other agents employed in terms of the powers: IN WITNESS WHEREOF

CERTIFICATE

This certificate is incorporated in the power of attorney subscribed by the granter, on [   ] 2004 which confers a continuing power of attorney on [   ] whom failing [   ] and [   ].

I certify that:

A.   I interviewed the granter on [   ] 2004 immediately before the granter subscribed this continuing power of attorney and;

B.   I am satisfied that, at the time this continuing power of attorney was granted, the granter understood its nature and extent. I have satisfied myself of this because of my own knowledge of the granter and;

C.   I have no reason to believe that the granter was acting under undue influence or that any other factor vitiates the granting of this continuing power of attorney.

[   ] 2004

Signatory's Name: [   ]
Profession: Solicitor
Business Address: 100 West Regent Street,
                       Glasgow G2 2QB

NOTE: Any person signing the Certificate should not be the person to whom the continuing Power of Attorney has been granted.

CERTIFICATE

This Certificate is incorporated in the power of attorney subscribed by the granter, on [   ] 2004 which confers a welfare power of attorney on [   ] whom failing [   ] and [   ].

I certify that:

A.   I interviewed the granter on [   ] 2004 immediately before the granter subscribed this welfare power of attorney and;

B.   I am satisfied that, at the time this welfare power of attorney was granted, the granter understood its nature and extent. I have satisfied myself of this because of my own knowledge of the granter and;

C.   I have no reason to believe that the granter was acting under undue influence or that any other factor vitiates the granting of this welfare power of attorney.

[   ] 2004

Signatory's Name: [   ]
Profession: Solicitor
Business Address: 100 West Regent Street,
                               Glasgow G2 2QB

NOTE: Any person signing the certificate should not be the person to whom the welfare power of attorney has been granted.

POWER OF ATTORNEY NO.2

I, [   ], residing at [   ] CONSIDERING that I am desirous of appointing a suitable person or persons to manage my affairs, and in the event of my being incapable in terms of the Act aftermentioned to take decisions about my personal welfare and having confidence in the persons afternamed DO HEREBY APPOINT [   ] whom failing in the event of him predeceasing me, or having taken up office under these presents thereafter being unable to act in terms of these presents for any reason, [   ] as my continuing attorney and also as my welfare attorney (and both hereinafter referred to as "my attorney" the singular including the plural where the context so requires) in terms of sections 15 and 16 of the Adults With Incapacity (Scotland) Act 2000 (which Act and any subsequent amendment thereof is referred to as "the Act") and that with effect from the date of these presents and that on the following terms and conditions:

ONE   My attorney shall have the following powers ("the powers").

    (a) To open, operate, overdraw and close any account in my name at any bank, building society or other institution, and to operate on, overdraw and close any existing such account in my name.

    (b) To execute and deliver deeds and documents, including without prejudice to the said generality, dispositions, leases or standard securities in respect of any heritable property belonging to me.

    (c) To maintain, and to pay any expense in connection with me and my property.

    (d) To deposit for safe custody in any bank or other depository any property or document and to withdraw any property or document deposited by me or on my account.

    (e) To effect, pay the premiums on, alter or surrender any insurance policy of any description, and to effect any new insurances of any description which my attorney may in his sole discretion consider appropriate.

    (f) To take possession of, and complete my title to, any interest in property.

    (g) To make, settle, compromise, discharge and refer to arbitration, and raise, defend, compromise and settle any court action and enforce any decree in respect of, any claim.

    (h) To make tax returns and settle, adjust and compromise and claim for tax, or any tax refund.

    (i) To attend and vote, in person or by proxy, at any meeting of any company or corporation in respect of any investment and to exercise any right arising from it.

(j)　To appoint a solicitor, accountant, stockbroker and other professional advisers.

(k)　To buy, lease, sell and otherwise deal with any interest which I may have in property both heritable and moveable.

(l)　To make, purchase, vary and dispose of investments (including any pension or life assurance policies held by me), whether stock exchange or unlisted investments or otherwise and to take up or refuse or renounce rights issues, to accept or reject offers and bids, to accept or renounce bonus issues and, without prejudice to the foregoing, generally to handle my investment portfolio; to arrange investment in or purchase of any insurance or product designed or intended to defray or to assist in defraying the costs of long term care for me.

(m)　To have access to any information regarding my financial affairs and to have access to confidential information regarding the provisions of my will and/or any codicil thereto, any trust in which I am a settlor or one of the beneficiaries, and any information held on me under any statute and in respect of which I myself would have been entitled to require the release.

(n)　To borrow and grant security for any sum, binding me and my executors or personal representatives jointly and severally in that regard.

(o)　To claim any social security benefits to which I may be entitled and to demand, sue for and recover all debts, claims and sums of money or property due or which may become due to me or be exigible by me on any account or in any manner of way and to give time for payment of any debt or claim and to grant receipts of discharges therefor; any persons paying money or transferring property to my attorney shall not be concerned with the application thereof by my attorney.

(p)　To engage in inheritance tax planning on my behalf including without prejudice to the said generality to make gifts of my property and assets of whatever nature and wheresoever situated to any of my children or remoter issue, or to any charity or organisation to whom I may have made previous such gifts as also to any trust established for the administration of my affairs; to make gifts or disposals into any trust created by me or in which I am one of the settlors; to establish any trust (including a discretionary trust) for the benefit of any of the foregoing persons or bodies and where appropriate in the judgement of my attorney to pay any tax chargeable or arising in respect of any such gifts or trust (including the expenses of creation or management thereof).

(q) To make payments of an alimentary nature to any of my children or remoter issue so far as my attorney may consider the same to be necessary or reasonable.

(r) Generally to do everything with regard to my estate and affairs which I could have done myself without limitation by reason of anything herein contained or any incapacity on my part, whether mental or physical, occurring after the date of the granting of these presents, it being my intention that the powers shall subsist and remain in full force and effect notwithstanding incapacity as defined by the Act on my part.

(s) (i)   To decide what care and accommodation may be appropriate for me.

(ii) To consent to any medical treatment or procedure or therapy of whatever nature my attorney may decide is for my benefit and may provide access for that, or may refuse such consent.

(iii) To make decisions about my dress, diet and personal appearance.

(iv) To make decisions regarding my taking part in educative or social activities, holidays, travel and other pastimes.

(v)   To exercise any rights of access which I may have in relation to personal data and records.

(vi) To take any proceedings, legal or otherwise, on my behalf in relation to my personal welfare and the above matters hereinbefore detailed.

(vii) To pay for holidays for me and one or more of my carers so far as my attorney in his or her sole discretion may consider appropriate.

(viii) To pay for items (including a motor car) or service which in the sole opinion of my attorney is for my benefit; the said power shall include power to pay for, repair, improve or replace any such item or service.

TWO   My attorney shall be entitled to exercise the powers until my attorney receives actual written notice of recall of his or her appointment in terms hereof.

THREE   All acts and deeds granted by my attorney in exercise of the powers shall be as binding upon me as if they were my acts or deeds granted by me.

FOUR   My attorney shall not be personally liable for acts and omissions as attorney unless he or she is shown to have been wilfully and grossly negligent and in particular my attorney shall not be liable for depreciation of investments made in virtue of this power of attorney or in terms hereof.

FIVE

My attorney (whether acting as continuing or welfare attorney or both) shall be bound by acceptance hereof to account to me for intromissions in virtue hereof and to make payment to me of whatever balance may be due to me after deduction of any remuneration for services including remuneration on the appropriate scale for any professional services rendered and all charges and expenses upon being relieved of all obligations and liabilities undertaken or incurred on my behalf; Further declaring that my attorney shall incur no responsibility whatever on account of or in respect of the actings, intromissions and management of any bankers, brokers or other agents employed in terms of the powers: IN WITNESS WHEREOF

CERTIFICATE

This certificate is incorporated in the power of attorney subscribed by the granter, [   ] on [   ] 2004 which confers a continuing power of attorney on [   ] whom failing [   ]

I certify that:

A.   I interviewed the granter on [   ] 2004 immediately before the granter subscribed this continuing power of attorney and;

B.   I am satisfied that, at the time this continuing power of attorney was granted, the granter understood its nature and extent. I have satisfied myself of this because of my own knowledge of the granter and;

C.   I have no reason to believe that the granter was acting under undue influence or that any other factor vitiates the granting of this continuing power of attorney.

[   ] 2004

Signatory's Name: [   ]
Profession: Solicitor
Business Address: 100 West Regent Street,
                       Glasgow G2 2QB

NOTE: Any person signing the certificate should not be the person to whom the continuing power of attorney has been granted.

CERTIFICATE

This Certificate is incorporated in the power of attorney subscribed by the granter, [   ] on [   ] 2004 which confers a welfare power of attorney on [   ] whom failing [   ]

I certify that:

A.   I interviewed the granter on [   ] 2004 immediately before the granter subscribed this welfare power of attorney and;

B.   I am satisfied that, at the time this welfare power of attorney was granted, the granter understood its nature and extent. I have satisfied myself of this because of my own knowledge of the granter and;

C.   I have no reason to believe that the granter was acting under undue influence or that any other factor vitiates the granting of this welfare power of attorney.

[   ] 2004

Signatory's Name: [   ]
Profession: Solicitor
Business Address: 100 West Regent Street,
                      Glasgow G2 2QB

NOTE: Any person signing the certificate should not be the person to whom the welfare power of attorney has been granted.

SPRINGING POWERS CLAUSE

My attorney is hereby authorised to obtain from a medical practitioner the certificate hereinafter specified but this apart, and notwithstanding the granting and delivery of these presents and the appointment of my attorney with effect from the date of these presents, the other powers hereby granted shall be suspended and shall be brought into effect only upon either:

ONE   My signing and delivering to my attorney a letter to that effect or

TWO   The issuing by a medical practitioner and delivery to my attorney of a certificate on soul and conscience that I am not capable of looking after my own affairs:

Author's Note Re: Style Powers of Attorney

The reader is referred to the general section on powers of attorney. The first draft is suitable for appointment of the granter's spouse whom failing adult children. In paragraphs (p) and (q) specific reference is made to the spouse. The second style makes no such reference to a spouse and would be more suitable for use in relation to a widow/widower. A warning note here—bear in mind that slavish use of styles is to be avoided. Use of the "non-spouse" style when there is, in fact, a spouse could occasion some difficulty (for example, if the attorney wished to make an alimentary payment to the spouse).

Bear in mind the cautionary note in the foregoing text regarding exercise of the powers detailed in paragraph (p). With regard to paragraph (s), this represents the "welfare" powers which will only come into effect on loss of capacity of the granter. Although the styles make no mention of this it might be appropriate, in certain cases, to amend the style to include specific reference to the relevant powers only coming into effect on loss of capacity—in some cases, the granter may see this as a "comfort"—the author has encountered one or two clients who have baulked in the first instance at granting power to an attorney to choose what pyjamas the granter will wear while the granter is still capable of making his/her own choice in that regard!

Some clients will mistake the provisions of paragraph (s) as being equivalent to an advanced medical directive/a living will. This is not the case. This should, perhaps, be pointed out to clients who may otherwise believe that by granting such a power of attorney they are "killing two birds with one stone".

DEED OF VARIATION NO.1
(in favour of a less wealthy member of the family)

DEED OF VARIATION

between

(FIRST) MRS MARION BAX-TER, residing at Eight Lawyers Row, Edinburgh as an individual (hereinafter referred to as "Marion")

(SECOND) ALAN MARTIN , residing at One Brown Street, Gourock as an individual (hereinafter referred to as "Alan")

and

(THIRD) MRS LINDA JOYCE , residing at Forty Lippey Terrace, Cupar, Fife (and hereinafter referred to as "Linda")

(FOURTH) the said MRS MAR-ION BAXTER as Executrix Nominate of the late MRS ISABELLA FORD MARTIN (and in that capacity hereinafter referred to as "the Executor")

WHEREAS MRS ISABELLA FORD MARTIN (hereinafter referred to as "Mrs Martin"), who resided latterly at Eighty-two Village Court, Crossmyloof, Glasgow died on the Twenty-third November Two thousand and three leaving a will dated First July Two thousand CONSIDERING that Marion is the executor acting under the said will conform to wonfirmation issued in her favour from the Commissariot of the Sheriffdom of Glasgow and Strathkelvin at Glasgow on Tenth January Two thousand and four FURTHER CONSIDERING that Mrs Martin was predeceased by her husband, JAMES MARTIN, who also resided latterly at Eighty-two Village Court, aforesaid and who died on First March Two thousand and two FURTHER CONSIDERING that in terms of her said will, Mrs Martin bequeathed the whole residue and remainder of her means and estate equally between Marion, Alan and Linda and that they have all survived to take in terms of said residuary bequest. FURTHER CONSIDERING that Mrs Martin had no other children and she is not survived by the issue of any predeceasing child, Marion, Alan and Linda being the only parties who can claim legal rights from the estate of the late Mrs Martin AND NOW SEEING with reference to section 142(2) of the Inheritance Tax Act 1984 and section 62(7) of the Taxation of Chargeable Gains Act 1992 as amended and the fact that Mrs Martin died within the last two years, Marion, Alan, Linda and the executor have agreed that they wish to vary the disposition under Mrs Martin's will THEREFORE in implement of the foregoing intention and with reference to the said sections of the said Acts, the parties hereto do hereby vary the will of Mrs Martin as follows:

ONE   The said will shall be deemed to have contained a residuary provision in favour of Marion alone, with no provision for any residuary bequests being made in favour of Alan or Linda.

TWO   Marion, Alan and Linda hereby acknowledge that they have had the opportunity to seek separate and independent legal advice as to the nature and effect of these presents but have declined to do so and they all hereby renounce and disclaim their respective entitlements to claim legal rights or any other rights in and to Mrs Martin's estate.

THREE   The parties hereby undertake to execute any further deeds or instruments required to achieve the purpose of this deed and Marion, Alan and Linda hereby request the executor to proceed to wind up Mrs Martin's estate in accordance with the foregoing provisions.

FOUR   With reference to the said section 142(2) and the said section 62(7), the parties hereby elect and give notice to the Board of Inland Revenue of their intention to have the foregoing deed of variation treated as if the variation hereinbefore detailed had been effected by Mrs Martin in terms of her said will.

FIVE   The executor hereby consents to and concurs in the provisions hereof.

SIX   The parties hereby declare these presents to be revocable and to have been freely granted by them: IN WITNESS WHEREOF

DEED OF VARIATION NO.2
(in respect of an intestacy)

DEED OF VARIATION

by

(*FIRST*) JOHN BLOGS, residing at One Welsh Street, Glasgow Executor Dative of the late MRS.JOSEPHINE BLOGGS, who resided at One Welsh Street, aforesaid (and in that capacity hereinafter referred to as "the Executor")

(*SECOND*) the said JOHN BLOGGS, as an individual (and in that capacity hereinafter referred to as "Mr.Bloggs")

(*THIRD*) DAVID BLOGGS, residing at Twenty one Green Crescent, Glasgow as an individual (and in that capacity hereinafter referred to as "David")

(*FOURTH*) FRASER BLOGGS, residing at Ninety Brown Road, Glasgow, as an individual (and in that capacity hereinafter referred to as "Fraser")

(*FIFTH*) JOANNA BLOGGS, also residing at One Welsh Street, aforesaid as an individual (and in that capacity hereinafter referred to as "Joanna")

WHEREAS

ONE   The said Mrs Josephine Bloggs (hereinafter referred to as "the deceased") died on First January Two thousand and three.

TWO   The deceased was survived by her husband, Mr Bloggs. She was also survived by her three children, David, Fraser and Joanna, being the only children ever born to the deceased, who was not survived by the issue of any predeceasing children.

THREE   The deceased died intestate. Mr Bloggs, David, Fraser and Joanna are her beneficiaries on intestacy in terms of the Succession (Scotland) Act 1964 as amended.

FOUR Mr Bloggs was confirmed the Executor Dative *qua* husband to the deceased in terms of Confirmation in his favour granted by the Commissariot of Glasgow and Strathkelvin at Glasgow on First April Two thousand and three.

LASTLY Mr Bloggs, David, Fraser and Joanna are the only parties whose rights are being varied in terms of this deed of variation.

AND NOW SEEING

That all parties hereto are of full age, capacity and sound mind and have resolved to enter into these presents under section 142 of the Inheritance Tax Act 1984 and section 62(6) of the Taxation of Chargeable Gains Act 1992:

THEREFORE the parties hereto do hereby agree as follows:

FIRST The parties hereby agree that the deceased's estate shall be treated as if she had made a will bequeathing:
(a) Legacies, free of all government taxes and duties but without interest of TWENTY FIVE THOU-SAND POUNDS (£25,000) STERLING to each of David, Fraser and Joanna;
(b) The residue of her estate to Mr Bloggs.

SECOND The parties hereby renounce and discharge their whole respective claims to *ius relicti*, prior rights or *legitim* from the estate of the deceased.

THIRD The whole expenses of preparation, granting, execution and intimation of these presents shall be paid from the estate of the deceased.

FOURTH The executor consents to and concurs in the provisions hereof.

FIFTH The whole parties hereto hereby confirm that they have been advised and have had the opportunity to seek separate and independent legal advice in respect of the nature and effect of these presents and they all hereby freely grant and enter into these presents which are declared by them to be irrevocable.

SIXTH The parties hereto elect and give written notice in terms of these presents to the Board of the Inland Revenue in terms of section 142 of the Inheritance Tax Act 1984 and also in terms of section 62 of the Taxation of Chargeable Gains Act 1992 of their election to have the foregoing variation treated as if it had been effected by the deceased: IN WITNESS WHEREOF

AUTHOR'S NOTE RE: STYLE DEEDS OF VARIATION

The first style is an example of a situation where "better of" members of the family decide to redirect more of their parents' estate to a less well-off sibling. The second is an example of how a Deed of Variation can be used to redirect an intestate estate. Both documents are fairly straight forward and, in truth, are simple examples. They could, however, be adapted for more complex situations (for example, redirecting an asset which otherwise carries "agricultural" or "business property relief" from the spouse to a non-exempt beneficiary).

DEED OF ASSUMPTION NO.1

WE, MRS JESSIE McPHERSON, Widow, residing formerly at Seventy Spring Road, Glasgow, thereafter at Ninety two Glasgow Road, Airdrie, and now at "Sula Bay", Six Hooters Road, Dundee, HUGH McPHERSON, residing sometime at Ninety two Glasgow Road, aforesaid and now at One hundred and eight Barrow Road, Glasgow and JOHN McPHERSON, residing formerly at Ninety two Glasgow Road, aforesaid and now also at One hundred and eight Barrow Road, aforesaid the trustees original and assumed acting under (FIRST) Trust Disposition and Settlement granted by John McPherson, Master Joiner, residing at Seventy Spring Road, aforesaid in favour of me, the said Mrs. Jessie McPherson, ALEXANDER WILLIAMS, residing at Lyddesdale, Six Yellowbrick Road, Glasgow (and who is now deceased) and JAMES ALEXANDER GOODE, Solicitor in Glasgow who declined to accept office under said Trust Disposition and Settlement, dated Twenty third May Nineteen hundred and fifty two and registered in the Books of Council and Session on Twenty fourth April Nineteen hundred and sixty one (SECOND) Deed of Assumption and Conveyance by me the said Mrs Jessie McPherson and the said Alexander Williams in favour of ourselves and the said Hugh McPherson dated Twenty second and registered in the Books of Council and Session on Twenty fourth both days of May Nineteen hundred and sixty one and (THIRD) Deed of Assumption and Conveyance by me the said Mrs. Jessie McPherson, the said Alexander Williams and me the said Hugh McPherson in favour of ourselves and me the said John McPherson dated Sixteenth and registered in the Books of Council and Session on Eighth January Nineteen hundred and sixty three Do Hereby ASSUME as a Trustee under the said Trust Disposition and Settlement MRS. MARY McPHERSON or STEELE, residing at "Sula Bay", Six Hooters Road, Dundee; And we dispone and convey to ourselves the said Mrs. Jessie McPherson, Hugh McPherson and John McPherson and to the said Mrs. Mary McPherson or Steele and the survivors or survivor of us as Trustees or Trustee foresaid ALL and SUNDRY the whole Trust Estate and effects, heritable and moveable, real and personal of every description and wherever situated at present belonging to us or under our control as Trustees under the said Trust Disposition and Settlement together with the whole vouchers, titles and instructions thereof; And I the said Mrs. Mary McPherson or Steele hereby accept office as Trustee foresaid IN WITNESS WHEREOF

DEED OF ASSUMPTION NO. 2
(incorporating resignation)

WE, IAN ALEXANDER, Solicitor, One hundred St Vincent Street, Glasgow and MRS CAROL SMART, residing at One Green Road, Glasgow CONSIDERING that in terms of her Will dated Fourth November Nineteen hundred and ninety five and registered in the Books of Council and Session on Fifth July Two thousand and four MISS PHYLLIS WILLIAMS, residing at "Glenisla", Twenty Blackrod Avenue, Glasgow and who died on Thirteenth May Two thousand and four appointed us the said Ian Alexander and Mrs Carol Smart as her Executors nominate FURTHER CONSIDERING that we have not yet expede Confirmation in our favour upon said Will but that we are desirous of appointing another suitable person to act along with us as Executor Nominate in terms of the said Will THEREFORE we do hereby ASSUME IAN SMITH, residing at Block One, Flat Two, Thirty Main Street, Milngavie, Glasgow as Executor Nominate along with us in terms of the said Will of the said the late Miss Phyllis Williams and as an Executor entitled to apply for Confirmation thereunder in terms of Sections 2 and 3 of the Executors (Scotland) Act 1900; And we dispone and convey to ourselves and the said Ian Smith the whole property under our control as such Executors under the said Will including our right to apply for Confirmation as Executors under said Will; And I the said Ian Smith do hereby accept office as Executor Nominate under said Will; And I the said Ian Alexander do hereby resign office as Executor Nominate under the said Will; And we the said Mrs Carol Smart and Ian Smith hereby accept intimation of the foregoing resignation IN WITNESS WHEREOF

Author's Note Re: Deed of Assumption No.1

In terms of the foregoing style, the trust in question was created under the Trust Disposition and Settlement by the late John McPherson dated May 23, 1952 and registered in the Books of Council and Session on April 24, 1961. The further terms of the Deed of Assumption narrate "earlier" assumptions of new trustees under the relevant trust, *i.e.* the Deed of Assumption is an example of the type of document which would be utilised in respect of a longstanding trust which not only would make reference to the original "trust deed" but also to those other "links in the chain" which reflect assumption, resignation or indeed perhaps death of previous trustees.

Author's Note Re: Deed of Assumption No.2 (Incorporating Resignation)

This is both a Deed of Assumption and Resignation. For one reason or another, the solicitor, Mr Ian Alexander, does not actually wish to act as an executor under the will of the late Miss Williams. However, Mrs Smart does not wish to act on her own as executor. That being so Mr Alexander has agreed with Mrs Smart that they will:

- Assume Mr Ian Smith as co-executor and having done so,
- Mr Ian Alexander will then resign as executor under the will of Miss Williams.

This style could be adapted for use where an individual nominated to act as executor (with no other additional parties being so nominated) indicates that he or she does not wish to act. Normally, the executry solicitor would seek to persuade that individual not immediately to decline office but rather to "accept" office purely for the purpose of assuming a new executor and thereafter immediately resigning, leaving the "new executor" in place as the sole executor who will administer the estate of the deceased.

DISCHARGE OF LEGAL RIGHTS

I, ROBERT CUTHBERT, residing at Nine Queensview, Glasgow CONSIDERING that in terms of his will dated Fifth October Nineteen hundred and ninety six and registered in the Books of Council and Session on Seventh March Two thousand and four March Two thousand and four, my father, the late WILLIAM CUTHBERT, who resided sometime at Two Beechlands Drive, Glasgow and latterly at Milngavie Care Home, Bearsden Road, Milngavie, Glasgow and who died on Fourth June Two thousand and four bequeathed the whole residue and remainder of his means and estate to my mother, MRS RHODA CUTHBERT, also residing at Two Beechlands Drive, aforesaid provided that my said mother survived him for one month following the date of his death. FURTHER CONSIDERING that my said mother has survived him aforesaid to vest in the residue and remainder of my father's estate FURTHER CONSIDERING that I have been informed of my entitlement to claim Legal Rights from the net moveable estate of my late father as also the estimated amount of my said entitlement. FURTHER CONSIDERING that I have been advised to take separate and independent legal advice in respect of my said entitlement but I have chosen not to do so THEREFORE that I do hereby discharge now and in all time coming my entitlement to claim legal rights from the net moveable estate to my said father and Do Hereby EXONER and DISCHARGE his Executors in that respect; and I confirm that these presents are freely granted by me and are irrevocable; IN WITNESS WHEREOF

Suggested Note on Legal Rights

In Scotland, the right to make a will has always been regarded as a fundamental freedom. However, it is not wholly unrestricted. In Scotland, we have what is known as the doctrine of legal rights. It is important that an individual maker of a will should be aware that the terms of that very important document are not absolute.

Purpose

The client making a will is of course likely to be surprised to find that the devolution of his estate will not be wholly controlled by the terms of his will. Why should this be? In essence, this is due to the fact that Scottish Law does not wish to allow a situation to arise whereby a spouse or child can be wholly disinherited for no good reason.

Who can claim?

The range of those who can claim legal rights is restricted to:-

- Spouses—this also includes estranged or separated spouses unless there is in place a valid separation agreement in terms of which both spouses on separation have waived their respective entitlements to claim legal rights from the estate of the other.
- Children—this includes both adopted and illegitimate children.
- The issue of a child who has predeceased the maker of the will.

How are legal rights calculated?

Legal rights can only be claimed against the net moveable estate, valued as at the date of death, of the maker of the will. In essence, the estate of the deceased person is divided into two separate categories being:

- Heritable estate—the value of land and buildings (against which legal rights cannot be claimed).
- Moveable estate—effectively anything which is not regarded as being heritable. This includes cash deposits, the value of stocks and shares, insurance policies, furnishings, jewellery and personal effects, artworks, stamp etc. collections (and note this list is not exhaustive).

Where the maker of the will is survived by spouse and children, their respective entitlements are as follows:

- The spouse is entitled to claim one third of the net moveable estate.
- The children or their issue (where a child predeceases the maker of the will) are entitled to claim one third between them.

Example

Let us take a typical family situation. The maker of the will A owns a dwellinghouse having a value of £200,000. He has net moveable estate as at date of death which amounts to £120,000. He is survived by his spouse

B and two children, X and Y. Neither B nor X and Y can claim against the value of the heritable property. They can, however, claim their respective entitlement to legal rights as against the value of the net moveable property. Thus:

- B can claim one third of the net moveable estate amounting to £40,000.
- X and Y can between them claim £40,000, *i.e.* £20,000 each. Note, however, that if, for example, X declines to claim his entitlement to legal rights this does not mean that Y can claim the total amount of £40,000. Y's claim is restricted to £20,000.

Further example

Let us take the same family save that unfortunately, A's child, X has predeceased him leaving two children of his own, D and E. As before, none of the beneficiaries who can claim legal rights can make any claim against the value of the heritable property. However, the moveable Estate against which he can claim remains the same. As before:

- B can claim £40,000.
- The legal right fund available to children and issue amounts to £40,000. This being so Y can claim £20,000 and D and E can both claim £10,000 each. Again, should Y choose not to claim, this does not increase the claims available to D and E.

The position changes where either there is no surviving spouse or no children nor issue of any pre-deceasing children. The result here is that where there is a claimant, his or her entitlement increases. Thus:

- Where the testator is survived only by his spouse but no children or the issue of any predeceasing child, then the surviving spouse is entitled to claim one half of the net moveable estate. In the example given above, B would there-fore be entitled to claim £60,000.
- Where there is no surviving spouse, again the claim available to children or the issue of a predeceasing child is one half of the net moveable estate. Thus, in the first example given above, X and Y could each claim £30,000. If X chooses not to claim, this does not increase Y's claim—this still amounts to £30,000. Where there is no surviving spouse and X has predeceased A, D and E would each be entitled to claim £15,000.

The meaning of "net moveable estate"

There is a tried and tested methodology for calculating the value of net moveable estate as at date of death. Firstly, the moveable estate is valued as at date of death. The figure as so calculated falls to be reduced by deduction of:

- Funeral expenses
- Debts due by the deceased as at his or her date of death (but excluding what are regarded as heritable debts—for example a mortgage)

- Costs incurred in valuation of the moveable estate (even although these costs are incurred after the date of death—for example the valuation of furniture, stocks and shares etc.)
- Legal expenses in relation to the winding up of the estate up to the point of obtaining confirmation (the Scottish equivalent of probate)

Can a beneficiary claim both legal rights and take his entitlement under the will?

The answer to this question is "no". Under the Succession (Scotland) Act 1964 as amended, unless the relevant will specifies otherwise, those who are entitled to claim legal rights are put to an election. If they claim the benefit left under the will, they forfeit their entitlement to legal rights. Conversely, if they claim their entitlement to legal rights, they forfeit any benefit left to them under the will.

The executor's obligations

The law on this matter is clear. Even where, for example, the testator has made it clear that he does not wish a particular "black sheep" child to have any rights against his estate, the executors are obliged to advise all who might have a claim to legal rights of their entitlement. Whilst it is appreciated that this can be awkward for executors, their duties are clear. They are not obliged to encourage a claim to legal rights and similarly, they should not bring pressure on a particular individual not to claim. Having advised the relevant individuals of their entitlement to claim legal rights, the executors are required to make available to those individuals of their legal agents the information which is required to enable such potential claimants to decide whether or not to claim. Should an executor fail in the foregoing respect, he may find himself being pursued by a potential legal rights claimant.

How long does the right to claim subsist?

The answer to this is simple—20 years. This can provide Executors with real difficulties where the potential claimant cannot be traced. In such circumstances, the executors may have no alternative but to retain on an interest bearing basis a sum to meet the potential claim of that missing beneficiary, notwithstanding the views of, or complaints on the part of, those who are beneficiaries under the relevant will.

Does the entitlement to legal rights earn interest?

Again, the answer to this is "yes". However, there is no statutory rate and if legal rights are claimed then they will carry a right to interest from date of death to date of payment. That rate of interest is, however, often difficult to calculate. Generally speaking the rate is equated to that which the remainder of the Estate gained interest during the relevant period. Obviously, however, if the remainder of the estate gained no interest (because it was invested, for example, in Premium Bonds, which are not interest bearing) then there is no entitlement to interest.

Can a claim to legal rights be defeated?

Again the answer is "yes". However, this can be difficult if not impossible to achieve. Where an individual dies leaving moveable estate then on the face of it, if there is a surviving spouse and/or children or the issue of predeceasing child, then the right exists. There are steps which can be taken in an attempt to defeat legal rights but, for the most part, these are impractical or might not be advisable. For example:

- The claim to legal rights only exists in respect of the deceased's moveable estate as at date of death. If the deceased deliberately expended his moveable estate prior to death in purchasing heritable property then legal rights cannot be claimed against that type of property.
- The testator may take steps to seek to secure that he has no personal moveable estate as at his date of death. However, Scottish Courts have shown themselves to be more than ready to "attack" what the courts regard as "sham" attempts to defeat a claim to legal rights.

Is a potential claimant obliged to claim legal rights?

The answer to this is "no". There is no obligation to claim legal rights. In fact, legal rights will normally be discharged where the benefit left to the potential claimant under the will is greater than the value of the entitlement to claim legal rights. Similarly, in most stable family situations, children will decline their entitlement to claim legal rights if they perceive that this will prejudicially affect the financial position of the surviving parent.

Conclusion

It is of great importance that the maker of a will should know of the existence of the entitlement to claim legal rights both on the part of a surviving spouse and children or the issue of a predeceasing child. If the existence of that entitlement causes concern, then the maker of the will should seek more specific advice as to his or her position and whether or not any practical steps could be taken to mitigate if not avoid the potentiality of such a claim against his or her estate to the potential detriment of the chosen beneficiaries under the will.

ADVANCED MEDICAL DIRECTIVE/LIVING WILL

For information on Living Wills please refer to the Voluntary Euthanasia Society (www.ves.org.uk).

MINUTE OF AGREEMENT

(to protect the inheritance of children by earlier relationship)

MINUTE OF AGREEMENT

By and Between

JOHN DOE, residing at 1 Scott Place, Anytown (hereinafter referred to as "John")

and

JANE BLOGGS, also residing at 1 Scott Place, Anytown (hereinafter referred to as "Jane")

WHEREAS John and Jane have cohabited with each other for several years without being married to each other CONSIDERING that John and Jane were previously married to other parties and are now both divorced from those parties but that they both have children from their respective previous marriages but have no children with each other FURTHER CONSIDERING that John and Jane are desirous of securing the financial position of the survivor of them on death of one of them and also that they wish to ensure that their respective children will all receive an equal share of the residue of the estate of the second of John and Jane to die AND NOW SEEING John and Jane have already granted wills to the foregoing effect respectively dated [   ], copies of which are annexed and subscribed by the parties as relative hereto THEREFORE John and Jane have agreed as follows:

ONE   John and Jane believe that the terms of their said wills are equitable and reflect their current wishes.

TWO   John and Jane hereby respectively confirm that these presents are granted in consideration of the financial support which they have given to each other in the past and which they shall continue to give to each other hereafter (including without prejudice to the said generality payment of the mortgage over 1 Scott Place, Anytown, and other costs, liabilities and expenses incurred or to be in relation to the said heritable property).

THREE   John hereby binds and obliges himself that he shall not at any time (including after the death of Jane should she predecease him) alter or seek to alter the terms of his said will in any way.

FOUR   Jane hereby irrevocably binds and obliges herself that she shall not at any time (including after the death of John should be predecease her) alter or seek to alter the terms of her said will in any way.

FIVE   The parties hereby confirm that they have been advised of their entitlement to seek independent and legal advice as to the nature and effect of these presents but have declined such advice.

SIX   The parties hereby agree that the terms of the these presents shall be binding on them both and do hereby confirm that it is their intention that the terms of these presents should create a *ius quaesitum tertio* in favour of each of their respective children (all as more particularly referred to/identified in their said wills).

SEVEN   John and Jane hereby confirm that they shall be jointly responsible for the expenses of the preparation and of the execution of these presents.

EIGHT   John and Jane respectively confirm that these presents are freely granted by them.

LASTLY John and Jane hereby respectively consent to the registration of these presents for preservation and execution: IN WITNESS WHEREOF

AUTHOR'S NOTE RE: SUGGESTED MINUTE OF AGREEMENT

The reader is referred to the text. The style presented makes reference to wills which have already been signed. Copies of the signed wills are annexed to the minute of agreement. In that respect the terms of the minute of agreement are "retrospective". The author accepts that some solicitors may feel that it would be preferable for the minute of agreement to refer to draft wills still to be entered into. It would appear that in the *Paterson* case, the agreement was that the successful litigant's mother would grant a will in particular terms. However, in the *McElveen* case also referred to in the text, the court appears to have made no adverse comment regarding the suggestion that a minute of agreement might have been entered into, binding Mr McQuillan not to depart from a will which he had already made. It is the view of the author that there is no reason why the agreement should not refer to the spouses having agreed that wills, already made, have been granted in implement of their intended binding obligations to each other. The style also refers to a consideration—the mutual financial support which the parties have and will continue to offer to each other. In the text, the author cites Eric Clive who makes it clear that in relation to a prenuptial Agreement in Scotland, consideration is irrelevant. However, the author does, however, consider it prudent to specify consideration for the minute of agreement—if this is unnecessary (which is, in fact, the author's view) then *superflua non nocent*!

Where clients wish to enter into such a Minute of Agreement, they must be warned of the possible distorting effect of a legal rights claim on the part of a child/the children of the first of them to die. In fact, such a claim could wholly distort the devolution of the estate of the survivor as:

- Children of the first to die would be entitled to claim their legal rights.
- However, the survivor might find himself/herself contractually "stuck" with a will which gives half of the estate of the survivor to the children who have already deprived the survivor of full benefit under the predecessor's will by making a legal rights claim in the first place.

I would suggest that the possibility of a legal rights claim should be covered either in terms of the minute of agreement (which could contain a provision which would allow the survivor to amend his or her will to take account of the possible "hostile" legal rights claim on the part of the children of the predecessor). Alternatively, the wills themselves could contain an appropriate provision allowing the executors of the survivor discretion to adjust the division of the residue of the estate of the survivor again to take into account the possibility of a hostile legal rights claim on the earlier death of his or her partner.

PETITION FOR APPOINTMENT OF FINANCIAL GUARDIAN

Sheriffdom of North Strathclyde at Dumbarton

THE ADULTS WITH INCAPACITY (SCOTLAND) ACT 2000

SUMMARY APPLICATION

By

JOSEPH BLOGGS, Solicitor, 100 West Regent Street, Glasgow   APPLICANT

The Applicant Craves the Court:

1. To appoint the Applicant as Financial Guardian under section 57 of the Adults with Incapacity (Scotland) 2000 Act (hereinafter referred to as "the Act") to LIAM BANKS, residing formerly at 27 Brown Street, Glasgow and now a permanent resident at Milngavie Care Home, Bearsden Road, Milngavie, Glasgow (and hereinafter referred to as "the adult").
2. To grant to the applicant power in terms of section 64(1)(d) of the Act to manage the property and financial affairs of the adult.
3. Without prejudice to the generality of the power detailed in second crave hereof, to grant power in terms of section 64(1)(a) of the Act to deal with the following particular matters on behalf of the Adult:

   3.1 To deal with, convey, sell, maintain, repair or manage the adult's interest in the heritable property known as and forming 27 Brown Street, Glasgow comprising ALL and WHOLE that steading of ground containing 30 poles or thereby in the Parish of Cathcart and County of Lanark more particularly described in Disposition by Robert Smith in favour of Wilson Jones dated 1st and recorded in the Division of the General Register of Sasines for the County of The Barony and Regality of Glasgow on 3rd June 1937 together with the dwellinghouse known as 27 Brown Street, Glasgow and the whole other buildings erected thereon owned jointly by the adult and his wife, Mrs Barbara Banks, also residing formerly at 27 Brown Street, aforesaid and now also a permanent patient also residing at the Milngavie Care Home, aforesaid, including but not limited to power to do everything reasonably required for the purpose, in relation to the said interest of the Adult, of marketing the house, negotiating, concluding and implementing a sale of the same including power to

      (a) employ, instruct and appropriately remunerate estate agents, solicitors, surveyors and any other tradesmen, specialists or experts whom surveyors might recommend to be instructed;

      (b) employ, instruct and appropriately remunerate removal contractors;

(c) arrange for termination of all services to the house;

(d) execute on behalf of the adult any disposition or other deeds or documents which solicitors as employed as aforesaid might advise should properly be so executed.

3.2 To open, operate and close any account containing the funds of the Adult and *ad interim* to operate in respect of the adult's interest therein:

(a) Account Number 1234 with Clydesdale Bank PLC at Station Road, Milngavie, Glasgow; and

(b) Account Number K 1256 with Abbey National plc at 488 Victoria Road, Glasgow.

Both standing in the sole name of the adult.

3.3 To make purchase, vary and dispose of investments whether Stock Exchange investments or otherwise and without prejudice to the foregoing generality to handle the investment portfolio Number BAN 5678 with Prudential Assurance, Craigforth, Stirling belonging to the adult.

3.4 To claim and receive on behalf of the adult all pensions, benefits, allowances, services, financial contributions, repayments, rebates and the like to which the adult may be entitled; and to vary or appeal arrangements for all such pensions etc.

3.5 To deal with the adult's income tax.

3.6 To obtain and pay for goods or services which are of benefit to the adult.

3.7 To take all necessary legal action to conserve, protect or vindicate the right of the Adult in and to any property belonging to the adult.

3.8 To do anything ancillary or consequential upon the powers above specified which may reasonably be necessary or appropriate for the full and proper exercise thereof.

4 . To find any person or persons challenging this application liable in expenses of the costs of the applicant.

5. To grant warrant to serve this application upon:

(a) The adult, residing at Milngavie Care Home, aforesaid;

(b) Mrs Barbara Banks, also residing at Milngavie Care Home, aforesaid as nearest relative of the adult;

(c) Homecare Limited, registered under the Companies Acts and having their Registered Office at 5 Clearview Gardens, Glasgow and a place of business at Milngavie Care Home, Bearsden Road, Milngavie, Glasgow as the current Primary Carer of the Adult;

(d) the Public Guardian.

(e) The Chief Social Worker, Glasgow City Council.

CONDESCENDENCE

1. This application is made under Part 6 of the Act. The applicant is a partner of a firm of solicitors which has acted for the adult and for the adult's wife, the said Mrs Barbara Banks for Twenty-five years.

The adult's primary carers are Homecare Limited aforesaid, providers of residential and nursing care. The Adult has been a resident at the said Milngavie Care Home since August 4, 2004. The said Milngavie Care Home is owned by the said Homecare Limited. Mrs Barbara Banks as wife of the adult has an interest in this application. The applicant and his said wife have no children or remoter issue The applicant has acted as solicitor to the adult and Mrs Barbara Banks for a period of six years. The adult is well known to the applicant and the applicant has an interest in the financial affairs of the adult.

2. The applicant seeks a Guardianship Order in terms of the Act in respect of the adult. The adult was born on September 3, 1924. The adult is 80 years of age. By interlocutor dated [   ] 2004 the Sheriff of Glasgow and Strathkelvin at Glasgow granted a Welfare Guardianship Order in favour of the Chief Social Worker for Glasgow City Council. The Powers granted in terms of Interlocutor were:

   (a) To require the adult to reside in a residential establishment;
   (b) To return the adult to such establishment should he leave and to prevent his removal without the consent of the Welfare Guardian;
   (c) To assist him in his self-care and personal hygiene.

   In exercise of the said powers, the Chief Social Worker of Glasgow City Council arranged for the adult to reside at the Milngavie Care Home, aforesaid. There is no prospect of the adult being able to return to 27 Brown Street, aforesaid and his wife, the said Mrs Barbara Banks, is now residing with the adult, also as a permanent resident at the Milngavie Care Home. No financial powers were granted to the Chief Social Worker of Glasgow City Council in terms of the said Interlocutor.

3. The dwellinghouse at 27 Brown Street, aforesaid is jointly owned by the adult and the said Mrs Barbara Banks and has an estimated value of £150,000. The adult has Bank and Building Society Deposits presently amounting to £15,000. The Adult has other investments in his own name with Perpetual, Abbey National, Lloyds TSB and Aviva, the approximate present total value of which is £12,000. The adult has joint investments with Mrs Barbara Banks with Legal & General and Norwich Union having estimated values in total of £10,500. Said joint investments cannot be surrendered by Mrs Barbara Banks alone. It is considered by the applicant that the best management option in relation to the said dwellinghouse at 27 Brown Street is for the same to be sold in order to fund Care Home costs for both the Adult and the said Mrs. Barbara Banks .

4. Due to the incapacity of the adult, no funds are presently available or accessible to pay his care home fees and associated expenses. The adult's care home fees amount to £450 per week. The adult has now been assessed by Glasgow City Council and is eligible to receive £145 per week by way of Personal Care Allowance and £65 by way of Nursing Care Allowance as from August 4, 2004. Said allowances are being paid and will be paid by Glasgow City Council direct to Milngavie Care Home. Arrears of Care Home fees in respect of the

adult to November 14, 2004 amount to in excess of £1,200. An interim order is therefore sought to operate on the above accounts with Clydesdale Bank PLC and Abbey National plc in respect of the interest of the adult therein in order that arrears of nursing home fees can be paid and a fund can be available to pay his ongoing care home fees pending a final order being granted.

5. The applicant holds a continuing power of attorney by Mrs Barbara Banks registered with the Office of the Public Guardian on 12 October 2003. However the applicant cannot operate alone in respect of the joint assets investments of the adult and the said Mrs Barbara Banks.

6. The adult is habitually resident within Milngavie Care Home aforesaid which is within the territory of this court. This court, accordingly has jurisdiction in terms of paragraphs 1 and 2 of Schedule 3 to the Act. To the applicant's knowledge no proceedings are pending before any other court involving the present cause of action and to which the applicant is a party or which relate to the adult. To the Applicant's knowledge, no agreement exists prorogating jurisdiction for the whole or any part of the subject matter of this application to another court.

7. Save as hereinbefore condescended upon, no other guardianship or intervention orders in terms of the Act and no appointments which have become guardianship appointments in accordance with the provisions of the Act are in force or have ever been granted in respect of the adult. The adult has no continuing or welfare attorney.

8. This application is supported by the accompanying reports as required by section 57(3) of the Act.

   (a) medical report;
   (b) financial report; and
   (c) mental health report.

PLEAS IN LAW

1. The applicant having an interest in the financial affairs of the adult is entitled to seek appointment as financial guardian to the adult.

2. The applicant, in the circumstances previously condescended upon to be appointed as guardian, decree therefor should be granted as craved.

3. It being reasonable in the circumstances condescended upon to operate the said Clydesdale Bank and Abbey National accounts, decree therefor should be granted as craved *ad interim* in terms of Crave 3.4.

IN RESPECT WHEREOF

Solicitor,
100 West Regent Street,
Glasgow,
G2 2QB.
AGENT FOR APPLICANT

PETITION FOR APPOINTMENT OF JOINT FINANCIAL AND WELFARE GURADIANS

Sheriffdom of North Strathclyde at Dumbarton

THE ADULTS WITH INCAPACITY (SCOTLAND) ACT 2000

SUMMARY APPLICATION

By

JOHN SCOTT, residing at Thirty Brown Place, Milngavie, Glasgow and ROBERT SCOTT, residing at Nine Queensview, Glasgow APPLICANTS

The Applicants Crave the Court:

1. To appoint the applicants as joint guardians under section 57 of the Adults with Incapacity (Scotland) 2000 (hereinafter referred to as "the Act") to FREDERICK SCOTT, residing formerly at Twelve Beech Drive, Glasgow and now at Milngavie Care Home, Bearsden Road, Milngavie, Glasgow (and hereinafter referred to as "the adult").
2. To grant the applicants a guardianship order so that the personal welfare of the adult can be protected by exercising the following powers:

    (a) To decide where the adult should live.
    (b) To require the adult to reside in a particular residential establishment.
    (c) To return the applicant to such an establishment should he leave and to prevent removal with the prior consent of the guardians.
3. To have access to confidential documents or information relating to the adult where he would have had such access to such documents or information on a personal basis.
4. To consent or withhold consent to medical treatment.
5. To have vested in the applicants the right of the adult to deal with, convey, maintain, repair or manage the heritable property belonging to the adult being ALL and WHOLE the subjects known as and forming 12 Beech Drive, Glasgow more fully described in Feu Charter by John Lawrence (Glasgow) Limited in favour of the adult dated August 2nd and recorded in the Division of the General Register of Sasines applicable to the County of the Barony and Regality of Glasgow on September 5, 1958.
6. To open and close and operate any account containing the adult's funds and *ad interim* to operate account number 01234 with Bank of Scotland, 836 Crow Road, Glasgow and account number X 6789 SCO with Abbey National plc, 354 Dumbarton Road, Glasgow, all for the benefit of the adult and to meet his expenses.
7. To make, purchase, vary and dispose of investments whether Stock Exchange investments or otherwise and without prejudice to the

foregoing generality to handle the investment portfolio belonging to the adult.

8. To claim and receive on behalf of the adult all pensions, benefits, allowances, services, financial contributions, repayments, rebates and the like to which the adult may be entitled, and to vary or appeal all arrangements.

9. To deal with the adult's income tax.

10. To obtain and pay for any goods or services which are of benefit to the adult.

11. To offer such financial assistance to Mrs Laura Scott, residing at 12 Beech Drive, aforesaid, the spouse of the adult in such manner as may be approved by the Office of the Public Guardian.

12. To do anything ancillary or consequential upon the powers above specified which may reasonably necessary or appropriate for the full and proper exercise thereof.

13. To find any person or persons challenging this application liable in the expenses of the cost of the applicants.

14. To grant warrant to serve this application upon:-

    (a) Milngavie Care Home, Bearsden Road, Milngavie, Glasgow as the current primary carer.

    (b) The said Mrs Laura Scott as nearest relative.

    (c) The Public Guardian.

    (d) The adult.

CONDESCENDENCE

1. This application is made by the pursuers under section 57 of the Adults with Incapacity (Scotland) Act 2000.

2. The applicants seek appointment as guardians with the powers set out above in respect of the following adult:

Frederick Scott, Milngavie Care Home, Bearsden Road, Milngavie, Glasgow.

3. The applicants are the only children of the adult and along with the said Mrs Laura Scott are his nearest relatives. The adult's spouse does not seek appointment. The adult's primary carer is Milngavie Care Home, aforesaid, providers of Residential Nursing Hospital care. The adult has been resident at Milngavie Care Home since June 5, 2004. Milngavie Care Home is a private Limited Company, having their registered office at [   ]. There are no other relatives having an interest in this application.

4. The adult is 86 years of age, his date of birth being July 16, 1918. In 2003 the adult was admitted to Bearsden Hospital, Bearsden, Glasgow for chest and urinary tract infections and for periods of rehabilitation followed by intensive support packages. On his discharge to 12 Beech Drive, however, owing to the adult's condition he was readmitted to hospital on November 1, 2003 where he remained until June 30, 2004. The adult has been diagnosed as suffering from chronic obstructive pulmonary disease, high blood pressure, and dementia with Parkinson features. The adult is frequently confused and disorientated, has difficulties with communication and has been verbally and physically aggressive to his carers

including his spouse. As a result of his mental disorder, the adult lacks capacity to manage his financial and property affairs. The adult cannot be cared for properly at home.

5. The adult is habitually resident within Milngavie Care Home, aforesaid which is within the territory of this court. This court accordingly has jurisdiction in terms of paragraphs 1 and 2 of Schedule 3 to the Act. To the applicants' knowledge, no proceedings are pending before any other court involving the present cause of action and to which the applicants are parties or which relate to the adult. To the applicants' knowledge, no agreement exists prorogating jurisdiction over the whole or any part of the subject matter of this application to another court.

6. No guardianship or intervention orders in terms of Act and no appointments which have become guardianship appointments in accordance with the provisions of the Act are in force or have ever been granted in respect of the adult. The adult has no continuing or welfare attorney.

7. The adult is the sole owner of the heritable property at 12 Beech Drive, aforesaid. Prior to the adult's admission to hospital, said heritable property had been the matrimonial home of the adult and his spouse, the said Mrs Laura Scott for forty-six years. The said property requires repair and maintenance but the adult's spouse does not have the financial means to secure the same. In particular the adult has various investments which although standing in the adult's sole name were truly joint investments between the adult and the said Mrs Laura Scott. Owing to the adult's mental disorder and the fact that all such investments stand in the Adult's sole name, no funds are presently accessible to allow for payment of the adult's liabilities or for any financial support in respect of his spouse. The adult's care home fees presently amount to £500 per week which, after deduction of the personal care and nursing care allowances of £210 per week, leaves a balance due on a weekly basis of £290 due by the adult. This liability is presently being met on a short term basis by the Social Work Department of Glasgow City Council as temporary measure only. An interim order is therefore sought to operate the above bank accounts in order to meet the care home fees and other liabilities due by the adult pending a final order being granted. The pursuers' application is supported by the attached reports as required by section 57(3) of the Act, namely:

- medical report;
- financial report; and
- mental health report.

PLEA IN LAW

The Applicants, in the circumstances previously condescended upon, are entitled to seek appointment as guardians, the Guardianship Order *ad interim* and decree should be granted in terms of the craves of this application all in terms of section 57 of the Adults with Incapacity (Scotland) Act 2000.

IN RESPECT WHEREOF

Solicitor,
100 West Regent Street,
Glasgow,
G2 2QB.
AGENT FOR APPLICANTS

Author's Note Re: Foregoing Style Petitions

It should be borne in mind that the sheriff who falls to consider the relevant petition has the responsibility to ensure that what is proposed largely meets the requirements of the "Gateway" Principles set out under The Adults With Incapacity (Scotland) Act 2000. So far as possible, the draftsman should seek to ensure that the petition will satisfy the sheriff in that regard. The following points are of note, bearing in mind those principles:

- The sheriff requires to be satisfied that the least intrusive option is being sought. This should be demonstrated by the terms of the petition. If the sheriff is not satisfied on this point then he may *ex proprio motu* decide that intervention, as opposed to guardianship, would be appropriate. The draftsman, therefore, should be satisfied that full guardianship, as opposed to simple intervention would, in the first instance, be appropriate.
- Bearing in mind that the past and present non-wishes of the adult should be taken into consideration, is it appropriate to present a petition on behalf of an individual who has had no previous contact with or knowledge of the adult?

In both of the styles presented it is clear from their terms that the applicants have had a long-standing connection (either professionally or through family relationships) with the adult.

One cautionary note—the **"Scott" Petition** craves power to offer financial assistance to the wife of the adult. The styles, of course, all relate to either anonymous or imaginary clients. However, the author did have occasion to consider this particular point. The particular power sought was never "tested" as unfortunately the adult died as the author was making ready to present the petition. The author would suggest that the power is entirely reasonable in the circumstances outlined in the **"Scott" Petition**. How the Office of the Public Guardian would react to such a power being sought is, however, unclear. In the "active" case referred to, the author wrote to the Office of the Public Guardian to advise as to the power which would be sought in relation to financial support of the adult spouse. The Office of the Public Guardian declined to comment at that point on the basis that this might been seen to be tantamount to offering "legal advice". However, the author considers that such a power is reasonable and is likely to be generally acceptable to the OPG, given that financial support for the spouse of an incapax under the previous curatory proceedings did not appear to occasion immediate or insuperable difficulty to the Accountant of Court.

SUGGESTED NOTE RE: REVIEW OF WILLS

A Job Well Done

Many people find the making of a will to be a difficult, stressful process. No one likes to have to contemplate their own death nor the possible earlier death of a loved one. However, the will having been made, it should not be regarded as having been written in a tablet of stone. A will does not take affect until death of the granter and, apart from a very limited range of circumstances, can be changed or even revoked in whole by the granter at any point prior to death.

Maxwell MacLaurin strongly recommend that clients should regularly review their wills. It is our practice to provide clients with copies of the completed documents. We recommend that the client should read over the copy of his or her will once a year. If the client is satisfied that the provisions of the existing will still meet his or her requirements, then nothing further may require to be done. Where the client is not so satisfied, then early contact with the drafting Solicitor is strongly recommended.

Quite apart from the annual review suggested above, there are other "life events" which should occasion a review of the existing will. These include:

- An "addition" to the family—for example, where the will in question has been made several years beforehand, it may not have taken into account the possibility of grandchildren coming into line of succession. The birth of the first grandchild is normally an event which focuses the mind of the grandparent on the question of succession.
- The death of someone named in the will—on occasions this will have no effect on the will. On other occasions it may be important that, for example, a new executor be nominated or the terms of the will be amended in some suitable fashion.
- A change in the client's financial position—at the time of making of the will, inheritance tax mitigation may not have played any part in the client's deliberations. However, a lottery or Premium Bond win or indeed a rise in the value of the client's dwellinghouse or inheritance from an older generation may well totally change the client's financial position and inheritance tax mitigation may suddenly become a matter of some interest if not importance to the client. The wills of husbands and wives can be structured so as to effectively save a large amount of inheritance tax on death of the survivor of them.
- A perceived change in how capital is taxed in the UK—the Treasury estimate is that 95 per cent of individuals in the UK are not affected by inheritance tax. This is not borne out by our experience in winding up estates. However, if the regime of taxation to inheritance tax becomes harsher, then clients may require to consider the terms of their wills in some detail.
- If you have disposed of any item you have bequeathed in your will.

The wills which we make for clients contain what is known as an "informal writings clause". This is a facility which allows the client to create his or her own simple codicils. These clauses are included because of the well known propensity of clients to resort to "self help" in relation to matters which they consider to be fairly simple. However, we do not in truth encourage clients to endeavour to create their own codicils—a client is not skilled in drafting techniques and may not properly execute the Codicil—where this happens then the whole purpose of granting the codicil in the first place is frustrated. If you are considering a simple change to your will but are unsure as to how to go about it we would recommend that you always make contact with us to obtain appropriate advice. This may avoid a loved one or friend being bitterly disappointed on death of the client.

SUGGESTED NOTE RE: VALUE OF GRANTING POWER OF ATTORNEY

The value of granting a power of attorney cannot be overestimated. Human longevity is increasing. In the recent Census, it was disclosed that there were more people alive over the age of 60 than under the age of 16. When we are young and have a young family we have no difficulty in accepting that it is appropriate to arrange life insurance to provide protection to our families in the event of early and untimely death. Similar considerations apply throughout life and in particular when we are older, to the granting of a power of attorney. Granting a suitable power of attorney can mean that our families avoid the horrendous difficulties which can arise where an individual loses capacity. In such circumstances, and if no suitable power of attorney is in place, the financial and business affairs of the older client can be impossible to manage in the short term. If a loss of capacity is permanent then the family of that older person will require to go through the complicated, long winded and expensive process of having a financial guardian appointed. This can be avoided if the older person has granted a power of attorney.

The granting of a suitable power of attorney will allow speedy and appropriate intervention on behalf of the older person. The power of attorney will remain in full force and effect notwithstanding the supervening incapacity of the granter and can allow the attorney to take part in the process of deciding what care etc will be appropriate for the older person.

Maxwell MacLaurin have a specific and recommended power of attorney for older clients. In that regard we would offer the following comments:

- The granting of a power of attorney is a protective step. It is not of itself a necessary acknowledgement of incipient inability. The document need not come into effect immediately and can in fact be "postponed" until the granter has lost capacity. Where required a clause to the foregoing effect can be included in the power of attorney itself.
- Our style of power of attorney contains very wide powers. It is our view that no one can predict the future or the circumstances which might apply at the relevant point in time. Given that one should not appoint another party to act as attorney unless full faith and trust is reposed in that person, there is no point in "hamstringing" the attorney from the outset.
- We recommend that a power of attorney should include a power to make gifts. This can be very important where the granter of the power of attorney is wealthy and would, for their own part, wish to mitigate the effect of inheritance tax as far as possible. The relevant gifting powers are detailed in clause 16 of our recommended format. Where a client does not find favour with the clause in question, the clause can be deleted. However, it is important to note that unless the power in question is included, an attorney will be prevented from engaging in legitimate inheritance tax mitigation, even where this might have been in line with the wishes of the granter of

the document. The reason for this is that without a specific power, the Inland Revenue will not recognise gifts made by attorneys with a view to mitigating IHT.

- The provisions of clause 19 are also of importance. These represent the new "welfare" powers authorised by the Adults with Incapacity (Scotland) Act 2000. The powers detailed in clause 18 only come into effect when the granter of the power of attorney has lost capacity. The powers in question do, however, allow the attorney to take part in the relevant decision making process regarding the care etc of the granter of the power of attorney. These welfare powers will not be available unless clause 18 is specifically included in the relevant document.

- All powers of attorney granted after April 2001 require to be registered with the Office of the Public Guardian. The Public Guardian if the official who has responsibility for overseeing the actings of Attornies. He can ask an attorney to provide an accounting for his or her actings and in a bad case, can seek the removal of an attorney who is considered to have misbehaved.

- It is a requirement of the Act of 2000 that anyone appointed to act as attorney should signify his consent so to do in writing. That being so, when a client grants a power of attorney it is our normal practice to send a copy of the same to the individual appointed as attorney, at the same time having the latter sign the form of consent required by the Office of the Public Guardian.

THE RESPONSIBILITIES OF THE ATTORNEY

Any individual who accepts appointment as attorney takes on weighty responsibility and, on occasions, an onerous task. The attorney requires to comply with the principles set out in the 2000 Act as also with The Code of Conduct promulgated by the Scottish Executive. Anyone appointed as an attorney should familiarise himself with both of the same. If he fails to comply with the Principles/The Code of Conduct and is also negligent, he could, at least in theory, be found liable in damages to the granter or to the executors of the latter. It is only fair that the attorney should be made aware that his task may not be an easy one and it is important that the attorney should be aware of the degree of responsibility and, indeed, the possible liability which he may be taking on. This cautionary note is not intended to dissuade individuals from accepting office as an attorney—an attorney who acts properly, adhering to the Principles and the Code of Conduct, and taking appropriate legal advice when required, has nothing to fear.

We should be happy to answer any queries which you may have in relation to our above comments or with regard to the format of power of attorney which we as a firm have adopted.

APPOINTMENT AS AN ATTORNEY

This note is not intended to be a learned treatise on the responsibilities of the main individual appointed (and accepting office) as an attorney. It is, however, intended to be a useful guide in order that an individual appointed and accepting office as attorney may be aware of his/her general responsibilities.

An attorney is no more than an agent for the person appointing them. However, since the passing of The Adults within Capacity (Scotland) Act 2000, it is arguable that the office of attorney now goes well beyond that of an "old-fashioned" agent.

As a first point, if the attorney should be aware of the fact that the 2000 Act sets out certain "gateway" Principles which every intervenor (including an attorney) is required to observe. Paraphrasing the Act, the Principles are as follows:

- Any decision or intervention taken by an intervenor must be for the benefit of the adult (in the case of a power of attorney, the granter of the document).
- The intervenor/attorney is required to take the least intrusive/ restrictive method of intervention on behalf of the adult.
- The intervenor is required to take into account the known past and present wishes of the adult.
- The intervenor should consult with "relevant others" (*i.e.* the nearest relatives of the adult, the primary carers, and any other appointee under the Act (for example, a welfare guardian). It should be noted, however, that the requirement to consult does not obliged the intervenor/attorney to simply follow the views of the "relevant others" (*i.e.* the intervenor/attorney must act in what he/she considers to be the best interests of the adult).
- The intervenor/attorney should endeavour to encourage the skills, training and education of the adult.

In truth, nowadays, the main purpose of granting a "protective" power of attorney is to ensure that the family of the adult do not require to be forced to resort to a financial guardianship. This involves court proceedings, is long-winded, expensive and is, frankly, the least favourable way of seeking to secure intervention. This is not intended to be a criticism of the 2000 Act—however, if an adult grants a power of attorney on a "protective" basis, the problems, bureaucracy and difficulties of a financial guardianship can be avoided and this can be a great boon to the adult's family/friends/ professional advisers.

In March 2001, the Scottish Executive published a Code of Practice for intervenors (which includes attorneys). That Code of Practice should be regarded as being a "bible" of best practice for attorneys. It is not our practice to supply each and every individual appointed to act as attorney with a copy of the Code of Practice for the simple reason that it consists of just under 80 pages. However, a copy of the power of attorney can be found on the Website of The Office of the Public Guardian (*www.publicguardian-scotland.gov.uk*) and the attorney is strongly recommended to make reference to the same. Although the legal status of the Code of Practice is not entirely clear, an attorney who does not follow the same may find it difficult to explain his/her actings to the Public Guardian (who has an over-all, supervisory jurisdiction in respect of the actings of attorneys).

An attorney must always make clear the capacity in which he is acting. An attorney who fails to make clear that he/she is acting purely as attorney for another person may, in fact, find himself/herself incurring personal liability to third parties with whom contracts are agreed. Thus, attorneys should always make it clear that they are acting in a representative capacity on behalf of their principal.

This note is intended to be helpful and of an informative nature. It is not intended to dissuade individuals from accepting office as attorney. An attorney who acts properly, complies with the principles and the terms of the Code of Practice and who takes appropriate legal advice, where necessary, is unlikely to encounter any difficulty. The message is simple—where you have been appointed to act as attorney, this appointment is intended to be in the best interests of the person who appointed you—they have reposed full faith and trust in you and they expect you to act appropriately, in their best interests, in taking into account the Principles of the Code of Practice which are, after all, conceived for the benefit of elderly/vulnerable individuals.

SUGGESTED NOTE RE: INHERITANCE TAX

Inheritance tax is a "wealth" tax. It has been with us since 1986. Prior to then its equivalent was capital transfer tax and before that and for many years the relevant wealth tax was known as estate duty. Basically, unless one of a number of exemptions or reliefs apply, where an individual (taking into account "chargeable lifetime gifts") leaves estate exceeding £263,000 on death, then inheritance tax will be charged. The rate of charge is 40 per cent.

The figure of £263,000 is known as the "nil-rate band". It is effectively the tax free section of an individual's wealth which can be passed on without incurring a charge to Inheritance Tax. The current level of £263,000 was announced by the Chancellor in his Budget Statement in March 2004. Immediately prior to that time, the nil-rate band had been £255,000. In announcing the increase in the nil-rate band, the Chancellor suggested that this would mean that 95 per cent of individuals would not be liable to inheritance tax (in 2002 his estimate had been 96 per cent). This is not my experience of advising individuals in this field and I suspect that the figure in question does not take into account the effect of aggregation of assets between spouses—transfers between spouses are wholly exempt. Most spouses bequeath their estate to the survivor. Thus, if a husband and wife both have personal estates separately totalling £263,000,at that point, neither of them will be liable to inheritance tax. However, if one spouse dies leaving his or her estate to the survivor obviously, the survivor will on inheritance have an estate which will be liable to a substantial inheritance tax liability on his or her death.

My experience of advising clients over the years has thrown up some interesting features:

- Many clients have never actually properly worked out their net value.
- Even with clients who have endeavoured to ascertain and value their assets, they often overlook various potentially valuable assets.
- Few clients know the reliefs which will be available to them.
- Few clients know about the "gifts with reservation" rules and some have already unwittingly fallen foul of the same.
- There is a misconception as to what amounts to a potentially exempt transfer (PET).
- Few clients have any idea of the value of making use of inheritance tax policies to cushion/mitigate the effect of inheritance tax.

Lets us examine these points:

Ascertainment and valuation of the client's estate

When an individual dies, the value of the whole of his or her estate requires to be ascertained for IHT purposes. Common misconceptions are:

(i) The value of furnishings, personal effects and even jewellery is not taken into account—this is not so and where inheritance tax is an issue, all such items require to be properly valued (normally by a skilled valuer). Beware section 213 of the IHTA 1984.

(ii) Many clients believe that where they hold property jointly with another (usually their spouse) such joint assets are excluded—not so; even where an individual has only a "partial" interest in an asset (such as a heritable property or a bank account) if inheritance tax is chargeable then the value of the interest of the deceased is taken into account in calculating the charge.

(iii) Clients commonly forget to take into account monies which would be payable under life assurance policies, death in service schemes or personal pension policies .Where such benefits come directly back into the estate of the relevant client, this can in fact move the client from a position of having no liability into perhaps having a substantial liability. The simple reason that many clients forget about such benefits is that they are not available to the client during his or her lifetime. Payment of the benefits is triggered only on death. One example of the potential effect can be seen where a client has assets totalling £200,000. If the client is employed and is a member of his employer's occupational pension scheme then very often a sum equivalent to four times the annual salary of the employee at death is payable by way of death in service benefits. If the client in question is earning £30,000 per annum the death in service benefits will be £120,000. If these benefits are added back to the client's other assets (totalling £200,000) the IHT liability will be £320,000 minus the nil-rate band (£263,000)—equals £57,000 taxed at 40 per cent—which gives an IHT liability of £22,800.

Overlooked assets

I have already indicated above the three "potential" assets which are more often than not overlooked by a client being:

(a) Life insurance policies—whether or not the value of a policy comes back into the estate of the individual will depend on whether the proceeds of the policy are payable to the executors/personal representatives of the deceased (in which case they will be taxable) or whether the benefit that is expressed to be payable to some other person (in which case they are likely to avoid taxation).

(b) Death in service benefits—see the example which I give above.

(c) Sums payable under retirement annuity or personal pension policies—normally such policies will provide for payment of a sum where the person who has purchased the relevant policy dies before reaching retirement age. The sum which is payable will depend on the terms of the policy. Some older policies provide for simply return of premiums paid. Other provide for return of premiums paid with interest at an agreed rate thereon. Most favourably from the point of view of the individual, more modern policies provide for payment of the value of the pension fund at date of death. This can amount in

382 Drafting for Succession

any case to a substantial sum of money which again may well be expressed to be payable to the executors or personal representatives of the deceased. If it is then again it will be taxable to IHT.

There are other "potential" benefits which many people overlook. Classic examples of this are:

(i) A potential direct inheritance from an elderly relative. No one really wants to contemplate the death of a loved one, particularly a parent or other elderly family member. However, as wealth within our society has increased, a greater proportion of the population does have a reasonable inheritance expectation. Thus, you may again find a situation where a client is not per se liable to inheritance tax having assets of £200,000. If, however, the client has a reasonable expectation of inheriting another, say, £100,000 from a parent or other relative then the receipt of such an inheritance will move the client from having no liability to having a substantial liability (in the example given IHT would amount to £14,800).

(ii) Clients often fail to mention that they are already beneficiaries under a trust but that the capital benefit due to them has not yet been paid.

(iii) A damages claim—although not particularly common, it is possible that the client is involved in a litigation (for example arising out of personal injury) which, if resolved in the client's favour, could amount to a substantial sum of money being paid to the client. Most individuals involved in such claims, particularly where a litigation has been ongoing for a period of time, tend not to "count their chickens" and therefore to overlook the potential benefits of a successful outcome.

From the advisor's point of view, it can therefore be seen that the client has to be encouraged to be full and frank in his or her disclosure of assets and potential assets. Some clients can see this as unduly intrusive but the fact of the matter is that without having all the details, an advisor cannot properly advise. I have already demonstrated a potential situation in which an advisor might conclude that there was no IHT liability when in fact, with a little more information, the advisor would have reached an entirely different conclusion.

IHT reliefs

Most clients are aware that they have an annual exemption of £3,000. However, in most cases this tends to be the full extent of the client's knowledge of the reliefs which are available. IHT mitigation is not a "one off" operation. It is an ongoing process and having a knowledge of the reliefs which are available can assist a client to mitigate reasonable sums of tax over a period of time. Important exemptions which clients should bear in mind are as follows:

- Gifts in contemplation of marriage—parents can gift up to £5,000 to a child in contemplation of marriage. A grandparent can gift up to £2,500 to a grandchild in contemplation of marriage. These payments are tax free and are quite separate from the annual exemption.

- The small gifts exemption—during any tax year a client can give as many gifts not exceeding £250 as they wish as long as they are to separate individuals (if you give two gifts of £250 to the same individual only one will qualify for the small gifts exemption).
- The normal expenditure out of income rule

Quite apart from the above, it is important that clients should understand that there are other important reliefs which can be brought to bear thus:-

- Agricultural relief
- Business property relief—this is not available for investments in businesses which deal in property (for example a property development company) or in investments (for example shares in other companies i.e. an investment trust).

The importance of business property relief cannot be overlooked. A client who has a business interest worth, say £300,000 and other assets worth £200,000 may perceive that he or she has a huge inheritance tax problem. If, however, the value of the business interest can be wholly relieved (*i.e.* 100 per cent business property relief is available) then the client moves from the position of having a potentially large IHT liability to having none.

Potentially exempt transfers and gifts with reservation

These two matters require to be considered together. A potentially exempt transfer is a gift or transfer at no consideration. Provided the gift is made on an absolute basis, without any strings attached and the donor survives for seven years from the making of the gift, the value of that gift will be wholly free of IHT on death after a period of seven years from the making thereof. If the donor dies within three years of making the gift, the whole value of the gift falls to be brought back into account in assessing the value of the deceased's estate for IHT purposes. For example, at death an individual may have assets worth £240,000. On the face of it there would be no liability to IHT. However, the same individual two years prior to death made a gift of £60,000 to a child. The whole value of that gift requires to be brought back into account—thus the chargeable estate will be as follows: £300,000 minus the nil-rate band £263,000 leaving a taxable estate of £37,000 at which tax is charged at the rate of 40 per cent, *i.e.* the tax charge is £14,800.

In some circumstances, there may still be benefit in making a large gift even although the donor dies within seven years. This is due to the fact that if the donor dies between three and seven years of making the gift, although the full value of the gift is brought back into account in calculating inheritance tax, the rate at which inheritance tax is charged on that gift reduces year after year obviously until the seventh year is reached when tax is no longer chargeable.

Many clients do have a passing knowledge of potentially exempt transfers but can fall into a classic trap. To most individuals, their single most valuable asset is the dwellinghouse in which they live. Many individuals have decided that, to take the value of their dwellinghouse out of charge to IHT they will adopt the seemingly simple step of conveying the title to the dwellinghouse to their children, reserving the right to occupy the dwellinghouse rent free until death. No only does this not work from the IHT mitigation point of view, it can be disastrous. The simple reason for this is that the Inland Revenue will apply their "gift with reservation" rules; the Inland Revenue will not accept such a transfer as being a potentially exempt transfer. Not only will the Inland Revenue not accept the transfer as being a "potentially exempt one", they will require that the dwellinghouse be valued as at the parent's date of death and that value added back to the parent's other assets to calculate the charge to inheritance tax. For example, a parent conveys his/her dwellinghouse to children when its value is £100,000. The parent continues to reside rent free in the dwellinghouse and passes on ten years later when the value of the house is £200,000. Not only will the transfer not be a potentially exempt transfer (even although legal title to the house has passed ten years beforehand) but the Inland Revenue will require that the value of the house as at date of death be added back to the parent's estate passing on death to calculate the charge to tax. Thus, if the parent's other assets passing on death total £100,000 when the value of the house is added back, the gross estate is £300,000 leaving £37,000 chargeable to tax—again a tax liability of £14,800.

Dwellinghouses are "lumpen" and difficult assets to deal with from the IHT mitigation point of view. It would not be true to say that there is nothing which a parent can do with his or her dwellinghouse but some of the schemes involved are complex, costly and some of them are not guaranteed to succeed. Use of a discretionary will trust with a "loan back" arrangement should be considered.

Insurance

As people get older, the willingness to purchase an insurance product decreases. However, there are some very valuable insurance products which can be purchased to mitigate the effect of inheritance tax on death.

Potential pitfalls

The mitigation of inheritance tax is a worthwhile aim but as with everything else in life, the process is a balance. There are various important considerations which require to be taken into account thus:

- A gift made unthinkingly with a view to saving inheritance tax could simply result in an immediate capital gains tax liability. Capital gains tax arises in respect of a "disposal"—many clients wrongly think that it is only of relevance when an asset is sold— this is not the case. This consideration is of particular importance in relation to investment such as stocks and shares. A gift of a shareholding is a disposal for capital gains tax purposes. If the gain in that holding exceeds the donor's annual exemption for CGT purposes, an immediate capital gains tax liability will have been crystallised.

- A part from capital gains tax considerations, care is required in relation to lifetime gifts. While such a gift can substantially reduce an anticipated inheritance tax liability on death, the nature of the asset requires to be carefully considered—for example, if the asset in question is an investment which is producing valuable income then the effect of loss of that income will require to be properly considered.
- Spouses engaging in IHT planning should always bear in mind the likely financial position of the survivor. This applies with particular force nowadays given the increasing longevity of our population. An individual retiring at sixty could easily have another thirty five years or so ahead of him or her. Given recent advances in genetic medicine, there are some geneticists who have indicated that within ten years, individuals might be born who might reasonably be expected to have a life expectancy of 120 years!
- IHT planning cannot be carried out in isolation. An individual who makes a gift with a view to IHT mitigation might, several years later, find themselves being "penalised" (under the "deprivation" rules set out in the National System Regulations 1992) if that individual requires to go into a nursing home and applies for financial assistance from the local authority in relation to payment of fees.

Appropriate steps

Bearing in mind the cautionary note outlined above, there are numerous steps which an individual can take with a view to mitigating inheritance tax. These include:

(a) Understanding and making full use of the various small exemptions/reliefs which are available.

(b) Making carefully considered potential exempt transfers, *i.e.* gifts.

(c) Writing existing life insurance benefits, death in service benefits and personal pension funds in trust. Such policies/benefits are often capable of being written in trust for selected beneficiaries (policies already assigned to a lending institution in connection with a mortgage cannot be written in trust or assigned to other third parties without consent of the lenders).

- With regard to life policies, the value of the policy as at the date of assignation (by way of gift) into a trust would be a potentially exempt transfer. If a period of seven years from date of the third party assignation or writing in trust passes before death of the original policy owner, the potentially exempt transfer will be wholly free of inheritance tax as will growth within the value of the policy during the seven year period in question.

- Death in service benefits under occupation of pension schemes are often subject and "internal" trust which would keep the benefits out of the estate of the employee on death. This is not necessarily the case and a check should be made with the scheme administrators. Very often the step can be taken by simply writing a letter of expression of wish. In some cases a more complex trust declaration might be required.

- As I indicated above, if a pension policy holder dies before retirement age there can be substantial benefits payable under the relevant policy. Again, it is very often possible to write these benefits in trust thereby ensuring that a large sum of funds does not come bouncing back into the estate of the deceased. If the benefits are written in trust then they will not form part of the estate of the deceased's personal estate and will be free of IHT.

(d) One of the simplest ways of mitigating IHT is to ensure that both spouses make at least partial use of the respective nil-rate bands. In many cases, spouses bequeath their respective estates to each other whom failing equally between their children. Whilst often that might be wholly appropriate, it is important that the spouses realise that they are effectively giving one "nil-rate band" (£263,000) back to the Treasury. As hereinbefore indicated, each person can pass a total of £263,000 of estate to non exempt beneficiaries without incurring any IHT liability. Transfers between spouses are exempt. However, transfers to other members of the family are not so exempt. There is a common misconception that only one tranche of £263,000 is available to spouses. This is not the case as each spouse has his/her own nil-rate band allowance.

Clients should therefore be encouraged to look at their wills. If they have bequeathed their whole estates to each other, then they should assess whether or not the survivor of them would require the whole estate. A brief example might be useful:

- A husband (H) has an estate worth £300,000. His wife (W) has an estate of her own worth £100,000. They have two adult children, A & B. If H passes on bequeathing his estate to W, she will then have an estate worth £400,000. There is no tax on the estate (£300,000) passing from H to W as it is spouse exempt. When W passes on her nil-rate band can be brought into play reducing the taxable estate (£400,000) to £137,000. The IHT payable on this before A and B take their benefit will be £54,800.
- We have the same scenario, however, having carefully considered their joint financial position, H amends his Will to the effect that on his death, his children, A and B each receive a legacy of £68,500. H passes on. £137,000 passes tax free (being below H's nil-rate band) to his children. The remainder (£163,000) passes to W. She then has an estate worth £263,000. When she passes on, her total Estate will be £263,000. As this is the amount of the nil-

rate band there will be no tax payable on her death, *i.e.* by a simple alteration to the will, a tax bill of £54,800 has been avoided.

- Not all spouses are in a position to take advantage of the "extreme" example hereinbefore detailed. However, H & W, having considered their respective financial position, might conclude that it would not be safe to leave £137,000 to the children on H's death. They do, however, feel that they are comfortable with their children each receiving £18,500 on death of each. This would mean that on death of H, a total of £263,000 would pass to W. When she passed on leaving £363,000 her taxable estate would be £100,000 on which the tax bill would be £40,000. Thus in this third example a total of £14,800 by tax has been saved.

Other possibilities

There are other steps which are presently still available to mitigate IHT thus:

1. Setting up of a lifetime trust. Section 260 of the Taxation of Chargeable Gains Act 1992.
2. Use of a deed of variation—under section 142 of the Inheritance Tax Act 1984, a family can get together and wholly rewrite the will of a deceased individual provided this is done in accordance with the provisions of the Act. An example of how a deed of variation might be used harks back to the examples given above. If, H, has left a will which simply bequeaths everything to W, the family could get together to rewrite the will in terms of a deed of variation in order to pass, say £100,000 by way of legacy equally between A & B. This would have the effect of saving £40,000 in tax when W passes on. This is an extremely useful device of which many families have taken advantage. However, it should be noted that since the early 1990's, there has been more than one indication given that the Inland Revenue do not like deeds of variation and on more than one occasion Chancellors (Norman Lamont and Kenneth Clark) have indicated that the facility to enter into a deed of variation might be withdrawn.
3. Investment in the alternative investment market (AIM)—many individuals do not know about this market. It is, however, a market for trading of shares of companies listed in the AIM. Shareholdings in many of the companies listed in the AIM will qualify for business property relief for IHT purposes. It should, however, be noted that it is considered that investing in the AIM is perhaps more risky than investing into the main London Stock Market.

Use of trusts in inheritance tax planning

It is a common misconception that Trusts are old fashioned vehicles which have little or no place in valid Inheritance Tax Planning. This is not the case. Some very complicated tax strategies have been developed, involving the use of lifetime trusts. Some of these plans are of doubtful value. As a first point, with regard to some of the very complicated plans, the success of the same is not guaranteed by those who promote them and the Inland Revenue are more than willing to go all the way to the House of Lords to challenge some of the plans in question. Whilst expert advice is required in relation to the creation of the lifetime trust, I would offer the following comments:

- A discretionary trust offers great flexibility. The individual can also avoid a substantial capital gains tax liability by placing in trust an asset which is pregnant with capital gains. The rules in relation to the inheritance tax position of a discretionary trust (as also taxation of income arising within the same) are complicated but with proper advice, a discretionary trust could be used to advantage.
- The use of a discretionary trust under a will can in fact result in substantial IHT savings where the principal "subject" of such a trust is the interest of a spouse in the dwellinghouse of the two spouses. Again whilst this could involve incurring legal expense in "splitting" a title deed and the setting up of an appropriate "loan back" arrangement substantial benefits can be achieved in IHT mitigation while still preserving the control of the surviving spouse as to whether or not the relevant matrimonial home is sold.
- Policy trusts are very effective and offer scope for flexibility and IHT mitigation.

Use of Insurance Policies

Again appropriate advice is required. However, the vehicles which can be used can range from the simple to the reasonably complicated. Brief examples are:

- Arranging a term assurance policy and writing the same in trust. The term assurance policy is one of the most inexpensive as payment under the same is, on an actuarial basis, unlikely. That being so the premiums can be relatively inexpensive. For example, if an individual arranges a term assurance policy for £50,000 over a period of ten years and immediately writes the proceeds of that policy in trust for his or her family, then those monies will not form part of his or her personal estate as payment on the policy is not guaranteed, the premiums are thereby smaller.
- A common way for spouses to arrange some "protection" against the effect of IHT is for the spouses to arrange what is known as a joint life second death policy. This can be arranged on the basis of payment of a single premium or regular premiums. The policy pays out only on death of the second spouse. Again, to be effective, the policy should be written in trust at the outset. If the policy is arranged on a single premium basis, payment of that premium will be a potentially exempt transfer. If it is arranged on a regular premium basis, then each annual (or other) premium will again amount to a potentially

exempt transfer. The benefit of such a policy is that growth of value within the policy itself will be free from IHT on death of the second spouse.

- Discounted bond trusts for older, high value individuals. These schemes can be particularly effective, involving immediate relief from IHT. Again, those schemes are not uncomplicated and, the usual "health warning"—appropriate, expert advice is required.

Care home fee planning and inheritance tax planning

These two areas have a real overlap. Some of the "informal" schemes which have been adopted by families may or may not be effective for the purpose of protecting assets from what are perceived to be the "predations" of local authorities where an older person requires to go into a nursing home—however, they will be wholly ineffective for inheritance tax planning. The insurance industry (as usual) is aware of the relationship between these two aims and have produced some ingenious products which assist not only in funding care home fees but also in securing a degree of inheritance tax mitigation—once again, the unwary beware—appropriate advice is required.

Conclusion

Clients should not be overwhelmed by the seeming complexity of this subject. IHT planning is really making a series of choices. No two clients will make the same choices. However, hopefully this note will make it clear that clients can take various steps which could substantially defray the ultimate liability on death of both spouses. If further advice on this matter is required, Maxwell MacLaurin will be happy to render the same. Please make contact with me on 0141 332 5666 or at my email address jkerrigan@maxwellmaclaurin.co.uk

SUGGESTED NOTE RE EXPLAINING DIFFERENCES BETWEEN *"PER STRIPES"* AND *"PER CAPITA"* SUCCESSION

The phrase *"per stirpes"* often appears in Scottish wills. To solicitors, the intention and effect of that phrase in a will is clear. However, it is distinctly unclear to most clients. The purpose of this note is to explain what *per stirpes* succession means.

A consideration of the examples attached to this note will explain how *per stirpes* succession operates. In each case A is to sole surviving parent.

In example 1, understanding the succession is simple. In terms of his will, A has bequeathed his estate equally between his three children, B, C and D. They each rake one third of A's estate.

In example 2, A's will follows the normal Scottish pattern, *i.e.* it declares that in the event of any A's children predeceasing A then his or her issue shall take equally between them *per stirpes*. For example if child C has predeceased his parent, A, child C survived by two children of his own namely X and Y. A division of A's estate in this example would be one third to child B, one child to third D and one third shared equally between grandchildren Y & Z. This type of succession is considered to be entirely equitable. There is, however, an alternative which can be seen in example 3.

In example 3, we have the same situation when A has been predeceased by his child C. Child C survived by children X and Y. If the will provides for **per capita** succession then in this case his succession would be one quarter of the estate to B, one quarter of the estate to X, one quarter of the estate to Y and one quarter of the estate to D.

If you stop for a moment to consider the effect of *per capita* succession you will see that one "strand" of the family (*i.e.* grandchildren X and Y) have been treated more favourably than immediate children of A, B and D.

To recap, an example, where *per stirpes* succession is specified in the will, each strand of a family receives the same benefit, *i.e.* one third. This is summing equity. Had C survived, he would have received one third of the estate. In the normal course of events, that one third would have "filtered down" to X and Y *per stirpes* succession is therefore considered merely to reflect what would have happened in normal life had C not predeceased his parent. As indicated, *per capita* succession can have a distorting effect on the relevant succession.

Example 1

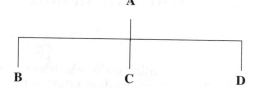

B, C and **D** each receive one-third.

Example 2
(*Per Stirpes*
Succession)

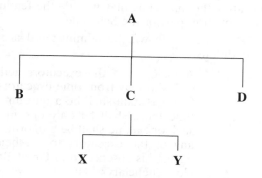

B and **D** each receive one-third.
X and **Y** each receive one-sixth.

Example 3
(*Per Capita*
Succession)

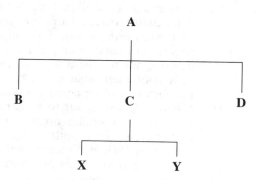

B and **D** each receive one-quarter
X and **Y** also each receive one-quarter (**more of
A's estate therefore goes to C's children than is
received by B and D).** it is suggested that this may
be a recipe for family dispute or fall out.

STYLE POWERS SCHEDULE*

Definitions

In this Schedule:-

"Will" means a deed or writing under which executors act. "executors" means the executors and trustees acting under the will.

"Estate" means the property, heritable and moveable, administered at any time under the will.

"Income" and "capital" refer to the income and capital respectively of the estate or any part thereof.

Words indicating the plural include the singular, and vice versa. Words indicating the masculine may include the feminine. Marginal headings do not form part of the Schedule.

CONDITIONS The estate will be administered according to the following conditions:

Quorum of executors	(A)	A majority of the executors acting under the will who may from time executorsto time be in Great Britain shall be a quorum, and if at any time there shall be only one in Great Britain such one alone shall be a quorum, the power of any of the executors to act being suspended during his absence from Great Britain.
Vesting of beneficiaries' interests and advances	(B)	No beneficiary shall take a vested interest in any part of the estate beneficiaries'until the due date for payment thereof, except that all advances made interestsby the executors in terms of powers conferred on them by the will and advancesshall vest in the recipient at the date of the advance.
Indemnity to executors	(C)	The executors shall not be liable for loss or depreciation of executors investments retained or made by them, nor for omissions, nor for neglect in management, nor for insolvency of debtors, nor for the acts, omissions, neglect or default of each other or of any banker, solicitor, factor or other agent employed by them.
Discharge	(D)	Where a legacy is left to a charity, unincorporated body or similar organisation the receipt of the treasurer or other appropriate official shall be sufficient discharge and my executors may make payment of any legacy or share of residue bequeathed to any charitable body which may have changed its name, been wrongly designed or amalgamated with any other body to that body, as my executors may in their sole discretion decide.

---

* Reproduced by kind permission of the Law Society of Scotland. This style was originally used in the Diploma of Legal Practice. Copyright remains with Law Society.

In the administration of the estate or any part thereof my executors shall in addition to the powers and discretions hereinafter expressly conferred upon them, and in addition to the powers, privileges and immunities conferred upon gratuitous executors in Scotland by statute or at common law, have the fullest powers of and in regard to investment, realisation, administration, management and division of the estate or any part thereof as if they were the beneficial owners thereof, and in particular but without prejudice to the foregoing generality my executors shall have the following powers:

Sale of estate	(1)	To sell the estate or any part thereof in such manner and on such terms and conditions as the executors think proper.
Purchase of estate by executor	(2)	To purchase the estate or any part thereof as long as the purchaser is not the sole executor.
Retention of estate	(3)	To retain any property comprised in the estate for such time as the executors think proper.
Investment	(4)	To lend or invest the whole or any part of the estate in the purchase or on the security of heritable or real property, whether situated in Great Britain or elsewhere, corporeal moveables, stocks, shares (including partly paid shares), deposits and securities (including securities payable to bearer), units of unit trusts, investments in property or other bonds and generally in investments or securities of any company, undertaking or body incorporated or carrying on business in any part of the world, and to sell, vary and transfer any such investments or securities.
Nominees	(5)	To have registered in the name of a nominee any part of the estate and to pay reasonable fees to such nominee.
Borrowing	(6)	To borrow on the security of the estate or any part thereof on such terms and conditions as the executors may think proper.
Policies of assurance	(7)	To effect or acquire policies of assurance, whether whole life, assurance endowment, term, accident, contingency or otherwise, on the life or lives of any person; to pay the premiums thereon out of income or capital orpartly from one and partly from the other; to cash bonuses on such policies; to convert such policies into fully paid policies for the same or reduced amounts or into any other form of assurance; to exercise any option available under such policies; to increase or decrease the amount of the annual premiums; to alter the period during which such premiums are payable; to surrender such policies and to do any such things notwithstanding that the sums assured may thereby be reduced.

Management of heritable property	(8)	To administer and manage any heritable or real property forming of heritable part of the estate; to repair, maintain, renew and improve the same property and to erect additional buildings and structures; to grant, vary and terminate leases and rights of tenancy or occupancy; to plant, thin and cutdown timber; to work or let minerals; all as the executors may think proper and as if they were absolute owners of the estate.
Companies	(9)	To exercise in relation to any company or corporation in which shares or securities are held by the executors all powers competent to them,including power to promote or concur in any reconstruction or amalgamation, with power to any of their number to continue or to be appointed as a director or officer of any such company or corporation and to retain personally any remuneration paid to him in respect of that office.
Proxies	(10)	To grant proxies in favour of any of their number or any other person to attend, act and vote for the executors at meetings of any company, corporation, trust or undertaking or in any bankruptcy or winding-up proceedings in which the executors may be interested or at any class meeting of shareholders, stockholders or debenture holders of any such company, corporation, trust or undertaking or of creditors in any such company, corporation, trust or undertaking.
Compromise of claims	(11)	To compromise or settle by arbitration or by the advice of counsel or in the discretion of the executors all disputed claims by or against the estate.
Apportionment between capital and income	(12)	To decide what money represents capital and what represents income and the proportion in which expenses are to be charged against capital and income respectively, notwithstanding any rule of law or practice to the contrary, and all similar questions which may arise in relation to the estate.
Loans to beneficiaries	(13)	To make personal loans with or without interest and with or without security to any beneficiary of the estate, provided the executors are at least two in number.
Accommodation for beneficiaries	(14)	To acquire for the occupation of any beneficiary in the estate any dwellinghouse which the executors may consider suitable and to improve, decorate, reconstruct or add to it in such manner as the executors may consider necessary or desirable.

Appropriation of investments	(15)	To set apart and appropriate specific investments or property of the estate to represent the whole or part of the particular share of any beneficiary or any share to which such beneficiary shall be entitled and that at such valuations as the executors shall determine, so that the particular share shall have the whole benefit and the whole risk of the appropriate investments or property. A minute signed by the executors, though not probative, shall be sufficient evidence of such appropriation.
Satisfaction of bequests in cash or in kind	(16)	To settle any pecuniary legacy or any share of a beneficiary in the estate either in cash or by conveyance or transfer of any part or parts of the estate, or partly in one way and partly in the other, all as the executors may decide and the valuation at which parts of the estate are so conveyed or transferred shall be determined conclusively by the executors.
Resignation of executors	(17)	To resign office as long as he is not the sole executor.
Appointment of agents	(18)	To appoint one or more of their own number (or in the case of Bloggs Trustees Limited one or more of its directors or shareholders) or any firm of which he, she or they may be a member, to act as solicitors in carrying out the purposes of this Will and to allow them their usual charges.
Payment of expenses	(19)	To reimburse any of the executors out of the estate for all expenses reasonably incurred by them in the administration of the estate.
General	(20)	To do everything the executors may consider necessary or expedient for the administration of the estate.
Business	(21)	To continue to carry on or to commence any business, whether alone or in conjunction or in partnership with any other persons, for such period as the executors may think proper; to appoint or employ any executor and any other person in any capacity in relation to such business and to pay to them suitable remuneration for services, including pension provisions for any employees or their dependants; and to delegate or entrust to any persons the control and management of such business to such extent as the executors may think fit; and

    (a) the executors may employ for the purposes of such business such part of the income or capital as they think proper;

    (b) the executors may enter into any agreement or partnership or other conditions;

(c) the executors shall exercise only such control or supervision of said business as they shall think fit;

(d) the executors shall be entitled to be relieved from the estate from all personal responsibility for any loss arising from such business operations, and

(e) any executor appointed or employed in any such business shall be entitled to retain personally the remuneration for his services.

Promotion of Companies   (22) To promote or concur in the flotation and reconstruction or amalgamation of any company with limited liability including, but without prejudice to that generality, any company formed to take over any business, company or concern carried on by the executors or in which they may be interested, and to subscribe for and hold the debentures, stocks, shares or other scrip or obligations of such new company or to accept the debentures, stocks, shares or other scrip or obligations of such reconstructed or amalgamated company in lieu of or in substitution for the debentures, stocks and shares or other scrip or obligations held by the executors prior to such reconstruction or amalgamation, and to contribute to the expenses of such flotation, reconstruction or amalgamation.

INDEX

Instruction for use of the companion disc

Introduction

These notes are provided for guidance only. They should be read and interpreted in the context of your own computer system and operational procedures. It is assumed that you have a basic knowledge of WINDOWS. However, if there is any problem please contact our help line on 020 7393 7266 and they will be happy to help you.

CD Format and Contents

To run this CD you need at least:
IBM compatible PC
CD-ROM drive
Microsoft Word 6.0/95

The CD contains data files of selected Styles and Suggested Notes from the *Appendix of Styles* in this book. It does not contain software or commentary.

Installation

The following instructions make the assumption that you will copy the data files to a single directory on your hard disk (e.g. C:\Drafting for Succession—Appendix of Styles).

Open your CD Rom drive, select and double click on setup.exe and follow the instructions. The files will be unzipped to your C drive and you will be able to open them from the new C:\Drafting for Succession—Appendix of Styles.

LICENCE AGREEMENT

IMPORTANT—PLEASE READ THIS DOCU-MENT CAREFULLY BEFORE BREAKING THE SEAL TO RELEASE THE DISK FROM THE WALLET. BY REMOVING AND USING THE DISK YOU THE PURCHASER ARE AGREEING TO BE BOUND BY THE TERMS SET OUT IN THIS DOCUMENT.

The disk and all data included thereon is supplied to you the purchaser by the publisher, Thomson/W. Green, based entirely on the Drafting For Succession book. If you do not wish to be bound by the terms and conditions of use of the disk and data please do not remove the seal from the wallet. The following terms shall apply to the use of the book, disk and data whilst it is in the possession or control of the purchaser:

1. The Purchaser is granted a non-exclusive licence by the Publisher to use the disk and data for the purpose for which it is intended in conjunction with the book in the normal course of business, namely for negotiating, drafting and creating contracts. This right is personal to the Purchaser and shall also permit the Purchaser to copy the files from the compact disk to their hard disk and also to make one security copy of the compact disk itself. The Purchaser shall not have the right to make any additional copies and/or to permit, authorise, sub-license, assign, transfer and/or otherwise exploit the book and/or disk and/or data in any form, whether for commercial purposes or otherwise. It is accepted by the Publishers that lawyers and others in practice and/or the energy industry may use the book and/or disk and/or data to provide legal advice and services to individuals and companies. However, there is no right to copy the disk, data and/or book for supply by the purchaser to such persons by photocopying or electronically supplying large sections of the book. Please advise your clients or company to purchase the book and disk.

2. The right granted is limited and personal to the Purchaser and does not permit the Purchaser to exploit the book and/or disk and/or data in any media of any nature at any time or to permit others to do so. The Purchaser shall not acquire any rights and/or interest in the book, disk and/ or data at any time which may be exploited by the Purchaser, and all rights not specified are reserved by the Publisher and not permitted or authorised under this Licence Agreement.

3. The Publisher and the Authors do not accept any responsibility for the use of the disk and/or data by the Purchaser at any time and shall not be liable for any direct and/or indirect damages, loss, injury or otherwise that may arise in respect of the Purchaser and/or any business in which the Purchaser may be involved and/or to which the Purchaser may supply material or advice for any reason. The Purchaser shall use the disk and/ or data entirely at the Purchaser's sole risk and expense and agrees that the Purchaser shall be liable for all its own costs and expenses or otherwise that may arise from any such use.

4. The Publisher concerns that all rights necessary for the specified use by the Purchaser of the disk and/or data have been obtained from the Author. The Publisher has endeavoured to ensure that as far as possible the data is based on the book. The Publisher and the Author do not accept any responsibility and/or liability for any errors, omissions, viruses, defects and/or any other matters of any nature in the disk and/or data which may be a legal, technical or material fault or problem otherwise. The Purchaser must use the disk and/or data entirely at its sole risk and cost and accept that the contract clauses are for reference and guidance only and are intended to be adapted and varied accordingly by each Purchaser to suit their particular circumstances. In the event that there is a technical defect in the disk itself, the Publisher agrees to replace the disk within 90 days of purchase provided that the disk and/or data has been treated with all due care and not mistreated in some manner or damaged by some other means at a later date after purchase. If the disk and/or data is incompatible with the Purchaser's hardware and there is no alternative product available then there is no liability on the part of the Publisher to provide any other disk and/or data or any refund or reimbursement of any nature at any time.

5. In the event of any claim, demand, action or otherwise by the Purchaser and/or any business for any reason arising from the use of the disk and/ or data, then the Publisher shall only be liable in total to repay the full purchase price of the book to the Purchaser. The Purchaser agrees that it is the Purchaser's responsibility to arrange and bear the cost of insurance cover for the benefit of the Purchaser, any business and/or third party for the use of the disk and/or data by the Purchaser and that the Publisher and the Authors shall not bear any responsibility and/or liability for the use of the disk and/or data by the Purchaser, any business, third party or otherwise which is supplied directly or indirectly by the Purchaser at any time.

6. The Copyright owner of the data contained on the disk is the Author of the book unless otherwise specified. The Author should be identified as John Kerrigan.

7. In the event that the Author and/or the Publisher become aware and/or have reasonable grounds to believe that the Purchaser, business and/or third party is using the disk and/or data in a manner which was not set out in this document and which is prejudicial and/or detrimental to the interests of the Publisher and/or Author and/or is in breach of any intellectual property rights including copyright of such parties, the Publisher and/or the Author shall be entitled without notice to the Purchaser to terminate the licence provided under this document without prejudice to any other rights and remedies of the Publisher and/or Author. The Purchaser shall be obliged upon written notice to surrender all copies of the disks and/or data to the Publisher and/ or Author.

8. The Purchaser agrees that it shall not use and/or authorise the use of the disk and/or data in any manner or nature which is inconsistent with the intended purpose of the licence given in this document. Nor shall the Purchaser deface, erase, remove and/or alter any part of the copyright notice, trade marks, Author and Publisher details displayed on any part of the disk, cover and/or data.

9. This licence shall be governed by the laws of the Scotland, whether this disk and/or data is supplied and/or used in the United Kingdom and/or in any part of the universe.